国家出版基金项目
NATIONAL PUBLICATION FOUNDATION

中華文化概覽

郑铁生（中）
陈法春（英）◎编著

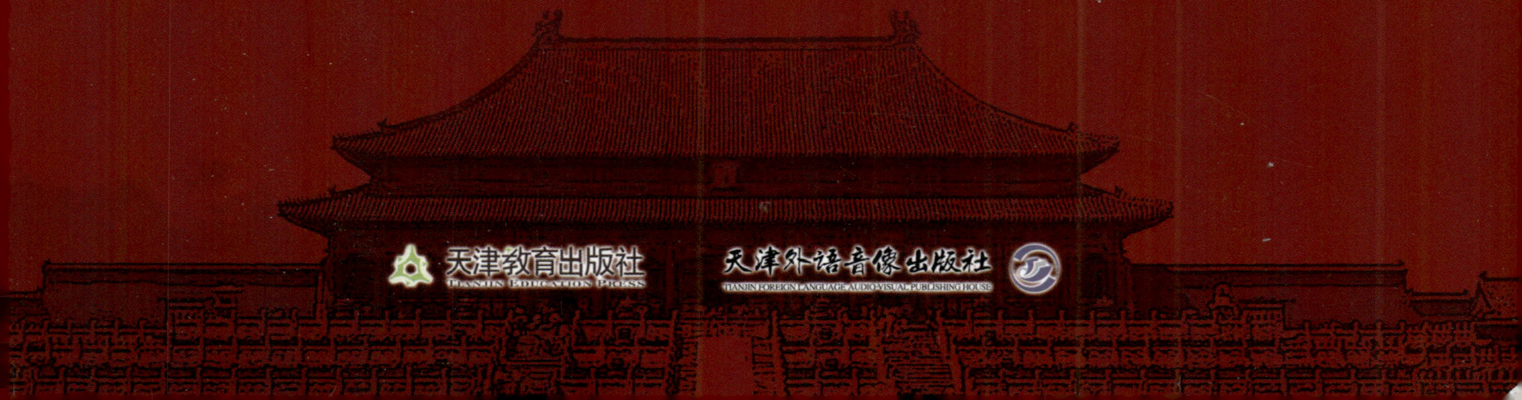

天津教育出版社 TIANJIN EDUCATION PRESS
天津外语音像出版社 TIANJIN FOREIGN LANGUAGE AUDIO-VISUAL PUBLISHING HOUSE

图书在版编目（C I P）数据

中华文化概览：汉英双语 / 郑铁生（中），陈法春（英）编著. —天津：
天津教育出版社，2010.8
ISBN 978-7-5309-6162-9

Ⅰ. ①中… Ⅱ. ①郑…②陈… Ⅲ. ①文化史—中国—汉、英
Ⅳ. ①K203

中国版本图书馆C I P数据核字（2010）第167503号

中华文化概览　汉英双语

出 版 人　修　刚　胡振泰

选题策划　夏　钢　于恪歆　胡振泰
编　　著　郑铁生(中)　陈法春(英)
责任编辑　马秀华　耿学明　贾永来
装帧设计　郭亚非　王　珺
封面题字　翟津壮

出版发行　天津教育出版社
天津市和平区西康路35号
邮政编码　300051
http://www.tjeph.com.cn

天津外语音像出版社
天津市河西区马场道117号
邮政编码　300204
http://tflaph.tjfsu.edu.cn

经　　销　新华书店
印　　刷　天津印艺通制版印刷有限责任公司
版　　次　2010年8月第1版
印　　次　2010年8月第1次印刷
规　　格　16开（889×1194毫米）
印　　张　21
字　　数　218千字

定　　价　286.00元

编 委 会 (The Editorial Board)

序

文化的存在是多元的，东西方文化存在巨大差异，这种差异的存在具有悠久的历史。如果任由文化差异的继续发展，势必造成深深的文化隔阂，甚至文化冲突。因此，随着经济全球化、世界一体化进程的不断进展，借鉴外来文化、宣传民族文化、加强文化交流成为国内外的一种共识。

随着对外开放的不断深入和经济社会的迅猛发展，在不断深入学习了解西方文化的同时，博大精深的中国文化吸引了越来越多的外国朋友。

为了向海外朋友介绍灿烂的华夏文明，帮助外国友人系统、便捷地了解中国文化，天津外语音像出版社、天津教育出版社联合出版了这部《中华文化概览》。

本书内容涉及的都是中华文化中最有代表性、最具民族特色的文化素材，如中国古代文化遗产，影响深远的儒、道、佛家思想，独具特色的中医、武术、戏剧文化，还有诸如货币、科技、工艺、饮食、美术、曲艺、对外交流等文化领域。

本书配有 DVD-ROM 光盘，分为汉英、汉日、汉韩三个版本，集图片、文字、声音于一体，声情并茂、图文并举，每一章节都在安排精短文章之外又增加了词语注释，便于外国朋友了解中国文化，学习汉语知识；与此同时，书中详细介绍了大量名词术语、史地概念、哲思理念，对于我国广大外语学习者深入了解祖国传统文化的丰富内涵，也具有重要的启发意义。

语言是文化的标记和符号，是文化的承载。本书既是文化交流作品，又是语言学习读物，既适合那些对中国文化具有浓厚兴趣的外国朋友，也适合国内有志于从事跨文化交际和文化传播事业的人士作为学习和工作之用。

当今，东西文化的融合已成为历史的趋势，各民族创造的文化都是人类共同拥有的文明宝库中的一部分，为此，希望《中华文化概览》在融通世界、传承文明的过程中能充分发挥它的积极作用。

是为序。

天津外国语大学校长 修刚

2010 年 5 月

目　录 / Contents

前　言

今天，是中国真正走向世界与各民族进行对话的伟大时代。愈是改革开放，愈是国人同外国朋友交往频繁，愈是感到弘扬中华文化迫在眉睫。另外，要提高国人的文化素质、自豪感、凝聚力和爱国心，也十分需要全面、系统地传授中华民族灿烂的文化。摆在你面前的《中华文化概览》，适逢盛世，用当其时。它既适合中国的广大读者阅读，也适合具有中、高级汉语水平的外国朋友阅读。

具体说来，编写《中华文化概览》双语读本，动机有二：

第一，随着中国对外开放的不断深入，中华文化的独特魅力吸引了越来越多的外国朋友学习汉语。不少外国留学生表示，提高言语能力，感到最难理解的是汉语中所蕴涵的中华文化因素。帮助外国留学生在学习汉语言的同时，较为系统和迅速地了解中国文化，是编写这本书的基本动机。

第二，多年来，无论是学外语的学生、教师，还是在中国国土长大的学者、官员、商人，在同外国朋友交流的过程中，既感到对中华文化知识的缺失，也不知道怎样用外语对其进行准确的表述，很难准确地把中华文化介绍给外国朋友。双语读本最大好处就是在展现中华文化知识的同时，也给他们提供了相应文化知识的外文表述范本。

中华文化历史悠久博大深邃，如何使本书做到既广博又精要，是我们遇到的首要问题。所谓广博，即尽可能系统地介绍源远流长的中华文化的基本特色，全书十八个章节基本上涵盖了中华文化的各个范畴。所谓精要，即选择最有代表性、最具亮色的文化素材，“以一目尽传精神”。遴选中华文化各个方面的精要内容，形成了本读本知识结构的搭建。

同时，我们遵循了三个原则，一、力避“选篇集萃”，突出文化内容的系统性和整体性；二、力避内容庞杂散漫，突出具体文化范畴的讲述；三、力戒专业性的艰深，做到通俗易懂。

当你阅读了《中华文化概览》，再到名胜古迹、博物馆、画廊、作坊、剧院、餐馆等场所，实地领略中华文化时，你会产生更加深刻具体的感受，也会对中华文化产生更浓郁的兴趣。

郑锦生

2010 年 5 月

第一章　龙的故乡

一、龙的文化

龙，作为中华民族的象征，起源于远古的图腾崇拜。甲骨文中的“龙”字，商周青铜器的龙纹，以及玉件上雕的草龙，都呈现出一种长躯、巨口、有角、有爪的兽形。从龙的起源和发展脉络可以看出，经过人们的想象和加工，创造出这种超自然、超人类自身的动物形象，具有神的伟力，受到人们的崇拜。传说龙能上天入海、兴风作雨、变幻无穷，有雷电之威、霓虹之彩。《说文解字》[1]：“龙，鳞虫之长，能幽能明，能细能巨，能短能长，春分而登天，秋分而潜渊。”今天常见的龙的造型，汉魏时代已奠定了基本形态，隋唐以后就基本上没有变化了。而作为祥瑞物的崇拜，可以说，中华大地是龙的故乡、龙的家园。龙文化伴随着中华民族走过了漫长的历史，中华民族的子孙都是“龙的传人”。

二龙戏珠

在中国古代社会里，“君子在位，则神龙出”，龙是帝王至高无上皇权的象征，所谓“真龙天子”，因而帝王要穿龙袍，坐龙椅，乘龙辇(niǎn)。但在中国漫长的历史进程中，龙的形象及蕴含的文化意义，随着时代的发展而发生演化，越来越多元化。在民间，崇拜龙的主要原因是龙可以兴云致雨。古老的中国是农业社会，人们总是希望风调雨顺，于是龙以体现民意的方式出现。人们向龙王顶礼膜拜，祈求降雨，并以赛龙舟、舞龙灯的方式欢庆或预祝五谷丰登。可以说，中华几千年农业文明孕育了中国龙，中国龙文化伴随着农业文明的发展不断走向成熟。

如今，龙文化渗透到中国文化的各个方面，不管是工艺美术、建筑名胜、歌舞影视，还是岁时节令、婚丧礼仪、服饰冠履，龙都作为重要的文化元素，以

赛龙舟

盘旋、腾跃、奋飞等多种形式，占据着醒目的位置，体现着龙文化的蕴涵。人们读龙书，演龙戏，唱龙歌，耍龙舞，栽龙树，以龙为名；人们说龙，写龙，画龙，雕龙，赏龙，立志成“龙”，望子成龙，处处有龙，时时见龙。直到今天，人们对龙依然表现出极大的兴趣，一些重大的庆典中，往往有龙的形象出现，年年春节、中秋等佳节，都喜欢舞龙！

龙是中国的象征、中华民族的象征、中国文化的象征。对每一个炎黄子孙来说，龙的形象都和自己有一种割舍不断、血肉相连的情感。

词语注释

【1】《说文解字》：是中国第一部由个人独立编纂完成的字典，成书于东汉和帝永元十二年（公元100年），作者是许慎，字叔重。全书收字9 353个，所释的字以小篆为主体分析字形结构，根据部首，归纳为540部，系统全面解释字的形、音、义的新体制，在中国文字学史上具有开创之功。

二、传说中的祖先——黄帝

轩辕黄帝

黄帝生活在距今五千多年的中国新石器时代晚期，姓公孙，号轩辕氏、有熊氏，居住在陕西北部的黄土高原一带，因为黄土地而得名。后来，他率领部落迁居到河北涿鹿[1]附近定居下来，开始发展畜牧业和农业。当时，中国黄河、长江流域一带住着许多氏族和部落，黄帝是传说中最有名的一个部落首领。

跟黄帝同时代的另一个部落首领叫做炎帝，姜姓，号神农氏。相传他改进农具，教人耕田，遍尝百草，总结了草药的各种用途，开辟了集市，使人们互通有无。炎帝最早住在中国西北方姜水[2]附近，后来，炎帝族和黄帝族发生了冲突，双方在阪（Bǎn）泉[3]打了一仗，炎帝失败。

这时候，有一个九黎族[4]的首领名叫蚩尤[5]

(Chīyóu)，十分强悍，常常侵掠别的部落。

黄帝联合各部落，在涿鹿与蚩尤展开了一场大决战。最后黄帝战败蚩尤，统一了中原部落，建立了部落联盟，黄帝因而受到了许多部落的拥护，从此，黄帝成为中原地区的部落联盟首领。

黄帝统一中原以后，率领他的部落生活在桥山[6]以及陕北黄土高原周围，并在这里繁衍生息。据说，黄帝创造文字，制造舟车，培育蚕桑，从事纺织，制定历法，研制算术，经过一番艰苦努力，建立了伟大的功绩。历史上尧[7]、舜[8]以及夏、商、周三代帝王，相传都是黄帝的后裔。西汉时期司马迁写的《史记》就是把黄帝时期作为中国历史的开端来记载的。黄帝统一了黄河流域和中原各民族，促进了中原地区最初的文化大融合，奠定了华夏史前文明。因此，中国人都尊崇黄帝为华夏族的始祖，自己是黄帝的子孙。由于炎帝族和黄帝族原来是近亲，后来又融合在一起供人祭祀，所以中国人又常常把自己称为炎黄子孙。

词语注释

【1】涿鹿：今河北省涿鹿县南。

【2】姜水：今陕西宝鸡地区境内。

【3】阪泉：今河北涿鹿县东南。

【4】九黎族：传说中的上古部落名。

【5】蚩尤：传说中的古代九黎族首领，与黄帝战于涿鹿，失败被杀。

【6】桥山：今陕西黄陵县。

【7】尧：传说中的上古帝王名。

【8】舜：传说中的上古帝王名。

三、中国最早的文字——甲骨文

甲骨文是世界上最古老的文字之一，也是中国最早的具有成熟形态的文字。清代末年，在北京做官的山东福山人王懿荣最早发现龟板上的甲骨文，并打听到龟板出土的地方——安阳。

甲骨文

这些龟板上的字，因为是商代至周初契刻在龟甲或牛的肩胛骨上的，所以叫"甲骨文"。由于它们大部分出土于商代都城的遗址——安阳，所记的都是占卜的事情，商亦称殷，所以又称殷墟卜辞[1]。商代的统治者对很多事情都要进行占卜，通过被烧灼的甲骨上的纹路来了解上天的意志，判断事物的吉凶。占卜完毕，就将占卜的时间、人名、所问事情、占卜结果以及事后验证刻在上面，形成了具有简明叙事特征的甲骨文。已经发现的甲骨文字有四五千个。经过文字学家和考古学家们的分析、判断，能够辨认的有一千七百多个。甲骨文有名词、形容词和数词等，主语—谓语—宾语的基本语序固定，也有一些复杂句；不仅有象形字、会意字，而且有了形声字。1977 年，陕西岐山、扶风两县间的周原遗址中，又出土了西周的甲骨文字。

甲骨文的使用，使中国历史开始了有文字记载的文明史，从中可以考证出殷商时代的社会制度、礼节、历法等。世界上一些古老民族在4 500年前也有使用过文字的，然而这些文字到后世都已失传，成为与后来通行的文字毫无关系的死文字。唯有甲骨文早在商代就以比较成熟形态的文字通用于我国中原大地，并与周代青铜器铭文，战国秦汉的简牍、帛书文字，魏晋的石刻文字发展相联系。汉字从甲骨文、金文、籀、篆、隶书，直至演变为今日通行的楷书，几千年来与时俱进，一脉相承，构成中华民族传统文化的重要组成部分。甲骨文是我们目前所能看到的中国最早的文字，研究甲骨文也成为一门专门的学问——甲骨学。

词语注释

【1】殷墟卜辞：殷人占卜，常将占卜人姓名、占卜所问之事及占卜日期、结果等刻在所用龟甲或兽骨上，间或亦刻有少量与占卜有关的纪事，这类记录文字通称卜辞。

四、《易经》

《易经》是中国文化最古老的典籍，推崇它的，称之“群经之首”；贬斥它的，认为是占筮（shì）之书[1]。传说远古时期伏羲氏画八卦，至周文王演为六十四卦，作卦辞。春秋时期孔子作《十翼》以解经。这就是说，《易经》的成书历时千余年，有一个漫长的历史演变过程，而且内容十分复杂，巫术、数学、史学等层面都有，是中国文化现象整合的产物。儒家和道教的学说都明显受到《易经》的影响。

伏 羲

《易经》创作经历三个阶段：首先是阴阳概念的认知；其次，八卦的创立；第三，卦辞、爻辞。因而，《易经》包括《经》和《传》两个部分。“经”，即易的本身，是由八卦推衍为六十四卦、卦形、卦名、卦辞，以及三百八十四爻和爻辞。“传”则是对“经”的最早的解说，包括彖[2]（tuàn）、象、系辞、文言、说卦、序卦、杂卦，七个题目十篇文章。“易象”的基本特征，一是来自于具体事物；二是具有象征意义。卦辞和爻辞的内容大体有三类：一是讲自然现象变化；二是讲人事的得失；三是判断吉凶的词句。它虽然包裹在神秘的形式之中，但蕴涵着一些合理而深刻的思维和观念。

中国哲学中阴阳观念以及相生相克、对立统一的基础理论，来源于《易经》。因为《易经》把整个自然界作为摹写的底本，能够把自然界变化发展的种种规律概括其中，因而含有朴素的辩证法思想。“易”

▶▶ 八卦图

就是变化的意思，因此外文翻译的《易经》大都把书名译为《变化之书》。《易经》核心部分是八卦。八卦是三画卦，代表天、地、人三才。天的作用在“化”，地的作用在“育”，人的作用在“赞”，三者互为用，即相生、相补、相克，达到阴阳平和，消长转化，五行有序，合而生物，从而构成了中国哲学思想的基石。以阴阳八卦[3]作为基础，演化为六十四卦，三百八十四爻[4]（yáo），卜官[5]以此为依据进行推理，以便测吉凶，探祸福。

《易经》对中国文化影响甚巨，特别是中医学的理论与易学一脉相承。阴阳五行学说在先秦并不是成熟的理论，它的完善化过程是一个相当长的历程。

词语注释

【1】占筮之书：讲述占卜活动的书。

【2】彖：《易经》中论卦义的文字，也叫“卦辞”。

【3】阴阳八卦：《易经》中的八种基本图形。用“—”（表示阳）和“--”（表示阴）两种符号表示的三爻卦。以此象征天、地、雷、风、水、火、山、泽八种自然现象，每种卦又产生多种象征意义。《易经》中六十四卦皆由八卦两两相重组成。

【4】爻：《易经》最基本的概念就是阴、阳。表示阴阳的两个符号阴爻“--”和阳爻“—”。卦的变化取决于爻的变化和交错，因此，爻是变化和交错的意思。

【5】卜官：掌管占卜的官员。

五、司马迁和《史记》

《史记》原名《太史公书》，司马迁撰。司马迁，字子长，夏阳（今陕西韩城西）人，是中国杰出史学家和文学家。

司马迁的父亲名叫司马谈，在汉武帝建元、元封年间为太史令[1]，曾有志于编写古今通史。司马迁十岁的时候，跟随父亲到了首都长安，从小熟读史籍。为了搜集史料，开阔眼界，司马迁从二十岁开始，就到处考察风俗，采集传说，游踪遍及南北。元封三年（公元前108年），他承袭父亲的职务，担任了太史令。太初元年（公元前104年）参与制定了《太初历》。此后，他开始著述通史。天汉二年（公元前99年），李陵出击匈奴[2]，兵败投降，司马迁为李陵辩护，触怒了汉武帝，遭受了腐刑（阉割），后来遇赦，担任中书令[3]。他忍辱负重，发愤著史。经过十多年的艰苦努力，终于写出巨著《太史公书》，东汉以后称为《史记》。不久，他就悲惨地离开了人世。《史记》成书之时，是“藏之名山，副在京师”的，没有可能在民间流布。汉宣帝时，司马迁外孙杨恽之“祖述其书”，才开始形成对它的阅读和研究。

▶▶《史记》

▶▶ 司马迁

《史记》是中国第一部纪传体通史，记叙了上自黄帝下至汉武帝太初年间，共计3 000多年的历史，全书共一百三十篇，包括十表、八书、十二本纪、三十世家和七十列传，共52万余字。《史记》取材丰富，借鉴了《左传》《国语》《战国策》《楚汉春秋》以及诸子百家的著述，既利用了国家收藏的档案、民间保存的古文书传，又增添了亲身采访和实地调查的材料。汉代以前，出现过多种体裁的历史著作，但从纪事的久远、内容的广泛、史实的翔实、材料的系统、组织的完善几个方面，都不如《史记》。在中国史学发展史上，《史记》堪称第一部规模宏大、体制完备的中国通史，具有开创之功，为我国传统史学建立了一座宏伟的丰碑。

《史记》同时是一部优秀的文学巨著。司马迁把古代文献中过于艰深的文字改写成当时比较浅显的文字。人物描写和情节描述形象鲜明，语言生动活泼，具有强烈的艺术感染力。作为一部传记文学，《史记》在我国文学史上占有重要地位，对后世的文学创作有很大的影响。

词语注释

【1】太史令：中国古代掌管文史星历和皇家图书的官。史官之设，起于西周。魏晋以后，修史之职归著作郎。

【2】匈奴：中国古代北方民族之一，战国时代在中国大漠南北兴起，秦汉时期最为强盛，称为“匈奴”，泛称“胡”。“匈奴”之名在南北朝后期渐渐消失。

【3】中书令：在宫廷中起草文书、传宣诏命，掌书记之责，故称“中书”，其长官为中书令。

第二章　孔子和儒家

一、孔子与《论语》

当代学者蔡尚思在《孔子思想体系》一书中指出："要了解中国思想史，就必须了解孔子的思想体系。"孔子（公元前 551 ～前 479 年），名丘，字仲尼。"孔子"是人们对他的尊称。在中国古代，在一个人的姓氏后面加一个"子"字，是对这个人的尊称，如老子、庄子、孟子等。孔子是春秋末年的政治家、思想家和教育家，儒家学派的创始人。孔子早年做过小官，从事"儒"（贵族丧事赞礼者）的职业；中年时开办私学，招收弟子讲学。孔子在教学中因材施教、诲人不倦，有"弟子三千，贤人七十"之誉。孔子五十岁在鲁国从政，政绩显著。后因与鲁国君臣政见不和，便开始周游列国，以求施展政治抱负，可惜一直未能实现夙愿。孔子六十八岁返回鲁国，致力于教育，整理《诗》《书》等古代文献，七十三岁病逝。

孔子死后，孔子的弟子将他的语录以及和学生们的对话录汇编成集，即《论语》。这本书是中国封建社会的典籍，被奉为像西方《圣经》一样的圣书。北宋宰相赵普曾经在与宋太宗谈论政治时说，半部《论语》治天下。《论语》在中国的作用与影响，实在是亘古未有。

孔子学说的核心是"仁政"，是以"克己复礼"为基本内容。学礼、复礼、传礼，是孔子思想体系和一生活动的主线，在《论语》中得到了集中的体现。《论语》记载：鲁哀公问孔子，要做些什么事才能使百姓服从呢？孔子说，把正直的人提拔起来，放在邪恶的人之上，百姓就服从了；如果把邪恶的人提拔起来，放在正直的人之上，百姓就会不服从。孔子认为，管理国家的人应该是贤人，他特别强调执政者个人的品德和修养的重要性，认为这对于政治的兴衰成败有决定性的作用。因为只有个人品行好的人才能施惠于民，

孔　子

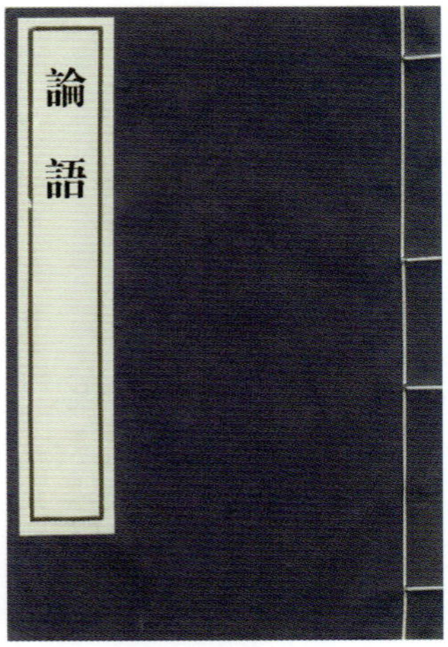

《论语》

把国家治理好；另一方面，也只有这样的人才能教化民众。孔子最理想的社会是“父子有亲，君臣有义，夫妇有别，长幼有序，朋友有信”的社会。

《论语》的内容十分广泛，有关于如何做人的思想和教诲；关于学习的态度、方法和目的；关于务政的思想及其价值；关于治国与安邦的道理，还有很多涉及人类社会的生活问题，如读书、音乐、郊游、交友等等。

《论语》的语言十分生动，形象性强，富于启发性、哲理性，语约义丰，言简意赅，都是生动精辟的格言式警句，概括了丰富的社会内容，传于后世，成为人们常用的习用语。如“人无远虑，必有近忧”[1]“温故而知新”[2]“巧言乱德。小不忍，则乱大谋”[3]“吾十有五而志于学，三十而立，四十而不惑，五十而知天命，六十而耳顺，七十而从心所欲，不逾矩”[4]“三人行，必有我师焉”[5]等。

孔子的学说在先秦时代，并没有成为主流思想。到了汉武帝时期，当时的中国已是一个强大、统一的中央集权制国家。为了适应大一统政权的需要，董仲舒提出“罢黜百家，独尊儒术”，从而将其定为国家正统的学说思想，影响中国两千多年。

词语注释

【1】人无远虑，必有近忧：一个人没有长远的考虑，事到眼前，必有忧患。

【2】温故而知新：温习旧的知识而能有新的体会和见解。

【3】巧言乱德。小不忍，则乱大谋：花言巧语就会败坏道德。小事不能忍耐，就会乱了大事。

【4】吾十有五而志于学，三十而立，四十而不惑，五十而知天命，六十而耳顺，七十而从心所欲，不逾矩：我十五岁立志学习，三十岁能在社会上立身处世做人，四十岁能懂得各种知识而不致迷惑，五十岁能知道天地间事物的运行规律，六十岁听到别人讲话能分辨是非真假，七十岁能随心所欲而不离准则。

【5】三人行，必有我师焉：每个人都有自己的长处，因此人们之间应该互相学习。

二、孔子与儒家学派

公元前484年，六十八岁的孔子从卫国返回鲁国，结束了十四年周游列国的生涯。返回鲁国后，其晚年所从事的最主要的工作，除教学活动外，就是潜心于典籍[1]的整理。

孔子以诗、书、礼、乐教授弟子，这些典籍全部在简牍和绢帛[2]上抄录流传，如果不加以选择、整理，则很难用于教学，而且随着当时礼崩乐坏、学术下移的社会情况，典籍散失的情况十分严重。为了保存、整理与流传典籍，孔子几乎投入了晚年全部精力。他从当时流传的大量典籍中，选取了最重要、最有代表性的六大类，加以认真系统的筛选、编辑、整理，形成了《诗》《书》《礼》《乐》《易》《春秋》六部书，全面总结了尧舜以来的礼乐文化，向后代提供了新的经典文本。

这六部书最初称“六艺”，后来称“六经”，是整个儒家学派最重要的经典，最重要的思想资源。《诗》即《诗经》，孔子将《诗经》删定为三百零五篇，分风、雅、颂三部分，使之具有“诗教”的作用，成为文学与政治、道德等密切相连的教科书。《书》即《书经》，也称《尚书》，选编了虞、夏、商、周时期的典章制度、施政史实等文书百篇；《礼》汇集修订了古代典章制度，以期建立社会伦理的规范。《乐》

即音乐，作为一门课程，包括弹琴、鼓瑟[3]、击磬[4]、弦歌[5]、舞乐等方面的知识技能，为规范礼乐制度，也为政治和社会生活服务。《易》即《易经》。《春秋》记载了从鲁隐公元年（公元前 722 年）至鲁哀公十四年（公元前 481 年）共 242 年的历史，成为最早的一部编年体史书。《春秋》只有一万八千余字，以极其概括的语言记述史实，含蓄而又不含糊地传达了自己的政治观点和好恶倾向。这种文笔曲折、微言大义，但带有一定倾向性的记述方法被后人所推崇，并称之为“春秋笔法”。

《春秋》

孔子对“六经”进行编定，体现出他对“六经”在社会政治生活中的作用十分重视。他向往建立上下有序的“有道”社会；他倡导仁，重视礼，把仁与礼作为解决人生困境和社会矛盾的良方，并且把“六经”作为其仁、礼思想的主要载体，从而建立起包括人生修养、伦理政治等内容的儒家知识系统和思想体系，创立了对中国历史乃至世界历史都产生过深远影响的儒家学派。

词语注释

【1】典籍：国家重要的文献，也泛指古代书籍。

【2】绢帛：古代丝织物的总称。

【3】鼓瑟：弹瑟。瑟是形似琴的一种拨弦乐器，常与琴合奏。鼓，弹奏。

【4】磬：古代打击乐器。其状如曲尺，用玉或石制成，悬挂在架子上，以槌击之而鸣。

【5】弦歌：古代传授《诗》学，均配以弦乐歌咏，因称之“弦歌”，后来借指礼乐教化、学习诵读。

三、曲阜与“三孔”

曲阜是孔子的故乡。孔子的嫡系子孙长期在这里聚族居住，世代受封，享受特权。所以，这里形成了中国最大规模的集祭祀孔子的寺庙、孔家的府邸和孔氏家族墓地于一体的建筑群——孔庙、孔府和孔林，俗称“三孔”。

曲阜孔庙被称为“中国第一庙”，是中国规格最高的祭孔场所。公元前 478 年，孔子死后第二年，鲁哀公将其故居改建为庙，内设孔子的衣冠礼器，“岁时奉祀”。西汉以后，孔子创立的儒家文化逐渐成为中国的正统文化，历代帝王不断扩建孔庙，到 18 世纪初，清朝的雍正皇帝下令大修孔庙，将其扩建为现在人们所看到的规模。

大成殿是孔庙的正殿，是整个孔庙最高的建筑，也是中国三大古殿之一。孔庙是九重庙堂，有九进庭院，大成殿九开间。在中国封建社会，“九”是皇帝的专用数，除了皇帝，别人使用“九”这个数字都要犯杀头之罪，但是孔庙是一个例外。孔庙正殿前修建了五重门，按照封建礼制，只有皇室建筑才能建五重门。北京故宫便是五重门，孔庙的五重门也是享用了皇帝的礼仪。孔庙保存了汉代以来的历代碑刻 1 000 余块，是研究中国封建社会政治、经济、文化和艺术的珍品。两千多年来，曲阜孔庙历经 15 次大修，31 次中修、百余次小修和随毁随修，从未废止。

孔府，旧称“衍圣公府”，位于孔庙东侧，是世袭“衍圣公”[1]办公和居住的地方。孔府始建于公元 1038 年，经过明、清两代的大规模修建，孔府不仅是中国仅次于故宫的最大贵族府第，而且是中国封建社会里典型的衙宅合一、园宅结合的封建贵族庄园，历代“衍圣公”恪守“诗礼传家”的祖训，收集珍藏了历代礼器法物共八万余件。除此之外，孔府最驰名的珍藏还有明清文书档案，它是孔府四百多年间各种

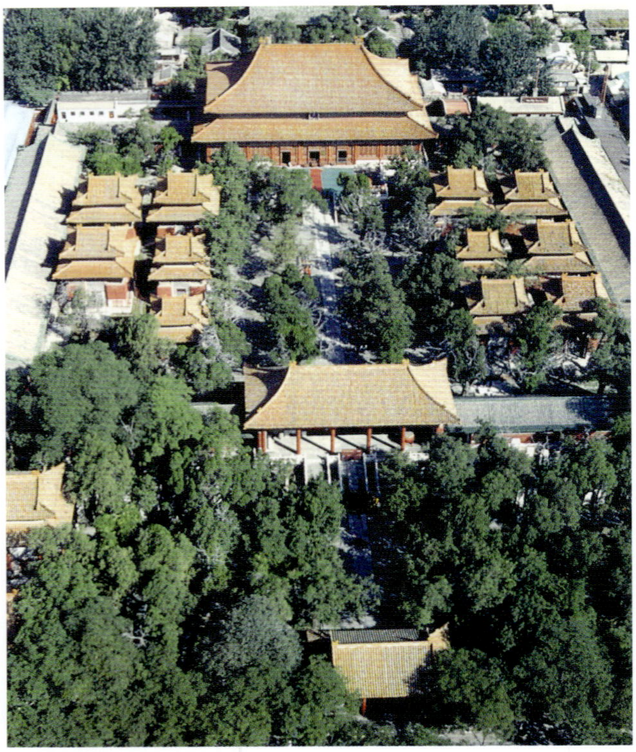

孔　庙

活动的实录，共六万余件，是中国数量最多、年代最久的私家档案。

孔林原名“至圣林”，是孔子及其家族的墓地，也是目前世界上延时最久、面积最大的氏族墓地。孔子逝于公元前479年，葬在了曲阜城北的泗水[2]边上，其后代也分别葬在孔子墓旁。孔林内墓冢累累，有周朝以来历代墓葬约十万座。汉朝以来，孔家子孙开始立墓碑，目前有宋、元、明、清、民国的墓碑3 600余块。因此，孔林又是名副其实的碑林，是研究我国历代书法艺术的珍贵资料。孔林也是一处古老而宏大的人造园林，孔子死后，弟子们纷纷把各地的奇异树种移植到此地，从孔子的弟子子贡为孔子庐墓植树开始，孔林内的古树已达万余株。自汉代以后，历代统治者对孔林重修、增修过13次，形成现在的规模，总面积约200万平方米。

曲阜每年都在孔庙举行祭祀孔子的仪式，曲阜的孔庙、孔林、孔府以其丰厚的文化积淀、悠久的历史、宏大的规模、丰富的文物珍藏以及科学艺术价值而著称于世，于1994年被载入世界文化遗产，对于研究中国历代政治、经济、文化的发展以及丧葬风俗的演变有着不可替代的作用。

词语注释

【1】衍圣公：孔子后裔的封号。宋仁宗将孔子第四十六代孙封为“衍圣公”，历经宋、元、明、清，至民国二十四年（1935年）改称“大成至圣先师奉祀官”。其职专主孔子祀事，明朝之前还兼地方官员。

【2】泗水：古水名，在山东省西南部，源出山东泗水县东，蒙山南麓，四源并发，故名。向西流经泗水县、曲阜市、兖州市，折南至济宁市东南鲁桥镇，入运河。

孔　林

第三章　老子与道教

一、老　子

老聃，尊称老子，春秋时期的思想家，被奉为道家的创始人。司马迁《史记》记载，老子姓李，名耳，字聃，楚国苦县（今河南鹿邑）人，传说他身材高大，长耳大目，宽额头，厚嘴唇。他曾做过周王室管理藏书的官，在当时是一个颇有声望的智者。后来，老子看到周王室日益衰落，就辞官离开国都洛邑（今河南洛阳市洛水北岸），开始了隐居生活。

老子一生阅读了周王室保存的大量古代文献典籍，同时，接触了不少如天文、历法等方面的自然科学知识，他对宇宙、人生和政治进行了认真的思考，并将其思想写入《老子》一书。《老子》又称《道德经》，上篇为《道经》，下篇为《德经》，合称《道德经》。全书共八十一章 5 000 多字，言简意赅，博大精深。老子以他独有的视角，探究了宇宙的形成、万物的本原、国家的治理等一系列重大的哲学和政治问题。提出了“道”[1]“自然”“无为”等著名的哲学概念，成为中国哲学的基石。

老子把“道”作为宇宙的最高本体。认为“道”超越了自然界和人类社会，超越了鬼神和天地，是宇宙万物、自然界和人类社会的总根源。他具有朴素的辩证法思想，指出事物都具有对立的两方面，如：美丑、善恶、有无、难易、长短、高下、贵贱、刚柔、黑白、明暗等都是矛盾对立的事物，并且是互相依存、联系在一起的。老子认为事物的变化就是向对立面转化的过程，但是他把这种转化看做是无条件的、绝对的，认为人们在转化中显得无能为力。这种思想也决定了他对待生活的态度，老子一生的追求是“道法自然”[2]，即依照自然本性，自然而然、自由自在地生活。这就要求保持低调，甘居下游，谦虚谨慎，拒绝竞争。

老　子

这种人生态度自然有合理的一面，它要求人们在人生征途上不要好高骛远，不要自高自大。不过，这种人生哲理中消极的一面也是很明显的，社会的历史是在竞争中发展的，没有竞争的社会就会死气沉沉，令人窒息。没有竞争的人生也将失去活力和光彩。

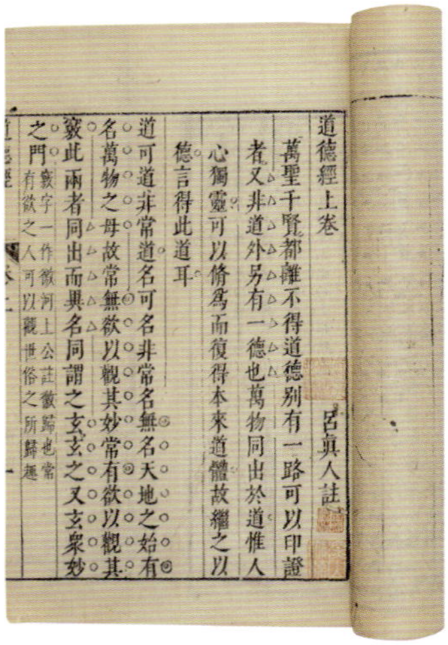
道德經上卷　呂真人註
萬聖千賢都離不得道德別有一路可以印證者又非道外另有一德也萬物同出於道惟人心獨靈可以脩爲而復得本來道體故繼之以德言得此道耳
道可道非常道名可名非常名無名天地之始有名萬物之母故常無欲以觀其妙常有欲以觀其竅此兩者同出而異名同謂之玄玄之又玄衆妙之門 竅字一作徼河上公註徼歸也常有欲之人可以觀世俗之所歸趣

《道德经》

《老子》对后世的影响非常深远，是中国道家的主要经典，又被道教奉为经书。而老子本人也被神化，唐代皇帝曾尊封老子为太上玄元皇帝[3]，宋代加号称太上老君[4]混元上德皇帝。道教尊老子为祖师，称为太上老君，又为道德天尊[5]，道教经书说老子从远古以来世代变化，降临人间演法弘道。

词语注释

【1】道：老子学说的中心概念或最高范畴。“道”在《老子》书中有三层含义：一是客观世界固有的东西，称为“恒道”；二是对客观事物的正确反映，即“论道”；三是把“道”正确论述出来，便成为道理。

【2】道法自然：老子的“道”既然是宇宙本体和客观规律，那么它的根本物性就是“自然”。

【3】太上玄元皇帝：唐高宗乾封元年（公元 666 年），亲自到亳州老君庙祭拜，并追号老子为太上玄元皇帝。

【4】太上老君：道家把老子尊为太上老君，即道教的教祖。

【5】道德天尊：即被尊为太上老君的老子。

二、道　教

道教是中国土生土长的宗教，对中国的历史文化产生过长久而重大的影响。道教是以“道”为最高信仰而得名，相信人们经过一定的修炼，可以得道成仙、长生不死。道教把老子尊为教主，奉为神明，并以老子的《道德经》为主要经典，对其进行了宗教性的阐释。此外，道教还吸收了阴阳家[1]、墨家[2]、战国时期以来的神仙方术、秦汉时期的黄老术和汉代的谶（chèn）纬[3]迷信思想。

道教产生于东汉中叶，一般认为汉顺帝时张道陵在鹤鸣山（今四川大邑县境）首创道教。道教最初有两个来源，一派是五斗米，凡是奉教者须交纳五斗米而得名。五斗米派奉老子为教主，张道陵被尊为“天师”。张道陵死后，其子张衡，其孙张鲁继续传道，世称“三张”道。到了张鲁的儿子张盛时，他从四川移居至江西，在龙虎山（今贵溪境内）继续香火，历代相传。另一派是太平道。河北平乡境人张角和他的两个弟弟，自称“大良贤师”，创立太平道，在十多年里，其信徒达数十万人，后来，张角兄弟利用道教组织发动农民起义，以头裹黄巾为标志，这就是历史上有名的黄巾起义[4]。黄巾起义失败后，太平道衰败；与此同时，五斗米道（后更名为天师道，也即正一道）却发展起来。

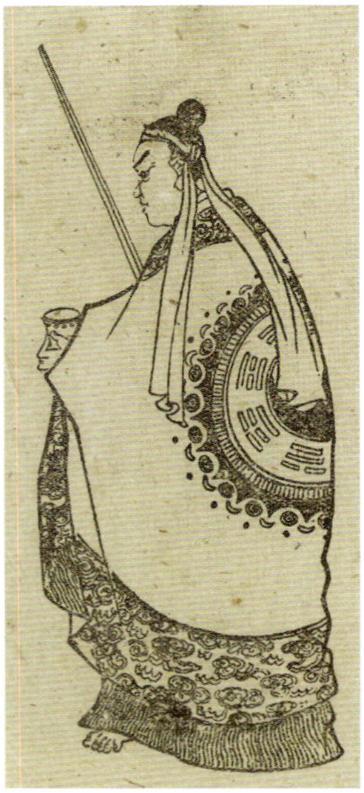

张　角

▶▶ 真武山道观

早期的道教经过改革，在经典、教义、戒律、仪轨以及组织等各方面趋于完善。公元 7 世纪后，在唐、宋几代皇帝的倡导下，道教发展到鼎盛时期。

公元 12 世纪以后，道教逐渐分为全真道[5]与正一道[6]两大系统。全真派讲究内、外丹的修炼，内丹即人身的精、气、神的修炼，是全真派的主要修炼方术；外丹即用铅汞和药物配制烧炼一种可食丹丸的方法。全真派道士按照最初的规定皆为出家道士，有四点基本要求：第一，不结婚；第二，不食荤；第三，平时也必须穿道装；第四，束发留须。他们都住在宫观里。

正一派道士以降神驱鬼、祈福禳灾的符箓活动为主。该派道士可以结婚，有家室，可以食荤，除上殿诵经、作经忏法事之外，平时可以穿俗装，不留胡须，发式随俗。

全真道主张出家清修，它的宫观建筑也大多仿照佛教寺院，并且建立起子孙庙和十方丛林两个系统。子孙庙中师傅即住持，收授弟子，称弟子为道童。十方丛林则不招收弟子，只为各小庙推荐来的弟子传戒。教规和财产管理都有严格的制度。

道教在近两千年的发展中，对中国文化产生过全面而深刻的影响。道教的神仙信仰，道家崇尚自然无为的思想，以及逍遥自由的精神追求，都极大地激发了中国文人的浪漫情怀，道教的许多典故为文学创作提供了丰富的题材。道教的俗神崇拜活动与中国普通民众的日常生活和文化娱乐水乳交融，息息相关；道教的服药炼丹方术，对中国古代化学和药物学的发展作出了重要的贡献。总之，道教对中国的社会心理、社会习俗、思维方式等各个方面都有过不同程度的影响，是中国古代文化遗产的一个有机组成部分，在中国传统文化中占有相当重要的地位。

词语注释

【1】阴阳家：战国时期提倡阴阳五行说的一个学派．以邹衍为首的阴阳家，认为人类社会的发展也受水、火、木、金、土五种势力的支配，提出“五德终始”“五德转移”说，用以论证社会历史的变革和王朝的更替，形成了唯心主义的历史循环论。

【2】墨家：先秦时主张“兼爱”和“非攻”等思想的重要学派。创始人为墨子。在当时为儒家的反对派，影响极大。墨家有严格的纪律，其弟子都能赴汤蹈火，舍身行道。后期墨家克服了墨子学说中的宗教迷信成分，对逻辑学、光学、几何学、力学等都有研究和贡献。

【3】谶纬：汉代流行的神学迷信。“谶”是秦汉间巫师或方士编造的预示吉凶的隐语或预言，“纬”指方士化的儒生所编辑的附会儒家经典的各种著作。

【4】黄巾起义：东汉末年张角领导的大规模农民起义。张角创立太平道，组织民众进行活动，公元184年发动起义，以头裹黄巾为标志，故称黄巾军。起义失败后，余部坚持斗争二十多年，沉重打击了东汉王朝的统治。

【5】全真道：公元1167年，王重阳在山东宁海（今牟平）全真庵讲道时创立。主张道、释、儒三教合一，以“澄心定意、抱元守一、存神固气”为“真功”，“济贫拔苦、先人后己、与物无私”为“真行”；功行俱全，故名全真。不尚符，不事烧炼。道士须出家居于宫观，不结婚并禁荤腥。

【6】正一道：原为张道陵所创的“五斗米道”。公元307~313年间，张道陵第四代孙张盛移居江西龙虎山，开“正一宗坛”，尊张道陵为“正一天师”，其名渐显，而以“天师道”著称。道士可居家也可出家山居，允许结婚，可在斋期以外食酒肉。

三、道教的养生术

在中国关于长生成仙的信仰由来已久，历史上流传着美丽的嫦娥奔月，飞升成仙[1]的故事。春秋战国时代，燕齐沿海地区流传渤海有蓬莱、方丈、瀛洲三神山[2]，山上有仙人游息，还有各种服之成仙而不死的灵药，于是形成一股求仙寻药的风气。道教继承了长生成仙的思想，带给人们一些信念：凡人经过现世的修炼能够长生成仙。养生术是沟通人神关系的桥梁。神仙是由凡人修炼而成的，而神仙的最大特点就是长生。若要长生，先要长寿，欲长寿必先养生。这就要采用各种养生方法来祛病健身，使身体和精神保持健康强盛。道教徒在追求长生成仙的过程中，通过无数实践，并随着道教的发展演化，形成了博大精深、蕴涵着高度健身疗疾价值的古代人体科学和健身方法体系，概括起来，有外丹、内丹、服食和房中术等内容。

外丹烧炼，是以炉鼎烧炼矿物类药物，制取“长生不死”仙丹（又称金丹、灵丹等）的一种实验方术。秦汉时，由于秦始皇、汉武帝等人迷信神仙之道，苦求不死之方，极大地刺激了外丹烧炼术。道教创立后，将它与符箓斋醮（jiǎo）等道教仪式和阴阳五行等结合起来，提升到新的高度并神秘化。虽然不死的仙丹没有炼成，但炼丹活动从客观上促进了古代冶炼和化学工业的发展以及火药的发明。

内丹炼养，是道教养生术中最富有特色的一类养生术。内丹，为行气、导引、呼吸、吐纳之类的总称。道教用人体做炉鼎，使精气神在体内凝结成丹而达到长生不死的目的。这种路数强调通过练吸、练呼、呼

炼丹

吸皆练，或者配合形体和意念的锻炼，来调整人体的生理功能，使阴阳平衡，改善脏腑的气血流通，虽不可能达到长生不死的目的，却可以健身祛病。受道教呼吸修炼理论和实践的影响，气功锻炼在中国代代相传，成为具有民族特色的传统养生术，经久不衰。

服食，指用服食药物以求长生。道书中记载了大量药酒、药茶、道菜、药膳[3]。道教服食派将用药物泡制的酒称为神酒，如：地黄[4]酒、胡麻酒、松脂[5]酒、天门冬[6]酒等。道教许多灵验的服食方还传入了世俗社会，并历代传承、演变，上至帝王，下至百姓，或保健养生，或治病祛疾，并且被录入中医著作，成为中医药学的重要组成部分。

道士们通过自己的修炼、行医的实践，在病理学[7]、药理学[8]方面作出了诸多贡献，其中医术高明者也不在少数。民间深信"十道九医"，一些道医被奉为医神或药王，享受祭祀。

从道教的性质以及道士修炼的目的来看，尽管在道士修炼方式的基础上所形成的道教医学，由于受神仙观念等影响而掺杂有许多非科学的糟粕，但是，也有与医学科学相通的一面。其在中医史乃至世界医学史上都占有重要地位。近几十年来，道教的炼养术被加以科学的改造，运用于医疗与气功养生，被证明有治病健身、延年益寿的效果，其影响日益扩大。

词语注释

【1】嫦娥奔月，飞升成仙：嫦娥，传说为后羿之妻，窃不死之药以奔月而为月神。后人称其为月中仙子。

【2】蓬莱、方丈、瀛洲三神山：《史记》等典籍中所提及的三座神山名。

【3】药膳：配有中药做的菜肴或食品，如参芪鸡、虫草鸭、银耳羹等。

【4】地黄：多年生草本植物，其块根为中药。

【5】松脂：松类树干分泌出的油脂，在空气中呈黏滞液态或块状固体，含松香和松节油。

【6】天门冬：百合科多年生攀援草本植物。

【7】病理学：研究疾病的原因、发生发展规律及其发展过程中人体的形态、代谢和功能变化的一门科学。

【8】药理学：药物在有机体内所起的变化，对有机体的影响及其防治疾病的原理的科学。

四、道教的洞天福地

道教追求得道成仙，希望通过这种方式超脱生死，过仙人的生活。道教所崇尚的神仙世界是一种仙境，充满了彩云亭台、琼楼玉宇，天上有神灵居住的帝乡天堂，地上有得道修仙的福地洞天。

在人间，洞天福地是道教提出的一个极具思想特色的学说，其源可以追溯到远古时期人们的山居传统，同时也与道教的人生追求相联系。道教对山特别偏爱，除了山的幽静、灵奇和方便采药、行气等原因，更因为山里万物生长、生机盎然，是自然大道的集中体现。道祖老子在描述"道"的表象时，就特别喜欢"山、谷、水"，因为它们分别象征了大道的虚静、宽容和柔弱、滋养。道教认为山中有神仙居住，道士住在这里可以修炼，得道成仙。总之，"洞天"的意思是：山中有

恒　山

武当山紫霄宫

洞室通达上天，贯通诸山。

因此，山在道教中的地位远比世界上其他宗教更为突出。古人云，“天下名山僧道多”，千百年来，历代道人隐居深山、潜心修道，把幽远的风景优美的名山作为修炼的地方，著名道士曾修炼的山岳常常流传着得道成仙的故事，带着一些神秘色彩。在这些地方往往会有一些道观胜迹，营造出理想的人间仙境，正所谓“山不在高，有仙则名”。

道教名山作为道教传播的势力中心，通常随着当地的道观规模的扩大、道文化的影响也越来越广，山就渐渐有了名声，最终成为“道教名山”。中国历史上有所谓“十大洞天”“三十六小洞天”“七十二福地”等著名道教仙山。历代的文人骚客也大多登临其境、心旷神怡，留下了大量的诗文。目前，中国最有影响的道教名山是：

山东泰山、湖南衡山、陕西华山、山西恒山、河南嵩山、江西龙虎山、江西阁皂山、江苏茅山、四川青城山、广东罗浮山、陕西终南山、湖北武当山、山东崂山和云南巍宝山。

泰山南天门

第四章　佛教在中国

一、玄奘取经

自唐朝以来，中国民间就流传着玄奘和尚西天取经的故事。小说《西游记》里的故事是虚构的，不过唐僧确有其人，取经也确有其事。玄奘（公元 602 年～664 年）俗姓陈，名祎（huī），河南偃师人。家中有四男一女，玄奘最小。他生性聪明，在父兄的熏陶和社会环境的影响下，养成了广泛探索学问的兴趣，尤其酷爱风靡当时的佛学。玄奘十三岁出家，遍访名师益友，很快就通晓了很多重要的佛教经典著作。但他并不满足，为了深入研究佛学，他决定亲自赴天竺（古印度）考察。那时，去印度没有任何交通工具，而且必须经过现在的甘肃、新疆，向西越过帕米尔，进入现在的中亚、西亚等地区，才能到达。公元 627 年 8 月，玄奘从长安出发，夹杂在返回西域的客商中混出玉门关，然后只身西行，经过著名的八百里流沙地，又从天山南麓横穿新疆终年积雪的别迭里山口[1]，走了将近一年的时间，历尽千辛万苦，九死一生，终于到达印度。在印度的佛教最高学府——烂陀寺，玄奘专心学习了五年，后来，又受戒贤法师[2]的委托，主持寺内的讲席。唐太宗贞观十七年（公元 643 年）春天，玄奘带了 657 部经书，踏上归国的征程。

贞观十九年（公元 645 年）正月二十四日，玄奘回到了阔别近十八年的长安。不久，唐太宗在洛阳的行宫接见了他。此后，他开始了佛经的翻译工作。他先后在弘福寺[3]和大慈恩寺[4]主持译场（翻译室），

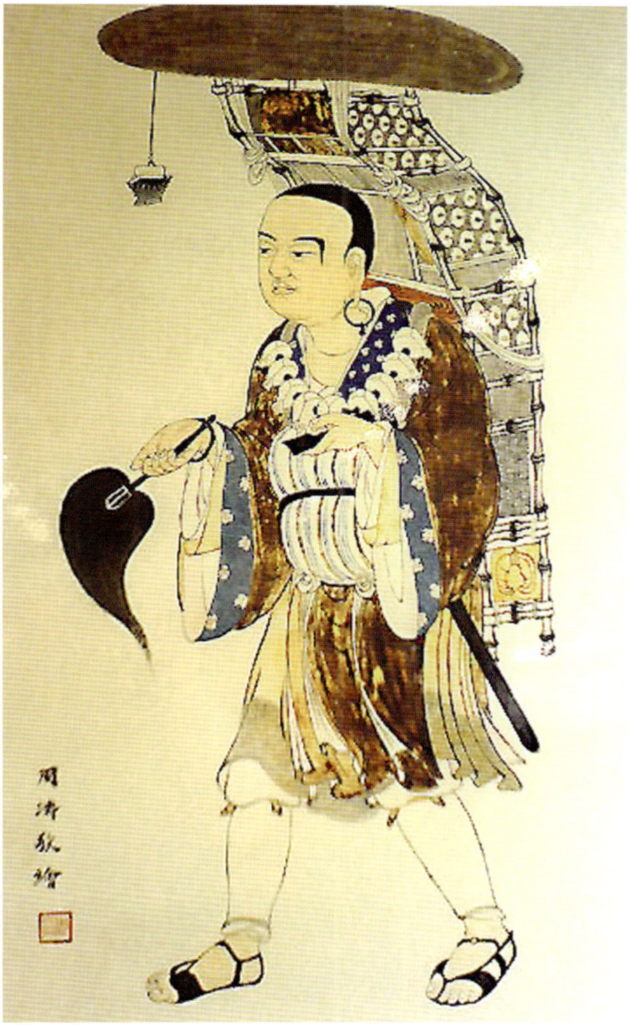

玄　奘

并在慈恩寺修造大雁塔，用来储备经书。从回国到圆寂的十九年间，他一共翻译了经书 75 部，1 335 卷，计 1 300 多万字。玄奘自己口述、由门徒执笔写了一本回忆旅途见闻的书——《大唐西域记》。这部书记载了他亲自游历的十一国和耳闻的二十八国的情况。所涉地域包括现今中国的新疆，以及阿富汗、巴基斯坦、印度、孟加拉国、尼泊尔、斯里兰卡等国家。《大唐西域记》被翻译成多国文字，成为一部世界名著。

佛教源于印度，是印度文化，但玄奘等佛教学者把佛经带回中国，用汉语言和哲理概念解释佛教，不仅保存了大量的珍贵的佛教典籍，而且创生了中国佛教。后来佛教典籍在印度大都失传，只有中文译本还保存完好，以至出现了佛教在印度式微而在中国兴盛的一种文化迁移现象。

词语注释

【1】别迭里山口：唐代长安通向西域“弓月道”的必经之路。

【2】戒贤法师：天竺的大学者。玄奘来到烂陀寺，跟随戒贤法师学了五年的佛经。

【3】弘福寺：弘福寺位于唐代长安城修德坊西北隅，即今陕西省西安火车西站附近，创建于贞观八年（公元 634 年），是著名的佛教寺院。贞观十九年（公元 645 年）玄奘自印度求法归来，奉敕在这里组织译经场。

【4】大慈恩寺：唐代寺院名。唐贞观二十二年（公元 648 年），太子李治（即后来的高宗）为追悼亡母文德皇后，在隋朝无漏寺的基础上扩建改造，改名大慈恩寺。

二、四大石窟

莫高窟大佛

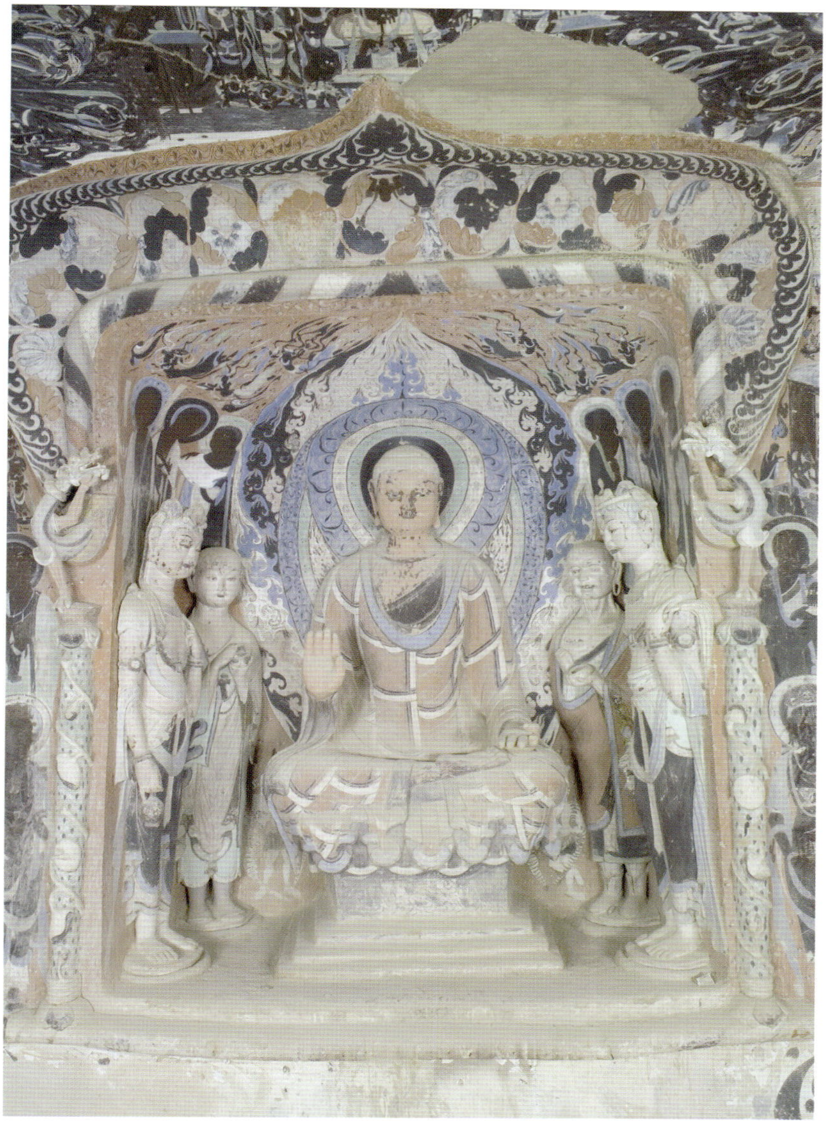

莫高窟佛像

公元 3 世纪前后，随着佛教在中国的兴起，集古代绘画、雕刻艺术成就于一体的石窟寺，也蓬勃发展起来，遍布全国，被誉为“东方艺术宝库”。敦煌[1]莫高窟、云冈石窟、龙门石窟和麦积山石窟，并称为“中国四大石窟”。其中前三个石窟已被载入“世界文化遗产名录”。

（一）莫高窟

莫高窟俗称千佛洞，“千”是概数，喻指很多很多。莫高窟位于甘肃省河西走廊西端，敦煌市东南 25 千米，在鸣沙山东麓 50 多米高的崖壁上。洞窟有上下五层，南北长约 1 600 米，是“四大石窟”中规模最大、内容最丰富的一座，集中反映了中国十几个朝代、历时近千年的石刻艺术精粹，是世界上规模最大、保存最完整的佛教遗址。莫高窟始建于前秦建元二年（公元 366 年），一位法名乐尊的僧人云游到此，他看到鸣沙山上金光万道，感悟到这里是佛的圣地，于是在崖壁上凿建了第一个佛窟。以后，经过历代的修建，到公元 7 世纪唐朝时，莫高窟已经有一千多个佛洞了，保存至今的有北凉至元代多种类型的洞窟 490 多个。

历朝历代的人们在开凿洞窟时，在洞窟内雕塑了大量的佛像，绘制了大批壁画。塑像千姿百态，服饰和表现手法各不相同，反映了不同时代的特色。壁画当中最有特色、最多的是佛教题材：各种佛、菩萨、天王的尊像画；佛经中各种故事的连环画；佛教在印度、中亚、中国的传说故事和历史人物相结合的佛教史迹画等等。此外，各个时代的壁画还反映了当时各民族各阶层的社会生活、衣冠服饰、古代建筑造型以及音乐、舞蹈、杂技等，也记录了中外文化交流的历史事实。因此，西方学者将敦煌壁画称为“墙壁上的图书馆”。保存至今的敦煌壁画有 4.5 万平方米，彩塑雕像 2 400 余尊。如果把这些壁画一一连接，可以组成近 30 千米长的画廊。

光绪二十六年（公元 1900 年）五月二十六日，寄宿在千佛洞中的游方道士王圆箓在引水冲沙时，无意中把水冲进了石窟甬道中，偶然发现墙壁里面是空的，因此发现了一个密室。此密室现编号为 17 号窟，也叫藏经洞，洞中有公元 4~11 世纪的经、史、子、集[2]各类文书和绘画作品等 4 万余件。其中的大部分后来被外国盗宝者劫到十多个国家和地区。

由于敦煌莫高窟位于当时沟通东西方的“丝绸之路”的要塞上，因此它也是东西方宗教、文化和知识的交汇处。各种外来艺术和中国的民族艺术水乳交融于莫高窟，使它具有珍贵的历史、艺术、科学价值，成为中华民族的瑰宝，人类优秀的文化遗产。

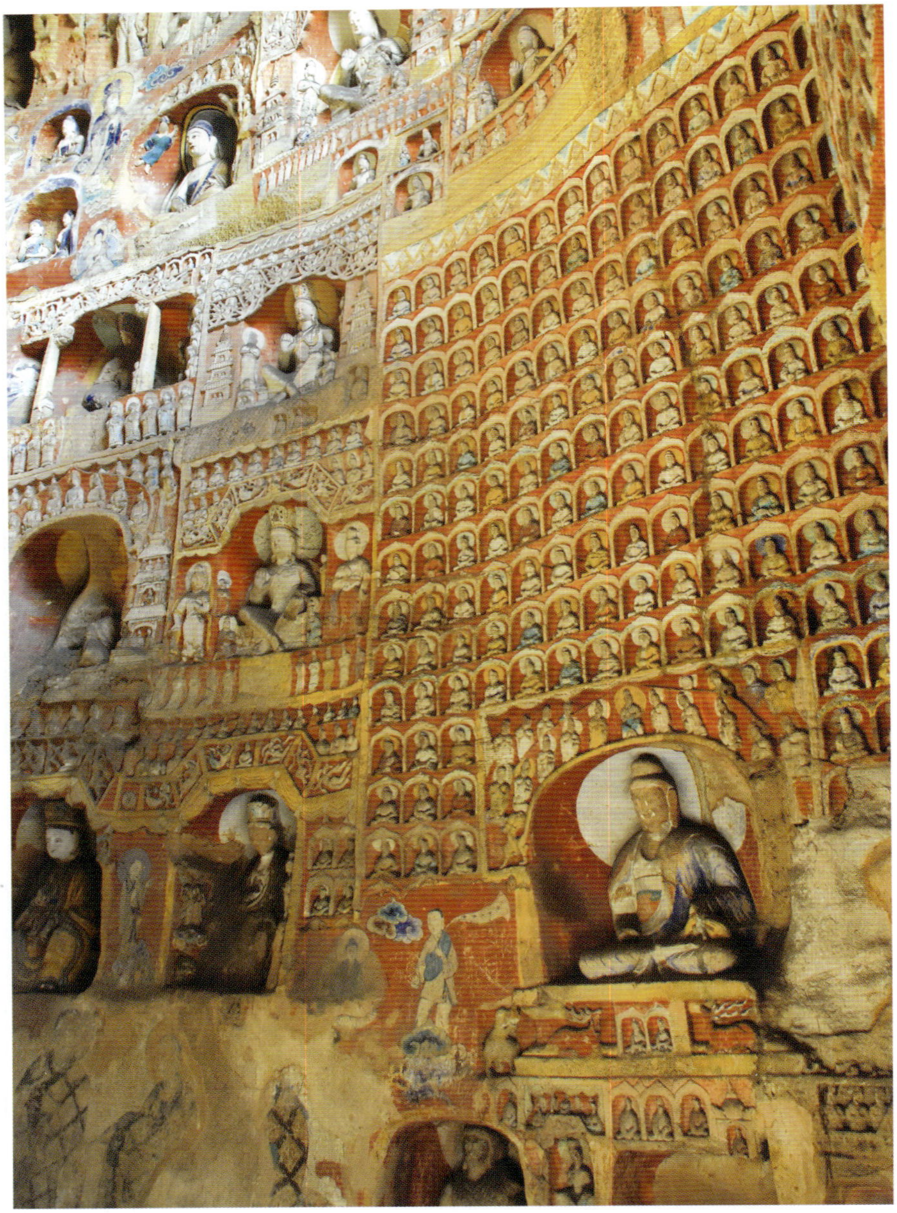

云冈石窟

（二）云冈石窟

云冈石窟位于中国北部山西省大同市以西16千米处的武周山南麓，始凿于北魏兴安二年（公元453年）。云冈石窟依山而凿，东西绵亘约1千米，气势恢弘，雕饰奇伟，是世界闻名的艺术宝库。北魏时期的高僧昙曜共开凿五窟，后世称为“昙曜五窟”，均为穹隆顶，椭圆形平面，仿天竺草庐式。现存洞窟53个，最大的是第3窟（魏孝文帝时开凿），由地面到窟顶高达25米，中央直立一个宽约60平方米的大塔柱，上端连接着窟顶，整个塔柱和洞壁嵌满了大小佛龛和多种装饰。

石窟中大小造像5.1万多尊，最大者达17米，最小者仅几厘米。窟中菩萨[3]、力士[4]、飞天[5]形象生动活泼。佛像的容貌一般是厚唇、高鼻、长目、宽肩，有雄健的气概，体貌表现了北方少数民族的特征。大佛像高大雄伟，显示了举世独尊、无可比拟的气概。石窟内的其他石像，按照等级一个比一个低，全体都服从于大佛像，再配上飞天和侏儒，为大佛服役。塔柱上的雕刻精致细腻，天花板、柱子上还刻满了神异的动物花纹。进入洞窟，恍如置身于一个神话世界。北魏著名地理学家郦道元在《水经注》中曾记载当年云冈石窟的壮观：“凿石开山，因岩结构，真容巨壮，世法所希。山堂水殿，烟寺相望，林渊锦镜，缀目新眺。”

（三）龙门石窟

公元5世纪末，北魏孝文帝迁都到河南洛阳，在伊水岸边的龙门山上，又营造了一个巨大的石窟群——龙门石窟，逐渐取代了云冈石窟，以后历经各朝营建，后人陆续在龙门山对岸坚硕的青石山壁上，

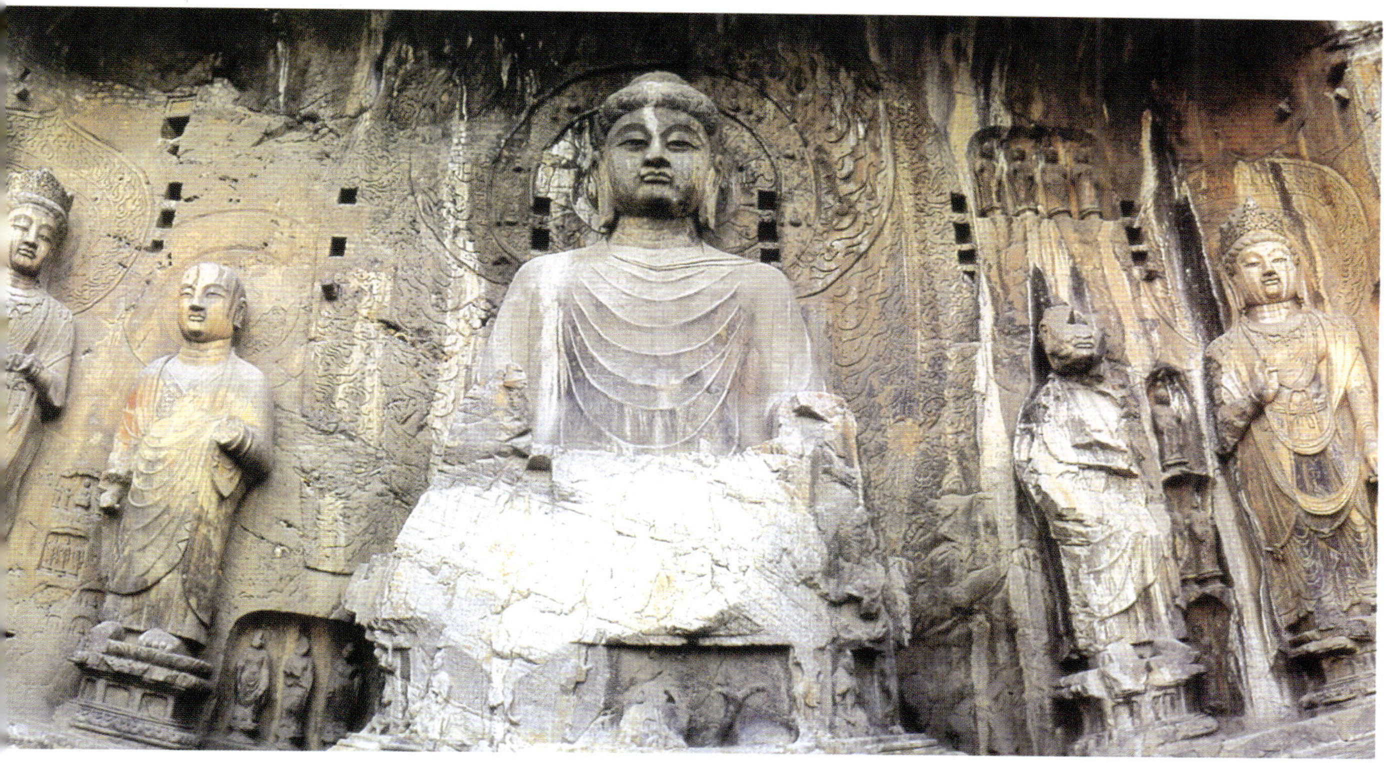

龙门石窟

密密麻麻地开凿了两千多个窟室，一共雕造佛像近10万尊。龙门石窟的佛像比云冈石窟的雕像表现出更多的中国艺术特点。其中唐窟最多，占石窟总数的60%以上。女皇武则天执政时期开凿的石窟占唐代石窟的大多数，这与她长期在洛阳有关。奉先寺是最具有代表性的唐代石窟，它位于西山最高处，其中的主佛为卢舍那佛[6]，佛高五丈有余，面部丰腴饱满，修眉长目，嘴角微翘，流露出对人间的关注和智慧的光芒。衣纹简洁流畅，两侧侍立的弟子，一为迦叶，老成持重；一为阿难，温顺虔诚；又有天王手持宝塔，力士左手叉腰，右手举拳，怒目相视，纷纷随侍左右。这座卢舍那佛像是唐代的武则天下令雕凿的，为了建造奉先寺，据说武则天资助脂粉钱两万贯，亲自率领朝臣参加卢舍那大佛的开光仪式。传说佛像是按武则天的长相雕刻的，因而庄严中透出几分女性风韵。龙门石窟还保存了碑刻题记三千多块，是我国书法艺术中的珍品。

（四）麦积山

麦积山石窟位于甘肃省天水市东南35千米处，是中国秦岭山脉西端小陇山中一座奇峰，因山形似麦堆而得名。周围风景秀丽，山峦上密布着翠柏苍松，郁郁葱葱；青松似海，云雾阵阵，构成一幅“麦积烟雨”的美丽图景，是四大石窟风景最佳的地方。

从公元4世纪起，历代在这座山上修造了二百多个洞窟，其显著特点就是都开凿在悬崖峭壁上，靠一层层的凌空栈道相通，极其惊险。现存北魏、西魏、北周石窟大约30个，麦积山石质不宜于雕刻，佛像一般都是泥塑。经过了一千多年，塑像仍然没有溃败。彩塑的佛像清秀洒脱，艺术水平很高。石窟内现存的古代雕塑有七千多尊，还有一部分壁画和精美的石刻造像碑。

麦积山比敦煌接近中原，中原较高水平的汉民族文化在这里给予佛教艺术的滋养是显而易见的。麦积山的雕塑有两大明显的特征：强烈的民族意识和世俗化的趋向。大多佛像都是俯首下视的姿态，和蔼可亲，虽是天上的神，却像世俗的人，体态和衣饰完全汉化。第44窟一座沙弥像着通肩袈裟，秀骨清相，神态安详，宁静谦和，笑靥可亲，被称为“东方的维纳斯”。

词语注释

【1】敦煌：在今甘肃省敦煌市。

【2】经、史、子、集：古代图书分类法的四大类别。

【3】菩萨：泛指佛和某些神；佛教指修行到一定程度、地位仅次于佛的人。

【4】力士：古代官名。主管金鼓旗帜，随皇帝车驾出入及守卫四门。

【5】飞天：佛教壁画或石刻中的在空中飞舞的神。

【6】卢舍那佛：卢舍那大佛是龙门石窟中艺术水平最高、整体设计最严密、规模最大的一处。

三、四大佛教名山

在中国，文殊[1]"大智"、观音[2]"大悲"、地藏[3]"大愿"、普贤[4]"大行"并称四大菩萨。四大菩萨都以拯救众生脱离苦海到达彼岸为宗旨，但各有自己显灵说法之地，即各有自己的"道场"。文殊菩萨的道场在山西省五台山；普贤菩萨的道场在四川省峨眉山；观音菩萨的道场在浙江省普陀山；地藏菩萨的道场在安徽省九华山。这四大菩萨的四大道场被称为四大佛教名山。

（一）五台山

位于山西省东北部五台县东北，以"东、西、南、北、中"五个台顶而得名，因为山上气候寒冷，又被称为"清凉山"，是驰名中外的佛教圣地，居于中国佛教四大名山之首。五台山佛教的发展开始于汉代。早在东汉永平年间（公元58年～75年），印度的两名僧人来中国传教，获得汉明帝的准奏之后，在洛阳建造了白马寺，之后，在五台山建立了灵鹫寺。从那时起，五台山就成为中国的一个佛教中心。五台山经过历代修建，寺院林立，五峰内外佛寺最多时达360座，僧尼达万人之众，堪称中国最大的寺庙建筑群。

五台山寺院有许多珍贵的文物，成为中国艺术史上的明珠。五台山显要的标志性建筑是白色喇嘛塔，矗立在塔院寺内，由于周身涂以白垩，俗称大白塔。塔高56.4米，塔的中层，建有塔殿三间，殿内有三大士[5]铜像、瓷质济公和尚[6]像、木雕刘海戏金蟾像和佛像。这座塔无论建筑之难还是工程之大，都是整个五台山之最。

佛光寺的正殿建于唐代。在中国，只有两座留存至今的唐代木结构建筑，也是中国最早的木构殿堂，都在五台山。佛光寺大殿是其中一座，是佛光寺建造时期存留至今的实证。

五台山作为中国首屈一指的佛教名山，融汇了印度佛教、藏传佛教、汉传佛教、民间宗教、儒教、

五台山

峨眉山金顶

道教和三晋文化的精髓，不仅是汉、藏、满、蒙等各民族的僧人聚居修学的道场，也是海内外广大佛教徒以及旅游者共同崇仰、朝拜的圣地。每年农历四月初四，文殊菩萨圣诞日，五台山都举办大型庙会。届时，中外香客络绎不绝。

（二）峨眉山

位于四川省西南部，距成都市130千米，以雄秀壮丽的自然风光和充满神秘传说的佛教文化闻名于世，是中国四大佛教名山之一，享有“峨眉天下秀”的美誉。汉朝末年，佛家就在这里建立寺庙，唐宋时期逐渐兴盛，到了清朝末年，寺庙多达150余座。将近两千年的佛教发展历程，给峨眉山留下了丰富的佛教文化遗产，使峨眉山逐步成为中国乃至世界影响深远的佛教圣地。

峨眉山的文物古迹绚丽多彩。其中，宋代的普贤菩萨铜像重约62吨，高达7.85米，规模宏大，造像庄严。元代的华严铜塔，14层，高5.8米，塔身铸有佛像4 700余尊和《华严经》[7]文。冶造精湛，巧夺天工。

峨眉山的主峰是金顶，最高峰又称万佛顶，海拔3 079米。有云海、日出、佛光、圣灯“四大奇观”。公元16世纪在这里修建了一座铜殿，因为殿顶鎏金，光耀夺目，人称金顶。铜殿及华藏寺都毁于火灾。现在的金顶华藏寺，是1986年～1989年按照原貌重新修建的。金顶金佛采用铜铸镏金工艺塑造，通高48米，总重量达660吨，由台座和十方普贤菩萨像组成。设计完美，线条流畅，堪称铜铸巨佛的旷世之作。金佛高48米，代表的是阿弥陀佛的48个愿望，“十方”意喻着普贤的十大行愿。

金顶是峨眉山最壮观的观景台，长约1 200米，总面积16 505平方米，由金刚嘴、舍身岩、睹光台、修心台四大观景平台组成，在3 079米的海拔高度，金顶如同飞来的巨石，这个能容纳数千人的观景台，可以说是独一无二。站在群峰环合的孤峰之上，观金殿、金佛、佛光、圣灯、日出、云海，千山万岭，起伏如浪，峨眉山的清神逸韵，尽收眼底。

（三）普陀山

位于舟山群岛的东部，与世界第三大渔港沈家门隔海相望，方圆12.5平方千米。山上景物奇特，风光秀丽，金沙绵亘，晚霞白帆，在佛教传说中，这里为南海，是观世音菩萨的道场（古时候的南海，现在地理上称为东海）。普陀山不同于其他佛教名山，是中国唯一一个以佛教名山为特色的海岛型国家重点风景名胜。

普陀山的宗教活动可以追溯到秦朝，自唐朝建立观音道场以来，经历代修建，寺院林立。鼎盛时期，全山除了有三大寺以外，还有88庵、128茅棚，4 000余僧侣，史称“震旦第一佛国”。现在全岛三大寺普济寺、法雨寺、慧济寺是为数不多的佛寺建筑中的精品。普济寺是最大的寺院，顶部金碧辉煌，大门有八扇，高大气派，建筑风格具有皇家建筑富丽宏大的气派。法雨寺庙宇都是依山而起，前后六重殿堂，

普陀山

九华山

最下面一层九龙殿内的“九龙盘拱”等结构，是清康熙年间从南京的明故宫拆迁到此重建的一座殿宇。慧济寺是普陀山最高的寺院，爬一千多级台阶才能到达。

普陀山还有许多大自然的巧夺天工，奇岩怪石。著名的有盘陀石、二龟听法石、海天佛国石等 20 余处。山海相接之处有许多石洞胜景，最著名的是潮音洞和梵音洞。

20 世纪末，新建成的“南海观音”铜像立于观音跳山冈。铜像总高度 33 米，重 70 余吨，采用漂海观音的形象，端庄慈祥，金光闪闪，成为普陀山的标志。

（四）九华山

位于安徽省长江南岸的池州市境内，方圆百里，山势雄伟，植被繁茂，瀑飞泉涌；气候温润，四季分明，有“东南第一山”之称。这座山原名叫九子山，因为唐代大诗人李白见此山“高数千丈，上有九峰如莲花”而赋诗，后来才更名为九华山。

传说唐高宗永徽四年（公元 653 年），新罗国（今韩国境内）国王近亲金乔觉来到九华，潜心修行 75 年，99 岁趺（fū）坐而圆寂，颜面如生，佛徒都传信他是地藏菩萨的化身，称为金地藏。僧徒在神光岭建塔，用三级石塔安置地藏肉身，开辟地藏王道场。自从金地藏驻山以后，九华山开始大规模兴建寺庙。以后历经宋、元、明、清，逐渐扩大，鼎盛时期，寺庵 300 余座、僧尼三四千人。现存古寺庙 99 座，佛像 1 万余尊，文物 2 000 余件，僧尼 700 余人。九华山历来高僧辈出，从唐朝至今，自然形成了 10 多尊肉身菩萨，现在可供观瞻的有 5 尊。在气候常年湿润的自然条件下，肉身不腐，为九华名山增添了一分庄严神秘的色彩。

地藏法会日为农历七月三十日，这一天是地藏菩萨金乔觉的诞辰日，又是圆寂日，各寺庙都举行隆重的佛事活动，来九华山参加地藏法会的善男信女正在逐年增多。

词语注释

【1】文殊：梵文，汉译为“妙吉祥”“妙德”。据说文殊在诸位菩萨当中以智慧和辩才居第一，尊号为“大智文殊”。其最典型的形象是骑一头雄健的青狮，象征智慧、辩才、锐利和威猛。

【2】观音：又称大悲菩萨、接引菩萨，传说，人在弥留之际口呼“南无阿弥陀佛”，观音菩萨就会来接引此人到西方极乐世界。在北魏以前观音菩萨为男性，因附和中国的生殖土壤，后慢慢幻化做女应身。

【3】地藏：又称地藏王。因其“安忍不动，犹如大地；静虑深密，犹如秘藏”故名。地藏菩萨之形象，或作喜菩萨，坐莲花座，光焰周遍，饰以宝冠、璎珞等；或作沙门形，着袈裟，左手持宝珠，右手执锡杖，或坐或立于莲花上。

【4】普贤：以“行愿”著称。主诸佛的理德、行德，与文殊的智德、证德相对，尊号为“大行普贤”。其最富特征的形象是骑一头六牙白象，作为他愿行广大、功德圆满的象征。

【5】三大士：佛教称西方极乐世界观音菩萨、文殊菩萨、普贤菩萨为三大士。

【6】济公和尚：小说《济公传》的主人公。又名济癫，俗姓李，名修缘。18 岁出家，投杭州灵隐寺为僧，法名道济。他不守佛门戒律，举止癫狂，衣衫褴褛，成天喝酒吃肉。他风趣幽默，喜嘲弄官府，爱打抱不平，济困扶危，除暴安良，被尊称为济公。

【7】《华严经》：全称《大方广佛华严经》，佛教经典。是中国佛教宗派之一华严宗据以立宗的经典。其性质与《大般若经》相近，也是在汇集一些原先单独流传的大乘经的基础上，逐渐增广而成的。

四、藏传佛教和喇嘛寺庙

藏传佛教，俗称喇嘛教。

最早将佛教引进西藏的是藏族的一个著名领袖——松赞干布。他统一西藏后，对当时的唐朝和尼泊尔国，采取了联姻通好的政策，于公元7世纪中期，先后娶尼泊尔王国尺尊公主及唐朝文成公主为妃。这两位公主都携带着佛像、经典、法器、僧侣进入藏地，于是松赞干布在拉萨为她们带来的佛像分别建造了大昭寺和小昭寺，并陆续请印度、尼泊尔和唐朝的高僧翻译佛经，兴建佛寺。

松赞干布（中）

此后，经过四个世纪的反复磨合，公元12世纪，佛教在西藏站住脚跟。佛教与当地的苯教[1]长期相互影响，相互斗争，以佛教教义为基础，吸收了苯教的一些内容，形成了许多教派，主要有：宁玛派，俗称红教。萨迦[2]派，俗称花教。噶举[3]派，俗称白教。格鲁派，俗称黄教等。其中以15世纪初宗喀巴对宗教进行改革后创立的格鲁派影响最大。该派后来形成达赖、班禅两大活佛系统。

藏传佛教文化是藏、汉、印三流汇融，主要传播于中国的藏、蒙古、土、裕固、纳西等族聚居的地区以及不丹、锡金、尼泊尔、蒙古人民共和国和俄罗斯的布里亚特等地。

喇嘛寺院的建筑大都佛殿高大，外墙很厚，窗户很小，大多依山修建，具有浓厚的西藏地方风格。最著名的建筑是西藏拉萨的布达拉宫，日喀则的扎什伦布寺和承德的外八庙。这些建筑规模宏大，气势雄伟，雕梁画栋，备极精巧。藏地寺院各种佛教造像艺术特别发达，无论雕、镂、塑、铸都能注重体型比例，栩栩如生，极为精美。大型造像如扎什伦布寺的大弥勒铜像高26米，北京雍和宫旃檀木雕大弥勒像高18米，造型生动庄严，工艺巧妙精湛，具有很高的艺术水平。其中西藏的布达拉宫已载入世界文化遗产名录。

布达拉宫的建筑艺术造型，因山就势，高低错落，由华丽的大小经堂、灵塔殿、佛堂和喇嘛寺院组成建筑群体，占地41公顷。尤其是主殿拔地凌空，巍巍高耸，气势雄伟。六座各具风格的塔顶，青铜作瓦，鎏以黄金，四角鳌突，兽吻飞檐，并配以各种鎏金的八吉祥、共命鸟、塔式宝瓶、龙凤呈祥等，四周排列着鎏金的经幢，悬挂着“五色”风马，喷射出万束金光，光彩夺目，气象非凡，既有震撼人心的威慑力，又有诱人登临的魅力。布达拉宫的内部空间彻底艺术化，藏有极为丰富的历史文物。数以万计的各种质料的雕塑、历史壁画、金银法器、经书宝卷以及明清以来历代皇帝和中央政府颁布的敕封、诰命、金册、玉印等，充实着每一空间，使布达拉宫成为一座珍贵的文化艺术宝库。

萨迦寺也是保存古代文物的世界级的宝库，被称为“敦煌第二”，1961年就被列为首批全国重点文物保护单位。寺内藏有大量手抄佛经和天文、历史、文学、医药、地理等各种典籍，从而成为西藏乃至全国屈指可数的文化典籍收藏中心。尤其令人瞩目的是其中大量的贝叶经，具有极其重要的历史价值。殿内还

大昭寺

保存着大量的元代壁画、雕塑、刺绣、瓷器及金银供器。其中瓷器约有万余件，且宋瓷、元瓷极多，质量上乘，堪称一个小型瓷器博物馆。

藏传佛教寺庙外观上注重色彩对比：寺墙刷红色，红墙面上用白色及棕色装饰；经堂和塔刷白色，白墙面上用黑色窗框，这种色彩对比渲染了藏传佛教的神秘色彩。寺庙建筑内容的组成与汉传佛寺有很大的不同。一座藏传佛教寺院内包括有信仰中心——佛殿（藏语为“拉康”）、佛塔（安放喇嘛遗体）；宗教教育建筑——学院（藏语为“扎仓”）；管理机构——活佛公署，以及辩经场[4]、僧舍、库房、厨房、管理用房以及转经[5]廊等。其中，僧众念经和供奉佛像的“扎仓”“拉康”是整座寺庙的主体，矗立于喇嘛寺的中心位置；其他建筑，特别是数以千计的低矮的喇嘛住房，围绕四周，从而使整座寺院的立体轮廓十分鲜明。

藏族地区的喇嘛教寺院一般依靠山势建造，根据地形较自由地布置寺院各类建筑，各个扎仓和活佛公署相对集中，没有明显的整体规划，不像汉地的寺院有明显的中轴线，讲究格局对称。元代以后，中原和蒙古地区的喇嘛寺逐渐受到汉文化传统建筑构思的影响，形成比较规整的纵中轴线布局。另外，因为藏地佛教寺院内容较多，一般的寺庙，经堂往往不止一个，经堂内可容纳上千名到数千名喇嘛念经，规模不等，成为汉地佛寺难以比拟的一大特色。

词语注释

【1】苯教：古代西藏的原始宗教，是一种原始的信仰，崇拜日、月、星辰、草木等一切自然物，特别重视部落神和地方神。公元 8 世纪后，苯教逐渐与佛教融合。

【2】萨迦：萨迦，寺名，以寺名命名的教派，是喇嘛教派之一。萨迦，藏语意为“白土”，因在白土地上建寺，故名。

【3】噶举：喇嘛教派之一。“噶举”，藏语意为“口授传承”，表示传承金刚持佛亲口所授秘咒教义。

【4】辩经场：教派之间辩论的场所。

【5】转经：藏传佛教的一种宗教活动。

布达拉宫

第五章　古代教育

一、官学与私学

中国在三千多年前的夏朝已经有了“庠”“序”“校”三种教育形式，但到清朝末年（19世纪70～90年代）才出现第一批现代学校。古代中国的学校教育，按其性质可以分为官学、私学两大类。

官学，就是古代各级官府主办的学校，主要培养官吏，大多设在官府内。汉以后历代封建朝廷都比较注重发展官学，使官学具备了中央官学和地方官学两级体制，形成了一套比较完备的学校制度，在培养人才、繁荣学术、弘扬文化方面起到了极其重要的作用。但各个朝代的官学的名称却有不同。例如，西周的官学称国学、乡学[1]，汉朝的称太学[2]，唐朝的称弘文馆[3]、崇文馆[4]，宋朝的称国子监[5]等等。

官学有严格的招生制度，平民百姓的子女一般不能入学。入学资格、年龄和修业年限都有严格限制。唐朝建立了完备的学制系统，其中国学地位最高，只有文武三品以上的“国公子孙”才有资格。其次是太

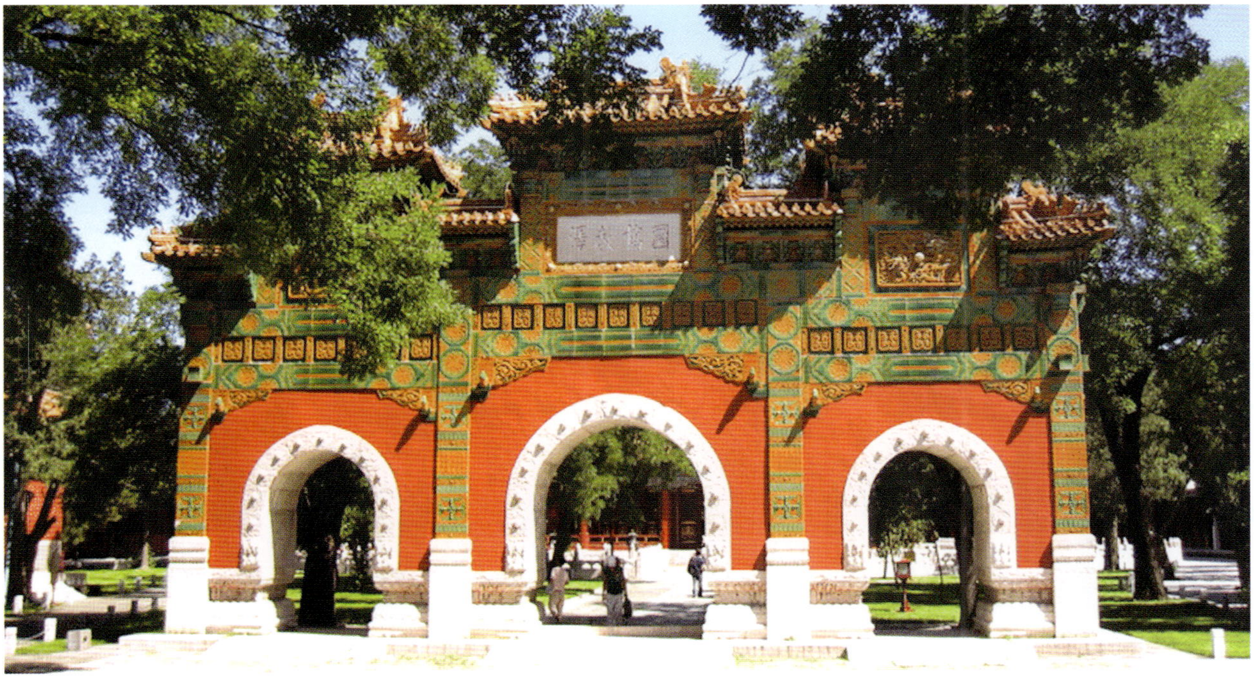

北京国子监

学，也要文武五品以上及“郡县公子孙”才能进入。宋、元、明、清基本上延续而下，清朝更规定：凡“娼、优、隶、卒及贱役子弟”，一律不准考官学，“违者治罪”。中央官学中，国子学和太学属于大学性质的教育，因此招收已经受过启蒙教育的王公贵族的子孙入学，官学的教师都是官府委任的。

官学的教学内容多是儒家的经典，《诗》《书》《礼》《易》《春秋》五经[6]之外，《论语》《孝经》[7]也是必修的。教学形式，有大家一起听课、学习突出的学生授课等，但主要靠学生自修。学生必须严守“师法”，精通五经当中的一经，通过考试，成绩优秀者可授予官职。

清朝在京城设宗学[8]（专收满族王公、将军以及宗室子弟）、觉罗学[9]（专收觉罗氏之八旗子弟）、旗学[10]（旗人学校总称）。地方官学分别为府学[11]、州学[12]、县学[13]。所有学校的课程设置和教学训练都是为科举考试作准备；学生入学动机和毕业去向都以获取功名、走上仕途为目的。教育的功能除了传导识字和教化学子外，实质上成了官员预备学校和科举的附庸。

中国私学的兴起晚于官学。春秋时，孔子开私人讲学之风。汉朝以后，私学已经成为封建教育制度的重要组成部分，因官学主要是围绕科举取士展开教学，这就给私学留下了一定的发展空间，启蒙教育几乎全在私学里进行，主要教授识字和基础知识。宋元以后，开始出现了一系列的启蒙教材，如《三字经》《百家姓》《千字文》《千家诗》等。清朝的私学大体有三种形式：一是“教馆或坐馆”，有钱人家聘教师在家教育子孙；二是“家塾或私塾”，教师在自己家里设塾，进行教学；三是“义学或义塾”，有钱人利用祠堂庙宇聘请教师教书。私学按程度分为两种：一是蒙馆，着重启蒙教育，主要教识字作文；二是经馆，专门学习一二种儒家经典。

私学的教师，有居官教授的，有隐居教授的，有辞官归家教授的，后两种形成了专业化的私学教师队伍。在相当长的历史时期内，不论在数量上还是知识传授上，私学都比官学庞大、全面，从而形成以私学为主、官学为辅、私学补充官学的格局。私学在中国存在了两千多年，是学校教育制度的重要组成部分，发挥过非常大的作用。它一方面使许多不为当朝统治者接受的思想、学术得以保存，在教学内容上比官学更多地承担了儒家学说之外的文化知识的传授，诸如黄老之学[14]、法律、天文、星历、图纬、医学等，另一方面也为平民子弟提供了更多受教育的机会，是中国封建社会知识、文化传播的重要渠道。

应天书院

词语注释

【1】乡学：古代的地方学校，与“国学”相区别。国学与乡学在培养目标上层次不同，国学造就国家高级官员，而乡学则培养普通权贵。

【2】太学：中国汉代设于京城由朝廷主办的最高学府。魏晋至明清，或设太学，或设国子学，或二者兼设，虽然名称不一，制度也有变化，但均为传授儒家经典的最高学府。

【3】弘文馆：唐高祖时为中央直接设立的旁系学校的一种，学生大都是皇亲国戚。学科与国子学相同，但地位高于国子学。

【4】崇文馆：官署名。唐太宗贞观十三年，于东宫设

崇贤馆，至高宗上元二年，避太子李贤讳，改名崇文馆。设学士，掌经籍图书，教授生徒；设校书郎，掌校理典籍。

【5】国子监：中国宋代最高的教育管理机关，又是中央最高学府。招收“京朝七品以上子孙”，称国子生。

【6】《诗》《书》《礼》《易》《春秋》五经：从汉朝称五经，并设五经博士，专掌对此五经的传授，始有五经之名，为五部儒家经典。

【7】《孝经》：中国古代儒家的伦理学著作。

【8】宗学：清代专为清宗室子弟设立的学校。

【9】觉罗学：清初为皇族子孙设立了宗学，后学生渐多，宗学不能容纳，乃于雍正七年（公元 1729 年）又专门创办一种为爱新觉罗氏子孙读书的学校，称觉罗学。课程与宗学相同，除授满汉文字、经史文艺外，兼习骑射。

【10】旗学：清代专为八旗子弟设立学校，有八旗官学、八旗义学、八旗学堂等八种。

【11】府学：古代官学之一种，由府一级政府设立。

【12】州学：古代官学之一种，由州一级政府设立。

【13】县学：古代官学之一种，供生员在此读书。

【14】黄老之学：中国战国时的哲学、政治思想一种流派。尊传说中的黄帝和老子为创始人，故名。

二、书院文化

书院是中国古代封建教育中一种很有特色的教育和学术研究机构。书院这个名称最早出现在唐玄宗开元十一年（公元 723 年）至开元十三年（公元 725 年）。那时，书院只是官方藏书和校书的地方，也有民间一些读书人借用这个名称，作为个人读书治学的场所。

五代时期，由于统治阶级割据混战，一些封建士大夫效仿佛教徒修身养性，选择山林名胜之地，筑屋建院，聚徒讲学，名为“书院”。从此之后，书院才具有学校的性质。

书院的发展有起有落。北宋初期，书院很兴盛，后期则比较衰落。南宋时，书院又非常兴盛，数目和规模都超过了以前。宋代一共建立书院 173 所，其中

岳麓书院

北宋建 37 所，南宋建 136 所。并且出现了著名的四大书院，它们是：岳麓书院[1]，位于湖南省长沙市岳麓山下；白鹿洞书院，位于江西省九江市庐山脚下；嵩阳书院[2]，位于河南嵩山南麓，登封县城北约 3 千米处；睢阳书院[3]（又名“应天书院”）。这其中朱熹[4]的功绩尤为突出，也使奠基于北宋的理学成了书院的主要教学内容。可以说，书院推动了理学的发展，理学促进了书院的建设。

元代，由于统治者的提倡，书院有所复兴。明代初期，统治阶级崇尚科举和官学，书院得不到振兴。从成化年间（公元 1465 年～ 1487 年）起，书院再度复兴。后来东林书院由于参与讽议朝政、裁量人物，引起了专制统治者的不满，先后出现了四次禁毁书院的事件。清代直到康雍两朝之后，书院才得以恢复，数量大增，超过了前代，但官学化的问题也更为严重与突出。随着时代的剧变，书院这种形式已不能满足时代的需求，从戊戌变法开始，全国各地的书院大多改为学堂。公元 1901 年，清政府宣布废止书院改办学堂，书院才逐渐完成其使命。

书院从宋初兴起到清末，存在了一千多年，对中国封建教育的发展起到了重要的作用。在办学形式、教学组织、教学方法方面，都积累了相当丰富的经验，对古代教育产生过深远的影响，不仅为历代王朝培养了大批官吏和人才，而且对中国古代文化的代代相传起到了不可估量的作用。

与官学和普通私学相比，书院在教学上保持着自身的特色。首先，学生以自学为主，教师指导为辅，学生由于仰慕大师的道德学问，不远千里前去拜师。入学以后，便各自埋头读书，刻苦钻研。教师为学生开列书目，指出读书的先后次序，读书的原则和方法，

白鹿洞书院

院址一般设立于文物荟萃的地区，选择在山水秀丽的地方。书院的园林建筑与宫苑、寺院、府署、宅第的园林建筑不同，讲求自然、宁静、清幽、雅淡的格调。书院里的景点大多要命名，富有诗的意境、文人的气息。因此，在书院兴起的同时，传统建筑方面也兴起了一种典雅的文人园林建筑的新类型。

让学生自学。其次，教学和学术研究相结合。由于书院是从藏书、校书和私人读书场所发展起来的讲学机构，历代书院的主持人和讲学者大都是当时著名的学者，因此，书院讲学多建立在学术研究的基础上，以学术研究促进教学，以教学带动学术研究。这种把教学与研究结合起来的做法，对后来的教育很有借鉴意义。其三，书院允许不同的学派共同讲学和自由听讲，讲学者和听讲者也不受地域的限制。比如，在白鹿洞书院主持教学的朱熹是正统理学派[5]，曾邀请心学理学派[6]的陆九渊[7]到白鹿洞书院讲学，朱熹不仅认真听讲，而且把陆九渊所讲的内容记下来，刻在山门石壁上，为不同的学派共同在书院讲学树立了典范。这种开放式教学，有利于学术交流，取长补短，开阔学术视野。

书院的环境优美宁静，利于陶冶性灵，清静潜修。

词语注释

【1】岳麓书院：宋开宝年间潭州太守朱洞创建，有讲堂、斋舍、藏书楼。朱熹曾在此讲学，传播理学，学生达千人。

【2】嵩阳书院：位于嵩山之南。嵩阳书院旧址在河南省登封县太室山南麓，建于五代。宋太宗至道元年七月赐额“太室书院”。仁宗景祐二年九月置学官，重修，诏令更名“嵩阳书院”，并赐额。

【3】睢阳书院：在今河南省商丘市（商丘旧名睢阳）。宋真宗大中祥符二年，曹诚建造学舍150间，广招生徒，讲习甚盛。范仲淹曾讲学于此。

【4】朱熹（公元1130年～1200年）：字元晦，号晦庵、紫阳。徽州婺源（今江西婺源）人。绍兴十八年（公元1148年）进士，仕途并不显达。然而他一生以著书讲学为主，学生众多。在哲学思想上，他将二程学说发展为完整的理学体系，为理学之集大成者，是中国封建社会后期影响最大的思想家。其学说在明清时代被官方奉为儒学正宗。

【5】正统理学派：宋明时期的唯心主义哲学思想，是以周敦颐、程颢、程颐、朱熹为代表的客观唯心主义流派。认为“理”是永恒的、先于世界而存在的精神实体，世界万物只能由“理”派生。

【6】心学理学派：宋明时期的唯心主义哲学思想，是以陆九渊、王守仁为代表的主观唯心主义流派。后者提出“心外无物，心外无理”，认为主观意识是派生世界万物的本原。

【7】陆九渊（公元1139年～1193年）：字子静，自号存斋。南宋哲学家，“心学”创始人。以“心”为构成宇宙万物的本原。认为宇宙便是吾心，吾心即是宇宙。其学说由明代王守仁继承发展，世称“陆王心学”。著有《象山先生全集》。

三、科举制

科举制度是中国古代王朝设科考试用以选拔官吏的一种制度，由于采用分科取士，所以叫科举。科举起源于隋朝（公元 587 年），唐朝开始逐渐完善，到了北宋，弥封、誊录、回避等科举立法全面完备，清除了举荐制残余，一切以考试为准，科举制度成熟定型。明、清两个朝代是科举制度发展到顶峰转而走向衰亡的时期。科举制度历时一千三百多年，曾经对中国的政治、经济、教育制度和社会生活产生过重大的影响。

明朝和清朝，是科举制最为成熟和发达的时代。在这一时期，考试制度更为严密复杂了。考试主要有三级，最低一级为“院试”，第二级是“乡试”，最高一级是“会试”和“殿试”。考生在进入三级考试以前，必须经过由知县[1]主持的“县试”和由知府[2]主持的“府试”。合格者因此获得“童生”的资格，之后，才可以参加由各省学政[3]主持的“院试”。

院试分为两场，一场正试，一场复试。各地考生在县或府里参加考试，由省里的提督学政主持。院试录取后，考生就成为“生员”，俗称“秀才”，从此就算是国家的正式学生，可以进入府学或县学学习了（这种学习有时只是名义上的），并且可以领取国家钱粮，准备参加各省举行的“乡试”。

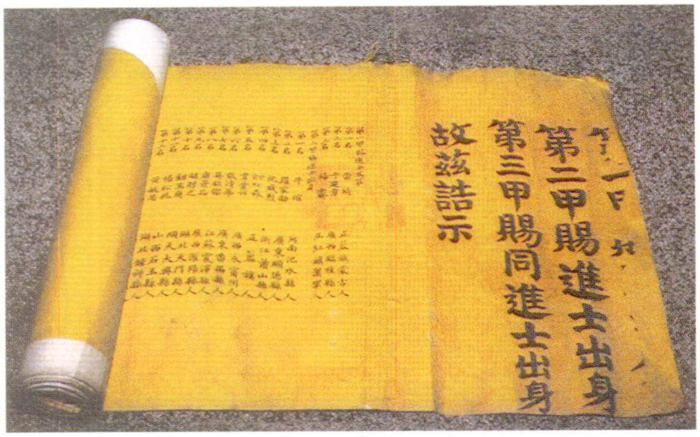

清朝用于公布殿试结果的大金榜

乡试每隔三年在各省省城（包括京城）举行一次。凡本省生员经过科考、录科、录遗三场考试合格的人，都可以参加乡试。考中者称为“举人”，其第一名叫“解元”。只有举人才有资格入京“会试”。

会试每三年在京城举行一次。考中者称为“贡士”，也就是社会上通称的进士，其第一名叫“会元”。明清两代，一般每隔三年举办一次会考，地点在京师。明洪武四年（公元 1371 年）是首届，在南京夫子庙[4]附近的江南贡院[5]举行。永乐九年三月，会试地点迁到北京。

考取贡士的人，同时要参加“殿试”。“殿试”是由皇帝在殿廷上对会试合格的贡士进行的考试，也叫“廷试”。殿试成绩分为一甲、二甲、三甲三等：一甲取三人，赐“进士及第”，第一名叫“状元”（也叫“殿元”），第二名叫“榜眼”，第三名叫“探花”。二甲、三甲各取若干名，赐“进士出身”“同进士出身”。

解元、会元、状元合称“三元”。读书人连中三元，是至高无上的荣耀。秀才、举人、贡士都不是官，只有经过殿试考中者，由朝廷决定授予官职的才算官。

科举考试情景

殿试揭晓时，在太和殿宣布名字，同时在长安街挂榜文三天。“榜”用黄表纸制成，称为“金榜”。因此，“金榜题名”成为每个学子的梦想。

到清朝末年，各级科场考试舞弊成风，买通考官、冒名顶替的丑行越来越厉害。另外，科举考试把规范严格的“八股文”[6]作为作文程序，极大地束缚了人的创造性思维。在朝野上下的强烈要求下，光绪二十七年（公元 1901 年），清政府废除八股，光绪三十一年（公元 1905 年）又下令废止科举。

科举制度从中国文化土壤中产生出来以后，再创造了中国文化。自唐代以来历朝历代，许多杰出的政治家、思想家、文学家、史学家等，很少不是通过科举考试而跻身社会上层的，他们为中国的政治、经济、文化的丰富和发展作出了巨大的贡献。应当说科举考试的形式是封建时代所能采取的最公平的人才选拔形式，它扩展了封建国家引进人才的社会层面，使大量出身中下层社会的人士能够进入统治阶级的队伍，为权力阶层增添了生气和活力。

词语注释

【1】知县：唐代佐官代理县令称知县事。宋代派朝臣充当县的长官称“知县事”（在这里是主持某县事的意思），简称知县。明代始正式用作一县长官名称。清代沿用。

【2】知府：地方行政中府一级的行政长官。府成为县级以上的行政区划，始于唐代。宋代将大郡升为府，遣朝臣出任长官，称知某府事，简称知府，后成定制。明代时成为府一级行政长官的正式名称，辖州县。清代沿用。

【3】学政：清沿明制，各省设提督学道，雍正四年改为提督学政。学政是一省教育管理的最高长官。清中叶以后，派往各省，按期至所属各府、厅考试童生及生员。

【4】南京夫子庙：南京贡院西街之西所建的孔庙。

【5】贡院：科举时代举行乡试或会试的场所。

【6】八股文：明、清两代科举考试采用的特殊文体。专取四书五经命题，行文格式有极严格的限制。每篇由破题、承题、起讲、入手、起股、中股、后股、束股八大部分组成。字数也有严格规定，如：清康熙二十一年（公元 1681 年）规定每篇 650 字，乾隆四十三年（公元 1704 年）增至 700 字，违者不予及格。

四、《百家姓》《千字文》《三字经》

《百家姓》《千字文》《三字经》是中国古代儿童启蒙的百科全书。自从孔子创私学以来的两千五百多年中，中国历代都十分重视启蒙教育，这是中国教育的一个重要传统。而在丰富的启蒙课本中，《百家姓》《千字文》《三字经》以其流传久远、传播广泛、影响极深而闻名于世。

《百家姓》是北宋初年钱塘（杭州）的一个书生编写的蒙学读物。原来收集的 411 个姓经过增补成为 504 个姓，其中单姓 444 个，复姓 60 个，据南宋学者王明清考证，这本书前几个姓氏“赵、钱、孙、李”的排列是有讲究的：赵是宋朝皇帝的姓，作为第一个；其次是钱姓，钱是五代十国中吴越国王钱俶的姓氏；孙为王妃孙氏之姓；李为南唐国王姓氏，所以赵、钱、孙、李四姓，优先上榜，以示尊敬。随后的周、吴、郑、王，冯、陈、褚、卫等各个姓氏，虽然用了四字一句、随口配韵的安排，但大致还是按照当时的大族或一般常见的姓氏排序的。《百家姓》收录的姓氏使用频率很高，虽然各句的内容没有实际意义，但由于姓氏知识切合于日常生活，应用性很强，所以大受欢迎。

《千字文》编写于南朝梁武帝时期。据说，梁武帝萧衍是个酷爱书法的皇帝，他对王羲之的书法特别推崇，命人从宫廷内府珍藏的王羲之书迹里选取了一千个字，这些字的笔画清晰、形体完美而又不重复，专门用来临摹。把这些字收集好以后，梁武帝又感到凌乱、没有次序，于是，便召来著名辞赋家周兴嗣，命他把这一千个汉字编写成韵文。《千字文》能够成为经典的识字课文，主要因素有三：

一、《千字文》250句，每句四言韵文都表达一个意思，每两句或者更多的句子之间保持一定的连贯性，简明地概括了律例、历史、道德、读书、地理、饮食、居处、园林、祭祀等知识，连缀成文。

二、魏晋六朝时期人们非常看重儒学经典的传授，而《千字文》则借助以往儒家经典和历史著作中的相关言语与事件编写而成，其内容远涉上古，近连魏晋，将一些流传较广的知识结合在一起。

《三字经·百家姓·千字文》

三、《千字文》所编入的一千个字中，可以说没有冷僻字。

《三字经》相传是南宋王应麟（公元1228年～1296年）所著，是我国古代蒙学教材中的代表之作。与《千字文》相比，《三字经》虽然有的字重复，没有华丽的辞藻，可是通俗易懂，老百姓比较容易接受。《三字经》总共一千多字，宗旨是强调学养的重要性，其中有伦理道德，历史沿革，生活常识，由于内容的启蒙性和通俗性，在道德伦理的灌输和人文知识的传授上具有实用价值。可以说，《千字文》的文采胜于《三字经》，《三字经》比《千字文》更为通俗。

《百家姓》《千字文》《三字经》具有共同的特点，都是韵语，朗朗上口，易于背诵，适合儿童的学习特点。《百家姓》采用四言体例，句句押韵，虽然它的内容没有文理，但读起来顺口，易学好记。《三字经》是三字句，文字简练、通俗易懂、整齐有韵，易诵易记，而且句句相连，表现力很强，广大民众容易接受。《三字经》开创了一种文体，各种课本、读物仿照其形式纷纷出现，比较著名的有《弟子规》《女儿经》等。《千字文》文笔流畅，读起来朗朗上口，文中字无重复，都是一些平时习见的常用字，便于对初学者进行启蒙教育。因此，无论是书家平时练字也好，课徒也好，作为一种艺术创作也好，《千字文》很受追捧，历代著名书法家如唐朝的欧阳询、怀素，宋朝的徽宗皇帝赵佶，元朝的鲜于枢、赵孟頫，明代的文征明等，也都写有《千字文》传世。

第六章　古代科技

一、四大发明

中华民族在漫长的历史进程中，创造了灿烂的古代文化，造纸、印刷术、火药、指南针是中国著名的“四大发明”，还有丝绸、瓷器、茶叶等，对世界文明的发展也作出了卓越的贡献。

（一）指南针和罗盘

指南针是一种磁性的指向器，与方向盘相结合就成为罗盘。指南针的发明对人类文明的发展具有举足轻重的作用。

中国人很早就对磁性有所认识，《管子》记载：“上有磁石者，下有润金。”这说明我国在公元前3世纪之前就知道磁石能够吸铁了。据记载，在战国时期，中国人就造出了人类历史上最古老的指南装置——司南。这是一种人工磁性指向器，造型像汤勺，将它放置在专用的光滑地盘上，它的柄就会指向南方。在汉朝，人们制成了带有方位标记的地盘，地盘的四周有二十四个刻度[1]，表示不同的方向，用来帮助司南定向。给司南配上带有方位的地盘，这是指南针发展史上的一大飞跃。

司南由于磁性弱，与地盘接触时的摩擦阻力大，效果不够好，没能广泛使用。后来，人们又用人工磁化的方法制成了更加先进的铁叶指向仪。先把薄铁叶制成鱼形，再磁化。使用时，把铁叶鱼放在水面上，就能指南了。指南鱼发明以后不久，有人尝试着把一根铁针放在磁铁上摩擦，这是人们最初掌握的让铁磁化的方法，使其磁化成为真正的指南针。北宋年间（公元9世纪～10世纪）造出的指南针有水浮、悬挂等几种形式。

司　南

南宋以后，曾经出现代表“天干”[2]的“天盘”（圆）、代表“地支”[3]的“地盘”（方）。出于测方向的需要，这些方位盘都比较简单、明了。圆形方位盘的每个字表示的方位偏角，都相当于现在的30度。盘的中央安置一根可以灵活转动的磁针，静止时，磁针总是指向南方，这样，就大大提高了指向的稳定性。指南针发明之后就被应用于航海事业。12 世纪以后，中国的指南针技术流传到世界各地，这种形式的罗盘至今仍然在全球广泛使用。

（二）火药的应用

火药的发明，起源于中国古代的炼丹术。炼丹术是古代炼制丹药的一种技术，是近代化学的先驱。人们在炼丹的过程中认识了炭、硝、硫的功能，大约在唐朝初期，中国人就发明了火药。

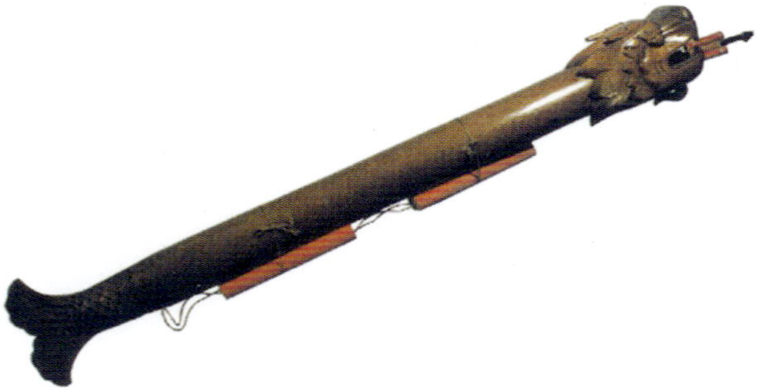

火 箭

唐朝末年，人们开始利用火药容易燃烧的特点制成发射的"火箭"。就是在箭上绑上火药，点燃以后发射出去，用来焚烧敌人的营地。后来，人们又把火药填在球状的容器中，点燃以后发射出去，从而成为中国原始的火炮。在宋朝频繁的战争中，人们又发明了能爆炸的火药武器，即用纸管做成爆炸火器，一半装火药，另一半装石灰，点燃后发出巨大的爆炸声，喷出的石灰粉能杀伤敌人。南宋时期，又发明了管状火器，即把火药装在竹子内，在战场上燃放，用来杀死敌人。后来，有人又发明了"突火枪"。元代（公元 13 世纪末 ~ 14 世纪初），人们开始使用铜、铁等金属铸造火炮，这种火炮的炮膛可以容纳更多的弹药，射程更远，杀伤力更大。

除了把火药用于武器，在宋朝，人们还利用火药制作烟火娱乐。据记载，南宋时皇家庭苑燃放烟火，一次曾经燃放了一百多架烟火，灿烂的光彩照亮了夜空。宋朝以后，制造烟火和鞭炮的技术不断提高，放烟火和放鞭炮成了人们娱乐和庆祝节日的方式。

在 13 世纪，火药传到印度，再经过阿拉伯传到欧洲。欧洲 14 世纪才有了火药。18 世纪末到 19 世纪，随着新型炸药相继发明和应用，火药大量用于建筑事业，对开矿、修路、建造房屋，兴修水利以及工业建设都起到了重大的促进作用。

（三）造纸与印刷术

在纸张发明以前，汉字的记载先后历经了甲骨、金石、竹木、帛等阶段。周朝末年，书籍多写在竹简上，一册书往往有好几十斤重，一辆车子也装不了几册书。孔子就是以车载书，周游列国，有许多学生跟随着帮助拉车、推车。据说，秦始皇统一中国以后，每天晚上都要亲自阅读大臣送上来的奏章，一个晚上就要读一箩筐的奏章。在纸张发明之前，人们的文化生活非常不方便。

大约在西汉初年，中国人用帛书写，可是帛的价格昂贵。后来，人们开始用麻的纤维造纸。考古学家在新疆和陕西都曾发现过这种早期的纸，这种纸的质地比较粗糙，不便于书写，还不能完全代替简和帛。寻求新的书写材料已成为时势所趋，造纸术因此应运而生。《后汉书·蔡伦传》记载，到了东汉和帝时，宦官蔡伦对纸张的改进起到了重大作用。

蔡伦字敬仲，东汉桂阳（今湖南郴州）人。此人很有才气，知识丰富，被任命为尚方令，即掌管皇家供奉的官员。这期间，他试着用树皮、麻头、破布、渔网等材料造纸，先把原料放在水里浸泡，使原料润胀，再捞出来，把这些材料剁碎，用水洗清，除去

活字印刷

造纸过程

其中的杂质，再用清水把细纤维浆液配制成纸浆。随后，把纸浆均匀分布在筛子上，经过干燥，一张纸就造成了。

东汉元兴元年（公元105年），工匠们在蔡伦的主持下，造出了价廉物美、适于书写的植物纤维纸张——一种真正意义上的纸。后来蔡伦被封为“龙亭侯”[4]，人们便把蔡伦制造的纸称为“蔡侯纸”，这种纸张的造价便宜，容易普及。自从蔡伦改进了造纸技术，纸张才被广泛用于书写、绘画。

中国发明造纸术以后很久，世界上许多地方还在用羊皮、树皮、树叶作为书写材料。公元7世纪初，中国的造纸术传到了朝鲜和日本，又过了一个世纪，传到了阿拉伯，再经过阿拉伯传到欧洲，然后传遍全世界。

纸的普遍应用直接促进了书写的激增和科学文化的传播，也促进了印刷术的发展。中国的印刷源于文字的雕刻技术。早在殷商时代，人们就把文字刻在甲骨上，以后，陆续出现了石刻、木刻、砖刻和印章篆刻等，雕刻技巧也日渐成熟。在公元4世纪左右，人们发明了把纸铺在石碑上用墨拓字（传拓）的方法。在印章和墨拓的启示下，公元6世纪末到7世纪初，发明了雕版印刷。即把写好字的纸贴在平板上，然后，用刀把木板上的字刻成反形的阳字（即凸起的字），这就成了雕版。印刷时，先将雕版的字涂上墨，再把纸贴在雕版上，然后用专门的刷子轻匀地在纸面上涂刷，文字就转印在纸上。现存世界上最早的雕版印刷品是公元868年中国印制的《金刚经》[5]。五代时，出现了雕版印刷的整部书籍。宋代的雕版印刷业十分发达，刻印的书，字体工整，装订精美。

北宋庆历年间（公元11世纪中叶），毕升发明活字印刷术，实现了人类印刷史上一次伟大的变革。毕升用胶泥刻成单字，字的厚薄如铁钱，每字一印，放到火里焙烧，使之坚硬而成活字字模。排版时，先在铁板上放置松脂、蜡和纸灰混合制成的药剂，铁框排满字模后，在火上加热至药剂烧化，再用一块平板按压字的表面，使整版字平如砥，冷却后即可印刷。印刷之后，可以拆散用过的字盘，经过重新排列组合，组成新的字盘，这样，就免去了一次次雕版的工作，这就是著名的活字印刷。活字印刷既节省了人力物力，又提高了印刷的速度。元大德二年（公元1298年）左右，王祯[6]创造了木活字，并且发明了能够转动的排字盘，减轻了捡字、排字盘的劳动，把活字印刷提高到一个新水平。中国印刷术大约在公元8世纪中叶流传到朝鲜、日本、越南，然后又传到欧洲等地。

词语注释

【1】二十四个刻度：古人用“天干”和“地支”，配以“八卦”中的干、坤、巽、艮表示二十四个不同方向。

【2】天干：指甲、乙、丙、丁、戊、己、庚、辛、壬、癸。

【3】地支：指子、丑、寅、卯、辰、巳、午、未、申、酉、戌、亥。

【4】侯：封建五等爵位的第二等。

【5】《金刚经》：全称《金刚般若波罗蜜经》，大乘般若类经典。因为用金刚比喻智能，有能断烦恼的功用，故名。中国禅宗南宗即以此经为重要典据。

【6】王祯：字伯善，山东东平人。是元代著名的农学家。他在地方做知尹（知县）时，很重视农业，并动手整理前人的农业文献及当时的种植经验，编成了《农书》，并创造性地采用木活字排印，提高了印刷《农书》的效率，推动了活字印刷技术的发展。

二、祖冲之和圆周率

祖冲之是世界数学史上第一次将圆周率[1]计算到小数点后七位的人，这一计算结果的提出，比欧洲要早一千多年。为了纪念祖冲之对中国和世界科学文化做出的伟大贡献，1967年，国际天文学家联合会把月球背面的一座环形山命名为“祖冲之环形山”，将国际永久编号为1 888的小行星命名为“祖冲之小行星”。

祖冲之

祖冲之（公元429年～500年），字文远，祖籍范阳遒县（今河北省涞水县北）。他生于建康（今江苏南京），生活在南朝宋齐时期。在西晋末年的战乱中，祖氏全家迁居到江南。祖氏历代在朝廷里掌管历法。祖冲之的祖父叫祖昌，曾经在朝廷里做过大匠卿，即负责营造的官吏。生活在这样的家庭环境里，祖冲之从小就有接触科学技术的机会。他在青年时代，就创制了中国古代精密的历法“大明历”[2]。公元464年，祖冲之三十五岁时，开始计算圆周率。

中国古代劳动人民在实践中知道圆的周长是直径的三倍多，但是到底多多少，意见不一。在祖冲之以前，数学家刘徽以“割圆术[3]”计算出圆周率约等于3.1416。祖冲之在刘徽研究的基础上，经过刻苦钻研，反复演算，把圆周率推算到小数点以后7位数（即3.1415926与3.1415927之间），并且得出了圆周率分数形式的近似值。祖冲之究竟是用什么方法得出这个结果的，现在已经无从查考。可以想象，在没有计算器的古代，用人工的计算方法把圆周率精确到千万分之一，祖冲之一定付出了巨大的心血。

祖冲之在数学领域的成就，只是中国古代数学成就的一个缩影。14世纪以前中国一直是世界上数学最为发达的国家之一。比如“勾股定理”，在早期的数学专著《周髀算经》（大约于公元前2世纪成书）中即有论述；在世界数学史上最早提出负数概念及正负数加减法，则在公元1世纪的数学专著《九章算术》中出现；13世纪时中国就已经有了十次方程的解法，而直到16世纪，欧洲才提出三次方程的解法。

公元500年祖冲之72岁时去世。他在世时，“大明历”还受到戴法兴等人的激烈反对而未被采用。最令人痛惜的是，他的数学著作《缀术》早在宋朝时便失传了。

词语注释

【1】圆周率：圆周长与直径的比值。是一个常数，用 π 表示。数学家刘徽用割圆术求得 $\pi \approx 3.14$，称为徽率。南朝数学家祖冲之算出 $3.1415926 < \pi < 3.1415927$，并以22/7作为约率，355/113为密率。

【2】大明历：祖冲之于南朝宋大明六年（公元462年）创制《大明甲子元历》，定一回归年为365.2488日。其特点一是改进闰法，更符合天象实际；二是制历时考虑岁差，一百年差一度。

【3】割圆术：刘徽首创的圆周率的计算方法。就是用圆内接正多边形的周长去无限逼近圆周，并以此求出圆周率。刘徽从圆内接正六边形算起，边数逐步加倍，一直算到圆内接正192边形的面积，算得了近似的数值3.1416。

三、郭守敬修订历法

郭守敬（公元1231年～1316年），字若思，顺德邢台（今河北邢台）人。元代著名的天文学家、数

郭守敬

学家、水利专家和仪器制造专家。他父亲去世很早，自幼承祖父郭荣家学，攻研天文、算学和水利，少年时代的郭守敬就对科学产生了浓厚的兴趣。

郭守敬杰出的成就在天文历法方面。元朝征服江南以后，由于南北的历法不一样，误差很大，连关乎农业生产的节气都推算不准。公元1276年，元朝政府决定对旧历法进行修订，命令郭守敬参与新历法的修订。当时，用来观察天象的大型仪器浑天仪[1]已经陈旧不堪了，不能获得可靠的数据。郭守敬为了修历而创制和改进了简仪、高表、候极仪、浑天象等十几件天文仪器仪表，又挑选了14个具有天文技术知识的官员，分为几个小组，带着轻便的仪器到各地去观测天象。当时，在全国从东到西，从南到北，一共设立了27个观星台。各地都把观测出来的数据报到大都[2]。郭守敬运用这些数据进行精密计算，花了四年的时间，于公元1280年编写出了一部新的历法，经忽必烈定名为《授时历》[3]。转年，颁布全国，通行360多年。这种新历法比旧历法精确得多，计算出一年有365.2425天，《授时历》和现在世界上通用的公历基本相同，但比公历早了300年，是中国元代最精确、最优秀的一部历法，也是世界上当时最先进的一部历法。

郭守敬在天文历法方面的著述有14种，计105卷。他在世界测量史上首次运用海拔概念，比德国数学家高斯提出的平均海平面概念早560年；他所创造的简仪是最早制成的大赤道仪，比丹麦天文学家第谷创造的同类仪器早300多年；他主持的纬度测量，比西方早620年。20世纪60年代，中国邮电部发行了两枚郭守敬纪念邮票；国际天文学会等组织为了表彰郭守敬对天文科学的贡献，将月球上的一座环形山和太阳系[4]一颗小行星分别用郭守敬的名字来命名。

词语注释

【1】浑天仪：观测天体的仪器。

【2】大都：元代京城，旧址在今北京附近。

【3】《授时历》：由郭守敬主持编写。他提出了“历之本在于测验，而测之器莫先于仪表”的主张。创制了十余种天文仪器，又在全国各地设27处测景所进行实测。历时五年，新历告成。

【4】太阳系：以太阳为中心的天体系统，由太阳、八颗行星及卫星、矮行星、太阳系小天体等构成。

四、李冰和都江堰

在四川都江堰岷江东岸的玉垒山麓，有一座二王庙，香火很盛。这是为了纪念李冰和他的儿子二郎治水的功绩而修筑的。

关于李冰的身世和当年修建都江堰的情况，历史上的记载比较少，人们只知道，秦昭王[1]五十六年（公元前251年）初，李冰是当时的蜀郡守[2]。他和儿子二郎共同修筑了著名的都江堰水利工程。

在民间，李冰治理都江堰的事迹被广为颂扬。李冰是一个体恤人民的地方官，也是一位杰出的科技专家。他担任蜀郡守以后，看到岷江两岸常有暴雨，特大洪灾发生的时候，大水冲溃堤岸、淹没农田，威胁了两岸人民的生活，就决心治理岷江，为百姓解决苦难。李冰和儿子二郎与百姓一起，跋山涉水，行程数百里，亲自勘察岷江的水情、地势。利用川西平原西北高、东南低的地理特点，李冰率领着广大民众，经过八年的艰苦奋斗，最后完成了都江堰工程，留下了水利工程史上的一个奇迹。

都江堰在今四川都江堰市。由分水（鱼嘴）、泄

古都江堰

洪排沙（飞沙堰）、引水（宝瓶口）三部分组成，形成一道长堤，竖卧在江心，把岷江一劈为二，分为外江和内江两部分。外江主要用于排洪，内江是人工建造的河道，主要用于灌溉。堤坝顶端扁平，像一个鱼嘴，是分江的关键部分。堤的末端有一座叫飞沙堰的大坝，宽200多米。内江进水量小的时候，飞沙堰可以把水拦进内江；如果进水量超过了坝面，就把洪水里的泥沙卵石排泄出去。紧靠着飞沙堰，有一道人工劈凿的峡口，名叫宝瓶口，上端连接内江，下端分成四条干渠，岷江水可以从宝瓶口流出，进入川西平原。上述这三部分工程相辅相成，自动引水分流，自动调控两江流量，自动防洪排沙，既保证了灌溉用水的需要，又极大地防止和减轻了洪水的威胁，成为中国史上科学治水的伟大创举和奇观。

两千二百多年以来，都江堰经受了无数次严峻的洪水考验，消除了岷江流域的水患，使川西平原成为“天府之国”。四川的老百姓为了纪念李冰父子，称他们为“川主”“巴蜀王”。后来，索性把他们神化，在神话传说中，二郎就是手握尖刀、长着三只眼的二郎神[3]。人们永远怀念他。1974年，在都江堰枢纽工程中，发现了李冰的石像，其上题记：“故蜀郡李府君讳冰”，“建宁元年闰月戊申朔二十五日都水掾”。这说明早在1 800多年前，李冰的业绩已为人民所传颂。

词语注释

【1】秦昭王（公元前324年～公元前251年）：战国时秦国国君，是秦统一天下、承上启下的一代有为的国君。

【2】蜀郡守：蜀郡最高长官，主一郡之政事。

【3】二郎神：传说战国时期，秦蜀太守李冰的次子曾奉父命在灌口斩蛟，为民除害，死后民间祀为二郎神，故事由此演化而来。

五、世界上最长、最古老的大运河

为了发展经济、便利交通，中华民族的祖先开凿了许多运河，其中规模最大、最为著名的是隋朝开凿的“京杭大运河”。大运河的开凿，是中国古代劳动人民利用水的伟大创举。它的出现促进了中国经济的发展、社会的进步和文化的繁荣。它是中国古代一项雄视百代、光耀千秋的伟大工程，与万里长城一起被列为世界最宏伟的四大古代工程之一。它孕育了一座座璀璨的历史文化名城和古镇，留下了丰富的历史文化遗存，大运河与长城同是中华民族文化身份的象征。

大运河从公元前486年开始开凿，至公元1293年全线通航，前后共持续了1 779年。它南起杭州，北达北京，也称为“京杭大运河”，流经浙江、江苏、山东、河北、天津，连贯钱塘江、长江、淮河、黄河、海河五大水系；全长1 794千米，是世界上最长的一条人工河道。这条运河经历了三次较大的兴修过程。第一次是在公元前5世纪的春秋时代，争强称霸的各诸侯国开始凿筑多条人工运河。第二次是公元589年，隋王朝统一全国后，大规模开凿了以洛阳、开封为中心，北起涿郡[1]（今北京附近），南达杭州的运河网，习惯上称为南北大运河。元朝建都今北京，统治者又以北京为中心改造运河，公元1283和1289年，开掘了济州运河、会通运河。元代还修通了从通州至大都（今北京）的通惠河。元代运河经过改造以后，从北京可以通过水路直抵杭州。这样，南方的漕粮[2]、商品可以直接运到都城。它比隋代运河缩短了900千米航程。

南北走向的大运河，是由通惠河（从北京到通州）、北运河（从通州到天津）、南运河（又称卫河，从天津到山东临清）、会通河（从临清到东平）、济州河（从东平到济宁）、中运河（也称台儿庄运河，从微山湖东口枣庄市台儿庄，到江苏徐州）、里运河（又称山阳渎，从江苏淮安南到扬州）、江南运河（又称江南河，从镇江到杭州）八段组成的。沿河兴起了城市和商埠，德州、临清、济南、扬州、镇江、杭州等都是运河边上重要的码头和城镇。大运河将中国东部各大水系连成一片，这在没有铁路、公路，海运不很发达的古代，对沟通南北、发展运输起了重要的作用。

词语注释

【1】涿郡：郡名，汉武帝置，所辖境相当于今北京房山以南，河北易县、清苑以东，安平、河间以北，霸县、任丘以西地区。

【2】漕粮：中国封建时代由东南地区通过漕运到京师的税粮。

京杭大运河杭州段

第七章　古代建筑

一、园林建筑

中国的园林建筑历史悠久，在三千多年前的周朝，就有了最早的宫廷园林。此后，中国古代园林大体有三种类型：一是皇家园林，面积较大，建筑宏伟，装饰豪华，金碧辉煌，表现出恢宏的皇家气派，如北京的北海、颐和园、承德的避暑山庄等；二是私家园林，风格因园主的情趣而异，建筑一般是玲珑淡雅，将秀丽、雅致的风格表现得淋漓尽致，如山东潍坊十笏园、山西榆次静园、苏州的狮子林、拙政园等；三是寺庙园林，如杭州的虎跑、成都的杜甫草堂。园林建筑的作用基本相同，主要有三个方面。

一是实用性。如亭、榭、舫等，可供人停留赏景。亭是供人休息和观景的园林建筑，造型相对小而集中，常与山、水、草木结合起来组景，周围开敞，作为园林中“点景”的一种手段。形式有四方亭、圆亭、多角亭等。水榭是供游人休息、观赏风景的临水建筑。其典型形式是一部分架在岸上，一部分以梁、柱凌空架设于水面上。平台临水部分围绕低平的栏杆，或设靠椅，或采用落地门窗，供休憩眺望。舫是依照船的造型建在水面上的园林建筑物，供游玩宴饮、观赏水景之用，宛如乘船荡漾于水中。

二是独特性。园林建筑以其有利的位置和独特的造型，为人们展现出一幅幅或动或静的自然风景画，

颐和园昆明湖西堤

▶▶ 武当山南岩宫

并与廊、桥、墙、径等形成一定的活动路线。廊一般是屋檐下的过道，或者延伸成独立的长廊。它是联系室内外建筑的通道，既有遮阴避雨、休息、连通的功能，又起组织景观、分隔空间的作用，是园林内游览路线的组成部分，按造型可分为直廊、曲廊、回廊、爬山廊、水廊、桥廊[1]等。桥在园林中点缀水景，增加水面层次，兼有交通和艺术欣赏的双重作用，在造园艺术上的价值，往往超过交通功能。基本形式有平桥、拱桥、亭桥、廊桥等。墙在园林中起划分内外范围的作用。精巧的园墙还可装饰园景，按材料和构造可分为版筑墙、乱石墙、白粉墙等。分隔院落多用白粉墙，墙头配以青瓦。用白粉墙衬托山石、花木，犹如在白纸上绘制山水花卉，意境尤佳。园墙还通常设有洞门、洞窗、漏窗以及砖瓦花格进行装饰，形成“借景”。借景是中国古代园林突破空间局限、丰富园景的一种传统手法。把园林以外的风景巧妙地引“借”到园林中来，成为园景的一部分。

三是园林意境。园林建筑将山水地形、花草树木、庭院、廊桥及楹联[2]匾额[3]等精巧布设，使得山石流水处处生情，意境无穷。正如《红楼梦》中说大观园：“偌大景致，若干亭榭，无字标题，也觉寥落无趣，任有花柳山水，也断不能生色。”中国园林的境界大体分为治世境界、神仙境界、自然境界三种。

治世境界折射了儒家传统思想对封建时代的园林建筑立意产生的深远影响。园林建筑的物质外壳如亭、堂、馆、轩、斋等，更多的是充当一种在文化礼仪及习俗上与“天地”及“先祖”沟通交流的物质媒体。而台的雏形是“灵台”，主要功用是祭奠天地祖宗。园林中的宫殿，讲求儒家“天人合一”所倡导的“顺天理，合天意”的礼制，强调中轴线意识及“天定”的尊卑等级秩序，反映的是唯我独尊的文化心理。重视道德伦理价值和政治意义的思想反映到园林造景上就是治世境界。体现这种境界的建筑布局喜欢用轴线引导和左右对称的方法求得整体的统一性。园林宫区的格局，包括结构、位序、配置皆必须依礼而制，建筑在设计上多取方形或长方形，在南北纵轴线上安排主要建筑，在东西横轴线上安排次要建筑，以围墙和围廊构成封闭式整体，展现严肃、方正，井井有条，这些是儒家的均衡对称美学思想在园林建筑中的反映。

神仙境界是指在建造园林时注重表现中国道家思想中讲求自然恬淡和修养身心的内容，例如圆明园中的蓬岛瑶台[4]、四川青城山[5]的古常道观、湖北武当山[6]的南岩宫[7]等，充满了求仙的神秘气氛。两晋南北朝是中国园林发展史上的一个转折时期。文人士大夫为避开政治动乱，大都崇尚玄谈，寄情山水，自然山水成了他们居住、休息、游玩的场所，于是就在园林中布置山水花木，既可以之寄托神仙境界，又可为超越尘俗、清心养虑之所。

自然境界重在写意，注重表现园林所有者的情思，这一境界大多反映在文人园林之中，如宋代苏舜钦[8]

苏州留园

的沧浪亭[9]，司马光[10]的独乐园等。唐宋时期文人墨客纷纷加入造园的行列，他们在设计中以诗画情趣入园，因画意而成景，园林与诗、画的结合更为紧密、精练，概括地再现了自然，并把自然美与建筑美相融合，创造了一系列诗情画意的园林景观，园林建筑获得了成熟发展。这时景物已不再是纯粹的线条、色彩、质感等的组合，而是在传统体验下给予人们以心理的暗示，造园时多采用象征的手法，不论景物的名称、形状或布置均别有深意，令人神思遐往、浮想联翩。

词语注释

【1】廊桥：加建亭廊的桥，称为亭桥或廊桥，可供游人遮阳避雨，又增加桥的形体变化。

【2】楹联：楹联是“对联”的雅称。楹联是由两个工整的对偶语句构成的独立篇章。其基本特征是字数相等、字调相对，词性相近、句法相似，语义相关、语势相当。

【3】匾额：匾额是古建筑的必然组成部分，相当于古建筑的眼睛，悬挂于门楣上作装饰之用，反映建筑物名称和性质，表达义理、情感。

【4】蓬岛瑶台：建于公元1725年（雍正三年）前后，时称蓬莱洲，乾隆初年定名蓬岛瑶台。在福海中央作大小三岛，岛上建筑为仙山楼阁之状。蓬岛瑶台结构和布局根据古代画家李思训的“仙山楼阁”画设计。

【5】青城山：青城山位于四川省都江堰市西南，成都平原西北部边缘青城山至都江堰风景区内，东距成都68千米，距都江堰市区16千米，古称丈人山。青城之幽素为历代文人墨客所推崇。

【6】武当山：武当山风景区位于湖北省西北部，在丹江口市境内，属大巴山东段。武当山，又名太和山、仙室山，古有“太岳”“玄岳”“大岳”之称。

【7】南岩宫：南岩宫属全国重点文物保护单位，是道教著名宫观，位于湖北省丹江口市境内的武当山的南岩上。南岩之上林木森翠，山色秀美，其上接碧霄，下临绝涧，是武当山三十六岩中风景最美的一岩。

【8】苏舜钦（公元1008年～1049年）：北宋诗人，字子美，宋梓州铜山（今四川中江）人，迁居开封（今属河南）。曾任县令、大理评事等职。因支持范仲淹的庆历革新，为守旧派所恨，御史中丞王拱辰让其属官劾奏苏舜钦，劾其在进奏院祭神时，用卖废纸之钱宴请宾客。罢职闲居苏州。他与梅尧臣齐名，人称“梅苏”。有《苏学士文集》。

【9】沧浪亭：世界文化遗产，位于苏州市城南三元坊附近，在苏州现存诸园中历史最为悠久。始建于北宋，为文人苏舜钦的私人花园，称“沧浪亭”。沧浪亭占地面积10 800平方米，园内有一泓清水贯穿，波光倒影，景象万千。

【10】司马光（公元1019年～1086年）：北宋时期著名政治家，史学家，散文家。北宋陕州夏县涑水乡（今属山西夏县）人，字君实，世称涑水先生。司马光一生最大的贡献是在史学上，他主持编纂《资治通鉴》，在史学史上享有崇高的地位。

二、宫殿建筑

北京故宫

如果站在北京景山之巅，向南眺望，一大片绿树掩映的古代建筑群顿时映在眼前。红墙黄瓦，金碧辉煌。殿宇楼台，画栋雕梁，高低错落，壮观雄伟，气势磅礴。这就是举世闻名的北京故宫，与法国凡尔赛宫、英国白金汉宫、美国白宫、俄罗斯克里姆林宫，一同被誉为世界五大宫殿，并被联合国科教文组织列为“世界文化遗产”。

故宫旧称“紫禁城”，是明、清两代的皇宫，明、清两代的491年间，24个皇帝（其中明朝14位，清朝10位）先后在这里居住、处理朝政。故宫占地面积72万平方米（长960米，宽750米），建筑面积近16万平方米，殿宇宫室9 000余间，是中国也是世界上目前保存最完整、规模最大的古代皇宫建筑群。

游览故宫，一般从天安门[1]往里走，沿着一条笔直的大道，穿过端门[2]，走过石板御道，就来到故宫的正门——午门，故宫的主要建筑都在午门内。故宫的主要建筑由外朝与内廷两大部分组成。前朝以太和殿、中和殿、保和殿三大殿为中心，东西文华、武英两殿为两翼，是皇帝发号施令和举行大典的地方。三大殿之后为内廷，有乾清宫[3]、交泰殿[4]、坤宁宫[5]、御花园以及东西六宫。东六宫之东还有皇极殿、宁寿宫，西六宫之西还有慈宁宫等宫殿，这里是皇帝、皇后、皇太后、嫔妃、皇子、公主生活的地方。

紫禁城全景

北京故宫太和殿

宫殿建筑庄严、宏伟，特别是太和殿、中和殿和保和殿三大殿，坐落在8米高的三层汉白玉石阶上，台基有三层，每层边缘都围绕着汉白玉栏杆，上面刻着龙凤流云[6]。台基每层设有1 000多个汉白玉龙头，龙嘴里都有一个出水口，是台基的排水管道，下大雨时，水从龙嘴里流出来，像是千龙喷水，既美观又实用，体现了中国古典建筑科学和艺术的完美结合，实在是一个无与伦比的杰作。它的平面布局、立体效果以及形式上的雄伟、堂皇、庄严、和谐，建筑气势雄伟，豪华壮丽，是中国古代建筑艺术的精华。它体现着中国悠久的文化传统，显示着五百多年前工匠们在建筑上的卓越成就。

故宫和当时北京城的修建是同时进行的，明清北京城的布局鲜明地体现了中国封建社会的都城以皇宫为主体的规划思想。当时北京城有三重——宫城（紫禁城）、皇城、京城。紫禁城位于北京城的中心，环绕紫禁城外围的是皇城，我们熟悉的天安门和地安门分别是皇城的南门和北门，皇城内部设有社稷坛、太庙、寺观、衙署等各类与皇家有关的建筑，另外，还有皇家园林，如北海、中南海、景山等也在皇城内。故宫周围环绕着10米多高的城墙和50多米宽的护城河，构成“城中之城”。城墙四角各有一座结构精巧的角楼，造型独特。皇城外面又有一道城墙环绕，称为京城。明中期在京城南边修建了一道外城，但由于财政匮乏，只修了南面，其余三面并未修建。这就使紫禁城成了一座至少有三重城墙包围的“城中之城”，这种布局显然是为了突出皇权的中心地位。

词语注释

【1】天安门：明、清两代皇城的正门。

【2】端门：宫城的正南门。

【3】乾清宫：在交泰殿之前，是皇帝处理朝政的宫殿。

【4】交泰殿：在乾清宫后，坤宁宫前，因在两宫之间，取“天地交泰”之义。清廷宝玺藏于此殿。

【5】坤宁宫：在交泰殿后。广九楹，有东西二暖殿，明代为皇后居处，清代曾为皇帝大婚的洞房。

【6】龙凤流云：龙凤在云中游动之势，栩栩如生。

三、陵墓建筑

中国古代多用土葬，中国古代人崇信人死之后，在阴间仍然过着类似阳间的生活，对待死者应该“事死如事生”，因而陵墓的地上、地下建筑和随葬生活用品均仿照阳间。河南安阳殷墟曾发现不少巨大的墓穴，并有大量奴隶殉葬和车、马等随葬。陵墓建筑可以说是中国古代建筑中历史久远的重要组成部分，先秦就有两座著名的帝王陵墓，一是陕西黄帝陵，一是浙江绍兴大禹陵，这都在《史记》中有记载。而后秦始皇陵，无论规模、形态、记述，都称得上是最伟大的帝王陵墓，在世界历史上都是罕见的。

在漫长的历史进程中，中国陵墓建筑得到了长足的发展，形成建筑、雕刻、绘画、自然环境融于一体的综合性艺术。其布局可概括为三种形式：

一、以陵山为主体的布局，如秦始皇陵周围建城垣，背靠骊山，轮廓宏大，气象巍峨。

二、以神道贯串，形成轴线布局。如唐高宗乾陵，以山峰为陵山主体，前面布置阙门、石像生、碑刻、华表等组成神道，衬托陵墓建筑的宏伟气魄。

三、建筑群布局。明清的陵墓都是选择群山环绕的封闭性环境作为陵区，将各帝陵谐调地布置在一处。在神道上增设牌坊、大红门、碑亭等，建筑与环境密切结合在一起，创造“王气葱郁”的氛围。

明清两代皇陵是中国帝王的陵墓中保存最为完整的。明朝皇帝的陵墓，即十三陵，为明代定都北京后13位皇帝的陵墓群，自1409年开始建造，至1644年明亡，历时二百余年，位于北京市昌平县城北天寿山下一个三面环山、向南开口的小盆地内。小盆地内的山坡上错落有致地分布着这些帝王的陵墓，占地面积达40平方千米。每个陵的建筑形式虽不太相同，但有好多共同之处。每个陵都称“宫”，外面也都用一道红墙围起来。宫门内是棱恩殿，这是祭祀行礼之地。棱恩殿后面是宝城，即帝后和众多的妃子、皇子、公主的埋葬地。明十三陵规模宏伟壮丽，景色苍秀，气势雄阔，是国内现存最集中、最完整的陵园建筑群。其中规模最宏伟的是明成祖朱棣[1]（dì）的长陵和明神宗朱翊钧[2]（yìjūn）的定陵。经挖掘发现，定陵地宫的石拱结构坚实，四周排水设备良好，积水极少，石拱无一塌陷，这充分展示了中国古人建造地下建筑的高超技术。

中国现存陵墓建筑中规模最宏大、建筑体系最完整的皇家陵寝群——清东陵，位于河北省遵化县马兰峪，占地78平方千米，埋葬着清朝5位皇帝及慈禧太后。清东陵中最大最辉煌的是乾隆的裕陵和葬有慈禧太后的定东陵。裕陵地宫由九券四门构成，四壁、券顶及石门上布满佛教题材雕刻及经文，人称“地下佛堂”，在明清帝陵地宫中唯其最富丽豪华、独具风格。定东陵中的慈禧陵最为华丽，大殿内外彩画中共有2 400多条金龙，64根明柱上均盘绕半立体鎏金盘

清东陵

龙，梁枋全都用名贵的黄花梨木制成。隆恩殿前的龙凤陛石，使用高浮雕与透雕手法，并打破传统龙凤并排格局，采用凤在上、龙在下图案，龙翔凤舞神态生动。其他陵墓建筑都很精美壮观，极为考究。清东陵以其无可辩驳的魅力和极高的历史、艺术和科学价值于2000年11月30日被联合国教科文组织正式列入“世界文化遗产名录”。

词语注释

【1】明成祖朱棣：明朝第三位皇帝，朱元璋第四子。初封燕王，镇守北平。建文元年（公元1399年）起兵“靖难”，四年，破京师（今江苏南京），夺取帝位，改元永乐，杀方孝孺等人。永乐十九年，（公元1421年）迁都北京，以南京为留都。极力肃整内政，巩固边防，政绩卓著。在文化事业上，加强儒家文化思想的统治，大力扩充国家藏书，编成《永乐大典》。

【2】明神宗朱翊钧（公元1563年～1620年）：明穆宗长子，六岁时被立为太子，穆宗死后，十岁的朱翊钧即位，改年号万历。朱翊钧在位四十八年，是明朝在位时间最长的皇帝。

四、万里长城

雄伟壮观的万里长城，是人类建筑史上罕见的古代军事防御工程，它以悠久的历史、浩大的工程、雄伟的气魄著称于世，被联合国教科文组织列入“世界遗产名录”，为世界八大奇迹之一。

人们一提到长城，往往想到秦始皇。的确，修筑长城是秦始皇统一天下以后的一项重大军事措施。其实，在秦始皇以前，长城就已经开始修筑了。远自春秋时代，各诸侯国相互防御，后来燕、赵、秦三国为防御北方的匈奴、东胡[1]等民族的骚扰而筑起高大的城墙。秦统一六国以后，以此为基础修筑成一道绵

八达岭长城

延万里的长城，奠定了今天长城的基础。以后历代对长城都继续修筑使用。明代，因为北方仍有蒙古族的进攻，东北又有女真族崛起，为了加强防御，将过去的土筑城墙部分改为砖石结构。

现在的长城就是明长城，东起山海关，西到甘肃嘉峪关[2]，横跨河北、天津、北京、山西、内蒙古、陕西、宁夏、甘肃等省（市）、自治区，翻山越岭，蜿蜒起伏，连绵6 700千米。在长城上，修筑了许多烽火台[3]。烽火台有的独立建在高山上，有的和长城城墙相连，是为传递军情设立的。若是敌人来犯，烽火台白天燃烟，夜间举火。临近的烽火台看见烟火以后，也点起烟火，这样，烽火台座座相连，即使远在千里以外，也可以在几小时之内把消息传到京城。

万里长城每隔7.5千米就有一座关城，其大小根据地势和军事重要性而决定。著名的关城有山海关、嘉峪关、平型关、雁门关、居庸关[4]等等。其中山海关为华北与东北交通的必经之道，号称“天下第一关”。居庸关距离北京约60千米，那里山峦起伏，树木葱郁，景色优美。居庸关原有南北两个外围关口，南面叫南口，北口就是八达岭。

词语注释

【1】东胡：春秋战国时期强盛一时的北方民族，分布在燕国的北部和东北，即今辽河上游，以畜牧业为主，兼狩猎。

【2】嘉峪关：明长城终点，附近有黑山石刻画像、魏晋壁画墓等。

【3】烽火台：古代边防用于瞭望和报警的建筑。

【4】居庸关：长城重要关口，在北京市西北。建于两山夹峙的深谷中，地势险要，为北京通往内蒙古主要通道，自古为兵家必争之地。

五、古都的建筑

（一）古都西安

西安是六大古都中最古老、建都时间最长的一个。从公元前11世纪起到公元10世纪初，这里先后建有丰京[1]、镐（Hào）京[2]，秦朝时这里是都城咸阳，此后，西汉、西晋、前赵、前秦、后秦、西魏、北周、隋、唐等共13个朝代都曾经在这里建都，作为统治中心的时间长达千余年。

在西安市东南灞河南岸公主岭发现的蓝田猿人化石，是距今五六十万年前的旧石器时期原始人类的遗迹；西安市东郊半坡村遗址和姜寨遗址，是属于距今五千年的仰韶文化和龙山文化的遗存，这证明西安是古老中华民族的发祥地之一。秦都咸阳及其阿房（Ēpáng）宫[3]由渭河[4]北岸延至今西安市西，现有阿房宫的殿基，反映出秦代建筑工艺的极高水平。唐长安城规模远大于今西安市，三大宫殿群的兴建，形成宏伟壮丽的长安城，成为中国封建社会发展到全盛时期的重要标志。加之当时文化、经济的繁荣，中外交流的开放，古“丝绸之路”的扩展，可说是长安发展史上最辉煌灿烂的时代。

大小雁塔为硕果仅存的唐代建筑，大明宫遗址位于今火车站之北；今西安市城墙及钟楼、鼓楼为明代建筑，城墙系国内保存最为完好的明代城墙。西安市

大雁塔

周围有秦陵 1 处、汉陵墓约 30 处，唐陵墓 30 处以上，为我国古代帝王及后妃、勋臣陵墓最集中的地区。这些陵墓一般都有很大的陵区，曾建有规模宏伟的地上建筑，多石像生[5]和碑刻，也有富丽的地下建筑和丰富的随葬品。现最闻名于世者当属骊山秦始皇陵和兵马俑。

西安还有中国最大、最古老的“石刻图书馆”——西安碑林，中国最早的伊斯兰教圣地化觉巷清真大寺，中国现代水平最高的国家级博物馆陕西省历史博物馆。

（二）古都洛阳

洛阳以位于洛水[6]北岸而得名。公元前 21 世纪夏代兴起，洛阳一带即为其活动中心。著名的仰韶文化，即首先发现在洛阳西北的仰韶村。“河图洛书”的传说，也反映河、洛流域历史文化的悠久。这里早在西周时期已形成城市，称洛邑。夏、商时期的二里头文化遗址，在洛阳一带已发现数十处。自公元前 770 年开始，先后有东周、东汉、曹魏、西晋、北魏、隋、唐、五代之后梁、后唐建都于此，历时 950 余年，故有“九朝古都”之称，为中国六大古都之一，是我国历史上第二个建都时间最长的城市。

城东白马寺始建于东汉永平十一年（公元 68 年），由天竺[7]（zhú）僧摄摩腾[8]、竺法兰[9]主持并在此译经，为中国第一座佛教寺院，故有“释源”及“祖庭”之称。城南关林为关羽首级葬地，始建于唐，明、清扩建重修。洛阳附近多历代帝王陵墓，其中以东周、东汉、北魏陵墓规模较大，出土文物很多。洛阳最著名的龙门石窟，始建于北魏太和年间（公元 477 年～499 年），经历众多朝代，开凿 400 多年，现有佛像 10 万余尊，是中国四大石窟之一。洛阳保存了大量优秀的历史文化遗产。宋代史学家司马光诗云：“若问古今兴废事，请君只看洛阳城。”洛阳从一个侧面反映了中华民族的灿烂文明和悠久历史。

（三）古都北京

北京，中华人民共和国的首都，是中国政治、经济文化中心，世界历史文化名城和古都之一。从古之蓟城到唐之幽州，从元之大都至明清之帝京、今日之北京，历经数朝的经营，历时 800 多年。一座厚重悠久的文化古城，一个朝气蓬勃的国际都会，传统与现代并存。

北京得名始于明代。明朝开国皇帝朱元璋定都南京后，当时北京是其子燕王朱棣的封地，称作顺天府。后来，朱棣策划发动政变，登上了皇帝的宝座。朱棣在南京即位后，立即将顺天府改称为北京。

白马寺

北京四合院

北京城是一座对称的城市，以故宫为中心，从永定门、前门、天安门、午门、神武门、景山、地安门、钟楼直到鼓楼为止，形成了一条中轴线。东四、西四等南北平行的大街，同一条条东西向的胡同纵横交错，分列在中轴线的两旁。北京古城分为内城外城两部分，今人称为凸字形城。凸字城的北边部分称为内城，建城较早，它是明朝初年在元大都的基础上参照明初都城南京城和明朝中都（安徽凤阳）的设计方案建设起来的。凸字形南边部分叫外城，建城较晚，它是在明朝后期嘉靖年间建设起来的。在古都北京内城之外的南北东西四个方位上，分别建有天坛、地坛、日坛、月坛四个古祭坛建筑。天坛位于北京内城之南，是明清两朝皇帝于每年“冬至”祭天、“孟春”祈谷[10]、“夏至”祈雨的地方。地坛位于北京内城之北是皇帝祭地神的地方。日坛位于北京内城之东，是皇帝在每年“春分”之日祭太阳神的地方。月坛位于北京内城之西，是皇帝于每年秋分之日祭月神和天上诸星宿的地方。祭祀天、地、日、月是中国历史上由来已久的习俗。

古都北京拥有众多的历史文化遗迹，构成了北京城市建筑上的独特风格和宏伟的气势，给人以稳重、博大、端庄的感觉。其中有当今世界上保存规模最大、最完整的皇宫——紫禁城；有中国现存最大的皇家园林——颐和园。颐和园兼有江南水乡的玲珑精致和北方园林的豪迈大气，园中山青水绿，景色宜人，在中外园林史上享有盛誉；天坛也是世界建筑艺术的宝贵遗产，那巍巍的建筑、经久不散的皇家气息，见证了古都北京曾经的辉煌。

明十三陵是北京最大的古墓群，尤其以定陵规模最为浩大。北京八达岭长城是中国长城保留最好的部分，为世界八大奇迹之一；北京的宗教建筑也久负盛名，有中国著名佛教圣地碧云寺、道教圣地白云观、喇嘛教圣地雍和宫[11]以及伊斯兰教的牛街清真寺等；特别是北京四合院民居，其间弥漫着浓浓的京味文化。

（四）六朝胜地南京

南京是中国最著名的四大古都及历史文化名城之一。

南京北临长江，南依丘陵，秦淮河沿西南城郭注

中山陵

入长江，古人曾以“钟山龙盘、石头虎踞”[12]形容其地势之雄伟险要，早在两千四百多年前的春秋时代即已建城。从公元3世纪起到15世纪初，曾先后有东吴、东晋、宋、齐、梁、陈在此建都，故历史上称其为“六朝古都”。以后南唐、明初也都定都在此。南京古称金陵，明朝以后始称南京。明朝初年朱元璋统治时期的都城——南京应天府，是南京第一次作为统一王朝的全国性都城，从公元1378年～1421年永乐迁都，一共43年。定都前后，朱元璋对南京进行了较大规模的营建，将其建成了一座具有世界水平的坚固的防御性城堡。

城市由三大部分组成，即旧城区、皇宫区、驻军区。后两者是明初的扩展。环绕这三区修筑了长达33.68千米的砖石城墙，即今南京明城墙。是为世界第一大城垣。南京城墙墙基用条石铺砌，墙身用10厘米×20厘米×40厘米左右的大型城砖垒砌两侧外壁，中实杂土。城墙沿线共辟十三座城门，门上建有城楼。城门与市内大街贯连，街道纵横交织，主次分明，井然有序。雄伟坚固高大的十三座城楼如同身着盔甲的勇士驻守在南京城的各个入口处。城楼中又以正南门“聚宝门”（今名中华门）最为奇特，它有三道瓮城，27个藏兵洞，每道门设有千斤闸，可谓“铜墙铁壁”。

南京城东盘卧着著名的钟山（紫金山，因山上页岩呈紫金色而得名），全山植被茂盛，形成一个不可多得的与繁华闹市相邻的风景区。钟山名胜古迹很多，大都分布在南麓。以中山陵为中心，东面是灵谷寺、邓演达[13]墓；西面是明孝陵和廖仲恺[14]、何香凝[15]夫妇墓及中山植物园。天堡峰上有太平天国天堡城遗址和闻名中外的紫金山天文台。钟山西段入城的余脉是六朝时皇家花园所在地，其北面有玄武湖[16]。

词语注释

【1】丰京：周文王旧都，在今陕西省长安县沣河以西。

【2】镐京：西周国都。

【3】阿房宫：秦宫殿名。其遗址在今西安市西5千米处，其前殿建于秦始皇三十五年（公元前212年），秦亡时整个建筑群尚未竣工，后项羽入关，焚毁。

【4】渭河：黄河最大支流。

【5】石像生：古代陵墓前的石雕人像。

【6】洛水：即今河南省洛河。

【7】天竺：古代印度。

【8】摄摩腾：印度高僧。

【9】竺法兰：相传为东汉明帝时来中国译经的印度僧人。

【10】“祭天”和“祈谷”：祭祀天神，祭祀上天。古代祈求谷物丰收的祭礼。

【11】雍和宫：在北京内城东北角安定门内，原为雍正皇帝藩邸，是北京最大的喇嘛教寺院。

【12】“钟山龙盘，石头虎踞”：形容古都南京气势雄壮。三国时代诸葛亮出使东吴，看到这一气象，叹曰：“钟山龙盘，石头虎踞，此帝王之宅。”（南京古称石头城）

【13】邓演达（公元1895年～1931年）：中国国民党左派领袖之一，在北伐战争中，任国民革命军总政治部主任；南昌起义中，任革命委员会委员。1931年被蒋介石杀害。

【14】廖仲恺（公元1877年～1925年）：现代民主革命家，曾任黄埔军校党代表、中国国民革命军总党代表、国民党中央执行委员会常委和工人部长、农民部长。1925年被国民党右派刺杀。

【15】何香凝（公元1879年～1972年）：现代革命家，廖仲恺的夫人。新中国成立后，历任全国政协副主席、全国人大常务委员会副会长、民革中央主席、全国妇联名誉主席。

【16】玄武湖：位于南京玄武门外，湖水来自钟山北麓。

第八章　古代工艺

一、青铜器

青铜是人类历史上一项伟大的发明，中国使用青铜的历史年代久远。1975 年，甘肃东乡林家马家窑文化遗址（约公元前 3000 年左右）出土一件青铜刀，这是目前在中国发现的最早的青铜器。商代和西周时期是中国青铜器最发达的时代，因此称其为“青铜时代”。

中国青铜器不但数量多，而且造型丰富、品种繁多，主要有工具、兵器、烹饪器、食器、酒器、水器、乐器、车马器、货币等等。单在酒器类中又有爵[1]（jué）、角[2]、尊[3]、壶、方彝[4]（yí）等二十多个器种，而每一器种在每个时代都呈现不同的风采，不同地区的青铜器也有所差异。在现存的商周青铜器中，司母戊方鼎[5]（dǐng）以其形制巨大而闻名遐迩。鼎，是古人用于煮熟、加温或盛放熟食物的器皿，后来演变为祭祀用器。用于盛祭品的鼎，因祭品的不同，分别有“鹿鼎”“牛鼎”等；鼎的形制有圆有方。司母戊方鼎是在河南安阳殷墟出土的，是商代后期的作品，高 133 厘米，重 875 千克，是中国现存最重的青铜器中形制最大的鼎。它的造型非常壮观，腹体方正，大耳，四足粗壮而上下相似，显示出一种不可征服的稳定和巨人般的力量。鼎腹的四个面的中心部位均为光洁的素面，四周环绕纹饰，最上面是个一首双身的饕餮[6]（tāotiè），口沿下四个角的转折处以及两侧鼎耳[7]（dǐng'ěr）连接口沿处，均为牛首图案，饕餮和牛首共计有 24 个。在奴隶社会的商代，能够制作如此巨大的铜鼎，体现了中国古代青铜铸造

方鼎

铜天觚

爵

技术的高超水平，在世界青铜文化史上占有很重要的地位。

中国的青铜器造型艺术非常独特。纹饰精美是商代和西周时期的青铜器物的突出特征。兽面纹也叫饕餮纹，本身就有浓厚的神秘色彩，是这一时期纹饰的主题。兽面纹的角部特别发达，有的几乎达到整个兽面纹的一半，眼、耳、嘴、鼻、躯体等部位也更形象化，特别是双目圆而大。龙纹、凤鸟纹也是常见的纹饰，各种动物如象、鹿、牛、蛇、龟、蝉等纹饰也有出现。另外，一些几何形图案也有了充分的发展，还有用细线雕刻狩猎、战争、宴会的图案。

马踏飞燕

与世界其他国家的青铜器相比，中国青铜器以礼器为主，在世界青铜文化中独树一帜。世界上发现的古代青铜器的代表作大都为武器，如戈、矛、刀、箭等，而中国却以铸造难度较大、纹饰复杂的礼器为主。尤其是鼎，为国家重器，是政权的象征。礼器是古代礼仪的重要载体，或陈于庙堂，或用于宴饮，或施于盥洗，还有一些专门作殉葬的明器，因而中国青铜器带有一定的神圣性。欧洲青铜文化以武器为代表，中国青铜文化以礼器为代表，从中也可以看出中西文化不同的取向。

作为礼器的中国青铜器的一个显著特点是铸有文字，即“金文”，铭文可以流传不朽，中国青铜器有铭文者仅出土的就达一万余件。这是与世界上其他国家的青铜器的一个明显的不同之处。青铜器铭文是从商代中期开始的，起初只是一两个字，即郭沫若先生称之为“族徽”的文字。商代晚期开始，铭文增多，最长也不过48字。西周时期是青铜器铭文大发展时期，鸿篇巨制不少，如篇幅最大的毛公鼎铭文长达487字。这些铭文字体，或粗犷放达、或渊雅静穆，具有很高的书法艺术价值。

词语注释

【1】爵：古代饮酒器。
【2】角：古代的盛酒器，外形像爵，有盖。
【3】尊：酒器。
【4】方彝：古代盛酒的器具。
【5】司母戊方鼎：商代晚期王室的祭器。1939年出土于河南安阳武官村。方形，四足，立耳，饰饕餮纹。为中国已发现的最大的青铜器，也是古代世界青铜文化中仅见的。方鼎结构复杂，鼎身和四足是整体铸造，耳则是在鼎身铸成后再在其上安模、翻范、浇铸成的。它集中反映了商晚期青铜器冶铸业的技术水平和生产能力。鼎腹内壁铸铭文“司母戊”三字，是商王为祭祀其母戊而作，现藏中国历史博物馆。
【6】饕餮：传说中的一种凶恶贪食的野兽。古代钟鼎彝器上多刻其头部形状以为装饰。
【7】鼎耳：鼎上两耳。

二、兵马俑[1]

秦始皇陵位于西安市的临潼（Líntóng）县城以东的骊（Lí）山脚下。秦始皇兵马俑坑是秦始皇的陪葬坑，位于陵园[2]东侧1 500米处，坐西向东，三个坑呈品字形排列。最早被发现的是一号俑坑，呈长方形。左右两侧各有一个兵马俑坑，统称二号坑、三号坑。

1974年3月底，当地农民打井，打到3米多深，

兵马俑战车

挖出了一些残破的陶人。有的说这儿以前是座砖瓦窑，有的认为这些“瓦人”是破庙里的神像，经过考古学家一年多的工作，终于发现了“世界上最大的地下军事博物馆”。

这里是秦始皇陵园的一个角落。据《史记》记载，秦始皇在十三岁（公元前 246 年）登上王位以后，就下令在骊山北麓[3]（lù）修建自己的陵墓。他驱使 70 多万人，从四川、湖北运进巨木，从渭河北的仲山、嵯峨山开采块石，全靠人力运到临潼。工程十分艰难，整整修了 39 年，直到他死后一年，工程方告结束。

1974 年以来，秦始皇陵周围出土了大量文物，尤其是兵马俑陪葬坑的发掘，震动了世界。秦始皇陵附近埋葬的兵马俑，是一个历史之谜，很可能象征着他生前拥有的千军万马，是秦国庞大军队的缩影。秦始皇凭借着强大的军事力量，以秋风扫落叶之势，兼并了六国，完成了统一大业。

1977 年，在一号兵马俑陪葬坑遗址上建成了秦始皇陵兵马俑博物馆。这个坑面积 14 620 平方米，据估测有兵马俑 6 000 多件，已出土的武士俑、战车、挽（wǎn）马等都仿真人和原物塑制[4]，展现了秦始皇威震宇内、统一六国的强大阵容。出土的武器是由精冶的青铜制成的，有的表面镀铬，银光闪闪，锋利得好像新制成的一样。另外，在陵旁还发现了两组铜车马和铜俑，单辕双轮，车上有篷盖，车前有骏马四匹，车上跪坐着长襦（rú）束带、握辔（pèi）、凝神的驭（yù）手。铜车重达 1 200 千克，车长 3.28 米，车高 1.04 米，马高 0.7 米，身长 1.2 米，是真马体量的一半。车马的 3 000 多个金属构件[5]几乎都是浇铸而成，厚薄仅在 2~4 毫米之间。专家认为这是“举世无双的古代青铜器珍品”。

秦俑坑的发现，证明秦代的工艺已经达到很高水平，国内外学者极为重视，誉之为“世界第八奇迹”。这证明早在 2 000 多年以前的秦代，中国彩色陶塑艺术就已经相当成熟了，改写了“中国雕塑受印度佛教传入的影响，而成熟于 1 500 年前的南北朝”以及“彩塑始于唐代”的说法。1987 年，联合国教科文组织将兵马俑与秦始皇陵一起列入“世界文化遗产名录”。

词语注释

【1】俑：古代殉葬用的木制或陶制的偶像。

【2】陵园：帝王或诸侯的墓地。现指以陵墓为主的园林。

【3】骊山北麓：骊山的北边。

【4】塑制：用泥或金属制成。

【5】构件：组成建筑物某一结构的物件。

兵马俑立俑

三、唐三彩

唐三彩的发现是在上个世纪初，发现之功首推中国学者罗振玉和王国维。光绪三十三年（1907年）罗振玉在北京厂肆得古俑两件，后续有所得。至民国五年（1916年）罗氏将历年所藏之精品，影印编成《古明器图录》四卷，并记录了发现的经过。唐三彩的发现惊动了世界考古界，风靡一时，唐三彩被公私收藏机构竞相搜求，高价收购。这些沉睡一千多年的艺术品不断流入北京。此后几十年中，河南、陕西、江苏等地又出土了大量的唐三彩，向人们展示了一个璀璨的艺术世界。

唐三彩是盛行于唐代的陶器，以黄、白、绿为基本釉色，后来人们习惯把这类陶器称为“唐三彩”。实际上，它所用的色彩还包括天蓝、赭黄、茄紫、褐红等。

唐三彩是因随葬的需要而发展起来的，是专为贵族葬礼特制的一种明器，品种很多，有动物、有人体塑像，也有生活用具。随葬和日用是唐三彩的两大用途。从唐三彩的造型看，器皿种类有水器、酒器、饮食器、文具以及建筑模型等，式样新颖，色彩绚丽。人物主要有妇女、文官、武士、伎乐[1]（jìyuè）、牵马俑、胡俑[2]、天王等，大体根据其社会地位，刻画出其不同的性格和特征。贵妇面部胖圆，肌肉丰满，梳各式发髻，着彩色服装；文官彬彬有礼；武士勇猛英俊；胡俑高鼻深目；天王怒目圆睁。动物有鸟、狮、骆驼、马、牛等。尤其是三彩骆驼，背载丝绸或驮乐队，仰首嘶鸣，那赤髯（rán）碧眼的牵驼俑，身穿窄袖衫[3]，头戴翻檐帽[4]，再现了中亚胡人的生活形象，使人回忆起当年“丝绸之路”上驼铃叮当的情景。

唐三彩俑

唐三彩盘

唐三彩的诞生，经历了几百年的时间。汉代发明了单色釉，即铅釉陶，釉呈黄褐色或翠绿色、红棕色，釉层清澈，光泽很强，到北魏才出现双色釉，能将不同颜色施于一器，以一种色釉为底，再在底釉上加彩，直到初唐时期才出现三彩釉。至今，唐三彩的生产已有一千三百多年的历史。它吸取了中国国画、雕塑等工艺美术的特点，线条粗犷有力，在陶坯[5]上涂上彩釉[6]，在烘制[7]过程中发生化学变化，色彩自然协调，花纹流畅，是一种具有中国独特风格的传统工艺品。

气度恢宏、壮丽辉煌的唐代文化记录了中外文化交流，唐三彩也反映了这种文化交融的过程，主要表现在唐三彩人物俑的创作上，留下了印度文化和西亚波斯文化的印迹。唐三彩的胡人有深目高鼻多须、头戴翻檐帽的阿拉伯人，辫发无须的西域人，还有白人、黑人，牵马拉骆驼的商贩、伶人，穿胡服，奏胡乐，跳胡舞。唐三彩还远销世界各地，目前所知，发现唐三彩的亚洲国家有印度尼西亚、日本、朝鲜、伊拉克、伊朗，以及非洲的埃及，欧洲的意大利。

词语注释

【1】伎乐：以音乐舞蹈为生的女艺人。

【2】胡俑：胡人的俑像。

【3】窄袖衫：初唐的女子服装，大多是上穿窄袖衫襦，有对襟、右衽交领两种，窄袖长至腕，衣身短窄，仅至腰部。这种服装开始在宫廷和贵族妇女中流行后才不分官庶、竞相仿效，成为一种时兴的服式，尤其在唐中期更为盛行。

【4】翻檐帽：一种把帽檐翻卷向上的帽子。

【5】陶坯：陶制器皿的生坯。

【6】彩釉：彩色的以石英、长石、硼砂、黏土等为原料制成的物质，涂在瓷器、陶器的表面烧制而成，有玻璃光泽。

【7】烘制：用火烘、烤使其干硬而制成。

四、瓷都景德镇和五大古窑

陶瓷与中国的关系深远，甚至“陶瓷”（china）便代表了中国。陶瓷的发明与发展，对人类的文明进程有重大的影响，而中国陶瓷发展史透发着中国历史文化的瑰丽。

青花瓷

景德镇是驰名中外的瓷都，它位于江西省东北部，邻接安徽省，是一座历史悠久的江南名镇，汉唐以来即以产陶瓷而著称于世。北宋景德年间（公元1004年～1007年）因真宗命进御的瓷器底书“景德年制”四字，遂天下皆称“景德镇瓷器”，景德镇也由此而得名。以后历经元、明、清三朝，景德镇一直是中国的制瓷业中心，生产出来的青花瓷[1]、釉里红[2]、五彩瓷[3]、珐琅（fàlánɡ）彩瓷[4]等，都是举世闻名的佳作，远销到欧美、东北亚、南亚、西亚、北非等地。景德镇对中国乃至世界陶瓷文化发展的贡献是巨大的。可以说，景德镇是千年窑火不断的产瓷圣地，是世界上唯一的以单一行业发展起来的城市。中华人民共和国成立后，景德镇成为国务院公布的中国第一批历史文化名城之一。

宋代是中国瓷业最繁荣的时期，名瓷名窑遍及大半个中国，名窑形成不同风格的系统。闻名于世的是宋代五大名窑，即钧窑、哥窑、官窑、汝窑和定窑。

官窑，是皇家、官方营建，主持烧造瓷器的窑场。窑址先在开封，后迁杭州。官窑制作精良，用料考究。胎骨有白、灰、红之分，白色胎骨多用含铁质深酱色釉护胎足。因而器皿口部边缘釉的最薄处隐约透露出胎色而呈微黑紫色。釉色以青为主，有天青、翠青、粉青，莹润如美玉；釉面又开泳纹，犹如微风吹皱的一池春水，泛出道道涟漪。作为宫廷的御用品，其可贵之处在于它既无精美的雕饰以哗众，又无抹彩涂绘以媚人，唯以体态造型之美，釉色纹片之俏，散发出艺术魅力。烧制时，不计工本，以最好的材料、最好的窑制、工艺最精良的工匠烧制。产品仅供给宫廷，严禁民间使用。

官窑青釉弦纹瓶

定窑，宋代属定州（今河北曲阳），故名定窑。

在宋代主要烧制白瓷，也兼烧绿釉、黑釉、褐釉，首创覆烧法[5]。定窑以丰富多彩的装饰花纹取胜，一向被视为陶瓷艺术中的珍品。定窑在当时规模很大，工艺水平很高，对各地瓷窑均有一定的影响，在宋代陶瓷工艺史上有突出的地位。定窑瓷器总的来说薄而轻，釉不很透明，白中泛黄。印花多采用模压，均为阳纹，题材以花卉为多，如牡丹、萱草等，以刻花者为贵，刻花简洁有力，常用的纹饰有莲花、海水、双鱼等。

汝窑，窑址在河南临汝。临汝在宋代属汝州，故名汝窑。其烧造的时间不长，仅从宋哲宗到宋徽宗时期烧造了二十多年，传世品不多，所烧陶瓷精美绝伦，在中国瓷器史上享有盛誉。北宋后期，汝窑专为宫廷烧制御用瓷器。汝窑胎质细腻，工艺考究，相传以玛瑙入釉[6]，色泽独特，随光变幻。其釉色如雨过天青，其他还有鸭蛋青、虾青、冻青、茶青、豆青等，古朴大方，其釉面，平滑细腻，如同美玉。

汝窑天青釉圆洗

钧窑，窑址在河南省禹县，古属钧州，故名钧窑，盛于北宋晚期。钧窑属北方青瓷系统，产品贵在“窑变”技术，素有“入窑一色，出窑万彩”“钧瓷无双”的特点。同样的釉色，入窑经 1 350℃高温烧成后，每件瓷器呈色不一样，并出现人们意想不到的视觉效果。钧瓷胎质极硬，叩之有声，色彩深灰带褐紫，或浅灰。釉的正色为雨过天青色，还有大红、玫瑰紫、月白等色。

哥窑，窑址至今说法不一。因兄弟二人开窑制瓷，便将哥哥开的窑称为“哥窑”。这一工艺盛于宋元时期。

哥窑高脚荷叶碗

哥窑器物主要是陈设瓷，多仿古铜器形制，如贯耳瓶、菊瓣盘、兽耳炉、长颈瓶。釉色以粉青和米色为正色，其他还有灰青、鱼肚白、油灰色等。哥窑器以纹片著名，纹多为黑色，俗称“金丝铁线”，按颜色分有鳝血、黑蓝、浅黄鱼子纹；按形状分有网形纹、梅花纹、细碎纹等。哥窑开片总的特点是平整紧密，片纹裂开成上紧下宽状；黑色纹片中有时闪蓝色。

词语注释

【1】青花瓷：白地蓝花瓷。

【2】釉里红：即先涂上一层白釉，再上一层红色，然后又上一层薄釉，最后再画上花卉纹饰。

【3】五彩瓷：五彩瓷可以分为青花五彩和纯釉上五彩两种。

【4】珐琅彩瓷：一种专为清代宫廷御用而特制的精细彩绘瓷器，部分产品也用于赏赐。采用景德镇烧制成的瓷胎，早期彩料从国外进口，在内务府造办处由宫廷画师精工绘画，经再次烧制而成。创始于康熙晚期，雍正、乾隆时盛行。

【5】覆烧法：瓷器的制作方法。口沿不施釉，俗称“芒口”，往往镶一圈金、银或铜为饰。

【6】玛瑙入釉：玛瑙研为细末加入釉中。

五、四大名砚

砚被称为中国的文房四宝[1]之一，不仅是文房用具，由于其性质坚固，传百世而不朽，又被历代文人作为珍玩藏品[2]之选。历代文人墨客大都喜爱砚，收藏砚，常与砚相随相伴。在种类繁多的中国砚中，从唐代起，广东的端砚[3]、安徽的歙（Shè）砚[4]、甘肃的洮（Táo）砚[5]、山西的澄泥砚[6]并称为四大名砚。其中尤以端砚和歙砚为佳。

石砚上丰富的石品花式与精湛的镌刻技艺，不但使砚台具有浓郁的书卷气息与艺术魅力，而且也博得了历代文人雅士的高度评价和喜爱。在四大名砚中，端砚成名最早，名声也最大。它产于广东肇庆东郊的端溪。因肇庆古属端州，端砚因此而得名。端砚石品优良，其优点一是下墨，二是发墨，三是不损毫。古人将端砚的特点概括为“温润如玉，叩之无声，缩墨不腐”，这表明端砚温和细致。端砚中的名贵石品有鱼脑冻、青花、蕉叶白，还有天青、石眼、金星、金叶等纹理。石眼对于砚没有直接的价值，但对技艺精湛的雕工来说，无疑可以通过意匠提高砚台的身价，利用砚材本身的形状、色彩和纹理雕刻适合的内容，保持内容与形式的统一。乾隆皇帝最喜端砚，甚至将珠宝钻翠[7]镶到端石上。

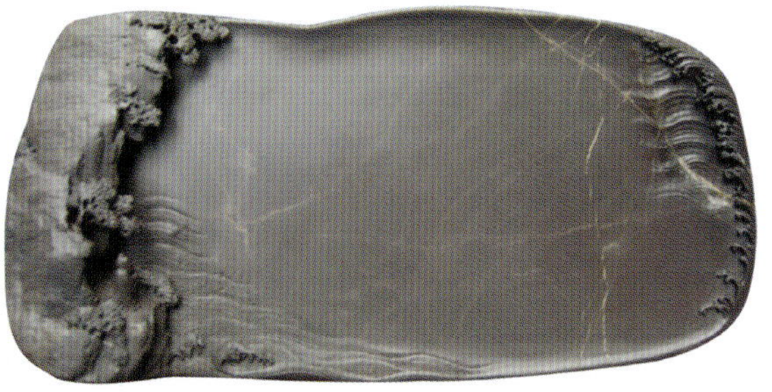

端 砚

歙砚的石料，称为歙石或婺源石，其产地在婺源县的龙尾山、仙霞山一带数百里范围之内，婺源属歙州，故称歙砚。歙砚天然生成的纹理主要有金星、眉子、水浪纹等。“金星”融结在砚石之中，形如谷粒，多如秋夜星星，闪闪发光；“眉子”似眉毛，粗、细、疏、密，各具神采；“水浪纹”如水的波纹，变化无穷。歙砚的雕刻艺术受徽州[8]砖雕和木雕的影响，有独特的艺术风格，造型浑朴，大方匀称。歙砚自它产生之日起，就作为贡品，博得了上自天子，下至文人雅士的欢心。

洮砚石产于甘肃洮河东岸喇嘛崖。此地山陡水急，采石异常艰难，故而珍贵。洮砚在唐代已名扬天下，它质地细密晶莹，有绿、红两种，尤以绿洮为贵，色呈墨绿，经研磨后可呈现云水样纹，具有发墨快亮而耐用、蓄水持久而不耗、利笔等优点。

澄泥砚

澄泥砚产于山西绛州，始于唐代，至今已有千余年历史，属于非石质砚材，其制作方法是，先缝绢袋置于汾水中，迎浪张开袋口，过滤水中泥沙，一年后袋内泥满，取出风干，制成砚坯，再烧制成质地似陶的砚台，最后经过雕刻、打磨等一系列工序，澄泥砚石质细腻、坚硬、光润，可与石砚媲美。其颜色以鳝鱼黄、蟹壳青和玫瑰紫为主。

早期的砚台注重实用性，装饰较少，明清两代的砚台制作又出现新的突破，朝着艺术化的方向发展。砚台制作讲究造型美观、雕刻精细、构图丰富多彩，而且镌刻砚铭的风气大为盛行，使砚台超出一般文具的实用性，而成为供人玩赏的艺术品。不少人以专藏各种各样款式的砚台为嗜好，闲时独坐书房中，品玩砚台，以为至乐。

词语注释

【1】文房四宝：指笔、墨、纸、砚四种书写和绘画工具。

【2】珍玩藏品：传世而为人珍藏的金石字画、珠宝瓷器等工艺品，被人把玩、品赏。

【3】端砚：用广东端溪地方出产的石头制成的砚台，是砚台中的上品。

【4】歙砚：砚的一种。因产于歙州（今安徽歙县）而得名。

【5】洮砚：古砚名。采甘肃省洮河中的绿石制成。

【6】澄泥砚：古砚名。以水澄结细泥烧制而成。

【7】钻翠：钻石和翡翠，泛指珠宝。

【8】徽州：古州名，宋宣和三年改歙州置，治今安徽歙县，以盛产墨闻名于世，其墨称徽墨。

六、中国的雕刻

砖雕[1]、石雕、木雕三种雕刻工艺是中国雕刻的简称。

（一）砖　雕

战国花砖

砖雕是在特制的质地细密的青灰砖上经过精致的雕镂[2]而形成的物像或花纹的工艺。中国自古就有战国花砖和秦砖汉瓦，上面都有图纹，这应是砖雕的起源。无论在宫殿、坛庙、寺观、陵墓还是居民住房的影壁[3]、门楼[4]、屋檐、屋顶、门楣等处都可以看到砖雕。砖雕艺术已成为建筑艺术不可缺少的装饰，远近均可观赏，具有完整的效果。砖雕雕刻的内容有神话传说、戏曲故事、民间风俗等，如《龙凤呈祥》《和合二仙》《刘海戏金蟾》《三阳开泰》《郭子仪做寿》《麒麟送子》《狮子滚绣球》。图案多采用中国民间吉祥的花卉，如松柏、兰花、竹、山茶、菊花、荷花、鲤鱼等，以及走兽。雕刻又可分为浮雕、透雕、线刻、镂雕、圆雕和镶嵌六种手法。有的砖雕多达九层，前后透视，层层深入。玲珑剔透的砖雕工艺不仅给建筑增添了一种诱人的魅力，也意味着居住在这样的宅院里将会是吉星高照[5]、福禄满门[6]。

中国砖雕艺术，由陶艺、石雕工艺发展而来，在历史的不同阶段，砖雕呈现出不同的工艺手法和风格特点。汉魏时期，砖雕艺术的成就主要表现在墓穴装饰，如画像砖艺术，多为模印制作，是砖雕发展的初始阶段。近来，南阳相继出土了近千块汉代画像砖，砖上的画面描绘出汉代丰富多彩的舞乐百戏[7]，由于民间匠师的精心雕琢设计，使静止画面上伎人的表演姿态无不充满着动感，富有浓厚的生活气息。戏车画像砖为车上表演走索[8]，动作惊险、演技精湛；拂袖舞伎，神态生动；还有些蹴鞠[9]（cùjū）者，边踢边舞，体态轻盈，优美潇洒；倒立者，或顶碗，或塌腰，表演无不柔和妩媚。画像砖中这些舞乐百戏，表现了汉代贵族们幻想死后到了另一个世界之后，继续驱使歌舞伎人供他们享受生前之乐的梦想。但它也给我们再现了汉代伟大的艺术成就，这些砖雕成为受

砖　雕

人瞩目的一大艺术奇观。

唐宋的砖雕也大都被用于佛塔和砖石墓装饰，是经模印后再加以雕刻，开始向雕刻工艺过渡。到了宋代，逐渐发展为多层浮雕。直到明清时期，砖雕艺术才被广泛应用于民居建筑，砖雕因其造价低廉、制作便捷而成为木雕装饰的主要替代品。民居砖雕开始注重情节构图，透雕层次加深，风格多样、手法细腻。可分南北两大体系：北方体系工艺纯熟，造型洗练，风格古朴豪放；南方技法丰富，造型精致，层次感强，风格典雅绮丽。

近代晋陕商人的崛起和商业资本的活跃推动了山西民居砖雕艺术的发展；徽州砖雕的发展同样得益于徽商雄厚的经济基础和儒商一体的文化氛围。江南民居形成了以黑、白、灰为主的典雅的装饰风格，而砖雕则是这种朴素风格理想的选择。总之，明清时代是砖雕艺术的鼎盛时期。

（二）木　雕

中国木雕艺术源远流长。早在史前时期就有不少具有雏形的工艺品，至战国时期，木雕工艺已由商代的简单刻纹和雕花的阴刻[10]，发展到立体圆雕工艺，各个部位整体和谐，刀法明快。秦汉以后的木雕工艺，在承袭春秋战国时期木雕工艺发展的基础上，又有了较大的发展和提高。

中国木雕种类繁多，遍布大江南北，以“四大名雕”为例，有浙江东阳木雕、广东金漆木雕、温州黄杨木雕和福建龙眼木雕。但大体分为工艺木雕和艺术木雕两大类。工艺木雕通常指民间木雕，具有艺术性与实用性相结合的特征，是木雕中的精华部分。其用途广泛、艺术表现形式之丰富，集中体现在其宽泛的题材内容上，体现了民间美术的共性，一般有三类内容：一类是吉祥图案，如山水人物、飞禽走兽、花卉虫鱼、喜庆吉祥等象征、寓意的图案，无所不包。大多都是表现人民群众喜闻乐见的事物，反映人们热爱生活、乐观健康、纯真善良的精神品质，以及对美好生活的向往和追求。最常见的有“吉祥”图案：用龙、凤、鹤、喜鹊等吉祥物寓意平安、富贵、长寿、人畜两旺、五谷丰登，其中龙凤之形尤为突出。二类是中国传统的民间英雄、神话传说、寓言故事、戏曲人物等寓教于乐的故事画，也都成为木雕的题材。三类是民俗民风题材作品，如纺织、放牧、娱乐等现实生活描写。

木雕菩萨坐像

木雕广泛地应用于建筑内外装饰、家具器皿用具上的装饰以及供人欣赏的木工艺品。传统木雕多用于建筑上，木雕在建筑外的装饰，主要是门、窗、廊、柱的雕饰。建筑内则主要装饰厅堂、隔扇[11]、屏风[12]等。中国南北方建筑的装饰各异，表现出地区的民族性格和审美特点。北方皇家建筑和各类官式建筑中的木雕往往刻工精细繁复，一般采用线刻[13]、浅浮雕[14]和贴雕[15]等手法，多采用如意[16]图案。垂花门[17]的垂花以圆雕手法雕刻出各种花卉图案，刻工精良，层次丰富，形象生动。北方居民建筑木雕则质朴敦厚，通常很少彩绘，大构件木雕简洁古朴，细部则精雕细刻，注重装饰性。江南民居木雕精致古雅，构思巧妙，有中国绘画的意境和趣味。装饰题材丰富多样，如民间传说、历史故事、虫草鸟兽、吉祥图案等，充满生活情趣。明清木雕主要以福建和浙江的雕刻为主，其中花板、窗花等木雕挂件是中国传统建筑中的精华，也是建筑中传统文化精神的集中表现。这些作品在简单中求丰富，统一中求变化。

木雕在家具器皿用具上的装饰，大的包括长条案、桌椅、床、衣柜、茶柜；小的包括梳妆盒、首饰盒等。家具中精美的雕刻，有的描金重彩，有的淡漆轻刷，均反映了祈盼祥和幸福的美好愿望。家居点缀以木雕挂件、屏风隔断和几件雕花案儿，就使家居蕴含着传统，明快活泼中透着沉静含蓄，简练中显露出渊博，犹如一曲“高山流水”，意境盎然。

中国的木材资源丰富，能用于雕刻的优质木材种类颇多，各种材质各异，有其不同的色泽和质地，用于雕刻也展现出不同的效果。如黄杨木雕，黄杨木质地坚韧，色黄，有如象牙，且经久不褪色，一般用于雕刻人物、飞禽走兽、花卉等比较细致的工艺品。在唐代，黄杨木还用于镶嵌“木画”，至今这种技法还在应用，并深受欢迎。

（三）石　雕[18]

人类艺术从起源就开始了石雕的历史。可以说，迄今人类包罗万象的艺术形式中，没有哪一种能比石雕更古老，也没有哪一种艺术形式比石雕更为人们喜闻乐见、万古不衰了。中国石雕艺术起源于新石器时代，商周时期的石雕艺术日趋成熟。河南安阳殷墟出土的商朝的虎纹石磬，刻在石磬上的虎造型优美，刀法纯熟洗练，线条流畅自然。秦汉至唐代是石雕艺术的高峰阶段，精致完美的菩萨立像、高大雄健的昭陵六骏、出神入化的赵州桥浮雕双龙献珠等均闻名于世。

中国石雕历史悠久，蔚为大观，从举世闻名的“四大石窟”到民间石艺，从皇家园林到庙宇庭院都有石雕艺术。古石雕的内容和形式极其广泛，其基本形式有圆雕、浮雕[19]、透雕[20]和线雕[21]，并形成“四大石雕之乡”。

浙江省温岭是我国四大石雕之乡之一，石雕工艺最早起步于宋代，至明代嘉靖年间，已盛极一时。

曾被文化部授予“中国石雕之都”的惠安石雕艺术融中原文化、闽越文化、海洋文化于一体，汲晋唐遗风、宋元神韵、明清风范之精华，形成精雕细刻、纤巧灵动的南派艺术风格，与建筑艺术交相辉映，成为中华优秀传统文化的一朵奇葩。其代表作有南京雨花台纪念馆《日月同辉》的大型石雕。

浙江省青田石雕历史源远流长，可以追溯到殷商时期，自 19 世纪以来，青田石雕多次在国际博览会上获金奖、银奖，赢得极高的声誉，1995 年被国务院命名为“中国石雕艺术之乡”。

河北省曲阳县 4 千米长的雕刻路上，两边或蹲或卧的石狮、鬃毛飘逸的石马、神态安逸的长颈鹿等各类动物石雕作品，件件栩栩如生，令人仿佛走进了“野生动物园”；石雕产品琳琅满目，又仿佛置身于“玉林石海”中。

西汉武帝大将霍（Huò）去病[22]墓的石刻造像

石　人

▶▶ 石　狮

是中国迄今为止发现的时代最早、保存最为完整的大型圆雕[23]工艺品，也是汉代石雕艺术的杰出代表。霍去病两次大败匈奴，为汉统一立下了汗马功劳。但是公元前117年，年仅24岁的霍去病不幸英年早逝。汉武帝为纪念这位杰出的军事将领，在武帝陵址旁不远处修建气势宏大的霍去病墓。墓前共有16件石刻，包括石人、石马、马踏匈奴、怪兽食羊、卧牛、人与熊等，题材多样，雕刻手法十分简练，造型雄健遒劲，其中“马踏匈奴”为墓前石刻的主像，长1.9米，高1.68米，为灰白细砂石雕凿而成，石马昂首站立，尾长拖地，腹下是一个手持弓箭匕首、长须仰面挣扎的匈奴人形象。这最具代表性的纪念碑式的作品，在中国美术史上占有重要的地位。

中国的佛教石窟的各种造像艺术在世界上享有盛誉。前面曾提到过的云冈石窟就是中国规模最大的石雕佛像群之一，被誉为世界伟大的古代雕刻艺术宝库。石窟有主题突出的佛像浮雕，有精雕细刻的装饰纹样，还有栩栩如生的乐舞雕刻，生动活泼，琳琅满目。其雕刻艺术继承并发展了秦汉雕刻艺术传统，吸收和融合了佛教艺术的精华，具有独特的艺术风格。石窟规模之宏伟、雕刻艺术之精湛、造像内容之丰富，堪称公元5世纪后半叶中国佛教雕刻艺术的“陈列馆”。

明清建筑石刻是中国古典建筑石刻集大成者。在宫廷建筑石刻中最常见的是龙、凤主题，此外还有莲耀纹[24]、朵云以及各种花卉。如北京故宫石栏杆的栏板上，就雕刻了小巧玲珑的龙纹，以牡丹花衬地，其间雕刻菊花、莲荷和茶花等花纹，代表了明清宫廷石刻的典型风格。最典型的雕刻就是故宫三大殿的御路石，其高浮雕的巨龙、流云所构成的华美磅礴的气势，堪称建筑石刻的古今之冠。

词语注释

【1】砖雕：中国民间工艺品之一。用工具在质地细密的青砖上凿打出人物、花木、鸟禽等图形，作为建筑构件的装饰。

【2】雕镂：雕刻，刻镂。

【3】影壁：也叫“照墙”。正对着大门做屏障及装饰的墙壁，有的底下有座子，可以移动。

【4】门楼：大门上边牌楼式的顶。

【5】吉星高照：吉星，指福、禄、寿三星；吉祥之星高高照临。

【6】福禄满门：福，福运、福气；禄，俸禄；满门，充满整个家族和家庭。

【7】舞乐百戏：南阳汉画像砖中的一种。

【8】走索：古代百戏节目。一条长绳系在两头梁上，悬于空中，演员在长绳上做高难动作，类似现代杂技中的“走钢丝”。

【9】蹴鞠：中国古代的一种球类运动，被认为是现代足球的起源。

【10】阴刻：将图案或文字刻成凹形。

【11】隔扇：在房屋内部起隔开作用的一扇一扇的木板墙，上部一般做成窗棂，糊纸或装玻璃。

【12】屏风：厅堂内做装饰的屏障。

【13】线刻：福建寿山石雕技艺之一。用尖刀或针刻画线条，以白描国画为“粉本”，酷似绘画之线描，图案清丽流畅。

【14】浅浮雕：浮雕中凸出部分跟周围平面差距不大，并无挖空部分。

【15】贴雕：用薄板雕出所需图案，再于底板上剔出浅槽，将图案嵌贴上去。

【16】如意：一种器物，象征吉祥，多用竹、骨、玉制成，多供玩赏。

【17】垂花门：垂花门就是沟通四合院内外院的门，俗称二门。门内两侧连接抄手游廊，把院落截然分为内外两部分。垂花门的装饰性极强，其向外一侧的梁头常雕成云头形状，称为“麻叶梁头”，梁头之下有一对倒悬的短柱，柱头雕饰出莲瓣、串珠、花萼云或石榴头等形状，称为“垂莲柱”，垂花门名称的由来大概就与这对特殊的垂柱有关。

【18】石雕：利用色泽光润、质地细腻、色彩丰富的天然石料，因材施艺，雕刻成山水、花卉、人物、动物等工艺品的一种技艺。

【19】浮雕：只有一个面向（观赏面）的雕塑形式，通常是指有一块底板为依托，占有一定空间的被压缩的实体所构成的雕刻艺术品。

【20】透雕：在浮雕作品中，保留凸出的物像部分，而将背景部分进行局部或全部镂空，称为透雕。透雕多以插屏的形式来表现。

【21】线雕：骨器上线刻是原始社会雕刻的萌芽，是现存最早的雕刻品种。

【22】霍去病：河东郡平阳县（今山西临汾）人，汉武帝时代的著名的抗击匈奴的大将（公元前140年～公元前117年）。

【23】圆雕：又称立体雕，是物体在雕件上的整体表现，观赏者可以从中看到物体的各个方面。

【24】莲耀纹：莲花形状的突出的雕饰花纹。

七、玉器文化

玉在中国人的心目中象征着纯洁、高贵、美丽和坚贞。中国人常说，黄金有价玉无价。中国人把玉本身具有的一些自然特性比附于人的道德品质，作为所谓“君子”应具有的德行而加以崇尚歌颂。“宁为玉碎，不为瓦全”。这正是玉美的“人格化”，它象征高尚的人格，君子的气节，优秀的品德，以及生活的理想。在古代诗文中，常用玉来比喻和形容一切美好的人或事物。如：以玉喻人的词有玉容、玉面、玉女、亭亭玉立等；也有不少人用玉给自己心爱的儿女取名字，如贾宝玉、林黛玉，还有百读不厌的那部感人至深的《红楼梦》，是作家曹雪芹把人生的理想寄托在一块顽石美玉里面了，对玉的爱在中国人的心目中扎下了深深的根。

汉代玉玺

中国古代，玉是权力、地位、财富、神权的象征。古代贵族祭祀、丧葬、征伐等礼仪活动中都要用玉制礼器[1]。天子的印章以玉为原料，所以称为玉玺[2]（xǐ）。因而，佩玉不仅是一种装饰、美化，而且是一种身份以及伦理、道德的象征。可见玉在人们文化和精神生活中占有一种特殊的位置。

距今五千五百年的时候，北方是“红山文化”，南方是“良渚文化”，都普遍地使用玉，玉在当时的政治生活中处在一个非常重要的位置上。在“红山文化”中，一种猪的头和蛇的身子复合而成的玉猪龙是当年最典型的玉器。在商代甲骨文的记载中，就有

▶▶ 翠玉白菜

了关于商王朝为玉石而征讨的文字，一片甲骨上记载着“取玉”的内容，而另一片甲骨上则记载了“征玉”的内容。

中国人对玉的玩赏有着特殊的爱好，喜爱玉甚于黄金和其他宝石。在古代，“君子无故，玉不去身”[3]，因此形成了中国人传统的用玉观念，这就是尊玉、爱玉、佩玉、赏玉、玩玉。玉作为装饰品，作为信物，作为法器，作为礼物被雕琢成各种形状，尤其是人们心目中的吉祥物形象，因而又形成了复杂的玉器制作的工艺过程，一般经过选料、设计、碾琢[4]、抛光等工序之后，形成各种式样的玉镯、玉器首饰以及各种玉石工艺品。如仕女、童子、佛像、植物、动物等。

今天玉器的主要产地是北京、上海、广州、扬州、岫岩等地。各地玉器的艺术风格也有差异。北京玉器风格浑厚、雅丽、端庄。上海玉器以仿青铜器为多，风格古雅。广州玉器吸收了西洋艺术长处，格调新颖，秀丽潇洒。扬州玉器则是线条流畅，玲珑剔透。不同地区的玉器工艺，世代相传，形成各有千秋的地方特色。

词语注释

【1】礼器：古时祭祀用的各种器物。

【2】玉玺：玺的俗称，自秦代以后专指皇帝的玉印。

【3】君子无故，玉不去身：古人认为君子是以玉来象征德行的，佩玉虽有等级差别，没有特殊原因，如服丧、死亡，身上应该随时佩带一块玉，象征洁身自好。

【4】碾琢：玉石材料加工制成工艺品的专门技术。

八、四大名绣

刺绣是中国传统的著名工艺品，在中国工艺美术史上占有重要的地位。中国是世界上发现与使用蚕丝最早的国家，人们在四五千年前就已开始养蚕、缫丝了。随着蚕丝的使用，丝织品的产生与发展，刺绣工艺也逐渐兴起，刺绣发展到清代已经形成不同特色的地方体系，其中著名的有苏绣、湘绣、蜀绣、粤绣，被誉为中国的“四大名绣”，各具特色，独具风韵。

苏绣是以苏州为中心，包括江苏地区刺绣品的总称。苏绣的历史悠久，根据出土的绣品来看，苏州的刺绣在五代时期已达到很高的水平，在宋代已具有相当规模，出现了绣衣坊、绣花弄、绣线巷等生产集中的坊巷。明代，苏绣已形成自己独特的风格，影响较广。清代是苏绣的全盛时期，真可谓流派繁衍，名家辈出。皇室享用的大量刺绣品几乎全出于苏绣艺人之手，在国内外久负盛名。苏绣素以精细、雅洁著称，其织品图案秀丽，色泽文静，针法灵活，绣像传神。其图案取材广泛，有花鸟、山水、人物、书法以及各种传统题材，针法多达40余种。清代以来，许多刺绣如粤

湘 绣

绣、蜀绣、湘绣，无不受其影响。

湘绣是以湖南长沙为中心的刺绣工艺品总称，其绣品丝细，是在湖南民间刺绣的基础上，吸取了苏绣和粤绣的优点而发展起来的。湘绣的特点是用丝绒线绣花，劈丝细致，绣件绒面图像具有真实感。亦称“羊毛细绣”。在配色上善于运用深浅灰及黑白色，加上适当的明暗对比，增强了质感和立体感，形成了湘绣水墨画般的素雅品质，传统题材是狮、虎、松鼠等，特别是以虎最为多见。

粤绣也称广绣，是产于广东地区的刺绣品。据传创始于少数民族，明中后期形成特色。其用线多样，除丝线、绒线外，也用孔雀毛做线，或用马尾做线。用色明快，对比强烈，色彩富丽夺目，讲求华丽效果，多用金线做刺绣花纹的轮廓线。装饰花纹，繁缛丰满，热闹欢快。常用百鸟朝凤[1]、海产鱼虾、佛手[2]瓜果一类有地方特色的题材。与其他刺绣不同，粤绣绣工多为广州、湖州的男子。

蜀 绣

蜀绣也称“川绣”，即以四川成都为中心的刺绣品总称。其产地主要集中于成都、重庆、温江，清朝中叶以后，逐渐形成行业。蜀绣以软缎和彩丝为主要原料，当时的产品品种主要是官服、礼品、日用花衣、边花、嫁妆（lián）、彩帐[3]和屏[4]等。屏是蜀绣中的代表作，有条屏[5]、座屏[6]、挂屏[7]。比如北京人民大会堂四川厅的巨幅“芙蓉鲤鱼”座屏和“蜀宫乐女演乐图”[8]挂屏、双面异色的“水草鲤鱼”座屏，刺绣技法甚为独特，至少有一百种以上精巧的针法。

发展到今天的刺绣艺术品，工艺精细复杂。例如双面绣《猫》，是苏绣的代表作品之一。艺人们将一根头发粗细的绣花线分成二分之一、四分之一，以至十二分之一、四十八分之一的细线绣，并将千万个线头、线结藏得无影无踪。无论从正面或反面都可以看到小猫调皮活泼的神态。绣猫最难的是一对猫眼睛，艺人们需用 20 多种颜色的丝线才能把猫眼绣得炯炯有神，栩栩如生。

词语注释

【1】百鸟朝凤：朝：朝见；凤：凤凰，古代传说中的鸟王。旧时喻指君主圣明天下依附，后也比喻德高望

重者众望所归。

【2】佛手：常绿小乔木，叶子长圆形，花白色。果实鲜黄色，下端有裂纹，形状像半握着的手，有芳香。可入药。

【3】彩帐：古代悬挂在床栏杆周围的彩色帐子，有遮蔽和装饰作用。

【4】屏：遮挡，遮挡物。

【5】条屏：条，长。条屏，挂在墙壁上的条幅，多为字画。

【6】座屏：放置在地上的屏风，起遮挡或装饰作用。

【7】挂屏：贴在带框的木板上或者镶在镜框里的屏条。

【8】蜀宫乐女演乐图：明代画家唐寅的著名绘画作品。

九、"泥人张"与惠山泥人

明清以后，民间彩塑赢得了老百姓的青睐[1]，其中最著名的是天津的"泥人张"和无锡[2]的惠山泥人。

（一）"泥人张"

"泥人张"是北方流传的一派民间彩塑，创始于清代末年。创始人叫张明山，生于天津，家境贫寒，从小跟父亲以捏泥人为业，养家糊口。张明山心灵手巧，富于想象，时常在集市上观察各行各业的人，在戏园观看多种角色，随身带着一团泥巴，偷偷地在袖口里捏制。他捏制出来的泥人个个逼真，酷似原型，一时传为佳话。张明山继承传统的泥塑艺术，从绘画、戏曲、民间木版年画等艺术中吸收营养，经过数十年的辛勤努力，一生中创作了一万多件作品。他的艺术独具一格，蜚声四海，老百姓很喜爱，亲切地送给他一个昵称：泥人张。

天津的"泥人张"已有一百六十多年的发展历史，它代表了中国北方民间雕塑艺术，自19世纪中叶起一直流传至今，历久不衰。"泥人张"着重刻画人物内在性格，善于捕捉人物刹那间的动态，不但接近社会下层民众的日常情感，而且综合了中国文化传统的抒情艺术。"泥人张"的作品享誉国内外，多次参加国际性展览，屡获殊荣。中国美术馆收藏"泥人张"的作品达九件之多，居民间艺术品之首，其中最精彩的作品是《钟馗嫁妹》[3]。这是一套长达5米、涉及40个人物形象的巨作，人物动作、性格、表情各不相同，或胖如蠢猪，或瘦如豺狼，或奸诈，或贪婪，或狡猾，或凶残，形形色色，面目可憎可笑，看了令人捧腹。

泥人张彩塑

（二）惠山泥人

无锡泥人是中国著名的传统民间艺术，已有四百多年历史，因起源于无锡惠山山麓，故名"惠山泥人"。据说从宋代开始，惠山就有泥人作品了。清朝以后，泥人的生产和销售达到了鼎盛时期。惠山泥人是用惠山脚下的泥土制成的。这种泥土不仅细腻，可塑性强，而且干而不裂，弯而不断。现在的惠山泥人，发展到用石膏制作，解决了惠山泥资源短缺的问题。

▶▶ 泥塑大阿福

惠山泥人大致可分为以下几类：手捏戏文、京剧脸谱、人物动物、实用玩具。题材多为戏曲人物、祈福避邪[4]的春牛、老虎、大阿福、寿星[5]等。惠山泥人造型简朴，粗犷略带夸张，夸大头部，着重刻画表情。匠人特别重视彩绘，常用的色彩有大红、绿、金黄、青等原色，对比强烈，主次分明，显露出浓郁的江南乡土气息。从"绘七塑三"的特点中，可以看出色彩的表现形式也是很重要的，用大红大绿的对比色彩，也用细致淡雅的调和色彩来衬托，所以色彩丰富，风格独特。

惠山泥人的代表作是一对男女儿童，即泥塑大阿福。刻画了两个手捧神兽、面带笑容、淳朴稚气的儿童形象。关于泥人阿福，当地还流传着这样一个传说：古时惠山有四只怪兽，即毒龙、恶虎、臭鼋[6]（yuán）和刁马，经常伤害人畜、践踏庄稼。后来有一对名为阿福的双胞胎兄妹入山与四怪搏斗，四怪被除，兄妹俩亦因流血过多，离开人间。人们捏制了他俩的生前形象，以作纪念。大阿福经过历代艺人的创作，栩栩如生，给人以健康、幸福和美好的感受。

1992年，惠山大阿福被定为中国国际旅游年的吉祥物。惠山大阿福漂洋过海，漫游世界，成了异国人民家中的珍品。一时之间，一股"阿福热"席卷全球。在"阿福热"的影响下，各种以阿福为标志或以阿福命名的风味小吃、生活用品，甚至餐饮场所也随之纷纷出现，如阿福饼干、阿福糖果、阿福香烟、阿福礼品、阿福酒家等等。惠山的主要街道——横街和直街有许多泥人店，成为远近闻名的"泥人一条街"，每天都要接待来自世界各地的许多旅游参观团和游客。

词语注释

【1】青睐：喜爱。

【2】无锡：在江苏省南部、太湖北岸、京沪铁路线上，京杭运河经此。

【3】钟馗嫁妹：钟馗是中国民间传说中能打鬼的神。钟馗生前有个同乡好友杜平，为人乐善好施，馈赠银两，助钟馗赴试。钟馗因面貌丑陋而被皇帝免去状元，一怒之下，触阶而死，跟他一同应试的杜平便将其隆重安葬。钟馗死后做了能打鬼的鬼王，为报答杜平的恩义，钟馗亲率鬼卒于除夕时返家，将妹妹嫁给了杜平。"钟馗嫁妹"是中国古代绘画和戏剧的一个重要题材，受到人们的普遍欢迎。

【4】祈福避邪：祈求好运，躲避厄运。

【5】寿星：对高寿人的尊称。

【6】鼋：动物名，亦称"绿团鱼"，俗称"癞头鼋"。

十、扎　染

扎染是白族人民的传统民间工艺产品。制作时，根据作者喜欢的花样纹式，用线将白布缚着，做成带有一定褶的小纹，再浸入染缸里浸染。如此反复，每浸一次色深一层。浸染到一定程度后，取出晾干，拆去缚结，便出现蓝底白花的图案花纹来。扎染以蓝白二色为基调所构成的宁静平和，不仅营造出古朴的意蕴，而且往往给人以“青花瓷”般的淡雅之感。白族的先民们选择了靛蓝色，这绝不是一种偶然。白族主要聚居和定居区是苍山洱海区域。蓝色的天，蓝色的海，蓝色的山，宁静而和平，造就了世世代代在苍山洱海生活的白族人民宁静和平的心理素质，也造就了白族人民对蓝色的特别喜爱。可以这样说，蓝色是白族传统审美意象的基调。

扎染主要用植物染料反复染制而成，产品不仅色彩鲜艳、永不褪色，而且对皮肤有消炎保健作用，克服了现代化学染料有害人体健康的副作用。被染的布一般就是生白布，先由民间美术设计人员根据传统和市场的需要，加上自己的创作，画出各式各样的图案，由印工用刺了洞的蜡纸在布上印出设计好的图案，再由村里的妇女把布拿走，用细致的手工把图案缝上，再送到扎染厂或各家染坊。周城是大理最大的白族聚居自然村，现有人口万人左右。几乎每个家庭都有从事手工织布和扎染工艺的妇女，“家家有染缸，户户出扎染”就是这里生产扎染的写照。大理周城被誉为“扎染之乡”是当之无愧的。

扎染工艺，兴于汉唐，盛于魏晋，已作为民族文化保留至今。随着市场需求的扩大，大理扎染的图案也越来越复杂和多样化，有数百种之多，各种尺寸大小都有，并且衍生出扎染包、扎染帽、扎染衣裙等琳琅满目的工艺品。白族扎染取材广泛，常以当地的山川风物作为创作素材，其图案或苍山彩云、或神话传说、或民族风情、或花鸟鱼虫，妙趣横生，千姿百态，图案新颖多变，具有古朴、典雅、自然、大方的特点。目前除保留传统的土靛（diàn）染蓝底白花品种外，又开发出彩色扎染的新品种。产品有色布、桌巾、门帘、服装、民族包、帽子、手巾、围巾、枕巾、床单等上百个品种。产品既有较高的艺术欣赏价值，又有较强的实用性。西南边陲的少数民族仍保留这一古老的技艺。除中国外，印度、日本、柬埔寨、泰国、印度尼西亚、马来西亚等国也有扎染手工艺。

扎　染

白族扎染是白族民族性的一个载体，它寄托着白族的民族理想和情趣，它是了解白族民族性的一道靓丽的风景。

第九章 古代文学

一、《诗经》和“楚辞”

中国是诗的王国，几千年来，产生了无数的诗人，也留下了难以数计的诗词歌赋，给世界文库增添了无价的瑰宝。其悠悠历史，万众瞩目；其辉煌成就，举世公认。

先秦诗歌的代表作是《诗经》和“楚辞”。

《诗经》是我国第一部诗歌总集，收入了从西周到春秋中叶的诗歌，一部分是司乐太师[1]所保存的祭歌[2]和乐歌，另一部分——较多也较重要的部分——是经过采集和整理的民歌。这些诗分为“风”“雅”“颂”三部分，共计305篇。

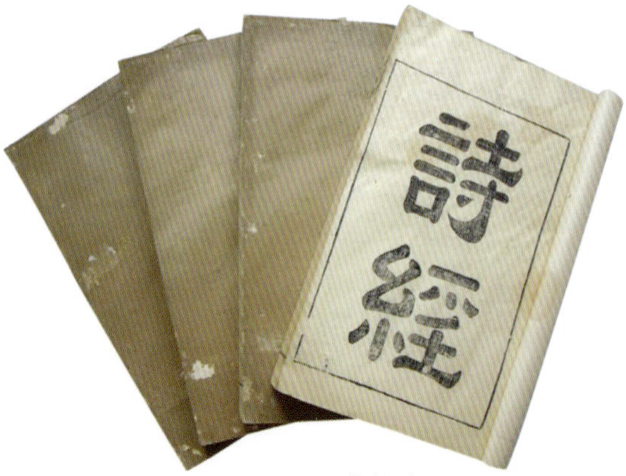

《诗经》

“风”是民歌。所谓“十五国风”，包括十五个地方的民歌。大都在黄河流域，共160篇。这些诗在《诗经》中占主要地位，比“雅”“颂”更富于现实性。其内容贴近当时的社会现实，富有浓郁的生活气息，是《诗经》的精华所在。如《七月》叙述了农奴一年四季的生产劳动，以及当时的物候、农作物、打猎、冷藏、酿造等生活侧面。《伐檀》《硕鼠》《相鼠》等，是对统治集团尸位素餐、贪得无厌的辛辣讽刺，表达了社会底层人们的不满和怨恨。《破斧》《击鼓》《东山》等是关于战争与劳役的诗篇，其中最集中的是关于恋爱和婚姻的诗歌，如《邶风 · 静女》《秦风 · 蒹葭》《卫风 · 氓》等。

“雅”分为“大雅”和“小雅”。“大雅”用于隆重盛大的宴会的典礼，“小雅”用于一般宴会的典礼，都是西周的乐歌。其中有叙事诗，有抒情诗，有对前代英雄人物的歌颂，有对当时政治的讽刺，共105篇，大部分是现实性的作品。

“颂”是“以成功告于神明”的祭歌，共40篇。这些诗，有祭祖先的，有祭天地山川的，也有祭农神的。

《诗经》对后世影响最大的是赋、比、兴的表现手法和艺术构思，在汉代以后构成了中国诗学发展的一条主线，产生了广泛而深远的影响。

《诗经》在汉代以前只叫“诗”或“诗三百”，“经”字是汉儒加上去的。如孔子说过的：“诗三百，一言以蔽之曰，思无邪。[3]”《左传》中也常引《诗经》中的诗，常有“诗云”字样。《诗经》和《尚书》《礼记》《易》《春秋》一起合成儒家的“五经”，是儒学

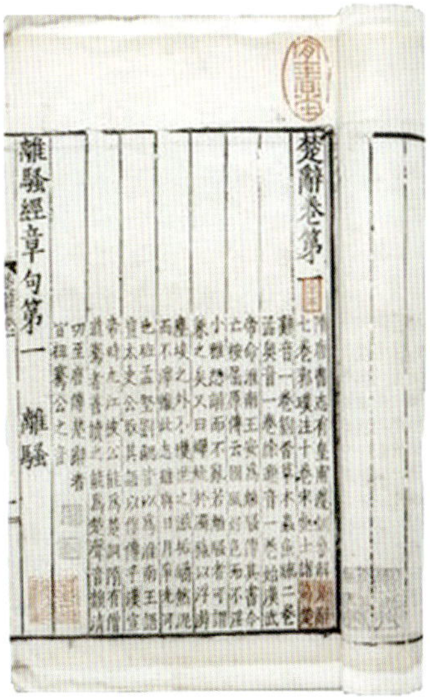

▶▶《楚辞》

必读的经典。

如果说《诗经》是黄河文化的代表作品，那么楚辞就是长江文化具代表性的作品。

战国后期，楚国出现了我国文学史上第一个伟大的诗人——屈原，他创造了一种新的诗体，就是后世所说的“楚辞”。楚辞是屈原在楚地民歌的基础上创造出来的，突破了《诗经》以四字句为主的句式，从形式上是一次解放，更适合于表达奔放、跳跃、激荡的情感世界。在句中或句尾多用兮字，成为楚辞显著的特征。当时写楚辞的人除屈原之外，还有宋玉、唐勒、景差等。他们的作品大都佚（yì）失[4]了，只有宋玉还留下了《九辩》《登徒子好色赋》《风赋》《高唐赋》《神女赋》《招魂》等篇。

屈原约生活于公元前340年至公元前278年之间，字平。他博闻强记，明于治乱，娴于辞令，因此深得楚王的信任。屈原二十多岁的时候，便担任左徒这样的要职。他怀有远大的政治理想，竭力主张举贤授能，修明法度，联齐抗秦，统一六国。屈原的一系列政治外交主张触犯了贵族保守势力，因而遭到诬陷，被谗见疏[5]，不被楚怀王信任，终遭流放。后虽被召回，但不久又被放逐[6]，直到公元前278年楚国都城郢被秦兵攻陷，屈原满怀悲愤，五月初五投汨（mì）罗江而死。屈原的代表作品有《离骚》《九章》《天问》《九歌》。

词语注释

【1】司乐太师：指官职，又名太宰。古代称太师、太傅、太保为“三公”。掌管礼乐的太宰，即为司乐太师。

【2】祭歌：平时禁止吟唱祭歌，只有在祭典仪式中才能唱。祭歌内容一般和打仗有关，歌颂战神，叙述战事及先人作为。

【3】诗三百，一言以蔽之曰，思无邪：孔子认为，《诗经》中的三百首诗，用一句话来概括，就是思想没有不纯正的。

【4】佚失：散失。

【5】被谗见疏：因被谗言离间，而感情与关系变得不亲近、冷淡。

【6】放逐：古时候把被判罪的人流放到边远地方。

二、唐　诗

唐诗是中国文化史的骄傲，是我国优秀的文学遗产之一，也是世界文学宝库中一颗璀璨的明珠。尽管距今已有一千多年了，但许多诗篇仍是广为流传，妇孺皆知。

唐代著名的诗人特别多。李白、杜甫、白居易固然是世界闻名的伟大诗人，除此而外，还有许多著名诗人，如陈子昂和“初唐四杰”；张扬盛唐气象的山水田园诗派诗人孟浩然、王维；边塞诗派的高适、岑参、王昌龄；中唐掀起新乐府运动的白居易、元稹，以及韩愈、柳宗元、刘禹锡、李贺，还有晚唐挥洒大唐余韵的杜牧、温庭筠、韦庄等。他们的作品，在清人编辑的《全唐诗》[1]中存有四万八千九百多首。据统计，全部唐诗，涉及作者两千八百多人，诗作四万九千多首。

唐代诗歌的发展，一般分为初、盛、中、晚四个阶段。

初唐，最先摈弃齐梁以来浮靡之风，以清新朴素的五言诗而成为唐代山水田园诗派先驱的是王绩，诗作如《野望》。继之初唐四杰，即王勃、杨炯、卢照邻和骆宾王，文学史上称他们为“王杨卢骆”。他们

李 白

是一批少年才子，才华横溢，精神昂扬，一出场就英气勃勃，而又是苦命诗人，时运不济，生活艰难。但都立志扫荡诗坛积秽，让诗歌具有激情和生气。他们突破了宫体诗[2]狭小范围，扩大了诗歌的题材，推出一批传诵千古之作，如王勃的《送杜少府之任蜀州》、杨炯的《从军行》、卢照邻的《长安古意》、骆宾王的《在狱咏蝉》等。四杰之后，陈子昂高举诗歌改革的大旗，提倡“汉魏”风骨，“风雅兴寄”，在诗歌理论上颇有建树。上追建安，下开盛唐，其作品《登幽州台歌》及《感遇》篇章，足以一新诗坛耳目。初唐确立了律体，发展了七言歌行。五言律诗的奠基人是王杨卢骆；七言歌行发展到刘希夷的《代白头吟》和张若虚《春江花月夜》，已趋于成熟。这是中国诗史上的一件大事。

盛唐，是唐诗最辉煌的时代，也是中国传统诗歌的巅峰时代。在五十多年的时间里，涌现出十几位大诗人。有继屈原之后最伟大的诗人李白和杜甫，有以山水隐逸为主要题材的孟浩然，有在山水诗开一代新风的王维，有七言绝句的名家王昌龄，有写边塞诗著称的岑参和高适，以及张九龄、张说、王翰、王湾、王之涣、崔颢、贺知章等著名诗人。孟浩然擅长五言诗，律绝俱佳，其《过故人庄》《宿建德江》《春晓》等诗，对自然景色和田园生活的描写极富情趣，妇孺皆知。王维则是状写山水田园大自然风光的大手笔，既有壮丽的描绘，如《使至塞上》《汉江临眺》《终南山》等，又有幽静禅意的刻画，如《山居秋暝》《渭川田家》《鸟鸣涧》等，显示了诗人精通音乐、书法、绘画而融入诗歌的艺术天才。高适的边塞诗具有深刻的内涵和真挚的情感，名篇有《燕歌行》《别董大》。岑参的边塞诗则更善于描写边塞风光，西域情调，名篇有《走马川行奉送出师西征》《轮台歌奉送封大夫出师西征》《白雪歌送武判官归京》。他是盛唐边塞诗成绩最突出的一位诗人，也是边塞诗数量最多的一位诗人，存诗 70 多首。

李白和杜甫是盛唐诗坛最杰出的诗人，是时代的歌手，诗国的巨人。他们的诗体现了大唐的气象，达到了唐代诗歌的巅峰，也达到了中国古典诗歌的最高峰。李白充满积极浪漫主义色彩的诗篇，是继屈原之后将中国古代积极浪漫主义推向新高峰的又一位伟大的诗人。丰富的想象，神奇的夸张，雄奇奔放的风格，多彩多姿的意境，创作出传诵千古的不朽之作。字里行间体现出一个中心主题是理想与现实的矛盾。他追求个人自由，反对权贵，要求人才解放，一种傲然不屈的反抗精神跃然纸上。如《蜀道难》《将进酒》《梦游天姥吟留别》《黄鹤楼送孟浩然之广陵》《望庐山瀑布》等。李白的诗具有极强的艺术感染力，正如杜甫称赞的“笔落惊风雨，诗成泣鬼神”。杜甫则是最伟大的现实主义诗人，真实地记录了安史之乱前后那个动荡的岁月，写出了忧国忧民的名篇，反映了人民的生活和疾苦，自古就有“诗史”之美称。如《自京赴奉先县咏怀五百字》《羌村三首》《秋兴八首》，以及“三吏”“三别”[3]，以沉郁顿挫的手法，将时代的绝唱、历史的画卷留给了后人。杜甫继承《诗经》和汉乐府的传统，同时也批判地吸收了六朝以来诗歌在音韵格律、遣词造句等方面的艺术技巧，可以说他是写七律的第一大家，其七律诗数量超过盛唐诗人写七律的总和，而且思想内容上一改歌功颂德或应酬之作，而抒发忧国忧民的情感，创造出沉雄、悲壮、激昂的风格，将现实主义诗歌推向了高峰，后人称其诗为“诗史”。

“安史之乱”像一条大河将盛唐和中唐分割开来，盛唐气象已不复存在，但作为盛唐诗歌的延续和发展，中唐诗歌呈现出流派众多的显著特色。以白居易为代表的“新乐府运动”，造就了中唐最大的一个诗歌流派。白居易在唐诗发展中最主要的贡献，一是倡导了新乐府运动，写下了叙述现实，抨击弊政的新乐府诗歌。二是掀开了长篇叙事诗新的一页，《长恨歌》《琵琶行》便是崭新的佳作。中唐另一个诗派韩孟诗派，他们共同的特点是深险怪僻，不失沉雄。韩愈以散文入诗，以议论入诗，时露诙谐，颇富机趣，开宋诗之先河。如《山石》《左迁至蓝关示侄孙湘》《听颖师弹琴》等。孟郊以苦吟著称，长于五律。

中唐还有一些杰出的诗人，虽不属于某一派别，却以各具特色的创作占据诗坛一席之地。刘长卿和韦应物都是中唐前期的诗人，以山水田园诗著称。唐代宗大历年间经济一度繁荣，政治呈现出一些升平的现象，于是一批诗人模仿盛唐之音。后人称为“大历十才子”，如李端、卢纶、钱起等。刘禹锡善于学习民歌，语言干净明快，写下一些伤今怀古的名篇，有《竹枝词》《西塞山怀古》《酬乐天扬州初逢席上见赠》，与他同为遭贬的“八司马”[4]之一的柳宗元，诗作多抒发个人愤郁，亦涉及民生疾苦，诗风幽峭明静，简古淡泊。代表诗有《登柳州城楼寄漳汀封连四州》《田家》《江雪》等。李贺是中唐浪漫主义代表诗人，以秾丽的语言、凄清的风格、奇特的想象，抒发感愤。其代表作有《雁门太守行》《梦天》《金铜仙人辞汉歌》等。

晚唐是唐诗的余光返照时期。最初尚有李商隐、杜牧两大诗人，为唐诗增光添彩。李商隐以七律见长，尤其是一组《无题》诗，独具朦胧意象，给人艺术享受。还有《夜雨寄北》《嫦娥》等是爱情题材的诗篇，对后世影响很大。杜牧七绝成就最高，如《过华清宫三绝句》《赤壁》《泊秦淮》《山行》，写景抒情，伤今悼古，小中见大。

白居易

唐诗的形式是多种多样的。唐代的古体诗[5]，基本上有五言和七言两种。近体诗也有两种，一种叫做绝句[6]，一种叫做律诗[7]。绝句和律诗又各有五言和七言之不同。唐诗的基本形式就是以上六种。古体诗对音韵格律的要求比较宽：一首之中，句数可多可少，篇章可长可短，韵脚[8]可以转换。因是前代流传下来的，所以又叫古风。近体诗有严整的格律，所以又称它为格律诗[9]。

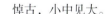

近体诗是当时的新体诗，它的创造和成熟，是唐代诗歌发展史上的一件大事。它把我国古典诗歌的音节和谐、文字精练的艺术特色，推到前所未有的高度，为古代抒情诗找到一个最典型的形式，至今还特别为人民所喜闻乐见。

词语注释

【1】《全唐诗》：清曹寅、彭定求等奉敕编纂。《全唐诗》是清朝初年编修的汇集唐一代诗歌的总集，全书共900卷，充分利用了胡震亨编《唐音统签》和季振宜编《唐诗》的成果。近年日本学者平冈武夫编《唐代的诗人》《唐代的诗篇》，将《全唐诗》所收作家、作品逐一编号作了统计，结论是：该书共收诗49 403首，句1 555条，作者共2 873人。这个数字是相当可靠的。

【2】宫体诗：以描写宫廷生活为内容的诗体，诗篇多写宫廷生活和男女私情，形式上追求辞藻靡丽，华而不实，因形成于宫廷而得名。

【3】三吏三别：组诗名。唐代诗人杜甫作。包括六篇：《新安吏》《潼关吏》《石壕吏》和《新婚别》《垂老别》《无家别》。诗中有对人民苦难的同情和对出征者的劝慰，表现了他爱国爱民的深厚感情。

【4】八司马：公元805年，李诵（顺宗）即位，重用王叔文、柳宗元、刘禹锡等人进行政治改革，但是革新运动很快便失败了。太子李纯（宪宗）即位后，将王叔文处死，又把刘禹锡、柳宗元等八人贬为远州司马。即“八司马事件”。

【5】古体诗：与近体诗相对而言的诗体。近体诗形成前，除楚辞外的各种诗歌体裁。也称古诗、古风。古体诗格律自由，不拘对仗、平仄，押韵较宽，篇幅长短不限，句子有四言、五言、六言、七言体和杂言体。

【6】绝句：又称截句、断句、绝诗。每首四句，通常有五言、七言两种，简称五绝、七绝，也偶有六绝。

绝句分为律绝和古绝，律绝是律诗兴起以后才有的，古绝远在律诗出现以前就有了。

【7】律诗：中国近体诗的一种。格律严密。发源于南朝齐永明时沈约等讲究声律、对偶的新体诗，至初唐沈佺期、宋之问时正式定型，成熟于盛唐时期。律诗要求诗句字数整齐划一，每首分别为五言、六言、七言句，简称五律、六律、七律，其中六律较少见。通常的律诗规定每首八句。

【8】韵脚：韵脚是每一句诗中押韵的字的韵母，也就是汉语拼音中的韵母。

【9】格律诗：包括律诗和绝句，被称为近体诗或今体诗，古人这么叫，我们现在也跟着这么叫，虽然它其实是很古的，在南北朝的齐梁时期就已发端，到唐初成熟。唐以前的诗，除了所谓“齐梁体”，就被称为古体。唐以后不合近体的诗，也称为古体。

三、宋　词

宋词是中国古代文学皇冠上光辉夺目的一颗巨钻，在古代文学的阆苑[1]（làng yuàn）里，她是一块芬芳绚丽的园圃。她以姹紫嫣红、千姿百态的风韵，与唐诗争奇，与元曲斗妍，历来与唐诗并称双绝，都代表一代文学之胜。

李清照

词是继唐诗之后的又一种特有的文体。词兴起于民间，称作“曲子词”。由于与音律结合，故而作词又叫“填词”，即按曲谱填写词句。每一种曲调的词都有不同的句式和字数，而这些曲调又各有固定的名称，叫“曲牌”或“词调”。20世纪初，在甘肃敦煌莫高窟发现了不少曲谱歌词，主要产生于唐代上下三百年的民间演唱，其中现存比较完整而有系统的写本曲子《云谣集》是中国古代最早的词集。民间词经过唐、五代文人的加工改造，发展到宋代达到了高峰，又被称为“长短句”。按其风格基本分为婉约派、豪放派两大类。婉约派的代表人物有柳永[2]、秦观、周邦彦、姜夔、李清照等；豪放派的代表人物有苏轼、辛弃疾、岳飞、陈亮等。

初期的词大都描写男欢女爱和相思之苦，流行于市井酒肆[3]之间，是一种通俗的艺术形式，五代时期的《花间集》[4]就很明显地展露词的“香”而“软”的特点，晚唐、五代是文人词取得长足进步的时期，温庭筠是致力于词的第一人，他精于音律，对词的规范化起过一定的作用。五代时文人词的创作中心有两个，一个在西蜀，形成了花间词派；一个在南唐，以南唐二主李璟、李煜和冯延巳为代表。南唐后主李煜在艺术上造诣颇高，纯以白描取胜，尤其是亡国之作，境界大开，抒国破家亡之感、发怨愤哀愁之音，极富

苏　轼

感染力，将词的创作推向了一个新的天地，留下了许多千古名句："问君能有几多愁，恰似一江春水向东流。"（《虞美人》）"流水落花春去也，天上人间。"（《浪淘沙》）"剪不断，理还乱，是离愁。别是一番滋味在心头。"（《相见欢》）等。

宋词分为北宋、南宋两个阶段。北宋前期，以晏殊、欧阳修为代表，一开始也是沿袭柔媚的词风，追求华丽辞藻和对细腻情感的描写。基本上承晚唐五代之余绪。然而真正给宋词带来根本性变化则是柳永。柳永郁郁不得志，一生流连于歌坊青楼之间，正是这种生活，使柳永以文人身份作词，又善于广泛吸取民间心声的优长，大量创制慢词，又以白描见长，善于铺叙，不避俚俗，曲直疏密，流转自如，开拓了词的表现空间。其代表作有《雨霖铃》《望海潮》《八声甘州》等。

随着词在宋代文学中占据越来越重要的地位，词的内涵也在不断地充实和提高。"人不寐，将军白发征夫泪。"范仲淹首开边塞词在宋词中的空间，使只闻歌筵酒席、宫廷豪门、都市风情、脂粉相思之类的世人一新耳目。到苏轼时期，宋词已经不仅限于文人士大夫寄情娱乐和表达儿女之情的玩物，更寄托了当时的士大夫对时代、对人生乃至对社会政治等各方面的感悟和思考。它彻底跳出了歌舞艳情的窠臼[5]（kē jiù），升华为一种代表了时代精神的文化形式。

苏轼以其极高的艺术才华，在传统的婉约柔丽词风之外，创立了豪放清旷的风格，大大开拓了词作的题材领域，丰富了词作的表现手法，成为北宋词坛的一代领袖。其代表作有《江城子（十年生死两茫茫）》《江城子（老夫聊发少年狂）》《水调歌头（明月几时有）》《念奴娇 · 赤壁怀古》等。同时的词林名家，还有"苏门四学士"中的黄庭坚、秦观，以及贺铸、周邦彦等，他们以各自不同的风格丰富了北宋的词坛。

南宋首屈一指的当为女词人李清照（号易安居士），她于柳永、苏轼、周邦彦等词坛大家之外独树一帜，创为"易安体"。其词作本色，如出天然，清新雅洁，善于白描，充满情感。其代表作有《如梦令（昨夜雨疏风骤）》《永遇乐（落日熔金）》《声声慢（寻寻觅觅）》等。两宋之交词坛最耀人耳目的，是以岳飞、辛弃疾为代表的爱国精神和豪放风格。岳飞的《满江红（怒发冲冠）》气壮河山，体现了以爱国主义为中心的豪放词风。尤其是辛弃疾，他上承苏轼豪放一派，下开沉雄悲壮之词风，以英雄之气，忠愤之心，旷世之才写词，把豪放词风推向了最高峰。辛词或是记叙战斗生活、或是登临怀古、或是送别寄远，都流动着一股浩然之气和浪漫激情。代表作有《水龙吟 · 登建康赏心亭》《摸鱼儿（更能消）》《永遇乐 · 京口北固亭怀古》等。与辛弃疾同时代的诗人陆游《诉衷情（当年万里觅封侯）》、张孝祥《六州歌头（长淮望断）》，以及陈亮、刘过、刘克庄、文天祥等也写下了大量的爱国辞章，抒发豪情壮志。

词语注释

【1】阆苑：阆风山之苑，传说中神仙居住的地方，旧时诗文中常用来指宫苑。

【2】柳永：崇安（今福建武夷山市）人。北宋词人，婉约派代表作家。原名三变，后改名永，字耆卿。排行第七，又称柳七。宋仁宗朝进士，官至屯田员外郎，世称柳屯田。由于仕途坎坷、生活潦倒，他由追求功名转而厌倦官场，耽溺于旖旎繁华的都市生活。作为北宋第一个专力作词的词人，他不仅开拓了词的题材内容，而且制作了大量的慢词，发展了铺叙手法，促进了词的通俗化、口语化，在词史上产生了较大的影响。其词多描绘城市风光和歌妓生活，尤长于抒写羁旅行役之情。词作流传极广，"凡有井水处，即能歌柳词"，著有《乐章集》。

【3】市井酒肆：买卖街市和酒店。

【4】《花间集》：晚唐五代词选集。十卷，选录唐末五代词 500 首。编者赵崇祚，字弘基。生平事迹不详。

在1900年敦煌石室藏《云谣集》发现之前，《花间集》被认为是最早的词选集。

【5】窠臼：老路子，俗套子。

四、明清小说

明清是中国古代小说史上的繁荣时期。从明代伊始，小说这种文学形式充分显示出其社会作用和文学价值，打破了正统诗文的垄断，在文学史上，取得与唐诗、宋词、元曲并列的地位。

《三国英雄志传》

小说是伴随城市商业经济的繁荣而发展起来的。宋代手工业和商业的发展带来了都市的繁荣，为民间说唱艺术的发展提供了场所和观众，不断扩大的市民阶层对文化娱乐的需求又大大地刺激了这种发展，从而产生出新的文学样式——话本。话本是说话人所用的底本，有讲史[1]、小说、公案[2]、灵怪等不同形式，已初具小说规模，在以后的流传过程中又不断加入新的创作，逐渐成熟。明代经济的发展和印刷业的发达，为小说脱离民间口头创作进入文人书面创作提供了物质条件。明代中叶，白话小说作为成熟的文学样式正式登上文坛。

明代文人创作的小说主要有白话短篇小说和长篇章回小说两大类。明代的长篇章回小说按题材和思想内容，又可分为四类，即讲史小说、神魔小说、世情小说和公案小说，代表性作品有《三国演义》《水浒传》《西游记》《金瓶梅》等。

历史演义小说是长篇章回小说中最早出现的一类，其代表作是罗贯中的《三国演义》。《三国演义》反映了东汉末至三国归晋近百年的历史，重点描写了魏、蜀、吴三国之间政治、军事、外交等方面的联合和斗争，表达了对仁政的向往和对暴政的批判，再现了这一特定的历史时期曹操、刘备、孙权、诸葛亮等一大批叱咤风云的英雄人物。战争叙事是《三国演义》最突出的特征，其次是文不甚深，言不甚俗，语言浅显。《三国演义》影响是巨大的，其后演义历史小说创作蔚然成风。《水浒传》是英雄传奇之作，塑造了一批性格化的人物形象，而且语言以白话为主，通俗明畅，极富表现力。在《水浒传》的影响下，英雄传奇小说的创作经久不衰，产生了许多读者喜闻乐见的小说，如《岳飞传》《杨家将演义》《说唐》等等。《西游记》通过大闹天宫和西天取经的故事，向读者展示了一个神奇瑰丽的神魔世界，投影式地反映了现实生活，其中又蕴涵着深刻而又令人玩味的人生哲理。《西游记》诙谐、幽默、生动的语言风格，令人爱不释手。"第一奇书"《金瓶梅》一问世，就被人骂作是一部"坏人心术""决当焚之"的"诲淫"之作；可也有人称赞它是"云霞满纸"的"逸典"。千百年来，毁之者把它视为"古今第一淫书"，悬为厉禁；崇之者则认为它"实在是一部可诧异的伟大的写实小说"，甚至是"中国小说发展史的极峰"。

明代的白话短篇小说也获丰收。冯梦龙辑纂的

《西游记·功满西天回》

▶▶ 红楼十二钗局部

《喻世明言》(一名《古今小说》)《警世通言》《醒世恒言》合称“三言”，收入宋、元、明话本及拟话本[3] 120篇。题材多取自稗史[4]或传说，有宋元旧作，也有明人拟作，经冯梦龙润色加工，反映社会问题非常广泛，折射出当时市民阶层的思想、生活和情趣，对后世的白话小说及戏曲都有很大影响。常与“三言”并称的是凌濛初编的拟话本集《初刻拍案惊奇》《二刻拍案惊奇》，合称“二拍”。“二拍”继承了“三言”多写市井、风情、公案、侠义等内容的特点，在表现商人的行业生活方面比“三言”更为细致。“三言二拍”之后，拟话本创作蔚然成风。

清初至乾隆时期是清小说发展的全盛时期，数量和质量、内容和形式、风格和流派与前代相比都有较大发展。清代小说基本是文人的创作，虽有历史、传说等素材的借鉴，但作品多取材于现实生活，较充分地体现了作者个人的意愿，在结构、叙述和描写人物各方面也多臻于成熟的境界。乾隆年间产生的《聊斋志异》和《儒林外史》《歧路灯》《红楼梦》，分别把文言小说和白话小说的创作推向顶峰。

《红楼梦》是中国古典小说发展到顶峰而出现的瑰宝，无论是在中国文学史还是世界文学史上都是不可多得的伟大著作。《红楼梦》的故事以贾府为中心描写了封建贵族家族的衰败史，展示了近代思想意识萌动下，一代具有叛逆性格的青年男女的爱情婚姻悲剧，以及女性群体在封建文化的桎梏下的挣扎和不幸。《红楼梦》在揭示中国封建社会的政治、经济和文化的深度和广度上，都达到了无与伦比的高度，在塑造群体个性化的人物性格方面达到呼之欲出的程度，语言的运用炉火纯青，成为“五四”新文化运动倡导的白话文的典范。

明清小说以前所未有的广度和深度反映了当时社会生活的各个方面，成为人民群众认识社会和文娱生活的主要文学样式。不仅对中国后世的文学、戏剧、电影有巨大影响，也对日本、朝鲜、越南等国的文学创作产生过巨大影响，其中的优秀作品被翻译成十几种文字，为世界文化交流作出了重要贡献。

词语注释

【1】讲史：宋元间“说话”的一科，讲说历代兴废和战争故事，据史传加以敷衍，亦称“平话”。记录时多用浅近文言，成为讲话本，是我国小说史上最早具有长篇规模的作品，后发展为演义小说。

【2】公案：本义为官府中判决是非的案例。此种言行录一如政府的正式布告，尊严不可侵犯，又可启发思想，供人研究，并且作为后代依凭的法式，故称公案。此一风气倡始于唐代，至宋代大为兴盛。

【3】拟话本：文人模仿话本形式编写的小说，鲁迅在《中国小说史略》中最早应用这一名称，指的是宋元时代产生的《大唐三藏法师取经记》和《大宋宣和遗事》等作品。它们的体裁与话本相似，都是首尾有诗，中间以诗词为点缀，词句多俚俗，但与话本又有所不同。鲁迅认为它们是由话本向后代文人小说过渡的一种中间形态。

【4】稗史：通常指记载闾巷风俗、民间琐事及旧闻之类的史籍，如清代人潘永因的《宋稗类钞》，近代人徐珂的《清稗类钞》，有时也用来泛指“野史”。

第十章　国画、书法、篆刻

一、中国画

中国画简称“国画”，一般是指用毛笔在宣纸[1]上或是丝绢上用墨色和中国画颜料所画的水墨画、淡彩画、重彩画或白描[2]。它在世界美术领域内自成其独特体系，是中华民族辩证形象性思维的结晶体，与武术、中医学构成了以中国哲学为基础的中华文化三大支柱。

中国画具有鲜明的民族形式和风格特点。在描绘物像上，中国画主要是运用线条和墨色来表现，具有高度的概括力和表现力。

经过数千年的发展，中国画把客体归为三类：山水、人物、花鸟，而且以山水居首。这一点很重要，因为相对于中国画的分类，西方绘画分为肖像、风景、静物，以肖像居首。中国画三大类都十分重视以形写神，以神写意。画家在表现时，各种客体材料都可以任其所需，各得其所。要表现磅礴气势时，可选择惊涛骇浪、高原巨木做客体；需要表现超然物外的心境时，可选择疏林修竹、小桥流水做客体；要表现高风亮节时，可以松竹梅菊为客体；要表现富贵喜气时，可以牡丹凤凰为客体，总之，中国画艺术追求的最高境界是：意境。所谓“意境”，就是画家淡淡的几笔，去追求一种情趣、一种格调、一种哲思。西方绘画讲环境对物体影响的“环境色”（光影、明暗、反光等）；而中国画则讲求对物体“固有色”的描绘及物体本质的表现，即所谓的“随类赋彩”[3]。西方绘画是用色彩的层次显示空间，用微妙的颜色表现物体受光和空气所形成的变化；而中国画“计白当黑”[4]，是利用空白让人产生想象和联想，来补充其空间，画面的前后层次是用笔墨的浓淡来显示的。西方绘画讲焦点透视；而中国画讲所谓“散点透视”，把不同的时间、空间表现在同一画面上。中国画发挥人的认知能力，就在于以白为无形，墨为有形。白为无色，墨为有色。而且用墨的浓淡层次去表现大自然的五光十色。例如《黄山图》，欣赏者可以从白、黑、浓、淡的水墨之中，获得无尽的想象，可以看出夏日的苍翠之色，冬日的肃杀景象，霞光中的五彩缤纷，雨雾中的空濛迷茫……

画者必须具备一定的传统文化修养和民族审美观，并且在绘画过程中要运用书法与篆刻功底入画，以达到“气韵生动”“形神兼备”的效果。作为单纯的视觉艺术，西方绘画（主要指油画）是纯绘画；而中国画（文人画）则是求诗、书、画、印一体，才成为完整的一幅画。西方绘画的点、线、面，都是为了塑造形体本身；而中国画讲求“骨法用笔”[5]“书画同源”，作画者必须有书法功底和修养，画出的线条讲力度和节奏，其本身就有审美意义。

中国画的发展史，如长河水涌，波澜壮阔，百年生变，一代数度，记述着中国画的美术家的灵性、体悟、思维、意境……进入20世纪以来，西方绘画

清 王翚《杜陵诗意》

出现所谓现代派，把视觉伸向东方，打破了 19 世纪前的纯粹绘画观念；中国画也大量运用西方绘画的科学性技法，产生着观念上的更新，创造着新的艺术类型。

词语注释

【1】宣纸：出产于安徽宣城、泾县的一种绵软坚韧的纸张，不容易破裂，吸墨均匀，一向为书画家所珍爱。

【2】白描：中国画中指纯用墨线勾勒，不加颜色渲染的画法。

【3】随类赋彩：是指色彩的应用，指根据不同的描绘对象、时间、地点，施用不同的色彩。

【4】计白当黑：一般在美术图案中限色的标准是计黑不计白，因为画图案的纸大多是白色，白色位置可以作留白处理，所以我们在白纸上画图案的时候即使用白颜料来画出白色，在设色中仍是忽略不计的。但在黑色纸上画图案的时候（也就是假设图案所处的位置是黑色时）就会反过来，计白不计黑，简称“计白当黑”。中国绘画的“计白当黑”，诗歌的“言有尽而意无穷”，音乐的“余音绕梁”，都是强调一种形式上化繁为简、以少胜多、以有限含无限的节制的美。

【5】骨法用笔：骨法原来是指人物的外形特点，后来泛指一切描绘对象的轮廓。用笔，就是中国画特有的笔墨技法。骨法用笔总地来说，就是指怎样用笔墨技法恰当地把对象的形状和质感画出来。

二、人物画

（一）画迹[1]留存第一人——顾恺之

顾恺之（约公元 345 年 ~ 406 年）字长康，小名虎头，世人多称他为顾虎头。晋陵无锡人（今属江苏），东晋时期杰出的文学家、画家，是中国绘画史上最早有画迹流传至今的著名画家。他生于官宦人家，天资聪慧，博览群书，有才气，工诗书，擅丹青。为人风趣、率直，因此当时人们称他为“才绝、画绝、痴绝”。其中“画绝”是顾恺之最令人称道的一绝。

顾恺之年轻时师从著名大画家卫协，名师的指点，加上他本人的天赋和努力，使他的画技很快超群出众。顾恺之在绘画创作上是个多面手，兼长画山水、花卉、人物。尤其是他的人物绘画，非常重视传神，能够深刻而细腻地表现人物的内心世界，在当时享有极高的声誉。他在绘画理论上最早提出“以形写神”[2]，强调眼睛的描绘对于传神的重要。画法上，他博采众长，在继承汉代传统与技法的基础上，首创了一种游丝般的线条，后人形容其笔如“春蚕吐丝”“行云流水”，充分发挥了毛笔的特性，改变了汉魏绘画先涂形色后勾线的画法，而是先勾轮廓后着色，为中国画用笔独立埋下了伏笔。东晋的绘画处在“尚韵”阶段，因此在形、色方面不刻意追求，而是追求鼓动飞扬的神韵。顾恺之的绘画就是杰出的代表。

顾恺之的作品真迹没有流传到现在，只存有一些摹本[3]，其中最著名的是《〈女史箴〉图》和《〈洛神赋〉图》。

《〈女史箴〉图》是顾恺之根据西晋张华所作的《女史箴》一文所画。张华撰写《女史箴》，是为了借歌颂古代贤德女子，来规劝晋惠帝皇后贾南风。顾恺之的画共十二段，每段均题写《女史箴》的一段原文，并且画出这段文字的故事情节，以描绘人物精神为主，笔彩生动传神。如冯昭仪挺胸趋前，以身挡熊，她的毅然不惧与汉元帝的惊惶神色形成了强烈对比。画家运用了绵密的线条，将人物的刚劲与柔媚刻画得惟妙惟肖。

《洛神赋图》是根据三国时期文学家曹植所写的《洛神赋》而创作的。曹植是曹操的次子，年轻时十分爱恋甄氏。而甄氏被曹丕纳为后妃，又贬入冷宫，最后郁郁而死。对此，曹植感伤不已，他途经洛水，追念旧人，写了《洛神赋》一文，借神女抒发自己的哀思。

顾恺之将这一文学名篇用画卷形式展现出来。在画幅的开始，描绘曹植在侍卫仆从的簇拥下，在洛河水畔下马歇息，信步走到水旁，神情忧伤、郁闷，面对着洛水的微波，若有所思。水面上，洛水女神步履轻盈地缓缓飘浮而来。随后，女神在空中、在山间翩翩起舞，曹植携随从相送。洛水女神坐在车上乘风而去。曹植一行在渡河的楼船内凝目远望，天各一方。这幅优美的画卷，不仅因为描写了一个情意缠绵的爱情故事，而且因为较早地在人物题材中加入山水背景而留名画史。

《女史箴图》局部

作为画坛一代宗师，顾恺之的绘画对当时以及后世都产生了极大的影响。

（二）吴道子与人物画

吴道子(约公元685年~758年)，又名道玄，阳翟(今河南禹州市)人。是盛唐时期最负盛名的画家之一。他幼年贫穷孤苦，浪迹四方，跟随民间工匠学习绘画。他刻苦用功，才艺出众，不到20岁，就以长于绘画而闻名。之后，他做过县尉，不久就辞官来到繁华的洛阳。唐代的洛阳正值佛教流行，大兴庙宇之际。吴道子就在这些寺院里从事绘画创作，显露了他的艺术才华，名声大振。后来被唐玄宗召入宫中，成为宫廷画师。他被后人尊为“画圣”。苏东坡说：“诗至于杜子美(杜甫)，文至于韩退之(韩愈)，书至于颜鲁公(颜真卿)，画至于吴道子，而古今之变，天下之能事毕矣。”

吴道子入宫以后，开始了他创作的黄金时光。他的一生创作了大量的壁画作品，仅在两京所作的宗教壁画就达三百多处，画中形象生动各异，没有雷同。此外，还有大量的卷轴作品。吴道子最著名的壁画是《地狱变相图》，据说，图中并未直接描绘屠杀的恐怖场面，但是使观者受到极大的震动，以至于长安的屠户、渔夫们看了这幅画以后，“惧罪改业”，可以想象，其绘画有着何等的艺术震撼力。

吴道子作画的速度也赫赫有名。据说天宝年间，吴道子随唐玄宗去四川，打算摹写嘉陵山水，数月后，他竟然两手空空地回到长安。玄宗责问他为何没有摹写嘉陵山水。吴道子胸有成竹地回答：“嘉陵美景，不用写生[4]，早已记在心上。”说罢，就在大同殿上画起来，不出一日功夫，居然完成了嘉陵江三百里山川的巨幅壁画，令群臣称奇。在他之前，著名画家李思训[5]也曾在殿内画过嘉陵江山水，那是用了好几个月的时间。玄宗不由感叹道：“李思训花了数月的功夫，而吴道子一天就完成了。”

在多年的艺术实践中，吴道子不仅集众人之所长，而且创造了自己的独特风格，其笔墨线条达到了前无古人的高度。吴道子用跟写毛笔字一样的笔法来描线，用力有轻有重，挥笔或快或慢，用色也不再是浓重绚烂，而是墨彩兼备，有的甚至是不着颜色的白描。画面上的线条有流畅也有顿挫，人物形象生动。吴道子的作品整体气氛和谐，有一种动感，画中人物的衣带飘飘若飞，常令人有“好似轻风拂衣一般”的感觉。人们以“吴带当风”来概括其特征。他的画风在很大程度上影响了盛唐以后的绘画和造型艺术，其不着色

《送子天王图》局部

的白描成为后世白描的先端。

由于时间久远，吴道子的大量作品已经失传，今天仅遗存《送子天王图》[6]《道子墨宝》等摹本，让后人还能瞻仰一代"画圣"的笔下风采。

（三）清明上河图

《清明上河图》是北宋的风俗画作品。作者张择端，字正道，东武（今山东诸城）人，宋徽宗时代的宫廷画家。他少年时到京城汴梁（今河南开封）游学，后习绘画，尤其喜欢画舟车、市桥，风格自成一家。《清明上河图》是其代表作，被人视为神品。

《清明上河图》纵 248 厘米，横 528.7 厘米，现藏于北京故宫博物院。该图描绘了清明时节北宋京城汴梁以及汴河两岸的繁华景象和自然风光。作品以长卷的形式，将繁杂的景物纳入统一而富于变化的画面中，画中人物衣着不同，神情各异，其间穿插各种活动。全图共分为三个段落：

首段，汴京郊野的春光。画面描绘了宁静的春郊，茅舍、草桥、流水、老树、扁舟[7]。两个脚夫赶着五匹驮炭的毛驴向城市走来。路边一片柳林，枝头刚刚泛出嫩绿，路上一顶轿子，内坐一位妇人。轿顶装

饰着杨柳杂花，轿后跟随着骑马的、挑担的，从郊外踏青扫墓归来。其环境和人物的描写，点出了清明时节的特定时间和风俗，为全画展开了序幕。

中段，繁忙的汴河码头。这是全卷最热闹的地带：汴河是北宋时期国家漕运枢纽、商业交通要道，在这一部分，画中人物由稀疏变密集，活计由闲散变繁忙，人们有喝茶休息的，有看相算命的，有停坐进餐的。河里船只往来、首尾相接，或纤夫牵拉、或船夫摇橹，有的满载货物，逆流而上，有的靠岸停泊，紧张卸货。横跨汴河上空的是一座规模宏大的木质拱桥，它结构精巧，形状优美，宛如飞虹。一只大船正待过桥，船夫们有用竹竿撑的，有用长竿钩住桥梁的，有用麻绳挽住船的，还有几个人正在放下桅杆，以便船只通过桥下。邻船的人指指点点地好像在大声吆喝着什么。大家都在为此船过桥而忙碌着。桥上的人也伸头探脑地张望，好像为过桥的紧张情景捏了一把汗。画家笔下名闻遐迩的虹桥码头区，车水马龙，熙熙攘攘，显示了水陆交通会合点的繁忙景象。

后段，热闹的市区街道。以高大的城楼为中心，两边的屋宇鳞次栉比，有茶坊、酒肆、脚店、肉铺、庙宇、公廨（xiè）[8]等等。商店中不光有专门经营绫罗绸缎、珠宝香料、香火纸马的，也有医药门诊、大车修理、看相算命、修面整容等各行各业，可谓应有尽有。街市行人，摩肩接踵，川流不息，在这里，有做生意的商贾，看街景的士绅，骑马的官吏，叫卖的小贩，乘坐轿子的大家眷属，身负背篓的行脚僧人[9]，问路的外乡游客，听说书的街巷小儿，酒楼中狂饮的豪门子弟，城边行乞的残疾老人。男女老幼，士农工商，三教九流，无所不备。交通运载工具，有轿子、骆驼、牛马车、人力车、太平车、平头车，形形色色，样样俱全，绘色绘形地展现在人们的眼前。在五米多长的画卷里，一共绘了五百五十多个各色人物，牛、马、骡、驴等牲畜五六十匹，车、轿二十多辆，大小船只二十多艘。房屋、桥梁、城楼等也各有特色，体现了宋代建筑的特征。

张择端的《清明上河图》，是一幅描写北宋汴京城一角的现实主义的风俗画，具有很高的历史价值和艺术水平。

词语注释

【1】画迹：指绘画作品。

【2】以形写神：用人物的外在描绘表达其内心世界，烘托人物的个性。

【3】摹本：按原本描摹的书画作品。

【4】写生：绘画术语。以实物为观察对象直接加以描绘的作画方式。

【5】李思训：唐代杰出画家，字建，陇西成纪（今甘肃秦安）人。唐宗室孝斌之子。以战功闻名于世，曾

《清明上河图》局部

任过武卫大将军，世称“大李将军”。

【6】《送子天王图》：吴道子的代表作品。这幅画的内容是描写佛祖释迦牟尼降生以后，他的父亲净饭王和摩耶夫人抱着他去朝拜大自在天神庙，诸神向他礼拜的故事。这幅传摹作品一变东晋顾恺之以来那种粗细一律的“铁线描”，突破南北朝“曹衣出水”的艺术形式，笔势圆转，衣服飘举，盈盈若舞，形成“吴带当风”的艺术风格，风行于当时。

【7】扁舟：小船。

【8】公廨：官署。

【9】行脚僧人：指步行参禅的云游僧。

三、山水画

展子虔和《游春图》

展子虔

展子虔，渤海（今河北河间县）人。生卒年不详，活动在公元550年～604年期间。一生经历北齐、北周、隋三朝，在隋文帝朝中任朝散大夫[1]，正四品，后改任帐内都督[2]，统领主帅左右的侍卫军士。与顾恺之、陆探微、张僧繇（yóu）齐名。据说，在唐代凡能称得上是收藏家的人，必须收藏有展子虔的作品。

展子虔擅长画车马、人物和山水。他的山水画有“咫尺千里”的气势，其中留下的《游春图》，是迄今所发现的中国最早、保存非常完整的一幅山水卷轴画[3]。这幅画生动地描绘了人们在风和日丽、春光明媚的季节，到山间水畔踏青游玩的情景。画面上花草树木漫山遍野，青山翠岭，湖水翠绿，在通往深山茂林的堤岸上，有的策马纵游，有的停立观赏阳春美景。水中有舟，舟中的仕女谈笑风生，画中人物姿态各异、生动有趣。将“仁者乐山，智者乐水”的旨趣转化成美丽的画卷。

《游春图》全画以自然景色为主。人物点缀其间，这与以前的绘画不同。南北朝时虽然也有独立的山水

《游春图》

画创作，但多以人物作为主体，风景则是人物的背景。而《游春图》的风格转变为以风景为主体，人物被缩小了尺寸，镶嵌到风景之中，反成为陪衬之物。这样，就改变了“人大于山”的现象，也拉开了近景和远景之间的空间距离，让山水本身彻底成为画卷上的主角。这种翻天覆地的风格变化，标志着独立的山水画的诞生。这种巨大的转变，又导致了许多技法形式方面的崭新创造。第一个技法进步是“笔法”的成长，从原来较为单一的“线描”变为各种不同形态的画法，包括线描、皴（cūn）染、转折的笔锋[4]等；第二个技法进步是全景构图中近大远小的透视关系[5]的改变，使景物的比例关系向适当方面发展。另一个技法进步是色彩，展子虔的山水画使用了青绿重彩，整个画面以青绿为主调，点缀以红、白等色彩，还施以金粉，使画面具有一种富丽辉煌的感觉。这些画技对唐代出现的李思训、李绍道父子二人的青绿、金碧山水画产生了直接影响，因此，展子虔的画被后世誉为“唐画之祖”。

北宋 赵昌《竹虫图》

展子虔的《游春图》在中国美术史上有着划时代的意义，在构图、用笔、用墨、用色等诸方面构建了基础骨架，全方位找到了合适中国文化国情发展的山水画一般法式。中国画的所谓“南宗”“北宗”都是由此流变而成的，通过《游春图》我们已窥视到中国山水画成熟的曙光。

词语注释

【1】朝散大夫：隋时设置的散官名。唐宋时文阶官之制，从五品下称朝散大夫。元朝时升至从四品下，明时废除。

【2】帐内都督：军幕中的将佐，军事长官。

【3】轴画：指装裱成卷的书或字画。

【4】笔锋：书画的笔势；文章的锋芒。

【5】透视关系：绘画术语。用线条或色彩在平面上表现物体的空间位置距离和轮廓投影的方法。因透视现象表现为远小近大，故也叫“远近法”。

四、花鸟画

中国花鸟画，可以说是世界上独一无二的画种，但在中国画中是出现并成熟得最晚的画科，一般认为发端于唐代，发展成熟于五代至宋，明清之后题材相对集中而风格多变。在中国画中，凡以花卉、

北宋 赵昌《写生蛱蝶图卷》局部

花鸟、鱼虫等为描绘对象的画，称之为花鸟画。花鸟画中的画法有“工笔”[1]“写意”[2]“兼工带写”[3]三种。

中国花鸟画集中体现了中国人与作为审美客体的自然生物的审美关系，具有较强的抒情性。其技法多样，曾以描写手法的精工或奔放，分为工笔花鸟画和写意花鸟画（又可分为大写意花鸟画和小写意花鸟画）；又以使用水墨色彩上的差异，分为水墨花鸟画、泼墨[4]花鸟画、设色[5]花鸟画、白描花鸟画与没骨[6]花鸟画。

中国花鸟画在长期的历史发展中，适应中国社会的审美需要，形成了以写生为基础，以寓兴、写意为归依的传统。为此，中国花鸟画的立意往往关乎人事，它不是为了描花绘鸟而描花绘鸟，不是模仿自然，而是紧紧抓住动植物与人们生活遭际、思想情感的某种联系而给以强化的表现。它既重视真，又非常注意美与善的观念的表达，强调其“夺造化而移精神遐想”的怡情作用，主张通过花鸟画的创作与欣赏影响人们的志趣、情操与精神生活，表达作者的内在思想与追求。

表现在造型上，中国花鸟画重视形似而不拘泥于形似[7]，甚至追求“不似之似”与“似与不似之间”，借以实现对象的神采与作者的情意。在构图上，它突出主体，善于剪裁，时画折技，讲求布局中的虚实对比[8]与顾盼呼应，而且在写意花鸟画中，尤善于把发挥画意的诗歌题句[9]，用与画风相协调的书法在适当的位置书写出来，辅以印章[10]，成为一种以画为主的综合艺术形式。在画法上，花鸟画因对象较山水画具体而微，又比人物画丰富，所以工笔设色更具写实色彩或带有一定的装饰意味，而写意花鸟画则笔墨更加简练，更具有程序性与不可更易性。

纵览花鸟画发展史，五代时蜀国的黄筌（公元903年～968年）与南唐的徐熙（公元937年～975年）是花鸟画独立形成过程中最著名的人物，是中国花鸟画主要风格形式的开创元勋。由北宋至南宋，花鸟画发生一次转变，宫廷画院对这次变化起过重要作用。宋徽宗赵佶（公元1082年～1135年）身为国君，却不理朝政，沉溺在书画中，亲自掌管翰林图画院，并以科举方式选拔画家，授以荣誉地位。因此，聚集了一批绘画人才，形成了一种反映宫廷精美、华丽、雅致的审美趣味，以工笔与雅丽色彩作画的“院体”风格，渐次成为画坛主流。

元代以后，花鸟画题材明显地集中在“松竹梅菊”上，王冕是画梅名家。真正能够充分发挥笔墨纸张特殊效应而创立水墨大写意画法的，归功于明代著名画家徐渭，他的特点不仅仅是他个人的坎坷和天才的禀赋造成的，也是新兴的文艺思潮与花鸟画发展的时代要求。其花鸟画走笔如飞、泼墨淋漓、直抒胸臆，赢得后人心悦诚服的赞叹。继徐渭之后，郑板桥（公元1693年～1765年）、恽寿平（公元1633年～1690年）、吴昌硕（公元1844年～1927年）、齐白石（公元1863年～1957年）都是花鸟画大家。

词语注释

【1】工笔：工笔花鸟画即用浓、淡墨勾勒精确的轮廓，再分层次着色。

【2】写意：写意花鸟画即用简练概括的手法绘写对象。强调以意为之的主导作用，追求像中国书法艺术一样淋漓尽致地抒写作者情意，不因对物像的描头画脚束缚思想感情的表达。

【3】兼工带写：介于工笔和写意两种画法之间的一种画法。

【4】泼墨：作为中国画创作的一种墨法，古已有之。泼墨法是用极湿墨，即大笔蘸上饱和之水墨，下笔要快，慢则下笔墨水渗开，不见点画，等干后或将干之际，再用浓墨勾勒。

【5】设色：是运用色彩的效果，表达物像的情境变化和韵味。古人称为“随类赋彩”“活色生香”。

【6】没骨：技法名。不用墨线勾勒，直接以彩色绘画物像。

【7】形似：与“神似”对称。术语，指艺术作品的外在特征。

【8】虚实对比：虚和实对书画的章法有着极其重要的意义和地位。所谓虚，其形态是疏和简，虚之极则归于无；所谓实，是密和繁的形态，实即是有。中国画最讲究章法，也就是虚实的对比程度不同的表现。

【9】题句：就一事一物或一文一图题写诗文以表达自己的感受。

【10】印章：图章。

五、中国书法

中国书法是一门古老而奇特的艺术，也是世界艺术苑囿里的一朵奇葩。是中华民族优秀的文化遗产中不可或缺的组成部分，是中华民族的象征。

书法艺术的自觉化虽然至东汉末才发生，但书法艺术的产生当与汉字的萌生同时。汉字的形成经历了很长的历史时期。为学术界公认的我国最早的古汉字资料，是商代中后期（约公元前14～前11世纪）的甲骨文[1]和金文[2]。从书法的角度审察，并具有了书法形式美的众多因素，如线条美，单字造型的对称美，变化美以及章法美，风格美等。甲骨文的章法最为人们称道，大小不一，方圆多异，长扁随形的单字组合在一起，错落有致而又统一和谐。最具有书法艺术价值的首推石鼓文，是战国时代秦国的作品。刻在十个鼓形石墩上，每一石鼓周围刻有一首四言诗。石鼓文笔画浑厚凝重，圆劲挺拔，结体略趋方正，章法均衡疏朗、朴实自然，为“小篆[3]之祖”。从商代后

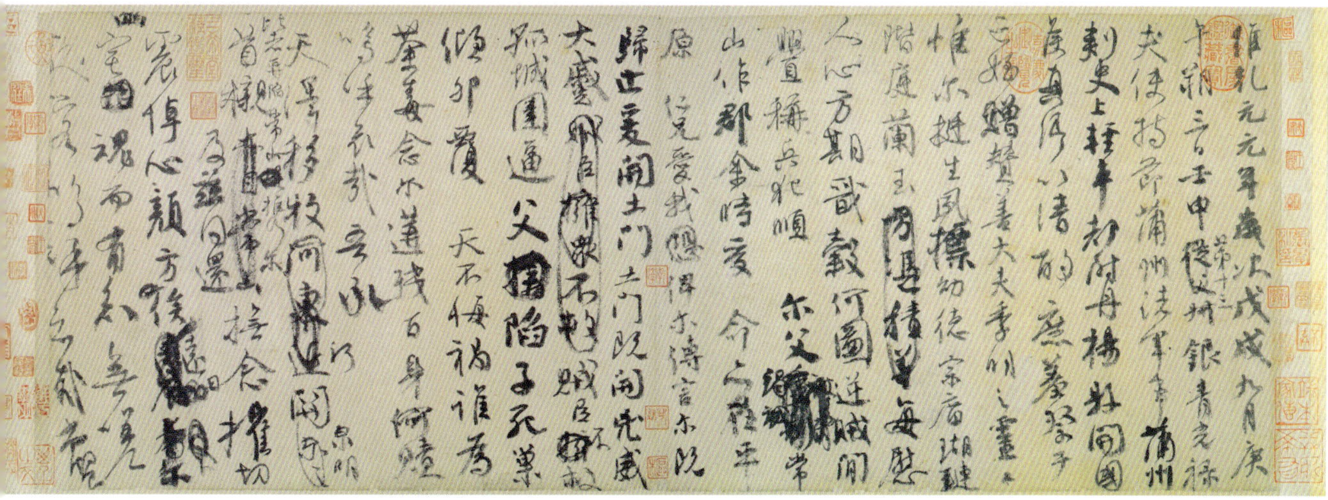

唐 颜真卿《祭侄文稿》

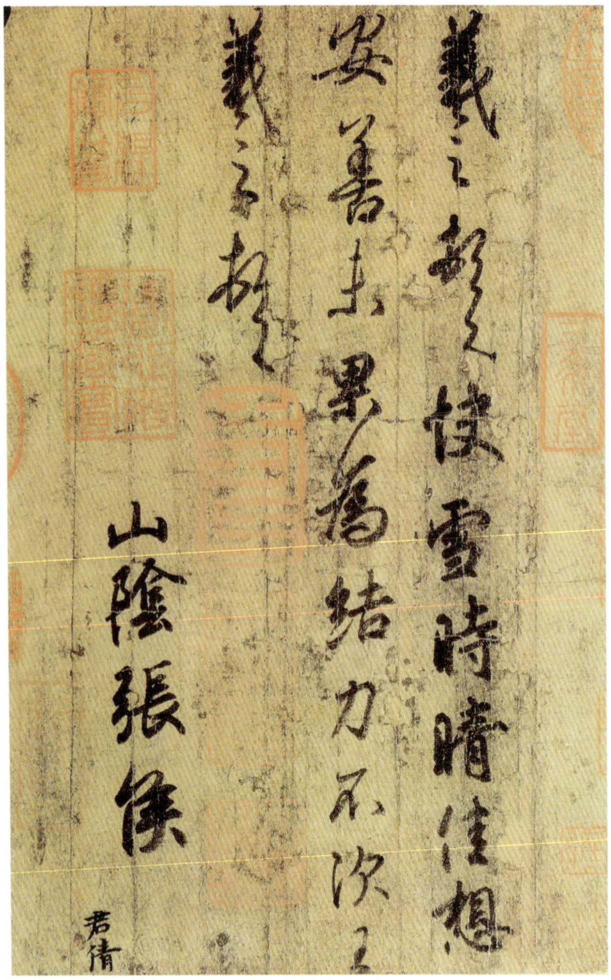

晋 王羲之《快雪时晴帖》

期到秦统一中国（公元前221年），汉字演变的总趋势是由繁到简。这种演变具体反映在字体和字形的嬗变之中。西周晚期金文趋向线条化，战国时代民间草篆向古隶[4]的发展，都大大削弱了文字的象形性。然而书法的艺术性却随着书体的嬗变而愈加丰富起来，备受推崇的是秦朝宰相李斯所厘定的小篆，结构平稳，上密下疏，圆润而遒健，可以说是秦时的美术体。汉碑是中国碑刻史上的第一个高峰。汉隶名碑，不下百通。如“汉碑第一品”的《华山庙碑》、秀美的《史晨碑》《曹全碑》、粗犷的《张迁碑》。

那么究竟什么是“书法”呢？我们可以从它的性质、美学特征、源泉、独特的表现手法方面去理解。书法是以汉字为基础、用毛笔书写的、具有四维特征的抽象符号艺术，它体现了万事万物的“对立统一”这个基本规律又反映了人作为主体的精神、气质、学识和修养。美学家李泽厚在《美的历程》中指出：“书法是把这种‘线的艺术’高度集中化、纯粹化的艺术，为中国所独有。这也是由魏晋开始自觉的。正是魏晋时期，严正整肃、气势雄浑的汉隶而为真、行、草、楷，中下层不知名没地位的行当，变为门阀名士们的高妙意兴和专业所在。笔意、体势、结构、章法更为多样、丰富、错综而变化。”魏晋时代书法艺术成为一种独立的艺术，进入了新的境界。由篆隶趋从于简易的草书[5]、行书[6]和真书，它们成为该时期的主流风格。

东晋大书法家王羲之的出现使书法艺术大放异彩，其艺术成就在唐朝备受推崇，唐太宗独尊王羲之，下诏重金广求王羲之书迹，所获甚多，并令太子临摹王羲之书法，还把书法当做铨选官吏的主要条件之一。这些都为唐代书法艺术的大发展推波助澜。同时，唐代一群书法家蜂拥而起，如：楷书有虞世南、欧阳询、褚遂良、颜真卿、柳公权等名家，草书有张旭、怀素等名家。在书法造诣上各有千秋、风格多样。宋代有四大书法家：苏轼、黄庭坚、米芾和蔡襄。元明清有赵孟頫、董其昌、邓石如等。经历宋、元、明、清，中国书法成为一个民族符号，代表了中国文化的博大精深和民族文化的永恒魅力。

词语注释

【1】甲骨文：甲骨文是中国的一种古代文字，被认为是现代汉字的早期形式，有时候也被认为是汉字的书体之一，也是现存中国最古老的一种成熟文字。

【2】金文：金文是指铸刻在殷周青铜器上的文字，旧称钟鼎文。

【3】小篆：秦始皇统一天下之后，实行了一系列的改革，其中，统一文字就是一项十分重要的政策。此种书体上承东周时秦国器铭与刻石文字，融会各地书风而成，为中国第一次统一之字体，居书体转变之关键。

【4】隶：隶书基本是由篆书演化来的，主要将篆书圆转的笔画改为方折，书写速度更快。

【5】草书：汉字的一种书体，特点是结构简省、笔画

连绵。形成于汉代，是为书写简便在隶书基础上演变出来的。有章草、今草、狂草之分。

【6】行书：介于楷书、草书之间的一种字体，可以说是楷书的草化或草书的楷化。它是为了弥补楷书的书写速度太慢和草书的难于辨认而产生的。笔势不像草书那样潦草，也不要求像楷书那样端正。楷法多于草法的叫“行楷”，草法多于楷法的叫“行草”，行书大约是在东汉末年产生的。

六、中国篆刻

中国篆刻是书法（主要是篆书）和镌刻（包括凿、铸）结合，来制作印章的艺术。一个非常特殊的现象是，入印的书体，从古至今，一般都用篆书，用隶书、楷书者很少。印章制作的材料有金、银、铜、铁、玉、石、骨、木等，以石材为最多。篆刻艺术发展到明代，已经完全成熟，并形成流派。篆刻艺术史可以上溯到两千多年前的春秋战国时代（公元前 770 年 ~ 前 221 年）。先秦时期印章最早叫玺（xǐ）印[1]，是古代人们在交往时，作为权力和凭证的信物。秦始皇统一中国后，规定“玺”的名称为天子专用。其他都只能叫印章，或简称为“印”或“章”。中国的篆刻艺术源远流长，自春秋战国时期，直至当代，风格各异，形式众多，流传不绝，出现过两大高潮时期，一是汉代，另一是明清。汉印数量多，艺术也达到了古印的高峰。汉印白文印最多，使用篆书而带有隶书笔意，其主调是笔画方正，布局均匀，气势饱满，端雅大气，被后世公认为初学篆刻的范本。

明代中叶，印章已发展为独特的篆刻艺术。它从实用品、书画艺术的附属品，而发展成为独立的艺术。篆刻艺术在明清两代好手如林、派别繁多。篆刻流派一般是以篆刻家的籍贯、姓氏、师承关系及其活动区域来命名的。在明代中叶到晚清的近五百年中出现了各种风格的流派，从而把中国古代篆刻艺术推向了又一繁荣时期。明代的文彭是书画家文征明的长子，诗书画均传家法，尤以篆刻擅名当代，后来的篆刻家奉他为篆刻之祖。

清代金石学[2]盛行，以及历代金石文物的大量出土，不少学者致力于这些文物和古代文字的搜集、研究、著述和流播，因而扩大了篆刻家的视野。可以说清代是中国篆刻史上的鼎盛时期，一时人才辈出，流派纷呈，艺术上出现全新的面貌。有邓石如、赵之谦、吴昌硕等金石大家。篆刻是一种“方寸之内，气象万千”的文字艺术，从广义上来讲，先有篆，后有刻；先章法，再刀法。篆书是篆刻的基础。刻是篆写效果的体现和抒发。从艺术上来讲“书画同源”[3]。书法和篆刻是两姐妹。书法是篆刻的根本。“印从书入，书从印出”。只有弄通书法尤其是篆法，才能治好印[4]，创作出像样的作品。书法讲究线条、结构、章法[5]布局，篆刻也同样如此。但是书法又不等同于篆刻，因为书法是用毛笔写字，篆刻是用铁笔；写字用的是纸，而篆刻用的是印石。再谈到篆刻与绘画的关系时，似乎更密切一些。在作品上钤（qián）[6]盖印章，不光是为了证明书画的真赝，更是为了充实和丰富画面，增加艺术效果。

龙钮石章

篆刻艺术自兴起至今，已成为欣赏艺术。篆刻艺术是一门实

琴罢倚松玩鹤

无功氏

磨兜坚室

豆花村里草虫啼

笑谈间气吐霓虹

壬辰进士

程守之印

实在在的学问，不是“雕虫小技”，当然也不是高不可攀。然而要使篆刻艺术达到较高境界，只有具备多方面的知识修养，才能真正地做到“有笔尤有墨”而不是只有“刀与石”。

词语注释

【1】玺印：印章亦称“图章”。古称“玺”。秦以前，无论官、私印都称“玺”，秦统一六国后，规定皇帝的印独称“玺”，臣民只称“印”。古代印章起源于中国的雕刻文字，最古的有殷的甲骨文，周的钟鼎文，秦的刻石等，凡在金铜玉石等素材上雕刻的文字通称“金石”。玺印即包括在“金石”里。

【2】金石学：近代考古学传入中国前，以古代铜器和石刻为主要研究对象的学问。近似欧洲的铭刻学，被视为中国考古学的前身。研究对象属零星出土文物或传世品，未经科学发掘；偏重于铭文的著录和考证，以证经补史为研究目的。形成于北宋，至清代正式有“金石之学”的命名。

【3】书画同源：中国书画术语。意为中国绘画和中国书法关系密切，两者的产生和发展，相辅相成，同质而异体也。

【4】治印：篆刻，刻印章。

【5】章法：指安排布置整幅作品中，字与字、行与行之间呼应、照顾等关系的方法，亦即整幅作品的“布白”。亦称“大章法”。习惯上又称一字之中的点画布置，和一字与数字之间布置的关系为“小章法”。

【6】钤：盖（印）。

第十一章　中国民间艺术

一、乐　器

中国乐器是对传统音乐器具的总称，中国乐器早在先秦就根据制作材料把乐器分为“金、石、土、革、丝、木、匏、竹”共八大类，故称“八音”。此种分类法起于周代（《周礼·春官·宗伯第三》），至近现代才划分为四大类“吹、拉、弹、打”。乐器发展的顺序是先产生打击乐器、吹奏乐器，后产生弹拨乐器，最后产生拉弦乐器。

编　钟

中国的乐器历史悠久，种类繁多。既有古代流传下来的华夏乐器，也有历代传入经过融合改造的异国乐器，还有奇异多姿的民间乐器。河南殷墟出土的乐器和甲骨文字，充分地证明了在三千多年以前，中国乐器的种类至少就有钟、磬[1]、埙[2]（xūn）、铜鼓、铃等十余种，到了西周时期，有记载的乐器达七十多种，有了比较发达的音乐文化。“琴瑟之乐”“钟磬之乐”是此时期的主要乐种。1978 年 5 月，在湖北省随县（今随州市）发掘了一座战国初期的古墓曾侯乙墓，墓中有一个完整的钟鼓乐队，珍贵乐器达 124 件。特别是其中有一套青铜铸的曾侯乙编钟[3]，有乐钟 64 枚，钟架通长 11.83 米，高 2.73 米。编钟大小不同，可以发出 12 个音调。因其精湛的工艺、宏伟的造型、优良的发音和完善的律制而震惊世界，被誉为“人间奇迹”。云南楚雄出土的战国铜鼓也是惊人的发现，至今发音洪亮，是当今已知年代最早的铜鼓之一。此外，还有瑟[4]、笙、排箫[5]和竹笛等乐器保存完好。竹笛、筝[6]也是这个时期产生的新乐器。

到汉朝和唐朝以后，伊斯兰教世界和印度的音乐和乐器开始大量流入，汉唐时统治者奉行开放政策，勇于吸收外来文化，来自异地的乐器如笛子、筚篥、琵琶、胡琴等大量为中国音乐采纳，并不断改造，大大丰富了中国的音乐文化。无论是民间音乐还是宫

▶▶ 埙（仿古）

廷音乐都空前繁荣，尤其弹奏乐器极为盛行。许多乐器如羯鼓、答腊鼓、箜篌、腰鼓、琵琶、筚篥、五弦等是异域传入的新乐器，它与国内的传统音乐结合而成为新型的民乐。在敦煌莫高窟的壁画和雕像中，可以看到大量的手抱琵琶[7]的飞天形象，可见当时琵琶已成为主要演奏的乐器。据记载，唐代乐器约有300种。

宋元时期，说唱音乐和戏曲音乐的崛起，带来了器乐艺术的发展，出现了三弦[8]、二胡[9]、京胡[10]等乐器，使中国传统乐器形成了吹、拉、弹、打四大类的格局。明清时期，西洋乐器也逐渐进入中国，如铜管[11]、钢琴、提琴、小号，与中国民族乐器交相呼应，扩大了中国的乐器领域和视野。中华人民共和国成立以后，国家非常重视民族乐器文化遗产，几十年来，拯救了一些失传的民族乐器，如葫芦丝[12]、陶埙、扬琴[13]、口笛[14]等乐器，使中国乐器作为中华民族文化的一部分，不断发扬光大。

词语注释

【1】磬：古代一种打击乐器，用玉或石做成。

【2】埙：古代用陶土烧制的一种吹奏乐器，大小如鹅蛋，六孔，顶端为吹口。

【3】编钟：古代打击乐器，青铜制，悬挂在木架上用小木槌打击发音。

【4】瑟：古代弦乐器，形状像琴。现在所用的瑟有两种，一种有二十五弦，另一种有十六弦。

【5】排箫：古代管乐器。也称箫。

【6】筝：一种弹拨乐器，一般有二十五弦。

【7】琵琶：弹拨乐器，用木料制成，有四根弦，下部为瓜子形的盘，上部为长柄。

【8】三弦：又称“弦子”，中国传统弹拨乐器。柄很长，音箱为圆角方形，两面蒙皮，张弦三根，侧抱于怀演奏。音色粗犷、豪放。可以独奏、合奏或伴奏，普遍用于民族器乐、戏曲音乐和说唱音乐。

【9】二胡：拉弦乐器的一种，比京胡大，琴筒用木头做成，前端稍大，蒙蟒皮或蛇皮，有两根弦，声音低沉，也叫南胡。

【10】京胡：又称胡琴，拉弦乐器。琴筒比二胡小，主要用于京剧伴奏。

【11】铜管：铜管乐器。

【12】葫芦丝：外形像葫芦和笛子的结合，音色独特优美，外观古朴、柔美、典雅。是云南少数民族的乐器之一，主要流传于云南省滇西傣族地区。

【13】扬琴：也叫“洋琴”，又称“蝴蝶琴”“扇面琴”。击弦类弦鸣乐器。相传源于西亚古亚述、波斯等国，约明末传入中国。

【14】口笛：以短竹管制作而成的吹奏乐器。

二、民　歌

民歌全称民间歌曲，是最大众化的音乐形式，是劳动人民在生活和劳动中自己创作、自己演唱的歌曲。它以口头创作、口头流传的方式生存于民间，并在流传过程中不断经受人民群众集体的筛选、改造、加工、提炼，随着岁月的流逝而日臻完美。

民歌按照题材来分，包括劳动工作的号子[1]，谈情说爱的情歌，流传于各族儿童中的歌谣，饮酒作乐的时曲，纪念亲人故友的挽歌[2]，劳动休闲时吟唱的小调[3]，还有民间经常唱的山歌[4]等等。

民歌具有很鲜明的民族特色和地方色彩。一般按

唱壮族山歌　迎八方宾客

照地区分为陕北民歌、东北民歌、河北民歌、青海民歌、新疆民歌、江浙民歌、湖南民歌等等。中国历史悠久，地域辽阔，人口和民族众多，所以民歌源远流长，浩如烟海。据统计，各地已经采集到的民歌，数量总计超过 30 万首。这些民歌具有浓厚的生活气息，手法简洁，容易上口，其中不少成为全国家喻户晓的、颇具代表性的作品，如:《茉莉花》《小白菜》《走西口》《小放牛》等。

中国汉族民歌《茉莉花》是清代以来十分流行的民歌。它不仅在中国各地广泛流传，而且从 18 世纪末叶流传到欧美亚各地，作为中国民歌的典型代表而广为传播。在外国出版的一些世界各国民间歌曲集子当中，常常可以找到《茉莉花》的歌谱。在华侨或华裔较多的国家里，《茉莉花》甚至成了当地的民间音乐。

《小白菜》是一首流行于河北一带的传统民歌，诉说了一个年幼的孤儿受摧残、想念死去的亲娘的哀伤之情。歌曲以三字为一句，共四句，基本上每字一音。曲调流畅，最后以两小节哀叹式的音调呼唤“亲娘呀，亲娘呀”做尾腔，烘托思念亲娘的悲切心情。这首曲调曾被采用改编为歌剧《白毛女》[5]的音乐主题“北风吹”，深受群众欢迎。

《走西口》是著名的陕北民歌。表现了一对新婚夫妇为生活所迫，丈夫决定到口外[6]去谋生，妻子与之依依惜别的动人故事。民歌反映了当地人“走西口”的生活。

《小放牛》是一首河北民歌，以牧童和乡村小姑娘相互对答的方式逗趣玩乐。歌中小姑娘向牧童问路，而俏皮的牧童故意刁难，要求小姑娘先回答他的提问才告诉她路怎么走。于是俩人就一问一答，边歌边舞地对起歌来。音乐灵活、音调明快、富于表情，歌舞的形式生动、活泼、风趣，充分表现出劳动人民的聪明才智和开朗乐观的性格。

民歌的音乐形态分为单声部和多声部两类。单声部即一首歌曲只用单一声部歌唱，中国民歌的绝大部分是这种形式。多声部即一首歌曲采用两个以上声部歌唱，在56个民族中，有20多个民族的民歌包含有数量不等的多声部唱腔，如壮族、侗族、仡佬族、布依族、瑶族、高山族、傈僳族、畲族、羌族的多声部民歌流传最甚。

民歌的价值表现是多方面的，它是一种富于生命力的口头创作，其优秀作品具有高度的艺术价值，如《诗经》，最有价值的部分被称为“风”，后世数千年来采集民歌的活动都称之“采风”。在中国文学发展史上，民歌是创作的源泉之一。诗、词、曲、赋等文学体裁都起源于民歌而后为文学家所采用。民歌是民族传统音乐的基础，许多各地的歌舞音乐、说唱曲艺、戏曲杂剧都受到民歌的深刻影响，如东北的“二人转”的基本曲调是由民歌构成的。还有的甚至由民歌发展而来，如湖南民歌基础上发展起来的湖南花鼓戏。

词语注释

【1】号子：集体劳动中，为统一步调、减轻疲劳而唱的歌曲。

【2】挽歌：挽柩者所唱哀悼死者的歌。后泛指对死者悼念的诗歌或哀叹旧事物灭亡的文辞。

【3】小调：主要指流行于城市和乡村的俗曲时调。在浙江也曾广泛流行。

【4】山歌：民歌的一种。一般在山野田间歌唱，曲调高亢，节奏自由。

【5】《白毛女》：歌剧剧本。延安鲁迅艺术文学院集体创作于1945年。贺敬之、丁毅执笔，马可等作曲。剧中讲述了恶霸地主黄世仁逼死佃户杨白劳，霸占其女喜儿，又企图将她卖掉，喜儿逃入深山多年，头发全白，后八路军解放了该地区，斗倒地主，喜儿获得翻身解放的故事。

【6】口外：张家口以西，内蒙古河套一带。过去，山西的贫苦农民为生活所迫，不得不于每年春天纷纷背井离乡，哭别亲人到口外去谋生，过着“走西口”的漂泊生活。

三、民族舞

中国是一个由56个民族组成的大家庭。在悠久的历史长河中，每个民族都萌生了自己风格独特、丰富多彩的民间舞蹈艺术。民族舞蹈来源于生活，如祭祀、聚会、择偶、婚丧等活动，产生并流传于民间、受民俗文化制约、即兴表演但风格相对稳定、以自娱为主要功能的舞蹈形式。民间舞具有朴实无华、形式多样、内容丰富、形象生动等特点，历来都是专业舞蹈创作不可或缺的素材来源。源远流长、多姿多彩的中国民族舞蹈，是中国数千年文化、艺术与美学的结晶。

蒙古族舞蹈

中国地域广阔，南方与北方、东部与西部的各民族具有鲜明的民族风格和浓郁的地方特色。北方民族舞蹈富于表现，雄健、明快、豪放，而南方民族舞蹈具有柔美、端庄、抒情的特点。西部民族舞蹈节奏刚劲、激烈，而东部的表现农业生活的民族舞蹈则动作柔和、节奏徐缓。中国舞台上常见的民族舞有豪放见长的藏族民间舞蹈、剽悍夺人的蒙古族民间舞蹈、热情奔放的维吾尔族舞、含蓄柔婉的朝鲜族舞……它们都以各自的特色表达着自己的民族特色和艺术。

蒙古族民间舞蹈具有浑厚、舒展、豪迈、粗犷的特点，蒙古舞肩部动作丰富，有上下、前后、环绕的动律。表演时男子多半表现骑手的风度，女子动作活泼动人。主要表演形式有筷子舞[1]和盅碗舞[2]，流行于内蒙古西部的伊克昭盟。配舞的音乐多为当地民歌，伴奏乐器有四胡[3]、马头琴[4]、笛子、扬琴等。

藏族舞蹈

新疆舞蹈别具一格，因新疆地处丝绸之路的要冲，中原文化、波斯、印度、阿拉伯等各种文化兼收并蓄，因此舞蹈具有绚丽多彩的风格。以维吾尔族为代表的舞蹈，擅长于头部和手腕的运用，通过移颈、头部的摇动和丰富多变的手腕动作，以及昂首、挺胸、立腰等姿态，加之眼神的传情达意，能表现出不同的人物性格和内心情感，同时，快速的旋转，使舞蹈动作柔和而优美。

藏族舞充分展示了藏族的服饰特点，长长的袖子甩动是藏族舞蹈突出的特征。男子舞者的上身动作非常讲究，不论是否手持道具，其“上身动作像雄狮”，威武雄壮，极富高原人剽悍的气质，给人以战胜一切艰难险阻的信念，而女子舞的上身动作则含蓄典雅，给人以健康和优美的感觉。藏族舞双手的动作非常丰富，极富活力，体现了千姿百态的舞蹈语言。由于藏民居住的地理、气候、方言、服饰的差异，以及宗教影响而形成种类众多的舞蹈，其中有广泛流传的民族民间舞蹈；有专供上层社会享用的歌舞；也有专为宗教仪式服务的舞乐，以及众多门派的藏戏[5]舞蹈。

朝鲜族舞蹈典雅优美，潇洒柔婉与刚劲跌宕兼而有之。如著名的“长缨舞”，舞者戴着特制的头盔，上有可以旋绕的长缨，舞时摆动头部，使长缨在头顶、身侧旋绕飞舞，有时舞者还作出各种动作，充分表现了劳动者乐观的精神风貌。朝鲜族的长鼓舞经常由女子表演，舞蹈之人将长鼓系在身前，左手拍击鼓面，右手用鼓鞭敲击鼓面，边击边打边舞，优美欢快。

孔雀舞是傣（dǎi）族古老的民间舞蹈，也是傣族人民最喜爱的一种舞蹈，每逢盛大的节日，如“泼水节”[6]和隆重的集会时，总要进行表演。傣族人民十分喜爱和崇敬孔雀，认为孔雀最美、最善良，把孔雀作为吉祥、幸福、美好的象征，以跳孔雀舞来歌颂自己的民族，表达自己的理想和愿望。在舞蹈中模仿孔雀飞跑下山、漫步森林、饮泉戏水、追逐嬉戏，以及拖翅、晒翅、抖翅、展翅、开屏、飞翔等等。

苗族民族舞蹈十分强调服饰和道具的运用。在《芦笙舞》《踩鼓舞》中，妇女佩戴银首饰、银头饰、银项圈，穿着多色彩的衣服，随着身体的摆动，嵌着银花的百褶裙闪光作响，与芦笙、鼓乐声、歌声相映成趣，形成了苗族文化典型的娱乐场景的生活习俗。

在中国，某些地区的少数民族还保留着古代的原始舞蹈——傩舞[7]。它是中国古代祭典中的仪式舞蹈，舞者面戴强悍、狰狞的面具，扮作鬼神歌舞，以表现神的身世事迹。如今，傩舞已经发展成的民间舞蹈和戏剧，广泛流传于江西、湖南、湖北、贵州、安徽和山东等地。

词语注释

【1】筷子舞：是蒙古族伊克昭盟人民具有代表性的传统民间舞蹈形式之一。表演者两手各握一把筷子，手持筷子的细头击打粗头。筷子舞凝结着蒙古族人民热爱生活的情意和美化生活的智慧，是蒙古族人民精神生活的组成部分。

【2】盅碗舞：根据流行于内蒙古伊克昭盟的民间舞"盅碗舞"，以及"顶碗舞"和"酒盅舞"改编加工创作。原民间舞为牧民在欢宴、敬宾时，酒酣兴浓时，即兴而舞。

【3】四胡：拉弦乐器。形状与二胡相同，因有四条弦，故名。第一、三两弦与第二、四两弦各同音，常用以伴奏大鼓等曲艺。

【4】马头琴：中国蒙古族民间拉弦乐器。蒙古语称"绰尔"。琴身木制，长约1米，有两根弦共鸣箱呈梯形，马皮蒙面。

【5】藏戏：是藏族社会生活中的重要文化内容，在藏语中被称为"阿吉拉姆"，在中国的西藏、四川、青海、云南等藏民集中的地区非常流行。而这种艺术形式，在表现手法和内容上，都有很强的藏传佛教色彩。

【6】泼水节：泼水节源于印度，曾经是婆罗门教的一种宗教仪式。其后，为佛教所吸收，经缅甸传入云南傣族地区。泼水节为傣历新年的庆祝活动，一般在阳历4月13日至4月15日之间。届时人们先至佛寺浴佛，然后互相泼水，用飞溅的水花表示真诚的祝福。到处欢声笑语，充满了节日气氛。

【7】傩舞：又叫"大傩""跳傩"，俗称"鬼戏"或"跳鬼脸"。源于上古氏族社会中的图腾崇拜，以后发展成原始巫教中的一种仪式，并逐步演变成有固定目的和内容的节令祭仪，是历史悠久的民间舞蹈。一般有两种表演形式：一种由主角四人表演，表演者头戴面具如冠，身着兽皮，手执戈盾，口中发出"傩傩"之声。另一种由12人组成，每人朱发画皮，手执数尺长麻鞭，甩动作响，并高呼各种专吃恶鬼、猛兽之神名，起舞时各有音乐伴奏。

四、秧　歌

"秧歌"，又叫扭秧歌，历史悠久，是中国最具代表性的民间自娱自乐形式。秧歌舞表演起来生动活泼，形式多样，多姿多彩，红火热闹，规模宏大，气氛热烈。秧歌出现得很早，陕西省出土的宋金时期的浮雕[1]砖刻中，已经发现有秧歌画像。画像中人物的衣着装扮、面部表情、五官特征以及舞蹈的造型和动态，都与今天陕北群众的服装、形象、性情以及陕北秧歌的表演相一致。由此可见，至今仍在民间流行甚广的秧歌，在八百年前的南宋时期就已经流行于民间了。

"秧歌"广泛地流行中国各地。在南方把"秧歌"称为"花灯"。在北方各省、各地的秧歌风格各异，具有独特的地方色彩。如陕北秧歌、东北大秧歌、河北地秧歌、山东的胶州秧歌、海洋秧歌等等。有的地方把"高跷"[2]也称为"秧歌"。这种自娱性民间舞蹈形式，一般都是由生、旦、丑婆等行当组成。由一人持一伞（象征风调雨顺）领头，其他人有的手持扇子、手帕，有的手持鼓、棒、彩绸等，在锣鼓的伴奏下，随着统一的节拍[3]在街头边舞边走。在广场表演时，开始先跑"过场"[4]，然后是变换各种队形和图案，形成一种大型的集体舞。其间，穿插有两三个人的表演，舞蹈表演生动活泼，趣味横生。

河北地秧歌《跑驴》，是深受当地人们喜爱的传统节目。表现一对农民夫妇回娘家探亲，妻子怀抱婴

陕北秧歌

儿、骑着毛驴，丈夫手持小鞭，相伴同行。当小两口高高兴兴赶路之时，毛驴陷在泥塘里，小孩哭、毛驴叫、大人急。正在无奈之际，另一位农民前来帮助，两人前拉后推，终于将毛驴赶出了泥塘，充满了浓郁的生活气息和强烈的喜剧色彩。

陕北秧歌的动作特点是扭动的时候步伐稳健大方，两臂甩动较大，挺胸昂头，有时头部还很自豪地晃动一下，给人以健壮、豪迈、朴实之感。如著名的"安塞腰鼓"。陕北安塞地区的"腰鼓"有多种形式和不同的打法，时常是两个腰鼓队展开激烈的竞赛，比鼓点，比技巧，腾空跳跃，热烈奔放，气势雄壮，鼓声、喊声震动山川，这是一种力量、意志的象征。

词语注释

【1】浮雕：是雕塑与绘画结合的产物，在平面上雕出的凸起的艺术形象。

【2】高跷：民间舞蹈，表演者踩着有踏脚装置的木棍，边走边表演，也指表演高跷用的木棍。

【3】节拍：音乐的节奏。

【4】过场：一种用法是戏曲中角色上场后，不多停留，就穿过舞台从另一侧下场。另一种用法是戏剧中用来贯串前后情节的简短表演。

五、舞　狮

舞狮是中国优秀的民间艺术，每逢元宵佳节或集会庆典，民间都以舞狮前来助兴。这一习俗起源于三国时期，南北朝时开始流行，至今已有一千多年的历史。白居易《西凉伎》诗对舞狮有生动的描绘："西凉伎，西凉伎，假面胡人假狮子。刻木为头丝作尾，金镀眼睛银帖齿。奋迅毛衣摆双耳，如从流沙来万里。"

北 狮

诗中描述的是当时舞狮的情景。狮子在百姓心目中的位置仅次于龙，被当做雄伟、威猛与吉祥的象征，以此驱魔避邪。因此，在宫庙前面或栏杆、桥头等处都安置有石狮。各种形式的舞狮流传于大江南北，专用于节庆场合。

中国的舞狮主要分为北派和南派。北狮在长江以北较为流行；而南狮则是流行华南、南洋及海外。北方舞狮狮子在造型上和真狮相似，全身以金黄的颜色为主，舞狮的时候，表演者一人或二人全身被狮被遮盖，下身穿着与狮子同样颜色裤子，双脚穿花靴。引狮者扮成武士，手拿绣球，在京鼓[1]、京锣[2]的打击乐中表演。基本动作有跌扑、翻滚、跳跃、搔痒、踏彩球、蹬高台等，配合着活泼、灵巧、愉快、轻盈的步法，把狮子舞得惟妙惟肖。北狮充满了中国北方浓郁的民情，以及柔美多彩、艺术性极高的民间舞蹈技术。南方舞狮以广东一带最为著名，南狮外形与北狮不同，重在狮头。南狮的狮头造型小于北狮，头上画着五颜六色的图案，额头吊着镜子再挂上绣花球，眼睛安上玻璃珠，更显威武凶厉。狮身是染上图案的布，缀满珠线。表演者两脚着地，举着狮头起舞。舞狮时，一人舞狮头，一人舞狮尾，头尾互相配合，并且以不同的招式表演各种南派武功。有出洞、上山、巡山会狮、采青、入洞等表演方式。在广东，舞狮拜年成为春节的习俗，时常是用红纸包着赏金，摆设成一个阵形，舞狮者必须以智慧和高超的舞艺，头尾通力合作，才能最后拿到赏金。南狮的形象表演重在神似，如狮子漫步的姿态，戏水的欢悦，采食的犹豫和贪馋的形态，都能生动地表现出来。

词语注释

【1】京鼓：打击乐器，多为圆桶形或扁圆形，中间空，一面或两面蒙着皮革。

【2】京锣：打击乐器，用铜制成，形状像盘子，用槌敲打。

南 狮

第十二章　中国戏曲

一、京剧艺术

中国传统戏剧中最具代表性的戏剧是京剧。京剧的形成有160多年的历史，它并不是北京土生土长的戏曲。公元1790年为庆祝乾隆皇帝80岁大寿，徽班进京演出，以汉剧为基础，又融合了秦腔、昆曲[1]的某些曲调和表演方法，最后才形成了京剧。由于北京是全国政治、文化的中心，所以京剧形成以后，在全国广泛流行，并逐渐传播到了国外。京剧虽然诞生很晚，却后来居上，被称为“国剧”，是中华文化的一种象征和标志。

京剧《将相和》

京剧是由中华民族民间文学、音乐、舞蹈、美术综合而成的舞台表演艺术，包括唱、念、做、打四种门类。唱，要用京剧特有的唱腔来唱，包括声腔和唱词；念，也称道白[2]；“做”包括表演和小幅度[3]的舞蹈，有一整套程式，概括为五个字，即手、眼、身、法、步；“打”是指格斗和战争场面，包括大幅度的舞蹈和翻跟头[4]。如果把京剧的音乐、美术（包括化妆、脸谱[5]、舞台设计、布景绘制）、灯光、服装（刺绣工艺）、道具（工艺品制作）等等都包括在内，所涉及的中国艺术的门类就更多了。做一个京剧演员需要具备很多条件，京剧演员既要是

京剧《贵妃醉酒》

表演家，又要是歌唱家、舞蹈家，甚至武术、体育、杂技，都得会一些，所以，一个优秀的京剧演员，必须从幼年就进行培养训练。

京剧有生、旦、净、丑四个行当。生行包括老生、小生、武生。旦行分为老旦、正旦、花旦、闺门旦和刀马旦。净行（俗称花脸）主要表现性格豪爽、粗鲁、刚烈、忠直或者奸诈的男性，大致分为大花脸、二花脸、武花脸三个分支。大花脸以唱为主，说韵白，勾脸谱，多扮演朝廷重臣、元帅、大将等人物。二花脸又叫架子花脸，以做功为主。一般说韵白，主要表现身份较高但性格幽默的人物和草莽英雄、绿林好汉。武花脸主要以武打为主，很少开口说话。丑行是喜剧角色，最突出的特点，是用白色在鼻梁窝处勾画脸谱，俗称“小花脸”，与大花脸、二花脸相排列，又称“三花脸”。丑行分为文丑、武丑，其主要特点，一是胡子短而稀，为了突出人物的喜剧色彩；二是不穿厚底靴，大部分表现社会地位较低的人。

京剧服装、扮相[6]、表演等都有固定的程序。每种角色都依据人物性别、身份、年龄等特征，安排其表演程序、装扮、服饰。京剧表演比任何戏剧都具有更多的虚拟性和夸张性，充分展现了京剧艺术的主体是“人”这个核心。人物、场景、时间、地点全靠演员的表演做交代，如，出门、进门，道具中并没有门，而是靠演员的动作来拟做出门或进门状。演员手里拿着一支船桨，舞台就象征水面；演员手里拿着枪、剑，舞台就象征战场；演员手里拿着书，舞台就表示书房。舞台在人物的运动和制约下，既可以由虚到实，也可以由实到虚，调动观众的生活积累来补充虚拟的空间。京剧的剧本、表演、音乐、化妆、服装，直到舞台设计和处理，都是夸张的。京剧所有的形体动作，包括身段、手势、步法，甚至运用眼神，也是非常夸张化的。如京剧中指人的动作，把手指头放在胸前，从胸到左肩，向上画一道小的弧线，把手指先引向演员的左后方，然后再从左肩上向下画一条大的弧线，再指向右前方演员所要指的那个对象。在这同时，眼神要密切配合，随着手指转动，动作幅度很大，都很夸张。这样表演的目的是为了让观众看得更清楚，感觉更美。

词语注释

【1】昆曲：流行于江苏南部（南昆）及北京、河北（北昆）等地的地方戏曲剧种，用昆腔演唱。也叫昆剧。

【2】道白：戏曲中的说白。

【3】小幅度：演员在表演时，舞蹈化的形体动作所展开的宽度小。

【4】翻跟头：身体向下翻转而后恢复站立。

【5】脸谱：戏剧中脸部化妆的图案。

【6】扮相：扮演角色后的形象。

二、京剧四大名旦

京剧中的旦角是京剧女角色的统称。在中国封建社会，妇女被禁锢在家里，不可能上舞台，因此戏剧的旦角均由男人扮演。即使到了民国初年，新思想有所抬头，但社会风气依然比较闭塞，连有些话剧舞台上的女角，也是由男人扮演的。

在辛亥革命之前，京剧中老生[1]是主角，旦角处于次要地位，在戏中多为配角。20 世纪 20 年代初，梅兰芳、尚小云、程砚秋相继崛起，他们三人在京剧界已成“鼎足”之势。原为“梆子花旦”的荀慧生改演京剧也成为后起之秀。此后，“梅”“尚”“程”“荀”并驾齐驱，闻名于北京剧坛。随之，旦角的地位也发生了变化，逐渐成为京剧中的主角。

1927 年，北京举办京剧旦角名伶[2]评选，梅兰芳、尚小云、程砚秋、荀慧生荣获“四大名旦”称号。名旦的出现，大大提高了旦角的地位，对京剧的发展起了很大的作用。他们刻苦钻研艺术，在艺术上不断进取，表演、唱腔精益求精，各有独门剧目，创造了各具特色的旦角四大艺术流派。京剧界一致评价“四大名旦”的艺术特点为：梅派雍容华贵，富丽堂皇；尚派刚健挺拔，洒脱大方；程派清秀典雅，柔中带刚；荀派活泼秀丽，自然洒脱。

梅兰芳（公元 1894 年 ~ 1961 年）生于北京的梨园之家，8 岁学戏，9 岁拜名旦吴菱仙为师，10 岁登台表演，20 岁时去上海演出。由于他唱腔清亮甜美，吐字清晰，扮相俊美秀丽，舞姿美俏，表演细腻、典雅大方的表演风格初露锋芒，一场《穆柯寨》演出轰动上海，从此一举成名。

在中国京剧艺术发展史上，梅兰芳是承前启后、继往开来的一位表演艺术家。他对京剧艺术最大的贡献是以极大的魄力改革了传统戏。传统的京剧中，注重唱而很少表演，梅兰芳从昆剧和其他地方戏剧中汲取了营养，在京剧表演中设计了很多载歌载舞的新戏，并与王瑶卿等创造了一个新的“综合行当”——把青衣[3]、花旦和刀马旦[4]的表演特点融为一体的“花衫”，将京剧艺术推向了一个新的高峰。

梅兰芳不仅艺术精湛，而且品德高尚，一生谦虚平和、刚正不阿。抗日战争时期，在民族存亡的时刻，梅兰芳排演了许多鼓舞中国人民抗战救国的优秀剧目，如《抗金兵》《生死恨》等。同时，为了拒绝给敌伪演出，他闭门谢客，蓄须明志，卖画为生，直到抗战胜利后才剃须登台，表现了一个艺术家崇高的民族气节。

梅兰芳

梅兰芳还是第一个把京剧推向世界的人，增进了各国人民对中国戏曲的了解。他于 1919 年、1924 年、1956 年先后三次赴日本演出，使京剧在日本家喻户晓。1930 年，梅兰芳自费率京剧团赴美演出，一时间，京剧艺术风靡美国。此次访美是经过燕京大学校长司徒雷登的介绍，所以受到美国教育界的极大重视。梅兰芳成为沟通中美文化的使者，他所到之地，各大学教授、专家抱着研究东方文化、探讨中国古典艺术的目的前来观赏，并在美国报刊上撰文大加称赞。梅兰芳不以赢利为目的，多次出国演戏，就是要向海外弘扬中国文化艺术。在他坚持不懈的努力下，国际文艺界逐步认识到中国戏曲的绚丽多彩、博大精深，从而对中国戏曲刮目相看。梅派经典剧目有《贵妃醉酒》《霸王别姬》《生死恨》《穆桂英挂帅》等。

程砚秋

程砚秋（公元1904年~1958年），自幼学戏，18岁成名，演青衣，受业于梅兰芳。他在艺术上勇于革新创造，讲究音韵，注重四声，追求“声、情、美、水”的高度结合，并根据自己的嗓音特点，创造出一种起伏跌宕、若断若续、节奏多变的唱腔，形成独特的艺术风格，世称“程派”。程砚秋擅长演悲剧，大多表现封建社会妇女的悲惨命运。程派经典剧目有《文姬归汉》《荒山泪》《六月雪》《春闺梦》《英台抗婚》等。

尚小云（公元1900年~1976年），幼年入科班学艺，14岁被评为“第一童伶”[5]。初习武生[6]，后改正旦[7]，兼演刀马旦。1927年入选“四大名旦”时才28岁。他功底深厚，嗓音宽亮，大胆吸收武旦、武生的动作，形成了唱腔铿锵有力、节奏鲜明，表演刚劲挺拔、洒脱大方的表演风格，世称“尚派”。他在舞台上塑造了一批巾帼英雄和侠女烈妇的形象。尚派经典剧目有《汉明妃》《梁红玉》《乾坤福寿镜》《双阳公主》等。

尚小云

荀慧生

荀慧生（公元1900年~1968年），幼年在河北梆子班学艺，10岁改演京剧，扮演花旦、刀马旦。他功底深厚，能汲取梆子戏旦角艺术之长，与京剧花旦的表演结合起来，以丰富京剧的唱腔艺术；念白方面，创造出一种介于京白和韵白之间的念白，吐字清晰，具有特殊的表现力。在表演方面，突破了京剧旦行过于稳重的表演程式，擅长扮演天真、活泼、温柔的妇女角色，世称“荀派”。荀派经典剧目有《红娘》《红楼二尤》《勘玉钏》《钗头凤》等。

词语注释

【1】老生：老生又称须生。演员所戴的假胡子叫“髯口”。老生主要表现中年以上的男性角色。

【2】名伶：著名的戏曲演员。

【3】青衣：戏曲中年轻女子角色行当。“正旦”的别称。

【4】刀马旦：传统戏剧中旦角的一种。扮演精通武艺的女性角色。

【5】童伶：儿童戏曲演员。

【6】武生：擅长武艺的男性角色。

【7】正旦：戏曲角色行当，旦行的一支。即旦行里的正角，剧中的主要女性角色。

三、京剧脸谱艺术

整脸脸谱

京剧脸谱是为了完成角色的艺术造型，在演员面部化妆的一种特殊形式。用以象征角色的性格、品质、命运。京剧艺术的化妆，按照一定的格式要求来勾画脸上的图案，这种格式就叫做“脸谱”。

脸谱的起源，要追溯到中国古代的面具和涂面两种化妆方法。据说在一千多年前的唐朝，就有了戴着面具表演的大型歌舞，因为面具可以掩饰人的面貌，夸大五官部位，突出面部表情，但是，面具也有缺点，因为它是固定的，没有面目表情变化。所以，人们又逐渐将色彩直接涂画在脸部，用来表达人的喜、怒、哀、乐的感情，最后形成了脸谱。随着京剧艺术的兴起，清朝的同治、光绪年间，脸谱技艺基本上形成了一种固定的格式。

京剧脸谱，是一种图案化的化妆艺术。画法非常夸张，无论是五官部位和轮廓的夸张放大，还是使用浓重、强烈的色彩，都是根据某种性格、性情或某种特殊类型的人物而采用相应色彩。早期脸谱用色比较单调，一般是用黑、红、白三种对比强烈的颜色，后来逐渐发展到红、黑、蓝、黄、绿、白等色，随着京剧的不断丰富，又增加了粉、紫、灰和用于神怪脸的金、银色。红色的脸谱表示忠勇义烈的人物，如关羽。黑色的脸谱表示刚烈、正直、勇猛，甚至鲁莽的人物，如包公和张飞。黄色的脸谱表示凶狠残暴的人物；蓝色或绿色的脸谱表示刚强、粗犷、暴躁的人物；金色、银色基本上是用于神仙、妖怪一类的角色，如孙悟空。白色的脸谱表示奸诈、阴险的人物，如曹操和司马懿。

三块瓦脸脸谱

在京剧艺术中，脸谱一般用于净行[1]和丑行[2]，至于生、旦两种角色则只是描眉，脸部涂些红色而已。京剧的脸谱构图样式丰富多彩，主要分为“整脸”、三块瓦脸和歪脸三种：“整脸”就是用一种颜色为主，只把眉毛（眉子）部分用另一种颜色勾画清楚。如果是红的或白的脸谱，就画黑色的眉毛，如果是黑色脸谱，就画白色的眉毛，达到两种色彩的鲜明对比。例如，关羽就是红整脸，曹操是粉白整脸，包拯是黑整脸。三块瓦脸谱是脸部的主要颜色分割成三个区域，有一种主要颜色作为底色，额部和两颊还留着主要颜色，其他部位用黑色代替，成为三块瓦片形状，因此得名三块瓦。第三种是歪脸。即脸谱左右两边的图形不对称，眉毛是歪的，眼睛是斜的，五官挪位，看上去图案的形状扭曲不规则，以此表示两种意思，一是表示极其丑陋，更多的是表示一些品质恶劣的坏人。

丑角脸谱

丑角脸谱。在丑角的鼻梁上面画个白粉块，有的是元宝[3]形的，有的是倒元宝形的，有的是方块形的，也有的是枣核形的。所有的丑角脸谱，都只不过是花脸脸谱的缩小，变成一小块，以表现各种不同性格的人物。丑角的脸谱，即鼻梁上抹白粉的人物，不一定是坏人，是用来表示他与一般人物的性格不同。

词语注释

【1】净行：俗称花脸，又叫花面，脸上勾画脸谱，扮演男性角色。

【2】丑行：又叫小花脸或三花脸。丑行分为文丑和武丑两类。

【3】元宝：我国古钱币的一种名称。

四、京剧服饰

中国京剧的服装，是以明代日常生活的服装为基础，参照了宋、元服装的样子，同时吸收了清代服装的某些特点，经过历代艺术家的概括、提炼、美化形成的。京剧界把服装叫行头，是各种角色穿戴的服饰总称，包括长袍类、短衣类、铠甲类、盔帽类、靴鞋类，以及辅助性服装。京剧的服装比较复杂，各种角色都有专门的服饰，形成了一整套类型化，或者说程式化的专用服装。服装的基本分类是蟒袍、帔、靠、褶（xué）子、衣。蟒袍，是帝王将相等高贵身份的人物所通用的礼服，其长袍阔袖的服装造型，具有庄重感。帔，即对襟长袍。比起蟒袍来，它突破了“全封闭式”的服装造型，以“对襟”造成自由开合的宽松感，文雅清秀，既符合人物闲居的需要，又不失其华贵。靠，就是武将所通用的戎服。衣分两片，上衣下裳相连，静则赋予人物以威武气概，动则便于夸张舞蹈动作。褶子，即斜领长衫，是广泛使用的便服，平民及士人皆用之。衣，四类之外其他所有的剧装都称为衣。无论哪部戏，同一个角色用同样的服装。比如，一套皇帝的服装，在这个戏里皇帝能用，在另一出戏里皇帝也能用；秀才穿的服装，无论哪出戏里的秀才都能穿。

京剧服装一般情况下不受时代的约束。无论哪个朝代，都可以穿这套服装。比如穿皇帝服装的，无论是春秋战国戏里的诸侯之类的角色，还是宋朝、元朝、明朝的皇帝，所有这些不同朝代的帝王，在京剧舞台上所穿的服装基本都是一样的。只要能表现出他们的身份为帝王就够了，其他问题都由剧本设计的台词和演员的表演去解决。

京剧中各种角色的服饰都有具体的规定，如，长袍有红的、黄的、绿的、白的、黑的、紫的、粉的等。各种颜色都有各自特定的意义，哪一类人穿什么颜色，都有大致的规定。比如，凡是皇帝、国王一类角色都穿明黄袍；亲王、太子一类角色穿用是深黄、杏黄

▶▶ 靠

▶▶ 盔　帽

色的袍；红袍表示庄严端正的色彩，是地位仅次于皇帝的王侯将相角色穿用的；穿绿颜色的大都是武人；穿白袍的大都是少年英俊的人物；穿黑袍的一般是性格比较粗鲁、刚猛的角色，而且穿黑袍的多半是花脸，为了配合其脸谱，服装为黑色。

在京剧舞台上，武将作战时穿的铠甲叫做“靠”。演员穿上这身铠甲，也有个专用名称，叫做“披靠”。在靠背的背后绑着一个皮鞘，里面插着四面呈三角形的靠旗，这种带靠旗的叫做大靠，或叫做硬靠。一般武将都穿大靠，再插上四面靠旗，看上去显得特别威武、勇猛。靠旗只是一种装饰性的舞蹈工具，是为了渲染武将的威风，显示表演者的技巧。穿什么颜色的靠，与角色的扮相、脸谱、身份、年龄、性格都有一定的联系。有的是根据年龄和性格而穿，比如年龄较轻、英武俊秀的武将都穿白靠，而黑脸人物则都穿黑靠。

帽子当中最有代表性的是乌纱帽，简称为纱帽。纱帽是古代官员戴的一种帽子。其中以宰相戴的帽子，也叫相纱帽最为典型，两旁的长方形翅子长约30厘米，宽约3厘米，翅的尾巴略为向上翘起，实际就是两根黑漆的平板。还有一种纱帽两侧是桃形的尖翅，戴这种纱帽的人物，一般是一些贪婪、狡诈、凶残的官员。

▶▶ 靴

京剧演员的靴子底大约有6～12厘米厚，均刷成白色。在生活里没有这样厚底的鞋，在舞台上把靴底加厚，是一种艺术加工。其作用是增加演员的身高，以便与宽大的、夸张化了的服装谐调。

在京剧中，不但服装是夸张的、放大的，而且装饰品也是如此特别多。例如舞台上的玉带，松松大大，悬挂在官员礼服外边袍子上，不起腰带的作用，而只是一种饰品和道具。

五、秦腔、皮影

（一）秦　腔

秦腔是流行在西北地区陕西、甘肃、宁夏和新疆等地的古老剧种，因以枣木梆子为伴奏乐器所以也称梆子。它起源于明代陕西、甘肃一带的民间歌舞，经过历代民间艺人的创造逐渐形成。秦腔的传统剧目大多出自民间文人之手，题材广泛，内容丰富，主要以反映历史事件的剧目居多，表现民间生活、婚姻爱情的剧目也占有一定比例。

秦腔的角色，生旦净丑，行当齐全，有“十三门二十八类”之说。仅小生就分为雉尾生、纱帽生、贫生、武生、幼生等等，各类角色都有独特的风格。秦腔具有鲜明的地方特色，表演技艺质朴、粗犷、细腻、深刻、优美，以情动人，富有夸张性。生活气息浓厚，程式严谨，技巧丰富。身段[1]和特技有趟马[2]、吐火、吹火、喷火、翎子功[3]、水袖功[4]、扇子功[5]、顶灯、咬牙等等。

秦腔的脸谱讲究庄重、大方、干净、生动和美观，颜色以三原色为主，在人物性格上，表现为红忠、黑直、粉奸。脸谱格调主要表现为线条粗犷，笔调豪放，着色鲜明，对比强烈，浓眉大眼，图案壮丽，寓意明朗，性格突出，与音乐、表演的风格相一致。

秦腔至明清时期已大大盛行。当时村村有戏楼，

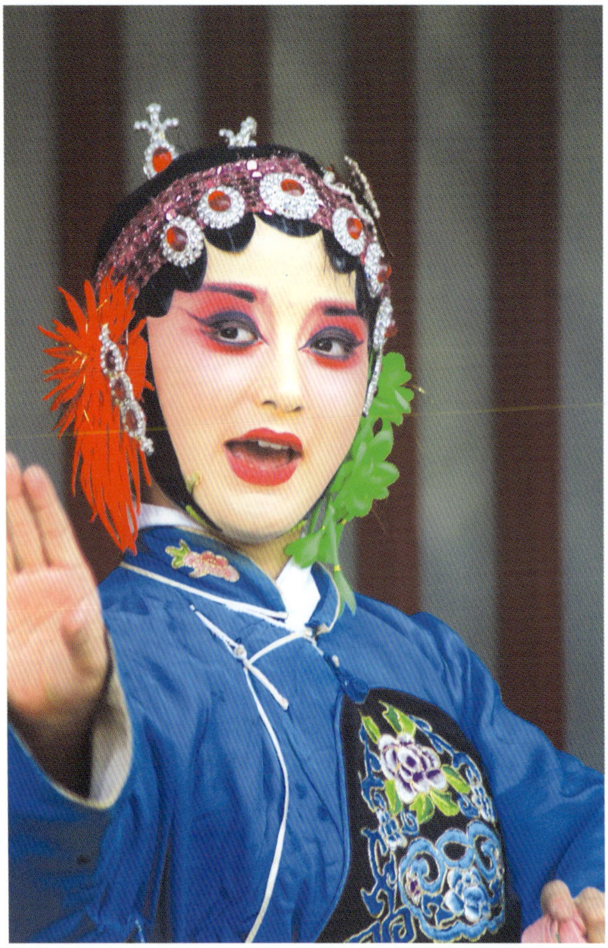

秦腔旦角

处处有庙会，逢会必有大戏演出，剧种以秦腔为主。据说公元1779年，著名的演员魏长生带秦腔入京，他的唱腔善于传情，生动感人，并在化妆、角色等方面让人耳目一新，因此名声大振，许多京城艺人改学秦腔，秦腔很快流传到山西、河北、河南、山东，甚至南方苏、浙、闽、川、云、贵等各地，因此秦腔成为各地梆子的始祖，如山西的四大梆子以及河北梆子。

（二）皮　影

“皮影”是对皮影戏和皮影戏人物（包括场面道具景物）制品的通用称谓。皮影戏是让观众通过白色布幕，用灯光照射驴皮、牛皮或纸板雕刻成的人物剪影以表演故事的戏剧。剧目、唱腔多与地方戏曲相互影响，由艺人一边操纵一边演唱，并配以音乐。而皮影戏中的人物剪影以及场面道具景物，通常是民间艺人用手工刀雕、彩绘而成的皮制品，故称之为皮影。

中国皮影戏已有一千多年的历史，至今仍在中国民间流行，它是戏剧和雕刻工艺的巧妙结合。皮影的制作体现了中国雕刻工艺的精湛，最初是用厚纸雕刻，后来采用驴皮或牛羊皮刮薄晒干，再进行雕刻，并施以彩绘。风格类似民间剪纸。皮影戏人物的手、腿等关节部位用线连缀在一起，能活动自如。好的皮影选用上等牛皮，经过刮、磨、洗、刻、着色等24道工序，手工雕刻3 000余刀而成。中国各种传统的图案常常出现在皮影人物服饰及道具中，如福禄寿[6]、五子夺魁[7]、麒麟（qílín）送子[8]、连生贵子[9]。为了配合戏剧的情节，皮影中还有彩绘精致的桌、椅、箱、柜及古朴的器皿等，各种服装、桌、凳图案刻镂得精美细致，令人赞叹。

皮影戏是中国出现最早的戏曲剧种之一，它的演出装备轻便，唱腔丰富优美，表演精彩动人，千百年来深受广大民众的喜爱，流传甚广。不仅如此，有不少地方戏曲剧种，就是从皮影戏唱腔中派生出来的。中国皮影戏所用的幕影演出原理，以及皮影戏的表演艺术手段，对近代电影的发明和现代电影美术片的发展也都产生过积极的影响。

皮影多见于北方农村以及四川、湖北、湖南等地，由于流行地区、演唱曲调和剪影原料不同而形成许多类别和剧种，以河北唐山一带的驴皮影和西北的牛皮影较为著名。其中，唐山皮影已发展成为具有精美的雕刻工艺、灵巧的操纵技巧和长于抒情的唱腔音乐的

皮影表演

皮影戏

综合艺术。

词语注释

【1】身段：戏曲名词。戏曲演员在舞台上表演的舞蹈化形体动作，如坐卧行走、上马下马等，均有一定的程式。

【2】趟马：戏曲表演程式，表现剧中人策马疾行。

【3】翎子功：翎子，戏曲中武将盔头上装饰的雉羽。作用在于加强表演的舞蹈性，表达剧中人物的感情。

【4】水袖功：戏剧表演特技之一。水袖是手势的延长和放大，演员利用水袖做出丰富的动作，夸张地表达人物的复杂表情和变化多端的心理活动。这种技艺叫做水袖功。

【5】扇子功：表演特技之一。扇子，是许多剧中特殊的舞蹈道具。基本动作大体有挥、转、托、夹、合、遮、扑、抖、抛等。通过这些动作的组合，配合身段，可以变化出各种舞姿，以表现人物情绪，刻画人物性格。以小生、花旦、闺门旦等使用最多。舞台上使用的扇子有大折扇、小折扇、团扇（宫扇）、羽扇、蒲扇、竹扇、鹅毛扇、芭蕉扇等。

【6】福禄寿：图案以“蝙蝠”“鹿”“寿星”图纹构成，蝙蝠喻福运；“鹿”被视为古代之瑞兽，以“鹿”与“禄”谐意，故寓“官禄”“俸禄”及“禄位”等。“禄”即古代官吏俸给之谓。“寿星”代表长寿。

【7】五子夺魁：吉祥图案。借历史上五个名人并列的习惯，画了五个童子争夺头盔（魁的谐音），以示子孙个个贤能，积极向上。满足旧时代人们渴望子孙争气，个个高升，光宗耀祖的心理。

【8】麒麟送子：传说中的麒麟是一种仁兽，能为人带来子嗣。

【9】连生贵子：吉祥图案。图中有莲花、桂花等。莲与“连”、桂与“贵”同音。莲蓬寓意连生，桂花寓意贵子。

第十三章　曲艺、杂技

一、相　声

相声起源于华北地区的民间说唱曲艺，以说、学、逗、唱[1]为主要艺术手段。相声语言幽默、诙谐，具有轻松、活泼、滑稽、风趣的特点，深受中国大众的喜爱。

所谓“说”，就是讲故事，还有说话和铺垫的方式。包括说灯谜[2]、对对联[3]、行酒令[4]、猜字意、绕口令[5]、俏皮话、反正话、笑话等等。“学”，学人言、鸟语和各种人物的音容笑貌、表情姿态，或学唱歌，跳舞。“逗”，制造笑料。甲、乙二人装成一客一主、一智一愚或一正一反来逗趣。“唱”，原指演唱太平歌词，是一种从属于相声的曲艺形式，大约形成于清代初叶，其曲调是从莲花落演变成的，流行于北京城区、郊区。它一直被作为相声的基本功，也是相声艺人招揽观众的主要手段之一，20 世纪 50 年代初渐渐消失，后来泛指演唱无伴奏的民间小调和地方戏曲。

相　声

相声的表演形式有三种，早期主要是一个人说的“单口相声”，类似于讲小笑话或幽默故事。后来出现了两个人合作表演的“对口相声”，其中一个人为甲方，称做“逗哏”[6]的，另一人为乙方，称做“捧哏”[7]的。“哏”指滑稽、逗人发笑的话或表情。“对口相声”的表演是在对话中制造笑料，给人启迪。另有一种三人或三人以上的多人表演的形式叫做“群口相声”，表演时一个人“逗”，多人“捧”。三种形式之中以“对口相声”的说演最为常见和普遍。

相声里引人发笑的言语段叫做“包袱”[8]，相声的主要艺术手段就是逗笑。因此没有情理之中、意料之外的语言“包袱”就不能称其为相声。一般说一段笑话，有一两个“包袱”就可以了。

相声艺术发展到今天，不仅在表演技巧上日益完善和丰富，而且涌现出一大批著名的相声表演艺术家，如已经故去的刘宝瑞、马三立、侯宝林等。

词语注释

【1】说学逗唱：相声的主要艺术手段，分说、学、逗、唱四个部分。

【2】灯谜：谜语的一种，将谜面贴于花灯上供人猜，故名。谜多着眼于文字意义，如一个字、一句诗、一种名称。

【3】对联：写在纸上、布上或刻在竹子上、木头上、柱子上的对偶语句。

【4】酒令：饮酒时助酒兴的一种游戏，根据酒令判断输赢，输了的人被罚饮酒。

【5】绕口令：也叫“急口令”“拗口令”，民间语言游戏。将声母、韵母或声调极易混同的字，组成反复、重叠、绕口、拗口的句子，要求一口气急速念出。

【6】逗哏：用滑稽有趣的话引人发笑（多指相声演员）。

【7】捧哏：相声表演时的配角，用话或表情动作来配合主角，逗人发笑。

【8】包袱：原指包裹用的布单，此处指相声等曲艺中的笑料。把笑料说出来叫抖包袱。

二、快板和快板书

快板，过去叫“数来宝”[1]，也叫“顺口溜”“流口辙”，是一种说唱故事的艺术形式，曲艺的一种，词儿要合辙押韵。唱时用竹板打拍子，不用舞台乐器伴奏，演员手拿两块板打拍即可。具有短小精悍、明快有力的特点。它是由旧艺人们沿街卖艺时，见景生情，口头即兴编词儿发展起来的。他们看见什么就说什么，擅长随编随唱，表述见解，抒发感情。从编演，到传唱，到后来进入小型游乐场所演出。快板原是单纯叙事的，没有故事情节，节奏较快。随着时代的发展，快板的内容增添了故事情节和人物形象以后，就形成快板书。

表演快板时用的竹板

快板艺术灵活多样，丰富多彩。快板的演出形式主要有一个人演唱和两个人对口演唱两种。对口还保留了“数来宝”的原名，也曾出现过三四个人演唱的“群口快板”和十几个人表演的“快板群”。有些地区还发展成用当地方言演唱的快板，如天津快板、山东快板、陕西快板等。

快板的语言具有节奏性强、生动流畅、通俗易懂、朗朗上口的特点，快板的句式以“七字句”为主，读起来要合辙押韵[2]。

1953年，天津市著名快板演员李润杰在快板的基础上，增添故事情节、塑造人物形象，创造了快板书，他表演的《半夜鸡叫》讲述了一个地主为了让雇工早起多干活，半夜偷学鸡叫的故事。

词语注释

【1】数来宝：曲艺的一种。流行于北方各地，一人或两人说唱，用竹板或系以铜铃的牛髀骨打拍。常用句式为可以断开的“三、三”六字句和“四、三”七字句，两句、四句或六句即可换韵。最初艺人沿街说唱，都是见景生情，即兴编词，后进入小型游乐场所演出，说唱内容有所变化。部分艺人演唱民间传说和历史故事，逐渐演变为快板书，与数来宝同时流行。

【2】合辙押韵：也作“压韵”。作诗词曲赋等韵文时在句末或联末用同韵的字相押，称为押韵。诗歌押韵，使作品声韵和谐，便于吟诵和记忆，具有节奏和声调美。旧时押韵，要求韵部相同或相通，也有少数变格。现代新诗押韵，不受古代韵书限制。

三、鼓 曲

（一）大 鼓

京韵大鼓

大鼓流行于中国的华北、东北等地区。一般用三弦伴奏，演员击鼓演唱。也有的不用乐器伴奏，只击鼓演唱。它是黄河流域的产物，盛行于清末，是从民歌小调发展变化来的。为什么起名为“大鼓”呢？大鼓是从农民的秧歌发展而来的，农民们有时敲着大鼓来引歌、送歌。秧歌鼓本来是很大的，后来参照和尚道士所用的扁鼓，把它改成小鼓了。

现在中国有二十几种大鼓，如西河大鼓、山东大鼓、京韵大鼓、乐亭大鼓、京东大鼓、奉调大鼓，以及东北、安徽、湖北、广西、胶东、淮南大鼓等。按乐器分有铁片大鼓、木板大鼓、梅花大鼓、梨花大鼓、清音大鼓等。

各地大鼓多由一人自击鼓、板，一至数人用三弦等乐器相伴奏，也有只用鼓、板为道具的。演出大多采取站唱形式，其唱词基本上为七字句和十字句。传统曲目题材很广泛，经常以历史战争故事和男女爱情故事为演唱内容。在唱腔上由于流行地区不同，也各自呈现出不同的风格，是民间颇为流行、很受欢迎的曲艺形式之一。

清末至20世纪40年代是鼓曲的黄金时代，当时在京、津两地，听鼓曲、看杂耍成为社会上一种主要的娱乐形式。20世纪30～40年代，北京民办电台里的鼓曲节目，约占整个节目的四分之三，市内的书馆、园子[1]遍地皆是。至于天桥、鼓楼、各大庙会的场子，更是以演唱鼓曲为主要形式。民间给老人办生日，给小孩办满月，往往也多是办场大鼓“堂会[2]”，来招待祝贺的亲友。

（二）弹 词

弹词，也叫“南词”。弹词盛行于中国南方。一般是由两个人用方言弹唱，一人弹三弦一人弹琵琶，有说有唱，称为双档。也有一个人自弹自唱的。

苏州弹词和扬州弹词，演出形式完全相同。书词中的散文部分，用“说”来表现；叙述和描写故事中人物的行为、思想和活动环境，称为“表”；人物语言叫“白”；书词中以七字句为主的韵文[3]，用三弦、琵琶自弹自唱，相互伴奏，称“唱”和“弹”；在故事中穿插喜剧因素，称做“噱”[4]；演员模仿故事中人物的表情、语言、语调及某些动作，称“演”或“学”，也称“做”。

清代初年，随着江苏城市经济的繁荣，弹词在扬州、苏州已经盛行。弹词的演出地域，南不出浙江嘉兴，西不过常州，北不越常熟[5]，东也超不过松江。地域小、艺人多，听众要求不一，迫使艺人在新书、新腔、新表演风格等方面进行各种探索，所以弹词在创腔上流派很多，各有特色。著名的弹词艺人杨振雄、

弹 词

杨振言兄弟二人，自小家境清寒，很小就学艺，数十年来配合默契，形成了杨派双档[6]艺术特有的风格，饮誉江、浙、沪。两人创作了长篇弹词《武松》和《西厢》[7]。演唱《武松》时粗声大气，顿挫分明；说《西厢》却是细声低吟，娓娓道来，表演女角色楚楚动人，令人折服。这两部风格反差极大的书词，均

取得了良好的艺术效果，反映了他们非凡的艺术功底。在1985年至1988年期间，杨振雄、杨振言分别接受了上海大学、加拿大多伦多大学的邀请，登上了高等学府的讲坛，讲解评弹艺术的特色、语言、文学特征，使在场的大学生和国内外文艺界人士惊叹不已。昔日被称为“开口艺人”的弹词艺人，如今走上了大学讲坛，一时传为佳话。

（三）单　弦

单弦是中国北方的一种曲艺形式，伴奏的乐器是三弦。主要表演方式是一弹一唱，采集民歌小调来演唱，通俗易懂。单弦演唱者手持的乐器叫做八角鼓，是一种打击乐[8]。

单　弦

单弦来源于清朝中期流行的一些俗曲。乾隆年间，由于满族军队士兵的军旅生活比较单调，他们就借单弦抒发孤寂情感，或者表达打胜仗之后的喜悦。满族统一中国后，单弦由军队流传到社会当中，后来出现了一系列的单弦票友[9]，基本全是八旗[10]子弟，这些人衣食无忧，把单弦作为自己的业余爱好，慢慢将它继承下来，开始在各种场合演唱、自娱自乐，在宫廷里也有演唱。后来，八旗子弟落魄，在票友当中产生出一些专业的演出者，他们不同于业余爱好者，把唱单弦作为一种职业。

一般唱单弦就是讲一个故事，多是传统故事，如宝玉探晴雯[11]、张生戏莺莺[12]和青蛇、白蛇的故事等。单弦采取以说为主、说唱结合的曲艺形式，很适合大众的口味，迅速在河北、山东等地流传开来，成为北方的曲艺形式之一。

（四）二人转

“二人转”最初是农民的“庄稼耍”，演唱时，一人耍扇子，一人耍手绢，边耍边舞边唱，音乐性和动作性都比较强。“二人转”通常由一男一女扮作一旦一丑，虽然化妆，却仍以演唱者的身份叙述故事，模拟角色。

二人转

东北“二人转”也叫“蹦蹦”，产生并盛行于东北三省（辽宁、吉林、黑龙江），受到东北群众，特别是广大农民的喜爱。它是一种有说有唱、载歌载舞、生动活泼的走唱类曲艺形式。唱本语言通俗易懂，幽默风趣，生活气息浓厚、富有地方特色。它的音乐唱腔是以东北民歌、大秧歌为基础，吸收了东北大鼓等曲调，亲切动听。舞蹈动作来自东北大秧歌，并吸收了民间舞蹈和武打成分，以及耍扇子、耍手绢等技巧。总之，“二人转”的表演特点最能体现东北劳动人民对艺术美的追求。

东北“二人转”迄今大约已有200年的历史。早期没有女演员，女子角色全部由男扮女装。上个世纪50年代，女演员开始出现并逐渐增多，“二人转”的演出基本结束了男扮女装的历史，男女开始分腔。早期演唱的曲目多是传统的爱情故事，近几十年来，又有大批新创作的反映群众生活的曲目，曲种建设取得了长足的进展，并开始成为东北地方戏的主要曲种之一。近几年，在著名演员赵本山的带动下，从东北到关内到处有“刘老根大舞台”，专场演出的“二人转”，受到越来越多人的喜欢和关注，“二人转”进入了最佳的发展时机。

词语注释

【1】园子：剧院。

【2】堂会：旧时的富贵人家每逢喜庆的日子邀艺人来家里演出。
【3】韵文：与“散文”相对。泛指用韵的文体，如歌谣、辞赋、诗、词、曲以及有韵的其他文体。
【4】噱：笑。
【5】常熟：在江苏省南部，北临长江。为中国历史文化城。
【6】双档：双档是苏州评弹的专有名词，台上坐于右侧者说书的称为“上手”，操三弦；坐于左侧者为“下手”是配角，弹琵琶；如此二人合演谓“双档”。
【7】《西厢》：全名《崔莺莺待月西厢记》，杂剧剧本，元代王实甫作。故事出于唐代元稹《莺莺传》传奇。叙述唐代书生张生在蒲东普救寺与崔相国之女莺莺相遇，产生爱情，经侍女红娘从中帮助，终于冲破封建礼教的束缚而结合。剧本以刻画人物性格和心理活动见长。明清以来，戏曲、曲艺多有改编。
【8】打击乐：凡用打击方式发声的乐器（弦乐器除外）统称为打击乐（器）。戏曲中称为武场。 京剧打击乐以鼓板（檀板与单皮鼓）、大锣、铙钹、小锣四大件乐器为主。
【9】票友：戏曲、曲艺界对业余戏曲、曲艺演员的一种称谓。
【10】八旗：清代满族户口以军籍编制，分正黄、正白、正红、正蓝、镶黄、镶白、镶红、镶蓝八旗。正白、正黄、镶黄为上三旗（亦称内府三旗），隶属亲军，其余五旗为下五旗。清初将归附之蒙古、汉人，又编为蒙古八旗和汉军八旗。
【11】宝玉探晴雯：小说《红楼梦》中的一个情节，表现贵族公子对自己丫鬟的同情和爱怜。
【12】张生戏莺莺：元杂剧《西厢记》中的主要情节，表现公子和小姐一见钟情的爱情故事。

四、评　书

流行于中国北方地区的评书艺术，大约形成于清代初期，也称评词，评书的特点是只说不唱，由一个演员讲故事，是口头说讲的表演形式。形成于北京，流行于北京、天津及河北、辽宁、吉林、黑龙江等地。

早先评书是坐着说的，所用的道具有三件：醒木（长方形的小硬木块，尺寸不一，一般长约一寸，宽约半寸）、扇子、手帕。醒木一般用在开头、结尾，用以吸引观众的注意力，渲染气氛。在讲述中间的紧要关头，又常常用它制造声势，强调一些惊心动魄的重要情节。扇子用来象征性地表现棍、马鞭之类，而手帕则帮助演员塑造妇女形象等等，同时这两件物品也是演员扇风、擦汗的辅助用具。

评书这种艺术形式一无布景，二无伴奏，也不论剧场、舞台，在什么地方都可以表演。全凭一个演员的说话来吸引听众，这就要求演员必须将故事讲得有声有色，所以评书演员对故事往往要经过自己的加工。

传统书目以历史故事和武侠故事为主，这些故事一种来自师承关系，即由师傅教授给徒弟，另外一种是艺人自己在文学著作的基础上创作的，如《岳飞传》[1]《杨家将》《穆桂英挂帅》等小说都是评书的内容。

评书一般都用普通话讲述，也有使用地方方言的，如四川评书、湖北评书、山东评书等。 著名的评书表演艺术家连阔如（公元1903年～1971年）说书时语重声洪，自成风格，在评讲方面见识独到，胜人一筹。他擅长的书目有《东汉演义》[2]《三国演义》等。他生前经常在广播电台播讲，誉满京都，曾有“千家万户听评书，净街净巷连阔如”的赞语。

鞍山市曲艺团女演员刘兰芳说的评书《岳飞传》，热情真挚地歌颂民族英雄岳飞，无情地鞭挞奸臣秦桧[3]（Huì）等败类，做到了老书新说、旧书新评，爱听众之所爱，恨听众之所恨，受到了亿万听众的欢迎。一个演员、一块醒木、一把扇子，就产生了“全凭一张口，满台风雷吼”的艺术魅力。

词语注释

【1】岳飞：南宋抗金名将。是中国人民崇尚的爱国主义的光辉形象。

【2】《东汉演义》：历史小说，明代谢诏作。

【3】秦桧：南宋奸臣，曾网罗罪名杀害岳飞等爱国将领，遭到世人的唾弃。

五、吴桥杂技

吴桥是中国著名的“杂技之乡”。

吴桥杂技历史悠久。1958 年在吴桥县小马厂村发现一座南北朝东魏时期（公元 534 至 550 年）古墓。古墓的壁画上对杂技艺术做了生动形象的描绘。其中倒立、肚顶、马术、蝎子爬等杂技表演极为精湛。

吴桥杂技在全国享有盛誉是在元朝（公元 1206 年 ~ 1368 年）以后。杂技艺术在吴桥有着广泛的群众基础，几乎村村都有杂技艺人。一些家庭全家从事马戏表演，吴桥流传着“上至九十九，下至刚会走，吴桥要马戏，人人有一手”的民谣。

历史上杂技艺人大多靠流浪街头卖艺，或参加庙会表演，后来人们在吴桥县建立了一个很大的杂技大棚，相传有五百年的历史，杂技艺人们开始了规模较大的登台表演。每逢佳节即掌灯三日，放烟火、表演杂技。

吴桥杂技中有驯兽、特技、高空表演等几大项。驯兽是传统节目，包括猴、羊、虎、熊、马、蛇等，其中最精彩的是马术。它起源于唐朝，兴盛于清朝末年，演员经过长时间的训练，能在飞跑的马上表演倒立、站立、横侧，表演各种翻身动作，扣人心弦。特技表演包括“转碟子”“蹬大缸”“顶碗”“车技”等。在这些节目中，演员通常使用日常生活用具，这说明吴桥杂技从一开始就与群众的生活有着不可分割的关系。“蹬大缸”是演员用双腿把 120 多千克重的大缸蹬起，缸内再坐 1 人，足有 200 多千克，仍能旋转自如。高空表演有叠椅子、走钢丝、打秋千等节目。最为壮观的是 100 匹形体高大矫健、毛色光亮美观的骏马，踏着音乐欢腾舞蹈，步伐整齐，令人惊叹。

在吴桥境内，无论城镇乡村、田间地头、家庭院落，也无论年龄大小、性别差异，到处都有人在练习杂技。正是由于这种群众性的活动，使吴桥杂技在中国久盛不衰。吴桥县向全国输送了很多杂技艺人，中国大的杂技团几乎都有吴桥籍艺人，因此民间流传有“没有吴桥人不成杂技班”的说法。目前，世界上至少有近 20 个国家的杂技团体里有吴桥籍杂技艺人。

1987 年，中华人民共和国文化部在石家庄举办了以吴桥命名的第一届“中国吴桥杂技艺术节”，至今已成功地举办了五届，使吴桥成为继巴黎、摩纳哥之后的世界第三大国际杂技赛场。

吴桥马术

第十四章 中医文化

一、阴阳五行与医学

阴阳五行学说在先秦产生以后，经历了一个相当长的历程得以完善，最完整的体系形式要在《黄帝内经》中才真正见到。阴阳五行学说，是中国早期的朴素的唯物辩证法，也是中医学的基础理论。

阴阳五行学说中的阴阳，是中国古代哲学的一对范畴。最初的含义是指日光的向背，向日为阳，背日为阴，后来引申为气候的寒暖，方位的上下、左右、内外，运动状态的动、静等。一切事物或现象都有阴阳的对立和消长，这是宇宙自然界的基本规律。

阴和阳的相对属性引入医学领域，将对于人体具有推动、温煦、兴奋等作用的物质和功能，归纳于阳；对于人体具有凝聚、滋润、抑制等作用的物质和功能，归纳于阴。中医学就是运用阴阳的对立制约、互根互用、消长平衡和相互转化四个方面来说明人体的生理活动、病理变化，并用以指导临床的诊断和治疗。由于疾病的发生、发展和变化的内在原因是阴阳失调，所以任何疾病尽管其临床表现错综复杂，千变万化，但都可用阴阳为纲来加以辨析概括。故《黄帝内经 · 素问 · 第五》说："善诊者，察色按脉，先别阴阳"。

应该指出，"五行"与"阴阳"的观念不是同步的。"五行"学说的提出要早于"阴阳"学说与"气"的概念。有了"气"的概念之后，才有了"阴阳"与"五行"之间的沟通。"阴阳"与"气"的结合，大大有利于"道——气"学说向自然科学方面倾斜，大大有利于医学理论取阴阳五行学说作骨架。

五行学说，即是用木、火、土、金、水五个哲学范畴来概括客观世界中的不同事物属性，并用五行相生相克的动态模式来说明事物间的相互联系和转化规律。中医学应用五行学说，主要在于运用五行的属性归类，以及生克、制化、胜复、乘侮等规律，来概括脏腑组织器官的功能属性，阐释五脏[1]六腑[2]系统相互联系的内在规律，并说明人体与自然界某些关系，特别是阐明人体脏腑[3]系统结构医学模式，对于促进中医学理论体系的发展及应用，指导中医临床的病证分析、诊断和治疗，则更具有深远的意义。

我国古代医学家，在长期医疗实践的基础上，将阴阳五行学说广泛地运用于医学领域，以"气"为人体的基本生理物质，化而为血、为精，所主持的人体正常生理功能活动为神。以"气"承载的四时阴阳与五行的运行规律，用以说明人类生命起源、生理现象、病理变化，指导着临床的诊断和防治，成为中医理论的重要组成部分，对中医学理论体系的形成和发展，有着极为深刻的影响。

词语注释

【1】五脏：指心、肝、脾、肺、肾。

【2】六腑：指大肠、小肠、胃、胆、膀胱、三焦。

【3】脏腑：中医总称人体内部的器官。

二、《黄帝内经》

《黄帝内经》是中医学的瑰宝，是预防、保健、护理、生理、病理、病原、针灸、药治、医疗方法之开端，是古代一部内容最丰富、影响最深远的中医典籍。简称《内经》，主要部分形成于战国时期，汉代略有补缀，是无数医学家共同劳动创造的结晶。由于中国人历来把黄帝氏族当做中华民族的祖先，因此将此书名冠以“黄帝”的名字。

《黄帝内经》

现今流传的《内经》，包括《素问》[1]和《灵枢》[2]两大部分。书中记述采取一问一答的形式。《素问》主要论述了自然界变化的规律、人与自然的关系等。《灵枢》的核心内容为脏腑经络学说。在《黄帝内经》中，注重整体和谐的观念，既强调人体本身是一个整体，又强调人与自然之间的密切关系，并运用阴阳五行学说解释生理、病理现象，指导诊断与治疗。

中国医学的基本理论，早在《黄帝内经》一书中就奠定了。包括道、气、形、神学说，天人关系学说，阴阳五行学说等，阴阳学说是《内经》阐述人体生理、病理、疾病、诊断、防治和养生等的重要理论，贯穿在各个方面。以五脏为中心，把六腑、五气、五神、五志、五体、五味、五色、五音、五声等构建成五脏系统，形成一个表里相依、内外相关的整体。在这个整体系统中，经络[3]是沟通表里、联络脏腑的渠道，精气神是维护和主宰这个系统的中流砥柱。中医学要求“四诊”——望诊、闻诊、问诊、切诊，《内经》最早对这“四诊”进行了详细的论述。《内经》还记载了多种病证，尤其对热病、疟（nüè）病[4]、咳嗽、风病、痹（bì）病[5]等病证的病因、病理、临床表现和治疗方法做了专题讨论，许多内容和观点至今仍然是临床实践所必须遵循的原则。

《内经》中丰富的医学理论，对中医临床工作有较大的指导作用，如果读通了《内经》，可以拓宽临证思路，提高辨证施治[6]水平。书中所体现的整体观、物质观、运动变化和防治等思想，具有朴素的唯物主义倾向和辨证观点，在中国医学上具有重要的地位。

《内经》中的很多篇章又是优秀的文学作品，所以，人们还可以把《内经》当做文学作品来阅读，借以提高文学素养。

词语注释

【1】《素问》：《黄帝内经》共十八卷，其中九卷名《素问》，今本二十四卷，载八十一篇。其中最主要的内容，是阴阳五行、五运六气、脏腑、经络、病机、病症、诊法、辨证、治则、针灸、方药、摄生十二个方面。

【2】《灵枢》：《黄帝内经》中的九卷名，又称《九卷》或《针经》等。

【3】经络：中医指人体里气血运行的通路。

【4】疟病：一种按时发冷发热的传染病，是由疟蚊把疟原虫传染到人的血液里而引起的。

【5】痹病：中医指风、寒、湿等引起的肢体疼痛或麻木的病。

【6】辨证施治：中医指根据病人的发病原因、症状、脉象等，结合中医理论，全面分析、作出判断，进行治疗。

三、神医华佗

▶▶ 华　佗

在中国，华佗是带有神话色彩的医生，其实，他是东汉末年的一位著名医学家，沛国谯（今安徽亳县）人。约生于汉永嘉元年（公元 145 年），逝于建安十三年（公元 208 年）。华佗自幼刻苦钻研医学，对内科、外科、妇科、儿科都很精通，尤其擅长外科，被称为“外科鼻祖”。

华佗生活在社会动荡、瘟疫流行的年代。他从小就立志要以医济世，为民众解除病苦。华佗行医的脚步遍及现在的安徽、江苏、山东、河南的一些地区，医术高明,深受群众的爱戴和推崇。他善于察声观色，根据病人的面目、形色、病状来判断疾病的轻重和如何治疗。据史料记载，有一位叫陈登的患者，胸中烦闷，面色发红，食欲不振。经过诊断，华佗说他肚内有虫，就给他配了些药让他喝下去，不久，这位患者果然排出许多寄生虫来。还有一位官员，患病已很长时间了，华佗诊断后认为，只有在盛怒之下，才能消除病人胸中的郁积，刺激他生气才能治好他的病，所以，华佗故意留下一封信骂这位官员，自己匆匆离去。这位官员读了信大怒，立即派人追杀华佗，但是没有追上，更加觉得气愤，不由吐出许多黑血，病一下子就好了。

由于华佗医术精湛，各地的病人都来请他看病。当时统治中国北部的曹操与华佗是同乡。他长期患头痛，每次发作，头昏目眩，许多大夫用尽各种办法治疗也不见效。后来，曹操把华佗请到许昌去给他治疗，华佗详细诊察病症以后，在曹操背上扎了一针，头痛立刻止住了。于是，曹操便打算留华佗在身边做侍医。但不久，华佗借故夫人有病，请假回家不归，曹操屡次催促，华佗仍然不返。于是，曹操一怒之下，派人把华佗抓进监狱，最后杀害了他。华佗死后，人们怀念他，在他行过医的许多地方建起了“华祖庙”。

华佗最大的成就是在外科方面。他发明了“麻沸散”，病人服用后会失去知觉，接受大的手术也不感觉痛苦。早在一千七百多年前，华佗就用这种麻醉剂成功地使病人全身麻醉,施行腹部外科手术。可惜“麻沸散”的药方早已失传了。

华佗也是中国体育疗法的创始人。两千多年前，华佗就已提倡用体育锻炼的方法来防治疾病，以达到延年益寿的目的。他发明了“五禽戏”（也称“五禽操”），一种仿生健身术，由模仿虎、鹿、熊、猿、鸟五种禽兽的神态和动作组成，每一禽戏由若干动作组成套路，将导引术与五行、脏象、气血、经络等学说相结合，以便活动筋骨、疏通气血，增强体质、防治疾病。“五禽戏”流传很广，深受人们的欢迎。

四、张仲景与《伤寒论》

张仲景，南阳郡涅阳（今河南南阳）人。大约生活在公元 150 年至 219 年之间。他从小读过许多书，在史书中读到扁鹊望诊齐桓侯的故事，对扁鹊高超的医道很是钦佩，从此对医学发生了浓厚的兴趣。后来，他跟随同族的张伯祖行医，学到许多医学知识和医术，“乃勤求古训，博采众方，撰用《素问》《九卷》《八十一难》《阴阳大论》《胎胪药录》并平脉辨证，为《伤寒杂病论》合十六卷”。其内容包括伤寒和杂病两部分，约成书于东汉末年（公元 200 年～210 年）。张仲景长期从事医学实践，既有临床经验又注重理论总结，终于成为当时最著名的临证医学家。

张仲景对医学的最大贡献就是通过对伤寒病治疗的科学总结，写成的《伤寒杂病论》一书。原书经历战乱而散佚，经过后世医家的整理，成为今本《伤寒论》和《金匮要略》二书。其中，《伤寒论》是专门论述急性热病治疗的著作，提出 397 法，113 方；《金匮要略》是主要论述杂病证治的专著，计 25 篇，载方 262 首。

《伤寒论》与《金匮要略》二书记载的方剂、用药，对药物的加工与使用，方剂的配置与变化都有很细致的要求。张仲景对外感热病与杂病的认识和临证治疗的指导思想与方法，被后世人概括为辨证论治体系，影响了中医学历史差不多两千年，对后世医学的发展产生了巨大的影响。他的《伤寒论》标志着中医辨证施治原则的基本确立。这是中医学的一大特色，后代尊他为“医圣”。一千七百多年来，《伤寒论》所确立的辨证论治的原则，始终指导着后世历代医学家。自宋以后，官办医学校还将它列为学生必读教材。后代医家对此书的研究，更为盛行，出现许多注释，阐发《伤寒论》的专著。后人为了纪念张仲景，在各地修建祠堂祭祀他。最著名的是河南南阳的“医圣祠”，现在被列为省级文物保护单位。分布各地的名医祠堂中都供有张仲景的塑像，反映了中国民间对张仲景的崇敬与缅怀。

张仲景

五、李时珍与《本草纲目》

李时珍

公元 1518 年，李时珍出生在蕲州（今湖北蕲春）。李家世代行医。李时珍童年时期，身体孱弱，曾患胸结核病，是医术高明的父亲挽救了他。李时珍从小就对医学感兴趣。他时常跟着父亲上山采药或给人看病。

李时珍是个好学的人，认真钻研过《内经》《神农本草经》《伤寒论》和《金匮要略》等古代医书，还经常向父亲请教各种疑难问题。

“本草”指的就是中药。中药的内容丰富，种类繁多，许多鸟兽虫鱼、金石草木，都可以入药。其中以草木类植物药占多数，所以中药被称为“本草”；凡是讲药物的书也都以“本草”命名。当时流行的“本草”书是汉代的《神农本草经》，这本书总结了秦汉以前中国人研究药物的成果，记载了 365 种药物。但是，到了明朝时，“本草学”早就有了大发展，人们掌握可治病的药物逐渐增多，分类日益严密。尤其在民间，世代流传着许多单方、验方，汉代的《神农本草经》已经不能反映新的医学成就了。于是，年轻的李时珍下决心编写一部全面总结明代以前医药学成果的巨著，即新的《本草》。

李时珍经常肩背药囊，手持刀剪锄镰，上山采药，蕲州一带的土地几乎被他踏遍了。他在家里开辟了一个小药圃，种了麦冬、蓝草、益母草、金银花以及从山上移植来的多种药物。后来，为了采集新药，李时珍干脆离开家乡，长途跋涉，足迹遍及大江南北，并访问了渔夫、猎户、樵夫、农民和药户，虚心向他们请教，收集民间偏方，采集药物标本。经过三十多年的不懈努力，公元1578年，李时珍终于完成了举世闻名的《本草纲目》。这一年他已经是60岁的老人了。

《本草纲目》共五十二卷，内容极为丰富，载入药方11 096首，并附药物形态图1 127幅。还详细地介绍了各种药的性、味、产地和栽培方法，以及方剂配伍。这部巨著是中国医药学宝库中的一份珍贵的文化遗产。

在《本草纲目》开始刻印的第二年，李时珍躺在了病榻上，切盼能亲眼看到这部书流传于世，但终未能如愿。公元1593年（明万历二十一年），76岁高龄的李时珍离开了人间。他去世三年后，即公元1596年，《本草纲目》一书才正式印行，即人们经常称道的金陵（南京）版，是《本草纲目》的最早版本。后来，这部书很快流传到国外，被陆续翻译成日文、英文、德文、法文、拉丁文、俄文等多种文字，成为世界医学史上的一部巨著。

六、望闻问切

中医在长期的医疗实践中，总结出了四种论断疾病的方法，这就是望、闻、问、切，合称“四诊”，这是中国传统医学体系中最基本、最重要的诊断术。

中医四诊建立在整体医治理论基础上，认为气血运行，感应传导，能传递病邪。反映病变的通路是经络，经络具有联络脏腑肢节、沟通上下内外的功能，联结成一个统一的整体，所以局部的变化通过经络可以影响全身，内脏的病变可以反映到体表，所谓“有诸内必形诸外”，相反，通过局部病变可以判断周身，内脏的病变能从五官、肢体、体表等各个方面反映出来，通过四诊而诊察疾病各个方面的征象，就可以了解疾病的原因、部位、性质和内在联系等，从而为辨证医治提供依据。这就是中医诊断疾病的理据。

切　脉

望、闻、问、切虽然排名有先后，尽管历代医学术士都强调“四诊合参”，然而在实际应用中，则比较偏重望诊和切诊。

望诊就是大夫运用视觉来观察病人全身或局部的神、色、形、态的变化。被列为四诊之首，内容包括望神气、望面色、望形态、望头颈、望五官、望皮肤、望脉络、望排出物等。但历来望诊的重点是望面色和舌诊，认为面、舌的各种表现，可以在相当程度上反映出脏腑功能的变化。

闻诊是医生运用自己的听觉和嗅觉，通过对病人发出的声音和体内排泄物散发的各种气味推断疾病的诊法。其内容一是听言语、呼吸、咳嗽、呕吐的声音，根据声音的变化，诊察与发音有关器官的病变；二是嗅气味，包括嗅病人的口气、分泌物、排泄物的异常气味，诊察人体脏腑、气血、津液产生的败气。

问诊，包括询问发病的时间、原因、经过、病史、家族史、病痛所在，以及生活习惯、饮食爱好等。在明代，从理论的角度扩大了问诊范围，总结为“十问”。即问寒热、汗、头身、便、饮食、胸、聋、渴、旧病、病因，用来区分阴阳、表里、寒热、虚实，成为辨证治疗的重要依据。

切诊，分为按诊和脉诊。按诊即按压或触摸病人身体的某些部位，以便了解局部疾病之所在。脉诊又称为切脉，是通过按压脉象的变化来了解体内病变的切诊方法。脉诊在四诊中成熟最晚，但最为常用，甚至成为中医的特征形象，中医认为全身血管四通八达，密布全身，在心肺作用下循环周身，只要人体任何地方发生病变，就会影响气血的变化而从脉上显示出来，中医通过诊脉也可以了解全身气血的情况。医家常常将脉诊列为四诊之首。

传统中医采用望、闻、问、切四种方法诊察疾病，这不仅在古代是十分先进的方法，即使在现代化检查手段迅速发展的今天，这四诊也很有实用价值。其中有些内容，如望舌、切脉等，是无法用科学仪器所替代的，充分体现了中医的特色。

七、针灸铜人

历史上最早的测定人体解剖部位及经脉穴道用的针灸铜人，于宋仁宗天圣五年（公元 1027 年）十月由医官院[1]铸成。它对中国医学教育有着重大的历史和现实意义，开创了世界针灸教学应用针灸铜人作为人体模型的先河。

针灸是中国医学的重要组成部分，至今已有几千年的历史。北宋以前，医生主要按照唐代《皇帝明堂经》指定的人体经穴进行针灸治病。然而《皇帝明堂经》因唐朝末年的战乱佚失，致使后来的针灸取穴失去了标准。为给针灸经穴重新制定国家标准，公元 1026 年，宋代著名的医学家王惟一开始组织校订古代针灸学的著作。不久，他就完成了新的针灸经穴国家标准——《新铸铜人腧穴针灸图经》。宋仁宗认为光有医书不够，还应该有实验道具，于是下令医官院“创铸铜人为式”。1027 年，两尊针灸铜人铸成了。针灸铜人铸成时正值宋天圣五年，所以这两尊铜人又被称为宋天圣针灸铜人。

针灸铜人身长共 173 厘米左右，造型为强壮的青年男子，姿势为直立裸体像。整个铜人的全身，被铸成前后两部分，利用特制的插头可以进行拆卸组合，体现了当时高水平的人体美学和铸造工艺。铜人标有 354 个穴位名称，所有穴位都凿穿小孔。胸腹腔可以揭开，内有木制的脏腑模型，与真人一样。全身的经络和穴位位置的名称均经过严谨核对。

为了测验应试学生的针刺技术，王惟一在铜人身上涂上一层黄蜡，把刻在上面的穴位全部遮住，同时，体腔内注满水或水银，测验学生对穴位的掌握。学生用针在铜人身上刺，只要刺深了或略微偏斜，水或水银就会随针流出。这是严格训练针刺技术的好办法。此

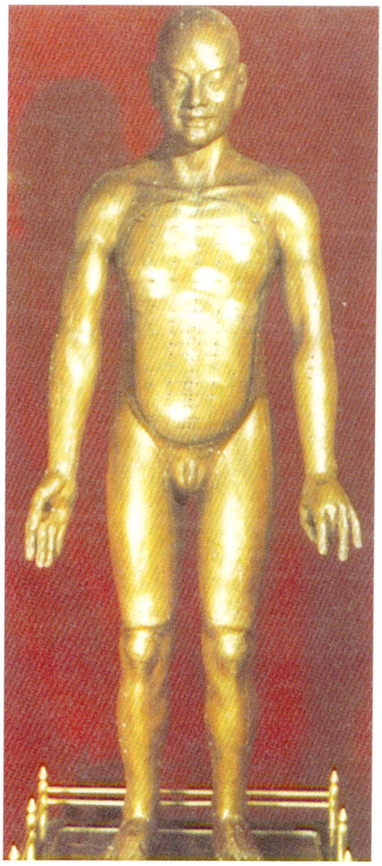

针灸铜人

后，铜人成为官医院、太医院的标准教具。针灸铜人不仅应用于针灸学，同时也可用于解剖教学，这比西方的解剖医学早了近 800 年。

针灸图经和针灸铜人是不可分割的一个整体，王惟一撰写的《新铸铜人腧穴针灸图经》，不仅是铜人的说明书，而且详细介绍了一些主要疾病的针灸治疗，成为总结公元 11 世纪以前针灸经络学说的一部专著。只有按照针灸图经上的穴位说明才能“读懂”针灸铜人，为了将针灸图经长久地保存，王惟一命人将针灸图经刻在十几块巨大的石碑上。

当时，一共制成了两具针灸铜人，分别被放置在翰林医官院和大相国寺[2]内的仁济殿里。公元 1126 年，发生靖康之乱[3]，北宋的首都汴京（今河南开封）被金人占领，两具天圣铜人从此历尽沧桑。

针灸铜人反映了当时的解剖学和针灸学成就，成为当时针灸、穴位的圭臬，朝廷命令医学界遵照实行，宋朝以后的几百年间，历代医家一直沿用。

天圣铜人问世后，历代都有人在仿造或制作针灸铜人。据记载，针灸铜人发明以后的主要用途是作为教具，但是，由于历代医家十分尊崇“铜人”，因此也用于观瞻甚至供奉。

词语注释

【1】医官院：北宋时期的医学机构。

【2】大相国寺：北宋首都汴梁府内规模盛大的一座庙宇，旧址在今河南省开封县东北。

【3】靖康之乱：公元 1226 年金兵攻破京师，宋钦宗、宋徽宗，以及后妃、宗室及大批官吏、内侍、宫女等被掳。同时，金兵掠去了大量礼器法物、天文仪器、书籍地图、府库积蓄。

第十五章　货币文化

一、贝币、布币、刀币、方孔铜钱、铜圆

夏商时代出现了中国最早的货币——贝币，是以海贝作为材料的货币。贝壳之所以成为货币，是因为它既是象征吉祥的贵重装饰品，又可以用枚作为单位计数，而且坚固耐久，便于携带。

商末周初，随着货币需求量的增大，还出现了各种材料的仿制贝，例如：兽骨制的骨贝，石头磨制的石贝，蚌壳磨制的蚌贝，陶制的陶贝，玉制的珧（yáo）贝，以及金贝、银贝、铜贝、包金铜贝等。贝币的计数单位是“个”和“朋”。《诗经·小雅·菁菁者莪》：“既见君子，锡我百朋。”

贝　币

贝币的使用持续到战国末期，而在云南一带，沿用到了清朝初年。贝币对后世产生了深远影响，这在文字上有明显表现。凡是与财富、价值、交换有关系的汉字，多用“贝”字旁，買（买）、賣（卖）、财、货、贵、贱、贩、贾、赊、赚等。

铜贝由于大小、重量与价值比较统一，因而具有其他贝币无法比拟的优越性。铜贝的出现和广泛使用，开启了金属铸币的先河，在中国货币发展史上具有非常重要的意义。当中国铜贝已经开始使用时，世界上其他国家尚未出现金属铸币，所以说，铜贝又是中国古代文明走在世界前列的重要例证之一。

布币是春秋战国时期主要在三晋、两周地区流通使用的一种青铜铸币，由于形状像铲子，又称铲币。布币由铲形农具——镈（bó）演变而来。“布”是“镈”的同声假借字，两个字在古代通用，因此得名布币。按照时间和型制，布币分为空首布和平首布两大类。空首布是早期的布币，春秋时期使用。形状好像铲子，头上的中间是空的，可以容纳铲柄，有尖肩尖足、平肩弧足、斜肩等形状，币的背上有三道纹。大多数空首布的币面上刻有各种文字记载，如干支[1]、数字、地名等。

平首布在战国时期使用，形状特点是币的底部分成两足，如同两只脚，基本上脱离了农具镈的原始形状。平首布的币首扁平，币身无直纹，刻有地名和货

币单位等文字，重量也比较轻。

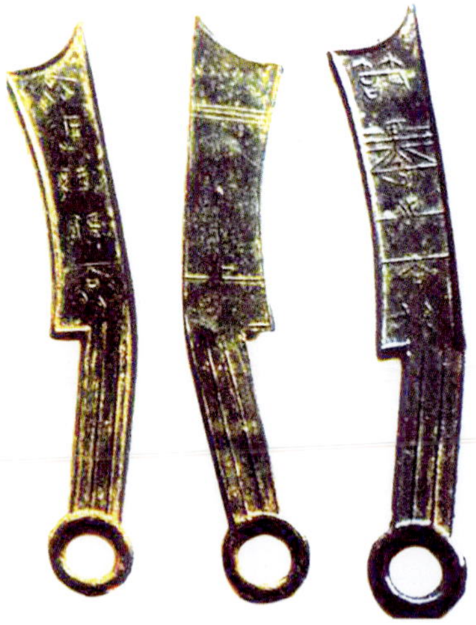

▶ 刀　币

刀币，顾名思义，就是形状像刀的货币。春秋战国时期流行于齐地（今山东半岛），燕赵（今河北、山西）。刀币起源于东方渔猎地区和手工业发达地区，是从一种叫“削”的刀类工具演变而来的。初期的刀币形状较大，顶端尖，柄端有环，可以穿绳，柄身有裂沟。晚期的刀币身小，平直，刀钝，头方或圆。按形制大小和铸造地区，刀币可分为四个类型：一、齐刀，俗称大刀，多在齐地流通，是先秦货币中制造最为精美的，每枚重 40 克以上。二、尖首刀，也称小刀，在燕国铸造通行，币身轻薄，刀首较为尖锐。三、明刀，也称燕刀，出现于燕地，按照刀身弧度分成方折刀、圆折刀。四、直刀，又叫圆首刀、钝首刀，多出现于赵地，刀体平直、短小，每枚重约 10 克。

方孔铜钱是秦代铸造的一种铜币。秦始皇统一中国以后，各地区的经济联系日益加强，但是货币的混乱给商品交换带来很多不便，也给国家的财政管理带来很大的困难。为了改变这种状况，秦始皇下令废除各地原来流行的货币，由国家统一铸造新币。按照当时所谓“天圆地方”的认识水平，铸造了象征天地的方孔圆钱。新币分为两种：一是黄金，名镒(yì)，以镒为单位，每镒二十两；一是铜钱，名“半两”，圆形方孔，直径一寸二分，有“半两”二字，这种圆形方孔的半两铜钱，在中国历史上沿用了两千多年，是中国封建社会影响最大的一种货币，在中国货币发展史上具有极其重要的意义。

▶ 南宋铜钱

铜圆从清光绪年间开始铸造，圆形，中间无孔，俗称“铜板”“铜子儿”，正面有“光绪元宝”四字，背面有盘龙纹；光绪后期改为“大清铜币”字样；民国初年，铜圆图案有交叉五色旗和 18 星旗（简称双旗）。日本侵略中国以后，大肆掠夺铜币，铜圆渐渐废除。

词语注释

【1】干支：天干和地支的合称。古人拿十干的“甲、丙、戊、庚、壬”和十二支的“子、寅、辰、午、申、戌”相配，十干的“乙、丁、己、辛、癸”和十二支的“丑、卯、巳、未、酉、亥”相配，共配成六十组，用来表示年、月、日的次序，周而复始，循环使用。干支最初是用来纪日的，后来多用来纪年，现中国农历的年份仍用干支。

二、金币、银币

金币：用黄金按照一定的形状、面额、重量铸成的货币。金币在中国的铸造史已有数千年，最早的金币是楚国的“爰(yuán)金”[1]。秦始皇统一货币以后，将货币分为两个级别，上币为黄金，下币为铜钱。此后，黄金在中国的货币史上始终占据着重要地位。但是，黄金只作为收藏手段而存在，不用于流通。在纸币流通的今天，金币同样也只具有保值和收藏价值。

银币：银币即白银，中国古代和近代的称量货币。

一般铸成元宝或直接使用碎散的银块，由于使用时要用秤来称斤两，按照重量计算，因此称为“银两”。最早见于战国时期的楚国，铸成铲形。汉武帝时期，曾经铸造银币“白选”[2]，但不久就废止了。后世多铸造成银铤、银锭、银饼，以自身重量为单位参与流通。明朝中后期，公元 1573 年 ~ 1620 年，货币流通以银为主的同时，西方的银圆大量流入中国，俗称“洋钱”“现大洋”等。清朝嘉庆（公元 1796 年 ~ 1820 年）之后，官商、私商都不断仿造。光绪十五年（公元 1889 年）仿铸的银圆，俗称“龙洋”，发行“光绪元宝”，是中国最早的正式银圆。此后，还有 1912 年的孙中山半身侧面像的开国纪念银圆和 1914 年的袁世凯头像银圆（俗称“袁大头”）。

银元宝

1933 年，国民党政府禁止银圆流通。1949 年，中华人民共和国宣告成立，中国人民银行发行人民币成为中国唯一法定本位货币。但建国之初，部分边远地区仍有银币行用，其主要集中于川、滇及西藏等地。1951 年西藏和平解放后，中央人民政府为尊重藏族人民在商品交换中长期使用银币的习惯，特许该地区暂时行用银币，缓解通货不足，且将原西藏地方政府所铸银、铜币等作为辅币流通。1962 年 5 月 10 日，西藏自治区人民政府公布《西藏自治区金银管理和禁止外币、银币流通暂行办法》，彻底废止银币流通，使之最终退出货币流通领域。

词语注释

【1】爰金：楚国的金币名称，是我国最早的金币，含金量 95%，流行于今湖北、安徽、浙江、江苏、河南、山东地区。

【2】白选：汉武帝时期铸造的银币，原名是“白金三品”，为银锡合金的圆形龙币。

三、纸　币

纸币：中国纸币的起源，最早可追溯到汉武帝元狩四年（公元前 119 年），发行的白鹿皮币，已带有纸币的性质。到唐宪宗（公元 806 年 ~ 820 年）时，出现了一种被称做“飞钱”的大牒[1]，类似今天的汇票[2]。

中国真正使用纸币是从北宋开始的。北宋仁宗天圣二年（公元 1024 年），最早的国家纸币——交子出现了。交子，也称为“会子”“钱引”。原来只是私人发行的信用兑换券，可以代替铁钱使用，因为铁钱太重，币值小，携带不方便，而持交子者随时可以到指定的地点兑换现金，便于贸易和买卖。最初出现在四川，交子是四川方言，意思是合券取钱的意思。继而由成都的 16 家富商联合发行铜版印刷的交子。交子上面印有房屋、树木、人物等图案，签有押字，作有暗记，用来防止别人仿印。宋仁宗天圣元年（公元 1023 年），由国家垄断发行官交子。官交子可以兑现成其他货币，流通范围基本上只限于四川、陕西、河东（今山西）

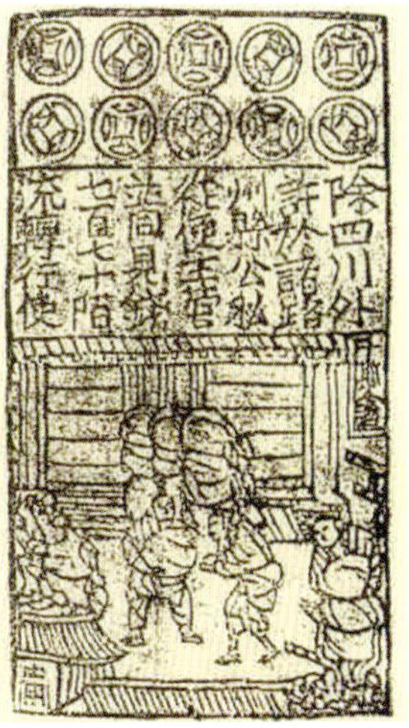

交　子

一带。北宋的交子是中国货币发展史由政府发行的最早的纸币，也是人类使用纸币的最早形式。纸币的出现是货币史上的一个进步。

南宋有多种纸币，有“会子”“川引”“淮交”“湖会”等名目，其中最为通行的是会子。会子是相会的意思，最初也是在民间自由发行的汇票性质的票券，开始由商人发行一种叫做会子的纸币，称为“便钱会子”，后来由政府发行，流行于江苏、浙江、安徽、湖北等地，币面印有发行机关、界致[3]（三年换一次称一界）、会子呈长方形，用红、蓝、黑三色铜版印刷，面额固定，原来只有一贯一种，后来又增发200文、300文、500文，票面上标明发行机关。总之，两宋的纸币都具有汇票和兑换券的性质，在国内相当大的地区流通，便利了商业往来，弥补了现钱的不足，可以说是中国货币史上的一大业绩，但渐渐发行失去控制，造成纸币价格低落。

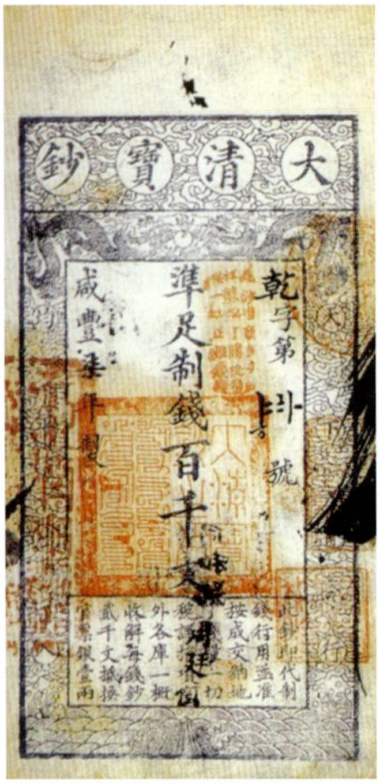

▶▶ 大清宝钞

元朝的货币制度以纸币为主，规定公私都行使纸币。所以元朝的大部分时间里只有纸币是合法通货[4]，金银铜钱都被禁止使用。元朝始终推行纸币制度，全国通行，基本上达到全国的货币统一。发行纸币作为本位制，从而为后代主辅币制度的形成开了先河。

明朝洪武八年（公元1375年）开始发行“大明通行宝钞”，这是明朝唯一的国家纸币。明中后期渐渐废止。

清朝咸丰年间（公元1851年～1861年），发行了“大清宝钞”，和“户部官钞”银票，合称钞票。钞票这个词由此产生。公元1879年，清政府成立中国第一个近代银行——中国通商银行，次年发行钞票，成为中国发行现代钞票的开始。

词语注释

【1】大牒：唐时的商业发达，当时没有纸币，携带金银赴外地贸易很不方便，同时禁止银币出境。因而产生了汇兑的办法，当时称为“飞钱”。唐代各道的军政机关都在京师设有贡院，为地方设在中央的联络处。商人把钱交给本道的进贡院，取得证券，可以凭券回到该道相应的机关领取。此证券称为“大牒”。

【2】汇票：银行或邮局承办汇兑业务时发给的支取汇款的票据。

【3】界致：宋代发行交子三年一换的期限。每次发行交子有一定的限额，以钦钱为现金准备，三年兑现一次，换发新交子，称为一界。

【4】通货：泛指在流通领域中充当流通手段或支付手段的纸币、硬币、支票、银行本票等。

四、纪念币

纪念币，是指一个国家为纪念国际或本国的政治、历史、文化等方面的重大事件、杰出人物、名胜古迹、珍稀动植物、体育赛事等而发行的法定货币，质量一般为精制，限量发行。它包括普通纪念币和贵金属纪念币。普通纪念币的材质是用于印刷钞票的纸张或铸造普通硬币的金属，是国家发行的可以流通但又具有纪念意义的法定货币。发行后，可以与人民币等值流通。贵金属纪念币包括金币、银币、铂币、钯币等贵金属或其合金铸造的纪念币，材质是金、银等贵重金属。这种币的发行价一般都等于面值的几十倍或上百倍。因此，面额只是象征性的货币符号，并不表明其真实价值，不能流通，其面值不记入市场现金流通量。

如北京2008年奥运会发行了金银铜纪念币，突出新北京、新奥运。特点是主题鲜明、工艺精致、数量较少、限量发行，人们一般把纪念币作为稀有工艺品收藏，或者作为一种保值手段和珍贵赠品。

中国最早的纪念币是光绪九年（1883年）在新疆铸造的“光绪通宝”，为迎接次年的新疆建省，库车局铸造了“新疆建省纪念币”。

中华民国元年（1912年），国民政府曾铸造过孙中山开国纪念币，由南京造币厂铸造，计有1圆、2角、1角。民国初期，天津、武昌、南京、云南等造币厂又曾先后铸造多种镌有时政要人肖像的银质纪念币章，品种名目甚多，竟成一时风气，形成中国货币文化发展进程中贵金属纪念章铸造高潮之一。其中除极个别币种曾行用于市外，绝大部分系满足军、政要员沽名钓誉及馈赠等所需，不曾参与货币流通。然此类币章风格各异，独具特色，铸工较为精湛，具有一定艺术与观赏价值，在一定程度上反映出其时代的中国铸币工艺水准。

中华人民共和国成立之后，于1979年首次铸造发行了中华人民共和国建国30周年纪念币。而后发行了10余个系列，有重大政治历史事件、杰出历史人物、大熊猫及珍稀动物、十二生肖、中国古典文学名著、古代科技发明、中国传统文化、宗教艺术、体育运动等，体现了我国五千年的文明历史和源远流长的中国文化。如中国人民银行从1984至1993年历时十年，盛大发行《中国杰出历史人物纪念币》，囊括了医药、军事、科学、地理、文学、水利，涵盖了民族、农业、工业、科技等各个方面，全面展示了中华民族各个历史时期杰出人物的精神风貌。构图精美，设计精湛，每一个图案都栩栩如生地刻画出了人物的内在特征，生动地再现了中华民族精明、睿智、豁达、沉稳、果敢、勤劳、坚毅、自豪等朴素的民族精神，币面设计既借鉴西方造型艺术浮雕写实技法，精心塑造主题人物形象，使之个性鲜明、生动传神；又借助中国传统绘画艺术构图之奇巧，虚实结合，令其别具风

2008年北京奥运会纪念币

采，情趣盎然；铸造方面，采用当代世界造币技术之新工艺，精心制作，确保币面浮雕层次丰富，明净无瑕，堪称中国现代金银纪念币珍品。

特别是改革开放以来中国发行的纪念币更是独具特色：

一、中国首套同时出现三个国家文字的纪念币。中华人民共和国恢复了行使对澳门的主权，1997年至1999年，发行了澳门回归祖国金银纪念币共3组，该项目的背面图案首次用了三个国家的文字，每组文字“一国两制”“平稳过渡，发展繁荣”“中华人民共和国澳门特别行政区成立纪念”分别为中文、英文和葡文。这是目前为止唯一的一套拥有三国文字的贵金属纪念币。

二、没有国名的中国金银铜纪念币。1980年发行的“第13届冬奥会金银铜纪念币”和“中国奥林匹克委员会金银铜纪念币”首次采用正面图案无国名，面额在正面设置的手法。继而，在1981年、1982年、1983年、1984年相继发行了正面无国名的“中国生肖鸡年”“中国生肖狗年”“中国生肖猪年”“中国生肖鼠年”金银币和1981年“中国出土文物青铜器”金银纪念币项目。

三、特别行政区发行的纪念币。这也是中国金银纪念币的一个重要组成部分。中国澳门特别行政区金融管理局宣布公开发售三款鼠年纪念币。此次发行的纪念币为全新一套农历年纪念币的首批。三款鼠年纪念币的正背面设计图案相同，但色调不一，正面铸有农历鼠年的生肖图案，而背面则为妈阁庙图案。

第十六章　饮食文化

中国饮食文化包括烹饪、饮食、食器、食俗、礼仪，以及更深层的文化隐义、智慧和艺术。我们这里以几个典型的饮食文化形态，如宫廷御膳、四大菜系、面点小吃、传统宴席、酒文化、品茗之道，来透视中国饮食文化的博大精深。

一、宫廷御膳

宫廷御膳（yùshàn）是指中国历代封建王朝专门管理帝王和后妃膳食机构所做的菜肴。在历代帝王宫廷和行苑中，每逢年节、庆典、寿日，或者祭奠、出巡、封赏，都要举行各种规格的宴庆，御厨[1]们绞尽脑汁，千方百计地精心烹饪、刻意创新，制作出各种奇珍美味来满足帝王与王公贵族、大臣、后妃们的美食之欲。连同熠熠闪光的金杯玉碟、珍稀器皿；官秩爵位、班然有序的宴席座次；庄严隆重的繁缛礼仪和热烈的气氛，构成了宫廷饮食文化，而其核心就是“宫廷御膳”[2]。每个时代的宫廷御膳实际上都可以代表那个时代的中国烹饪技艺的最高水平。

满族八大碗

宫廷菜作为中华民族饮食文化最优秀的产物，其用料上乘，制作精细，形色美观，极精致鲜美，多山珍海味。既有白煮烧烤，又有煎炒烹炸，奢侈靡费，强调礼数，这是历代宫廷御膳的共同点，而清宫御膳尤为突出。清宫的御膳房[3]共分九局：干果局、鲜果局、点心局、粥局、饭局、蘸吃局（专司用酱油、醋等调味作料）、汤局、素局、荤局。这是一个庞大的、完整的御厨系统。御膳不仅用料名贵，而且对菜肴的造型艺术十分讲究，在色彩、质地、口感、营养诸方面都相当强调彼此间的协和归同。清宫御膳风味结构主要由满族菜、鲁菜和淮扬菜构成。

在帝王日食单[4]中，记载的中国皇帝的御膳达千种之多。单单一只羊，也能巧立名目，烹制出上百道菜。平日皇帝最普通的一顿饭也要摆上大约20种菜。据记载，仅乾隆皇帝一日两餐饭，就上了76种菜点，若再加上两顿小吃就更多了。御膳每道菜肴都是讲究异常，如慈禧太后喜爱的“八珍糕”[5]，小巧玲珑、十分精致，味道清淡又易于消化。帝后们所食用的大米分黄、白、红数种，有的是远方的贡米，有的取自皇帝的“试验田”[6]。清宫还专门为皇帝养殖牛羊，供应牛乳、牛羊肉等食品。

清宫最盛大的宴席要数“满汉全席”[7]了。据史料记载，清朝每逢军队凯旋，皇帝驾崩，后妃去世都要办满汉全席。清宫御膳宴礼名目繁多，唯以千叟宴规模最盛，排场最大，耗资亦最巨。为了显示皇帝的气派，御膳房要把全国各地进贡的满汉名菜集中起来办。王公重臣须盛装赴宴，在御膳房总理[8]的指挥下，依照品位的高低，分两路进入宴席。皇帝驾到时，百乐齐鸣，群臣向皇帝行三跪九叩之礼[9]。御宴备有山珍、海味、珍禽、异兽、鲜蔬。据说，到清末，菜肴最多达200余款。除精致鲜美的菜肴外，用于吃饭的器皿也是精美无比。清宫餐具多为金银玉器，珍美宝贵，且造型美观，具有很高的艺术价值。

如今，宫廷御膳房随着社会的变迁已同帝王们一起走进历史的档案。但是御膳食品已成为中国丰厚的饮食文化的组成部分。

词语注释

【1】御厨：御膳房的厨师。
【2】御膳：帝王的饮食。
【3】膳房：掌握帝王膳食的厨房。
【4】帝王日食单：帝王一日三餐的菜单。
【5】八珍糕：用精细的玉米面、小米面、糜子面、小麦头道面和栗子面加上不同风味的调料等八种原料制作而成，所以称八珍。
【6】试验田：皇宫附近中南海丰泽园试种名稻之田。
【7】满汉全席：满汉全席起兴于清代，是集满族与汉族菜点之精华而形成的历史上最著名的中华大宴。满汉全席原是官场中举办宴会时满人和汉人合做的一种全席。满汉全席取材广泛，用料精细，山珍海味无所不包。烹饪技艺精湛，富有地方特色。突出满族菜点特殊风味，烧烤、火锅、涮锅几乎是不可缺少的菜点；同时又展示了汉族烹调的特色，扒、炸、炒、熘、烧等兼备，实乃中华菜系文化的瑰宝。
【8】御膳房总理：帝王专用厨房的领班。
【9】三跪九叩之礼：古代臣子向皇帝行的大礼，分别跪地三次，每次磕头三次。

二、四大菜系

中国烹饪是文化，是科学，是艺术。四大菜系是鲁菜、川菜、淮扬菜、粤菜的总称。这些菜系因地理、气候、习俗、特产的不同形成了各自的地方风味。

（一）鲁　菜

鲁菜历史极其久远。《尚书·禹贡》中载有“青州贡盐”，《诗经》中已有食用黄河的鲂鱼和鲤鱼的描述，而今糖醋黄河鲤鱼仍然是鲁菜中的佼佼者。以其味鲜咸脆嫩，风味独特，制作精细享誉海内外。鲁菜在烹饪技艺上重视爆[1]、炒、扒[2]、塌。“塌”是山东独有的烹调方法，其主料要事先用调料腌渍入味[3]，再沾粉或挂糊[4]。两面塌煎至金黄色，放入调料或清汤，以慢火㸆[5]尽汤汁，使之浸入主料，增加鲜味。山东广为流传的锅塌豆腐、锅塌菠菜等，都是久为人们所乐道的传统名菜。

鲁菜 葱烧海参

鲁菜善于以葱香调味，在菜肴烹制过程中，不论是爆、炒、烧、熘，还是烹调汤汁，都以葱丝（或葱末）爆锅，就是蒸、扒、炸、烤等菜，也借助葱香提味，如“烤鸭”“烤乳猪”“锅烧肘子”“炸脂盖”等，均以葱段为作料。山东厨师多以淡水鱼、猪肉、蔬菜为原料。依靠山东的丰富食料，如大明湖的茭白、蒲菜、藕、章丘的大葱、黄河的鲤鱼、泰安的豆腐、北园的蔬菜等。其代表菜肴为糖醋黄河鲤鱼、锅烧肘子等。鲁菜系中的胶东菜以烹饪海鲜著称，无论是用名贵的海产珍品如鱼团、海参、燕窝、干贝，还是用小海味如鳞、虾、蟹，都能烹饪出精细鲜美的名肴。其代表菜肴如绣球海参、红烧干贝、芙蓉虾仁等。胶东菜烹制海鲜有独到之处，对海珍品和小海味的烹制堪称一绝，如胶东沿海生长的比目鱼（当地俗称“偏口鱼”），运用多种刀工处理和不同技法，可烹制成数十道美味佳肴。以小海鲜烹制的“油爆双花”“红烧海螺”“炸蛎黄”等，都是独具特色的海鲜珍品。

鲁菜系除了沿海的胶东菜（以海鲜为主）之外，还有济南菜和孔府菜。曲阜的孔府菜用料讲究，刀工细腻，烹调程序严格、复杂，口味讲究清淡鲜嫩、软烂香醇、原汁原味，对菜点制作精益求精，始终保持传统风味，也是鲁菜中的佼佼者。原曾封闭在府内的孔府菜，20世纪80年代以来也走向了市场，济南、北京都开办了“孔膳堂”。

（二）川　菜

四川古称天府之国，得天独厚的自然条件，古老的巴蜀风俗，先民的饮食习惯为川菜的形成奠定了基础。天府之国，美食丰盈，味甲天下。饮誉中外的川菜是中国饮食文化园地中的一朵奇葩。一提到川菜，人们马上就会想到麻辣、鱼香、怪味……它味浓、味美、味重、味多，有百菜百味之美誉。

四川人创造出众多的口味丰富、醇美并富于特色的食品，如保宁的食醋、涪（Fú）陵的榨菜、重庆的辣酱、郫（Pí）县的豆瓣、宜宾的芽菜等。厨师用这些调料以普通的鱼肉禽菜烹制出许多朴实无华、经济实惠，却极有特色的菜肴，不仅为四川人所习惯，而且受到其他地区人们的欢迎。回锅肉、鱼香肉丝、宫保鸡丁、麻婆豆腐、水煮肉、蒜泥白肉等，物美价廉，又很下饭。因此川菜可以说是最大众化的菜系。

川菜多用复合味，如咸鲜、糖醋、麻辣、酸辣、椒盐、

川菜 爆炒腰花

酱香、五香等，可列数十种之多。其烹饪技艺擅长小煎、小炒、干烧。“小炒”的特点是，烹饪食物不过油、不换锅、急火短炒、一锅成菜，如炒肝尖、炒腰花都只需一分钟左右，成菜嫩而不生。“干煸”（biān）主要用来加工纤维较长的食物，如牛肉、萝卜、苦瓜、四季豆等。

（三）粤　菜

粤菜是以广东省的广州、潮州、东江（又称客家菜）三地的菜系为代表而形成的。广东地处中国南端沿海，境内高山平原鳞次栉比，江河湖泊

纵横交错，气候温和，雨量充沛，故动植物类的食品源极为丰富。

粤菜的食物原料、烹调技法、调料运用都有异于其他地区之处，因此粤菜的第一特点是“怪”。粤菜选料广博奇异，品种花样繁多，令人眼花缭乱。天上飞的，地上爬的，水中游的，几乎都能上席。

粤菜 烤乳猪

粤菜的另一特点是用量精而细，配料多而巧，装饰美而艳，而且善于在模仿中创新，品种繁多，早在 1965 年“广州名菜美点展览会”上介绍的粤菜就有 5 457 种之多。

粤菜的第三个特点是注重质和味，口味比较清淡，力求清中求鲜、淡中求美。而且随季节时令的变化而变化，夏秋偏重清淡，冬春偏重浓郁，追求色、香、味、型。食味讲究清、鲜、嫩、爽、滑、香；调味遍及酸、甜、苦、辣、咸。

粤菜的著名菜肴有：烤乳猪、龙虎斗、太爷鸡、香芋扣肉、狗肉煲[6]、五彩炒蛇丝等。广州的北园、大同、广州、大三元、泮溪（Pànxī）、陶陶居、蛇餐馆等酒家，均以经营粤菜闻名。

（四）淮扬菜

淮扬菜系是淮安（今楚州）、扬州、镇江三地风味菜的总称。淮安、扬州、镇江三地位于长江南北，紧挨京杭大运河，从地理上看是连接南北西东的重要交通枢纽。

古运河把海、黄、淮、江、钱五大水系贯通，扬州汇聚了全国烹饪人才、技艺，占据原料交流枢纽的位置，北方的豆、麦、杂粮，油料南下，南方的粮、茶、果、盐、水产北上。而隋炀帝三幸江都，将长安、洛阳中原美食，随龙舟带进扬城隋宫，再加上州县上贡珍馐，厨师刻意斗妍。特别是唐朝以后，扬州已为富商云集之地，讲究饮食排场，大多盐商家皆有名厨，往往都能烹制一两种令人叫绝的菜肴。故盐商请客设宴往往从各家请厨师取其擅长，以凑出市肆不能买到的筵席。淮菜、扬菜正是在消费水平极高的富商的奢侈需求下逐渐培植起来的。

明清以后，淮菜和扬菜开始相互渗透、逐渐融合，熔南北风味于一炉，从而形成了统一的菜系。

淮扬菜以烧、焖[7]、炖[8]、蒸、烩等见功，加工时间较长。其名肴如“火腿炖甲鱼”“腌鲜鳜鱼”“火腿炖笋”“雪冬烧山鸡”“毛峰熏鲥（shí）鱼”“栗子黄焖鸡”“荷叶蒸肉”“扬州狮子头”等，都带有此特点。因此淮扬菜注重原汤原汁，要求鸡有鸡味，鱼有鱼味，突出主料的味道，再恰当地配以辅料，其选料精严，讲究刀功、造型，显得富贵气十足。扬州还以其皮薄、汁浓、味鲜的各色点心闻名，俗语道“川菜扬点”。

淮扬菜口味偏甜，但不过分，而且往往糖盐并用，使得菜肴鲜味悠长，口味清鲜平和，咸甜浓淡适中，南北皆宜。并且，淮扬菜的选料尤为注意鲜活、鲜嫩；制作精细，注意刀工；调味清淡，强调本味，重视调汤，风味清鲜；色彩鲜艳，清爽悦目；造型美观，别致新颖，生动逼真；回味无穷。

淮扬菜 花雕酒酿蒸鲥鱼

词语注释

【1】爆：一种烹调方法，用滚油炸或滚水煮。

【2】扒：煨烂，炖烂。

【3】腌渍入味：用盐等浸渍食物使其有味道。

【4】挂糊：中国烹调中常用的一种技法，即在经过刀工处理的原料表面挂上一层糊浆。有蛋清糊、蛋黄糊、全蛋糊、水粉糊等。

【5】㸆：烹调的一种方法，慢火熬干汤汁。

【6】煲：用文火烧煮或熬。

【7】焖：烹调方法，把锅盖盖紧，用小火把饭菜煮熟。

【8】炖：烹调方法，加水烧开后用文火久煮使烂熟（多用于肉类）。

三、面点小吃

中国的面点小吃历史悠久，风味各异，品种繁多。面点小吃的历史可上溯到新石器时代，当时已有石磨[1]，可加工面粉，做成粉状食品。到了春秋战国时期，已出现油炸及蒸制的面点，此后，随着炊具和灶具的改进，中国面点小吃的原料、制法、品种日益丰富。如北方的饺子、面条、拉面、煎饼等；南方的烧麦[2]、春卷[3]、汤圆等。此外，各地依其物产

汤　圆

及民俗风情，又演化出许多具有浓郁地方特色的风味小吃。如：北京的焦圈、蜜麻花，豌豆黄、艾窝窝；上海的蟹壳黄、南翔小笼馒头；天津的狗不理包子、耳朵眼炸糕、桂发祥麻花；山西的栲栳栳、刀削面、揪片；西安的牛羊肉泡馍、乾州锅盔；兰州的拉面、油锅盔；河南的枣锅盔、白糖焦饼、鸡蛋布袋；新疆的烤馕；山东的煎包；江苏的葱油火烧、蟹黄烧麦；浙江的重阳栗糕；湖北的云梦炒鱼面、热干面、东坡饼；四川的龙抄手、担担面、赖汤圆；云南的过桥米线等。

面点小吃较之菜肴，地方性更强，与当地的物产、气候、地理、历史等因素密切相关。比如陕西被秦岭分为三大自然区域，中部关中平原号称“八百里秦川”，汉代起就盛产小麦，因之，面点小吃中以小麦面粉为主要原料的居多，如今遍及关中各地的石子馍，是我们的祖先由生食转入熟食后，用石子导热，上烫下烙焙制而成的一种食品，其渊源可以上溯至新石器时代，被称为人类食品中的化石。由于石子馍具有酥脆甘香，营养丰富、经久耐贮、易于消化等特点，历来都是馈赠亲友的佳品，同时兼及米类（大米、糯米、小米、黑米等）、豆类（大豆、绿豆、豌豆、小豆、豇豆、扁豆）、杂粮类（玉米、荞麦、糜子、谷子等）、薯类（土豆、红薯、山芋等）。在熟制方法上，有煮、蒸、炸、烤、烙、烩、煎、炖、熬、煨、涮、炙、浸、泡、汆、氽等，而其成型工艺则有揉、卷、盘、包、擀、捏、切、按、摊、撕、揪、叠、抻、扯、削、搅、旋、模印等。面点小吃数量多达 1 000 多种。

在中国北方的面食小吃中，山西的面食以花样多、品质好、影响大而出名。最负盛名的是刀削面，堪称山西面食一绝，已有数百年的历史。传统的操作

刀削面

方法是一手托面，一手拿刀，直接削到开水锅里，其要诀是：“刀不离面，面不离刀，胳膊直硬手端平，手眼一条线，一棱赶一棱，平刀时扁条，弯刀是三棱。”1985年山西面食技术比武时，饮食行业的削面高手每分钟削118刀，每小时可削25千克面粉的湿面团。刀削面柔中有硬，软中有韧，浇卤（lǔ）、或炒或凉拌，均有独特风味，若略加山西老陈醋食之尤妙。

此外，各地依其物产及民俗风情，又演化出许多具有浓郁地方特色的风味小吃。如北京的面点多与御膳有关，栗子面窝头传说就是宫廷小吃品种，是慈禧太后当年吃过的小窝头。这种小窝头用的是上好的新玉米面，再掺上好黄豆面，蒸的时候加桂花白糖，一斤面要蒸出一百个小窝头才够“小”。吃起来香甜可口，百吃不厌。芸豆卷本是民间小吃，据传，清光绪年间一个夏日，慈禧太后偶尔听到宫墙之外有铜锣声和吆喝声，就问是做什么的，得知是卖芸豆卷的，即唤来卖货人，品尝了他的芸豆卷，觉得很好吃。于是，将此人留在宫内为她专做小吃，芸豆卷也就成为清宫御膳珍品。

栗子面窝头

在中国南方的面食小吃中，上海小吃早在南宋时便有记载，清代以来，上海成为对外通商口岸，相继吸取了各地风味小吃精华，几乎包括了全国各主要地方的特色，并加以发展和提高，应时适令的各类米、面类小吃品种更为丰富，形成自己的特色。如大众小吃蟹壳黄，是用发酵面加油酥制成皮加馅的酥饼，饼色和形状酷似煮熟的蟹壳，成品呈褐黄色，入口酥、松、香。早期上海的所有茶楼、老虎灶（开水专营店）的店面处，大都设有一个立式烘缸和一个平底煎盘炉，边做边卖两件小点心——蟹壳黄和生煎馒头，深受茶客喜爱。20世纪30年代后期，出现了单卖这两个品种的专业店，如黄家沙、大壶春、吴苑等，名噪一时。

词语注释

【1】石磨：将粮食等磨碎的石材工具。

【2】烧麦：福建长汀著名的风味小吃。烧麦状似石榴，以皮薄馅爽、芳香扑鼻、令人垂涎而得名为“三特石榴果”“三里香”。原叫“烧卖”，因用很薄的面皮包馅儿，再捏成折儿，蒸熟，便改叫“烧麦”。

【3】春卷：用上好白面粉加少许水和盐拌匀揉捏，放在平底锅中摊烙成圆形皮子，然后将制好的馅儿心（肉末、豆沙、菜猪油）摊放在皮上，卷成长卷，下油锅炸成金黄色即可。春卷皮薄酥脆、馅儿心香软，别具风味，是春季的时令佳品。

四、传统筵席

筵席，古代是以酒肉款待宾客的一种聚集活动。隋、唐以前，古人不使用桌椅，屋内先铺在地上的粗料编织物叫筵，加铺在筵上规格较小细料编成的叫席。宴饮时，座位设在席子上，食品放在席前的筵上，人们席地坐饮。后来使用桌椅，宴饮由地面升高到桌上进行，明清时有了“八仙桌”“大圆桌”，宴席形式已经改变，宴席却仍被沿称为“筵席”，座位仍沿称“席位”，筵席成为专用名词。

传统筵席形成了一整套饮食文化习俗，宴席上的

宴 席

珍馐佳肴，不仅色香味形俱佳，而且命名要典雅喜庆，多取谐音，以求吉祥。菜谱要配套完整，有酒、有菜、有主食、有点心、有饮料，上菜有一定的顺序。民间每逢婚、丧、喜、庆，常要办筵席宴客。筵席在菜式和上菜方式上都有讲究。筵席上菜的顺序一般是先凉后热、先咸后甜、先贵重后一般。头道热菜为主菜，是筵席中最贵重的菜，最后一道热菜为饭菜，连同主食一起上，热菜之后为汤菜。席上的人见到上来了汤菜，就知道菜都上完了。用餐还有规矩和礼仪，也有一套规则，常常与官秩、名位、尊贵、老幼相关，营造出热气、香气，洋溢在人们的脸上喷发出红润，满足不同层次人的心理需求，因为筵席本身就是一个繁文缛礼的过程。中国人习惯使用八仙桌，对门为上座，两边为偏座。请客时，年长者、主宾或地位高的人坐上座，男女主人或陪客者坐下座，其余客人按年龄顺序坐偏座。在中国，左为尊，右为次；上为尊，下为次；中为尊，偏为次。目前城市酒家的筵席，则是用圆桌子，人数也较灵活。在用餐的过程，还要讲究揖让周旋之礼。从传统习俗上说，中国人请客，不但按长、尊、主、次围桌而坐，而且主人还要频频劝酒，客人谦让礼到。中国人觉得这样的宴客方式才能体现主人的热情和诚恳。另外宴客时崇尚热闹欢快的气氛，讲究面子和排场。排场之大，气氛之热闹常常令人叹为观止。

较随便的形式则是主人邀上三五知己，到家中由女主人炒几个菜，小酌一番。这种随便的宴客形式不讲究礼仪，不讲究座次，不讲究饭菜，只讲气氛的和谐、主人的热诚、主客谈话的投机。当然，近年来西方的一些宴客形式，如酒会、招待会、自助餐或冷餐也传到了中国，但这些多是官方或单位出面组织的宴请形式，家庭中还少有实行。

五、酒文化

中国是酒的王国。酒，形态万千，色泽纷呈，品种之多，产量之丰，皆堪称世界之冠。中国是酒人的乐土，地不分南北，人不分男女老少，饮酒之风，历经数千年而不衰。每逢佳节，或封功庆典、或宴请宾客、或祭奠逝者、或饯别亲朋、或迎亲嫁娶，上自王公贵族，下至庶民百姓，几乎生活的每一个方面，都以酒助其兴。古往今来，许多文人墨客更喜欢借酒当歌、酒后赋诗。曹操《短歌行》说“何以解忧，唯有杜康”，即指杜康酒。李白用“兰陵美酒郁金香，玉碗盛来琥珀光”[1]的诗句来歌颂兰陵酒。杜牧用“借问酒家何处有？牧童遥指杏花村”[2]来指明杏花村汾酒，等等。甚至行将就死的囚犯也要喝

斗酒图

三碗“上路”酒才受戮，因此，时时处处在中国人的生活中都可以寻找到酒文化的踪迹。酒，作为一个文化符号，一种文化消费，用来表示一种礼仪、一种气氛、一种情趣、一种心境。随着历史的演进，形成了中国独特的酒文化现象。

在中国绘画和中国文化特有的书法艺术中，酒神的精灵更是活泼万端。传说，画家郑板桥的字画不能轻易得到，于是求画者就拿狗肉与美酒款待，在郑板桥的醉意中求字画，即可如愿。“书圣”王羲之酒醉时挥毫而作《兰亭序》[3]，“遒媚劲健，绝代所无”，而至酒醒后“更书数十本，终不能及之”。

中国人饮酒，自古就非常讲究礼仪，几千年来约定俗成，主要有以下通行的酒人礼数：

一是未饮先酹（lèi）酒[4]。酹，指洒酒于地。在拜神、祭祖、祭山川江河时，必须仪态恭肃，手擎酒杯，默念祷词[5]，先将杯中酒分倾三点，后将余酒洒一半圆形；这样用酒在地上酹成三点一长勾的“心”字，表示心献之礼。

二是饮酒时应干杯。即端杯敬酒，讲究“先干为敬”，受敬者也要以同样方式回报，否则罚酒。另外，为客人斟酒应从长者开头，接受主人敬酒要双手扶杯。接受长者斟酒更应一边扶杯，一边微微欠身；与人碰杯时注意比对方酒杯端得低一些，以示尊敬。

三是行酒令以助兴。酒令是中国特有的宴饮的艺术，是中国酒文化的独创。用来活跃气氛，调节感情，促进交流，斗智斗巧，提高宴饮的文化品位。其中，游戏令包括传花、猜谜、说笑话、对酒筹等（即据酒筹上所刻文字限定罚酒人）；赌赛令[6]包括投壶、射箭、掷骰（tóu）、划拳[7]、猜谜等等。

词语注释

【1】兰陵美酒郁金香，玉碗盛来琥珀光：唐代诗人李白《客中行》中的诗句。兰陵：山东省最南部。郁金香：单子叶植物，百合科。多年生草本。花大而美丽，形似高脚酒杯，有黄、白、红或紫红等色，可供观赏。琥珀：质量轻，一般呈蜡黄及黄褐色，透明，有树脂光泽。是一种树脂化石。有的内含昆虫遗体。能做绝缘材料、化工原料、药材等，色美质优的可用作工艺雕刻材料。

【2】借问酒家何处有？牧童遥指杏花村：唐代诗人杜牧《清明》中的诗句。

【3】《兰亭序》：东晋永和九年（公元353年）三月三日，王羲之与谢安、孙绰等四十余人在山阴兰亭举行祓禊（fúxì）活动。参加雅集的多为当世名士，大家一道曲水流觞（shāng），饮酒赋诗，事后这些诗篇汇编成集，《兰亭序》就是为这个诗集写的序文。《兰亭序》书法本身的艺术魅力：点画注重提按顿挫，精到而多变，同一点画，写法多样，无法而有法，能寓刚健于优美。结构强调欹（qī）正开合，生动而多姿，同一字形，绝不重复，能尽字之真态，寓欹侧于平正。章法疏密有致，自然天成。

【4】酹酒：以酒浇地，表示祭奠。古代宴会往往行此仪式。

【5】祷词：求神者在向神祷告时所默诵的经句或愿词。

【6】赌赛令：喝酒时的游戏。

【7】划拳：饮酒时的一种博戏。两人同时喊数并伸出拳指，以所喊数目与双方伸出拳指之数相符者为胜，败者罚饮。

六、品茗之道

中国是茶的故乡，制茶、饮茶已有几千年历史。茶在历史上有许多名称如“茗”等，而人们将它正式定名为“茶”，却是唐代的事。但在人们把它作为艺术行为来享受时，习惯还是称之为“茗”。茶道艺术具体包括茶具、验水、点茶、煎水和烹茶艺术，它与饮茶、品茗、食啜艺术一起，共同构成了古代的茶文化。

饮茶始于中国，茶叶冲以煮沸的清水，顺乎自然，清饮雅尝，寻求茶的固有之味，重在境界，这是品茶的特点。同样质量的茶叶，如用水不同、茶具不同或冲泡技术不一，泡出的茶汤会有不同的效果。中国自古以来就十分讲究茶具、茶的用水、茶的冲泡，积累了丰富的经验。泡好茶，要了解各类茶叶的特点，掌握科学的冲泡技术，使茶叶的固有品质能充分地表现出来。

喝茶是一种艺术，三分解渴七分品。品茶即品茗，需要好茶，精髓就在于品茶的色、香、味、形，解渴则在其次。“品”茶时，不但是要鉴别茶的特色，而且也带有神思遐想和领略饮茶之情趣。生活在现今社会的人们，工作繁忙，能在百忙之中泡上一壶茶，择雅静之处，自斟自饮，对消除疲劳、振奋精神大有裨益。

“以茶待客”是中国悠久的习俗。中国古代的文人名士很多喜欢品茗之道，他们时常以茶会友，茶助诗兴，这种风尚自唐以来愈加兴盛。宋代由于文人雅士的倡导，逐步形成了自成体系的茶文化。宋代诗人陆游就是一位嗜茶诗人，他在《剑南诗稿》中有关茶事的诗词多达320首，是历代写茶诗、茶词最多的人。明清时代，不仅上层社会品茗风习极盛，市井百姓中也是饮茶成风。茶楼茶馆沿街遍布，不亚于酒肆（sì）。居家待客，敬茶成为必尽礼仪。有客来，端上一杯芳香的茶，是对客人的极大尊重。在中国许多地方的风俗中，甚至把饮茶与定亲、结婚等紧密地联系在一起，不少地方有“饮茶定终身”之说，女方接受男方聘礼叫“吃茶”或“喝茶”；结婚仪式中，谒见长辈要“献茶”，以表儿女的敬意。长辈送见面礼，称为“茶包”。《红楼梦》中凤姐就对黛玉说：“你吃了我家的茶，为什么不给我家做媳妇！”可见，茶与中国人的日常生活的关系十分密切。

▶▶ 茶 道

第十七章　中华武术

中华传统武术是中华文化的瑰宝，它博大精深、源远流长，不仅具有严密的哲学思想、系统的技击理论、完整的锻炼体系，具有强身健体、祛病延年、防身御敌、制人取胜、修身养性、悟道怡情等一系列神奇的功效，而且还跟军事、宗教、教育、医疗、艺术、游戏等活动紧密相连和相互渗透，表现出中国人特有的文化精神、思维智慧、社会心态、风俗民情、审美情趣。

一、拳　术

拳术是中国武术的一种，在民间成为流派，是在宋以后，盛于明清。拳术主要以踢、打为主，是一种徒手技击术。由于受到地域因素的影响形成了各种地域性拳术，显示出不同的地区特点，其中最显著的是南北拳术的区别。人们常说的"南拳北腿"[1]，实际上就概括了南北地域武术的差别。从技法上看，南方人个子较矮，下身稳固，而身法敏捷，动作灵活。他们的四肢均比北方人短些，于是注重手法灵活，贴身靠打[2]。北方人身高力大，臂长腿长，但重心较高，于是善于以迅猛多变的腿法击人。

"南拳北腿"之说只是粗线条地表述了南北武术的差异，而无法概括诸多地域性武术的特点。中国武术在漫长的历史发展过程中，先后形成了多个地域性的大拳系，如以黄河下游的豫、冀、鲁三省为中心的少林拳[3]系，以闽、粤二省为中心的南拳系，以四川为中心的峨眉拳[4]系，以湖北、江苏、四川为中心的武当拳[5]系，以河南、北京为中心的太极拳[6]系，以北京为中心的八卦掌[7]系等等。

少林拳系最早形成，影响也最大，因此有"少林拳术甲天下"之称。少林寺位于河南省登封县嵩山五乳峰脚下，建于南北朝时期。当时创建此拳术只是为了和尚健身。由于长期静坐，和尚们不免精神疲倦，又因身居山林，时或受到毒蛇猛兽的威胁和袭击，禅僧达摩[8]便根据山林中各种动物的特性和动作，如虎跃猴攀、鸟飞虫爬，又吸收了劳动人民锻炼身体的各种方法，初创了一些简单易学的舒展筋骨的健身法，

少林拳

号称“达摩十八手”，从此开创了少林寺僧人健身习武之风。据传，少林寺第一次以武扬名是在隋末唐初。唐太宗李世民曾在白葛庄被围困[9]，少林寺挑选了13名武功高强的和尚去救驾，解救了被围困的李世民，为大唐统一立下了汗马功劳。李世民当皇帝后，不忘旧恩，特许少林寺可以拥有僧兵，自成体系的少林武术闻名遐迩，成为中华武术的代表之一。

从少林强身健体变为技击绝学，始于“少林五拳”，即龙拳练神、虎拳练骨、豹拳练力、蛇拳练气、鹤拳练精。能于此五拳精熟，则身坚气壮，手灵足稳，眼锐胆实，倘与人搏，出其一指半足之功，便可以压倒群流。

武当是道家的武术派别，创造出一套“以静制动”“以柔克刚”“ 借力打力”的内家拳法。偏重精、气、神的内部修炼；注重意念的训练，风格是文雅、安舒、沉稳、圆活；注重后天克服本能的训练，主静、主慢、主曲、主柔。值得注意的是少林、武当两派，内、外两家拳法的区别，从根本上讲，是佛、道两大宗教思想在拳术上的体现。

“太极拳”一词最早出现在1852年王宗岳《太极拳论》。太极拳采用道家健身养生的方法，是一套导

太极拳

引吐纳术。太极拳是一种摒弃一切暴力的技击术，这是独一无二的。其本质是“以柔克刚”；其练习特点体现为“松”“慢”“用意不用力”。

词语注释

【1】南拳北腿：中国的武术分为南北两类，南方的武术以拳部的变换为主，北方的武术以腿部的变换为主。

【2】贴身靠打：用身体的某一个部位如肩、背、胯、臀等去靠打对手，是传统武术高级实战技法。

【3】少林拳：亦称“外家拳”。武术门派之一。源于唐代少林寺而得名。具有刚健有力、朴实无华、招式多变、内静外猛、利于技击等特点。技法以进攻为主。拳术套路有大洪拳、小洪拳、罗汉拳、梅花桩、虎战拳、炮拳等，还有技击散打、气功和以棍术见长的各种器械术。

【4】峨眉拳：武术门派之一。动作讲究刚、柔、曲、直。该拳技击性强，不先出手击人，以后发制人为根本。

【4】武当拳：武术门派之一。是一种集武术、养身为一体的精妙拳法，有以静制动，以柔克刚，以四两拨千斤，后发先制的武术特点，亦有动如行云流水，绵绵不断，刚柔相含，含而不露的武术风格。

【6】太极拳：武术门派之一。是由两仪、太极、无极，三种不同层次的拳术、功法组合而成的一套由外至内，由动至静，从初级到高级，动静结合，内外兼修完整的修炼功法。

【7】八卦掌：八卦掌是河北文安县人董海川所创，是一种以掌法变换和行步走转为主的拳术。它将武功与导引吐纳融为一体，内外兼修。八卦掌的运动特点是：一走、二视、三坐、四翻。这些特点为训练人的柔韧、速度、耐力，特别是下肢的力量提供了必要的锻炼条件。

【8】达摩：达摩，天竺人，禅宗始祖。是把禅学带入中土的第一人。他为弘扬佛法历尽艰辛，后终在少林寺后山面壁九年得悟大道和高深武艺。

【9】白葛庄被围困：唐朝李世民在白葛庄被围困，少林寺挑选了13名武功高强的和尚去救驾李世民，后来李世民当上皇帝后，为了感谢少林寺和尚救命之恩，加封少林寺为“天下第一名刹”。

二、武术与养生

养生健身是武术的价值功能之一。人们习武练武，不仅是获得一种自卫防身的手段，而且也是为了健身强体，延年益寿。武术在其发展中受到了中国传统养生文化的极大影响，传统养生理论和方法与武术相互融摄，形成了武术的养练观。主张以刚柔、动静、虚实、开合等为运动规律，打通经络，流畅气血，协调阴阳，从而达到提高机体健康水平的功效。

五禽戏

中国传统的精、气、神论、经络原理，融摄于武术之中，构成武术理论的内涵，并发展成为“内练精气神，外练筋骨皮”的武术练养理论。武术养生重视导引形体，讲究动静结合、内外结合、练养结合、形神结合，使武术有技击之术的单一功能向养生之术、健身之术、修身之术演化，形成具有健身功能含义的融技击与养生为一体的活动，成为中国武术文化的重要组成部分。其特征：

一、形神共养是中国传统武术理论中重要的练养原则。中国古代养生理论认为，气是生命的本质基础，阴阳二气在人体内外不停地流动运行，人体内阴阳二气的平衡与和谐，是健康状态的基本表现，也是健康长寿和古代养生的基本要求，所以要形神共养。形指身体；神指人的心性、精神、意识、思维等，这都是气的种种外在表现和神韵。形神共养不仅注重形体养护，更要注意精神的调摄，促使人体内部阴阳平衡、调和，健康长寿，来实现生命和潜能的开发与完善。

二、内功养生。内功注重于意念、气息、脏腑、经络、血脉等人体内部机能的锻炼，以求内壮的养生功法。武术内功的出现，以内家拳为标志。如：形意拳、太极拳、八卦拳、意拳等称为内功拳。锻炼的效果不在肌肉的发达，而在内脏的坚实和舒适。中华武术门派众多。人们常常把少林拳术、南拳等称为外家拳术[1]。把太极拳、八卦拳等称为内家拳术[2]。与外家拳术相比，内家拳术更适于强身健体，它是集体育性、医疗性、艺术性和娱乐性为一体的强身健体、延年益寿的一种拳术。太极拳术演练的时候，要做到心与意合，意与气合，气与力合，内外一致。它的发力是推进的，借力打力，在劲力上体现的是内气内力，所以内家拳一般体现的都是松柔、中和、轻缓的打拳姿态。所以有人说，内家拳实际上就是高级的养生气功。而外家拳术则讲究手、眼、身法等的灵活，即手与眼合、眼与心合、肩与胯合、上与下合、身与步合。手足的变化，其劲如箭离弦，发力于身，是碰撞之力，是瞬间之力，而不是推力。这种拳术更适于年轻人武练，时常出现在体育竞技的场合中。

三、导引养生。导引是以肢体运动为主，配合呼吸吐纳的传统健身法，此法历史悠久。1973 年湖南长沙马王堆汉墓群三号墓出土的帛画《导引图》绘有 44 个不同人物的运动姿态，既有徒手的动作，又有使用器物的导引，其外还有大量模仿动物形态的动作。魏晋之时，导引术已包括肢体运动、吐纳内视、按摩咽液。如五禽戏[3]是华佗模仿虎、鹿、熊、猿、鸟五种动物的形体特点而创造的一种具有强身保健作用的锻炼方法。坚持做“五禽戏”，可使血流通畅，精神抖擞，而且可保持行动敏捷、体态均匀。再如太极内功[4]是太极拳的内练功，是一种动静功结合的武术，主要通过以意运气[5]、呼吸锻炼等方法，以增强内气而产生祛病强身等功效。武术的养生价值已成为中华民族的一种健身文化，同时也是东方体育健身的一大派系。宋至明清导引术日趋求实和简约，比较典型的有宋代的“八段锦”，明清时代的“十二段锦”“十六段锦”以及“太极拳”，保留了中国导引术“导气令和，引体令柔”的特色，动作缓慢，以意导气，以气运身，疏通经络，调理脏腑，以期养生健身。

词语注释

【1】外家拳术：拳术的著名流派之一。相传外家说法起源于少林拳术，以主动攻击搏人为主，重而紧猛，练外家拳的人则肌肉结实丰满，以钢筋铁骨为精髓。

【2】内家拳术：拳术的著名流派之一。相传起源于宋代张三丰，拳法以静制动，使犯者应手而仆，以柔克刚为精髓。

【3】五禽戏：也称“五禽操”。一种仿生健身术。由模仿虎、鹿、熊、猿、鸟五种禽兽的神态和动作组成。每一禽戏有若干动作组成套路。由汉代名医华佗将导引术与五行、脏象、气血、经络等学说结合创编而成。

【4】内功：锻炼身体内部器官的武术或气功，对外功而言。

【5】以意运气：重视意念的作用，以气催力，意到气到力到；非以力使气；全身意在精神，不在气，在气则滞；有气则无力，无气则纯刚。

三、武术与兵法

孙　武

中国人经常提到：“声东击西”“敌进我退”“知己知彼，百战不殆”[1]“因敌制胜”等，这都是中国古代的兵书中出现的术语。中国古代战争频繁，出现了许多军事理论家，撰写关于战争谋略学的兵书。其内容之丰富，在世界上当是首屈一指。《汉书·艺文志》著录古代兵书有53家，790篇。可见古代兵法流派众多，内容丰富。由于这些兵书植根于中华传统文化沃土，武术技击原理和军事战略、战术息息相通，一脉相承。加之不少武艺高强者参军实战后，增长了兵法知识，成为将帅之才，岳飞、戚继光便是其中佼佼者。古谚所谓：“古来习拳知兵法，不知兵法莫练拳。”即是古代兵法对武术深刻的反映。

武术与兵法早在先秦时代就有着极为密切的联系。《庄子·说剑》就涉及许多兵法之道，如诱敌来攻，因敌应变，后发制人。《孙子兵法》中朴素的军事哲学思想、灵活机动的战略战术，对武术技击理论的形成有重要的影响。《孙子兵法》提出的“知己知彼，百战不殆”，“攻其无备，出其不意”，“后人发，先人至”等，都被武术家作为武术技击的基本法则，备受推崇。其中《计篇》论述了用兵打仗是一种诡诈之术。简介了诡道十二法，能打，却装着不能打，要打，却装着不想打。而《太极拳经谱》中亦有“佯输诈败，制胜权衡，顺来逆往，令彼莫测。”《太极拳经总歌》中也有“佯输诈走谁云败？引诱回冲制胜归。”其文字虽异，说理相通，皆言战争与武打的特性——诡诈性，目的相同，那就是克敌制胜。《水浒传》中林冲棒打洪教头即为“诡道”应用范例。披枷戴锁的八十万禁军教头林冲，面临咄咄逼人的洪教头的挑战时，先说不敢，交手仅几个回合，又跳出圈外认输。开枷后正式比武，还是先往后退，诱得洪教头志得意满，轻敌冒进，连续攻打。待其步乱后，林冲只一棒就把洪教头打翻在地，此为后发制人。

《孙子兵法》还提出：兵为凶器，不可轻易发动战争。作战要知己知彼，才能百战百胜；不知彼而知己，一胜一负；不知彼不知己，每战必败。战争对于败方或胜方都有重大的损失等等。自此书问世以后，不仅被中国历代军事指挥家奉为经典，而且闻名于世界，并被译成日、法、英、德、俄、捷等多种文本，在国外广为流传，被誉为“东方兵学鼻祖”“兵学圣典”“世界古代第一兵书”，在世界军事史上占有重要地位。

总之，古代兵法对武术影响较大的几个方面：审时度势，知己知彼，胆气为先，兵之情主速，先发制人，避实击虚，诡道诱敌等。

在古代战争短兵相接[2]的条件下，为要求战场上统一的指挥和协同动作而产生了阵法。中国古代很讲求阵法。所谓“阵”，就是军队在投入战斗时，根据地形条件、敌我实力等具体情况而布置的战斗队形。中国古代作战是非常讲究作战队形的，称之为“布阵”。布阵得法就能充分发挥军队的战斗力，克敌制胜。其中著名的有八卦阵、撒星阵[3]、鸳鸯阵[4]等。如《三国演义》中诸葛亮与八卦阵的故事，说的是刘备在夷陵兵败，当陆逊追击蜀军夔门关不远，发现前面临山傍江，一阵杀气，冲天而起，疑有伏兵，令大军撤退待命。几次派人侦探，并无一卒一骑。找来土人询问，才知此是诸葛亮设下八卦阵[5]。吴军几十万大军进入诸葛亮的八卦阵，刹那间，飞沙走石，遮天盖地，横沙立土，重叠如山。江声浪涌，有如剑鼓齐鸣。陆逊大惊，却无法寻觅外出之路，后来由于高人的指点，吴军才摆脱了困境。

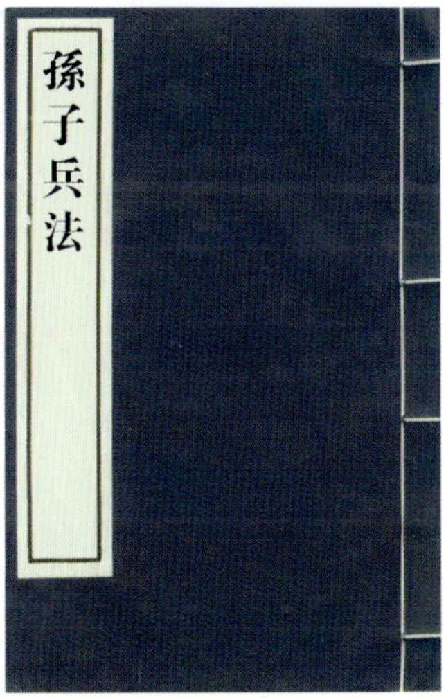

孙子兵法

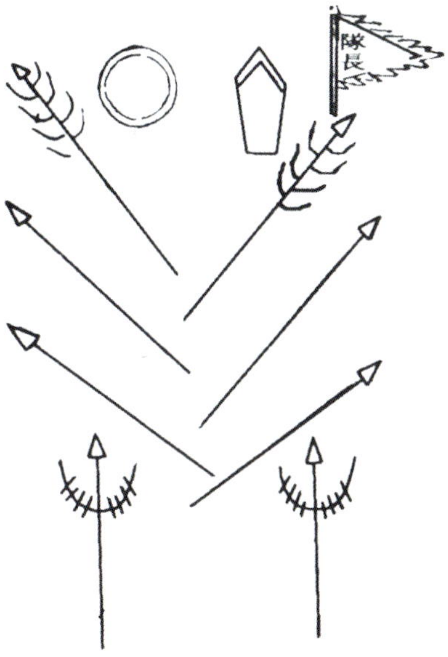

鸳鸯阵法图

词语注释

【1】知己知彼，百战不殆：原意是如果对敌我双方的情况都能了解透彻，打起仗来就可以立于不败之地。泛指对双方情况都很了解。

【2】短兵相接：双方用刀剑等短兵器进行搏斗。

【3】撒星阵：是南宋名将岳飞破金兵“拐子马”（骑兵的一种）的阵法。撒星阵的队形布列如星，连成一排的“拐子马”冲来时士兵散而不聚，使敌人扑空。等敌人后撤时散开的士兵再聚拢过来，猛力扑击敌人，并用刀专砍马腿，以破“拐子马”。

【4】鸳鸯阵：是明代将领戚继光为抗击倭寇而创设的一种阵法。他把士兵分为三队，当敌人进到百步时第一队士兵发射火器；敌人进到六十步时第二队士兵发射弩箭；敌人进到十步时第三队士兵用刀矛向敌人冲杀。这些变化反映了中国作战阵法从传统的方阵向多兵种的集团阵法演变的过程。

【5】八卦阵：也称八阵，这是战国时期的大军事家孙膑创造的，据说孙膑是受了《易经》八卦图的启发创造了此阵法，所以就称八卦阵。具体阵势是大将居中、四面各布一队正兵，正兵之间再派出四队机动作战的奇兵，构成八阵。八阵散布成八，复而为一，

分合变化，又可组成六十四阵。当年诸葛亮还用石头在四川奉节布设过八阵的方位，作为教练将士演习阵法之用，名为“八阵图”。

四、十八般兵器

“十八般兵器”之称是从“十八般武艺”一词演化而来，所谓十八般兵器是中国民间对古代兵器的泛称。今天，武术界普遍对“十八般兵器”的解说则是：刀、槊（shuò）[1]、枪、剑、戟（jǐ）[2]、斧、钺（yuè）[3]、钩[4]、叉、鞭[5]、锏（jiǎn）[6]、锤[7]、殳（shū）[8]、镋（tǎng）[9]、棍、棒、抓[10]、流星[11]。

最早出自汉武帝时期（公元前107年），经过严格的挑选和整理，筛选出18种类型的兵器。到了三国时代，又根据兵器的特点，对汉武帝钦定的“十八般兵器”重新排列为九长九短。九长：刀、矛、戟、槊、镗、钺、棍、枪、叉；九短：斧、戈、盾、箭、鞭、剑、锏、锤、抓。

从以上各说法来看，十八般武艺所列兵器大同小异，形式和内容却十分丰富。有长器械，泛指其长度等于或超过练武者直立时从脚底至眉的高度的器械，如长棍、枪、大刀、方天戟等。短器械，武术短柄器械的统称，其长度一般指超过练武者的小臂，而短于练武者直立地面至眉的高度，如短刀、剑、钩、锏等。软器械，泛指各种以环、链和绳索为中间环节串联而成的器械。如三节鞭、九节鞭、梢子棍等。双器械，泛指双手持握形制相同、左右对称的器械。如双刀、双剑、双钩、双鞭等。有带钩的、带刺的、带尖的、带刃的；有明的、暗的；有攻的、防的；有打的、杀的、击的、射的、挡的。

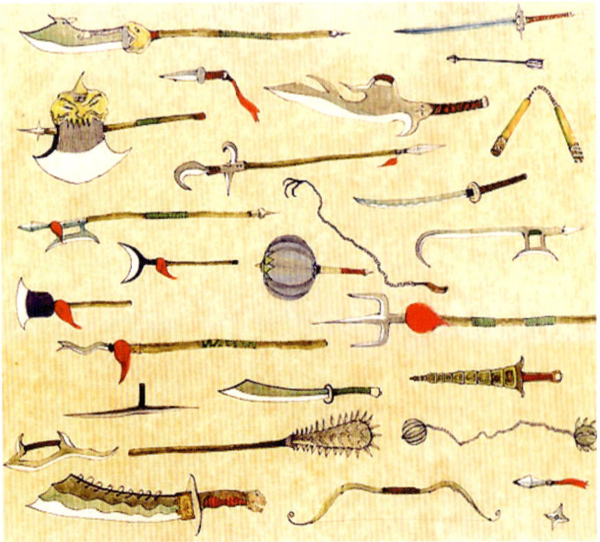

十八般兵器

在中国漫长的历史长河中，由于战争实践决定了对兵器的弃劣存优，十八般兵器中的一些兵器后来成为仪仗队专用品，有的则不被采用而散失民间。但是作为兵器演练却成为一门专门的艺术，在中国戏剧、杂技舞台表演中仍占有一定的地位。兵器的性质不一，使用对象也多有区别。中国武侠小说中柔和纤弱的女性、温文尔雅的书生，通常使用轻便灵活的“剑”；身材魁梧、性格粗爽的大汉，则不是用威风凛凛的“刀”，就是用沉重的“狼牙棒”[12]。在中国古典小说中，兵器甚至成为人物的象征，青龙偃（yǎn）月刀[13]是关羽的，方天画戟[14]是吕布的，金箍棒[15]是孙悟空的，这些兵器与人物的定型化在中国家喻户晓。有些兵器技能一直流传至今，在群众中有雄厚的基础，成为群众热爱的体育运动项目。

中国传统武术是从使用兵器开始的，形成与战争中使用兵器完全不同的特点：（一）武术是个体对打，讲究刀剑一招一式的功夫，枪法、剑法不乱；（二）技击双方对峙是常有的，有所谓“以静制动”“后发制人”；（三）战场上使用兵器容不得虚假，而武术中可以虚虚实实、真真假假。

词语注释

【1】槊：古代兵器，长杆矛。

【2】戟：是一种既可刺杀也可钩啄具有双重性能的古代兵器，在长柄的一端装有青铜或铁制的枪尖，旁边附有月牙形锋刃。

【3】钺：古代兵器，青铜或铁制成，形状像板斧而较大。

【4】钩：古代兵器，弯曲带尖的兵器——似剑而曲，所以钩杀人。

【5】鞭：古代兵器。用铁链做成，有节而没有锋刃，鞭打、击杀人时有如挥动的赶牲畜的鞭子。

【6】锏：古代兵器，方形有四棱，连把有1米多长，因形似简故名。与鞭同属短兵器，因为二者形制相似，所以历代都把鞭、锏相提并论。

【7】锤：古代兵器，柄的上头有一个金属圆球形重物，用以击杀人。

【8】殳：古代兵器，一种用竹或木制成的，八棱，顶端装有圆形金属，无刃。也有装金属刺球，顶端带矛的。起撞击作用，或作依仗。

【9】镋：古代兵器。一般头的两边形似马叉，中间似剑状。上有利刃，长0.5米，尖锐如枪，横有弯股刃，两锋中有脊。锋与横刃互镶，并嵌于约2米多长的柄上，柄下端有长约20厘米的梭状铁钻。

【10】抓：古代兵器。又称挝，在民间流传较广。抓头形似爪，缚以长绳或木柄。抓分长械及软械两种。长械有“金龙抓”，杆长约2米，杆端有抓形如人手，中指伸直，四指屈挠。软械叫双飞挝，系暗器的一种，用金属打造，像鹰爪，缚以长绳，用于击人马，脱手掷去，着身后收回，使其不能脱走。近代这一器械演练者已很少。

【11】流星：流星锤，是一种将金属锤头系于长绳一端或两端制成的软兵器，亦属索系暗器类。

【12】狼牙棒：古兵器名。用坚重之木为棒，长约1.5米，上端长圆如枣，遍嵌铁钉，形如狼牙。

【13】青龙偃月刀：刀类兵器名。因形如偃月，并雕有青龙，故称。

【14】方天画戟：古代兵器。是一种在戟杆一端装有金属枪尖，一侧有月牙形利刃通过两枚小枝与枪尖相连的利器。使用者有三国时期的吕布和唐朝的薛仁贵。

【15】金箍棒：神魔小说《西游记》中孙悟空使用的兵器。

五、十八般武艺

在中国古典小说戏剧和传统评书中，常常可见“十八般武艺样样精通”之类的词句，元·杨梓《敬德不服老》第一折：“凭着俺十八般武艺，定下了六十四处征尘。”明·施耐庵《水浒传》第二回：“史进每日求王教头点拨十八般武艺，一一从头指教。哪十八般武艺？矛锤弓弩铳，鞭锏剑链挝，斧钺并戈戟，牌棒与枪杈。”是对武将本领高超的一句赞语。这和用“才高八斗”之类的词语来形容文人博学多才一样。现在也经常用来形容某个人物的本领高强。

“十八般武艺”一般指使用十八般兵器的技艺，是中国古代对各种武术技艺的统称。其实，十八般武艺中的数字十八，并不止十八个，这和中国民族传统中的习惯用语有关。古人认为九是数字之极，历来喜欢用九或九的倍数来表示高深广众的事物，因此“十八般武艺”同十八罗汉[1]、一百零八将等说法同出一源，这是一个概数，即笼统地指多数，有时还有夸张或强调的意思。中国古典小说中，经常将武侠好汉描写成十八般武艺样样精通。比如宋代英雄杨家将当中的杨五郎曾被描述为“十八般武艺无所不拈，无所不会”。少林正宗[2]功夫中也包括十八般武艺。

一代少林高僧海灯法师[3]习武的毅力、恒心和刻苦精神十分令人钦佩。他貌不惊人，年近八旬时还容光焕发，十八般武艺样样皆能，剑和三截棍[4]尤

十八般武艺

有独到之处。早年还练袖剑，百发百中。他的轻功[5]也出奇惊人，普通平房，他一跃而登屋顶，竟然毫无痕迹。他的散打以空手夺刀最为拿手，套路有百余种，出拳力大无穷。早在20世纪50年代，海灯法师就已享有盛名。

实际上，现实生活中真正精通十八般武艺的人并不多。每位古代英雄往往精通一两种兵器，但是一种兵器就有几十种花样。如枪，就有长枪、短枪等十几种，而枪的技法更是种类繁多，著名的有赵云、杨家将、岳飞等人的枪法，使用枪的花样品种多得让人眼花缭乱。《水浒传》中的李逵长期使用板斧，充分掌握了斧头的使用技巧，有劈、剁、搂、抹、云、片等，舞动起来姿势优美，风格粗犷、豪放。有些梁山好汉的绰号取名也都与兵器有关，兵器几乎成了表明其身份、个性的名片。

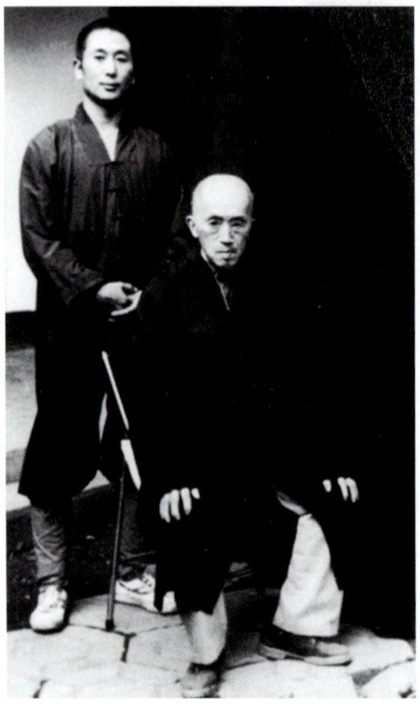

海灯法师及其弟子

词语注释

【1】十八罗汉：佛教称如来佛的十六弟子和降龙、伏虎两罗汉为十八罗汉。

【2】正宗：佛教禅宗称初祖达摩所传的嫡派。后也指行业、学术、思想的嫡传正派或传统事物。

【3】海灯法师：高僧（公元1902年～1989年），原名范无病，四川江油县人。幼年多病，跟舅父薛久志学剑，以武功强身。17岁毕业于绵阳南山师范学校，后相继就读于法政学院（四川大学前身）文学系和省立警监专科学校。只因父亲范绍安被恶霸黄团练迫害致死，为报父仇，他历访名师学武。20岁投昭觉寺智化上人座下学佛，披剃出家。1989年1月11日圆寂。

【4】三截棍：属武术软器械的一种。它由三条等长的短棍中间以铁环连接而成，又称“三节鞭”。

【5】轻功：属武当内家功中的一项功夫。以练内气为先，用意将丹田气往上引提，使身体飘逸，百念俱弃，气通百脉，而身轻似燕。其功可使人心境开阔爽朗，乐观无忧，益寿延年。

第十八章　古代中外文化交流

在中外文化交流的历史长河里，中外文化交流曾出现三次大的高潮。张骞出使西域后，打开了中西交通的新纪元，中华文化源源不断地传向中亚、欧洲，促进西方世界文明的进步；同时中国也吸收西方先进的人类文明成果，不断丰富和促进中华文明。随着海陆两途丝绸之路的发展与繁荣，中外文化交流出现了历史上的第一次高潮。中国丝绸、冶铸和水利技术远播中亚、朝鲜、日本和欧洲地区。汉字也传入朝鲜。儒学经典传到日本。佛教、象牙、香料、宝石和多种植物等传入中国。唐、宋、元时期，中外文化交流进入一个十分活跃的新时期。中国的造纸、纺织、印刷术、指南针、火药传入朝鲜、日本、印度、阿拉伯和欧洲。印度的制糖、天文、医学、音乐、舞蹈、佛教等传入中国。明末清初，伴随着外国传教士来华，欧洲的科技文化在中国的传播使中外文化交流出现了第三次高潮。明清之际的科技著作《本草纲目》《天工开物》被译成许多种文字流传国外。当时中国先进的技术、文化传入南洋。原产美洲的甘薯、玉米、马铃薯、烟草传入中国。明朝还引进欧洲的水利方法以及科技著作。纵观历史，国力强盛是对外文化交流的前提，是世界文明进步的趋势。在中外文化交流的历史长河里，我们只能撷取几朵浪花，透视中外文化交流的壮阔波澜。

一、东渡日本的鉴真和尚

鉴真生于公元 688 年，扬州（今江苏扬州）人。他的父亲是个商人，也是非常虔诚的佛教徒。鉴真从小受父亲影响，对佛教产生了浓厚兴趣，14 岁即到扬州大云寺出家。21 岁到长安、洛阳等地游学，潜心研究佛经。22 岁在长安一座佛寺里受具足戒[1]。26 岁回到扬州，为大明寺（今法净寺[2]）的大师。由于渊博的学识和高尚的品德，当他 45 岁时，已经成为名扬四方的高僧，受其传戒者前后有 4 万余人。

隋唐时期，中、日两国人民的友好往来更加密切。从唐太宗贞观四年（公元 630 年）到唐昭宗乾宁元年（公元 894 年），日本派出遣唐使共 12 次，每次都在 100 人以上，最多的一次有 650 人。很多日本留学生进入唐朝的最高学府国子监深造，有的在中国居住 20 年以上，有的留在唐朝做官。当时，日本受中国影响，大力提倡佛教。他们仿照唐朝修建佛寺，派遣僧徒到中国学习佛学，并打算聘请中国的高僧去日本传授戒律。唐玄宗天宝[3]元年（公元 742 年），在中国留学的日本僧人荣睿（ruì）、普照[4]，受日本天皇派遣，专程来到扬州大明寺，邀请鉴真去日本传法。当时鉴真已经 54 岁，他欣然应允，其弟子祥彦

▶▶ 鉴真和尚

有畏难情绪，说：“日本和中国有大海阻隔，路途危险，往者很少能安全到达。”鉴真坚定地说：“为传法这样的大事，怎能顾惜生命，你们不去，我自己去。”在鉴真精神的感召下，他的弟子纷纷表示愿意随师傅前往。

鉴真和尚东渡，先后失败过五次。鉴真并未因他的得力助手日本僧人荣睿和弟子祥彦相继去世而灰心丧志，又过了5年，66岁高龄的鉴真双目失明，毅然决定再度出航。这次同航的有四只船，一号船又在航行中遇难。鉴真等人乘的是二号船，经历了漂海的艰难航程，于天宝十三年（公元754年）初到达日本九州萨摩国阿多郡秋妻屋浦（今日本鹿儿岛县）。鉴真一行在前后12年当中，六次启行，五次失败，航海三次，先后有36人献出了生命。但是他百折不屈，虽然双目失明，终于实现了毕生的心愿，在68岁高龄时踏上了日本国土。

鉴真一行到达当时的京都奈良，受到以天皇为首的举国上下的热烈欢迎，轰动了日本全国。鉴真在日本生活了10年，他除了向日本传布佛教，还带去了灿烂的盛唐文化。鉴真带去了王羲之、王献之[5]等人的书迹50余帖，大大推动了当时日本佛教和民间风行的“王体”书法。孝谦天皇题的《唐招提寺》匾额就是王体，至今日本朝廷还珍藏着鉴真带去的王羲之书迹。鉴真东渡日本还带去了许多药材和验方，他为光明皇太后治过病，为圣武天皇会诊。他还受朝廷委托，对日本药物口尝、鼻嗅，鉴别真伪。此外，鉴真还带去了扬州寺院盛行的豆腐制作技术，至今日本还奉鉴真为豆食制作祖师。鉴真将中国的建筑、雕塑、医药等介绍到日本，为中日文化交流作出了卓越的贡献。

公元763年，鉴真圆寂[6]，为了纪念这位高僧，日本将鉴真的坐像供奉在鉴真和尚亲手主持兴建的唐招提寺中，雕像高90分米，面向西方，双手拱合，结跏（jiā）趺（fū）坐[7]，闭目含笑，两唇紧敛，表现了鉴真圆寂时的姿态，现已被定为日本国宝。1980年，唐招提寺第81代长老森本孝顺亲自护送此像回中国探亲。在1 200多年以后的今天，中日两国人民还如此尊重鉴真、怀念鉴真，正是因为他在沟通中日两国文化、加强两国人民的友好关系方面作出了巨大贡献。

词语注释

【1】受具足戒：具足戒，即佛教戒律。受具足戒，是佛教高级受戒仪式，受戒者经此仪式而取得正式僧尼资格。

【2】法净寺：原名大明寺，又名中天竺。位于杭州天竺路中段。始建于隋开皇十七年（597），据说南宋初，佛教护法神二十诸天的第十六位女神“感应显灵”而备受朝廷尊宠，成为著名的寺院。

【3】天宝：唐玄宗的年号。

【4】日本僧人荣睿、普照：荣睿，日本美浓（今日本岐阜县）人，奈良兴福寺和尚。唐玄宗开元二十一年（公元733年）他和日本僧人普照随遣唐使团来中国留学。

【5】王献之：东晋书法家（公元 344 年～ 386 年），字子敬，会稽山阴（今浙江绍兴）人。为王羲之第七子。王献之的书法博采众家之长、兼善诸体之美，赢得了与王羲之并列的艺术地位和声望。历来与王羲之并称“二王”，或尊称为“小圣”。

【6】圆寂：僧人去世。

【7】结跏趺坐：佛教徒坐法，将右脚盘于左腿上，左脚盘放于右腿上的坐姿。

二、丝绸之路

“丝绸之路”是中国古代经由中亚通往南亚、西亚以及欧洲、北非的陆上贸易交往的通道，由于大量的中国蚕丝和丝织品经由此路西传，所以被称为“丝绸之路”。

中国是丝绸的故乡，是世界上第一个发明丝绸的国家。早在战国时期，精美的中国丝绸已经由欧亚草原的游牧民族传向西北部地区，受到其他民族的喜爱。而到了西汉年间，汉武帝派遣张骞 (qiān) 出使西域[1]以后，逐渐开辟了丝绸之路。成批的汉朝使者和商人，满载丝绸，从京都长安出发经玉门关到达西域。

张骞出使西域图（莫高窟第323窟）

当时的“丝绸之路”南道可西行到现在的阿富汗、乌兹别克斯坦、伊朗，最远可到达埃及的亚历山大城；另一条路经过巴基斯坦、阿富汗喀布尔，到达波斯湾头；如果从喀布尔南行，可以到达现在的巴基斯坦卡拉奇，转海路也可以到达古波斯和古罗马等地。据说丝绸传到古罗马后备受贵族喜爱，他们争相竞购，使得丝绸在罗马城中与黄金等值。

丝路的畅通，不仅使中国丝绸源源输往西方，同时也将毛织品、香料、宝石、金银铸币、金银器、玻璃器等输入中国。西亚和中亚的音乐、舞蹈、饮食、服饰等也经由丝绸之路源源传入中国。沿着丝路还传来了新品种的植物和动物，中国古代文献中记载的一批带有“胡”字的植物，如胡桃、胡瓜、胡椒、胡萝卜等，大多来自西域。特别是来自乌孙[2]的“西极马”和来自大宛[3]的“天马”[4]等优良马种，对中国古代马种的改良具有较为深远的影响。与此同时，中国古代的许多重要的发明、物产和技术也经过“丝绸之路”传到各地，像丝绸、农桑、造纸术、印刷术、漆器、瓷器、火药、指南针等，为世界文明作出了重大的贡献。

西晋以后在皇室的大力支持下，开始了丝绸之路沿线诸地的开窟造像[5]之风。现存的重要石窟如云冈石窟、敦煌莫高窟、天水麦积山石窟、永靖炳灵寺[6]等，都保留有大量魏晋时代的雕塑和绘画作品，成为中国佛教艺术的宝库。丝绸之路沿线石窟寺的兴旺情景，正反映出当年这条商路的通畅繁荣。宋代以后，中国经济重心南移，造船航海事业也有了极大发展，海上航路的畅通、便利，人们逐渐放弃了陆路那横越大漠荒山的艰苦旅程，丝路贸易日趋衰落。

词语注释

【1】张骞出使西域：闻名世界的“丝绸之路”，是张骞出使西域时开辟的。公元前 138 年，张骞以郎（皇帝侍从官）的身份第一次出使西域。公元前 119 年，受汉武帝的派遣，张骞率领随行人员 300 多人，带着

大批物品再次出使西域。到了那里以后，他们分头访问了许多地区。

【2】乌孙：中国古代西北地区国名，位于河西走廊西部张掖至敦煌一带。

【3】大宛：中国古代西北地区国名。大约位于今塔吉克斯坦共和国费尔干纳一带，为西域三十六国之一，北通康居，南面和西南面与大月氏接，产汗血马。

【4】乌孙的“西极马”和来自大宛的“天马”：这两个地区的马历史上被称之为西极马和天马。

【5】开窟造像：开凿石窟、雕造佛像。

【6】永靖炳灵寺：位于甘肃永靖县以西 35 千米、黄河北岸积石山中。历经北魏、北周、隋、唐、宋、西夏、元、明、清各代都有不断的开凿与修缮，现存泥塑造像 800 尊、壁画千余平方米。

三、马可·波罗到中国

马可·波罗出生在意大利水城威尼斯的一个巨商家庭。当时东方的文明，中国的丝绸早已通过“丝绸之路”传到欧洲，在欧洲人的心目中，东方是神秘的、

马可波罗碑

是黄金和财富的蕴藏地，然而东方又是稀奇古怪的。公元 1275 年，年仅 17 岁的马可·波罗怀着好奇的心情跟随父亲和叔父开始东方游历的艰苦行程。他们走过荒无人烟的沙漠，越过帕米尔高原，再往东，经过中国的新疆、甘肃等地到达元朝的上都（今内蒙古自治区正蓝旗东北），受到在那里避暑的元世祖忽必烈[1]的欢迎和友好款待。从此，马可·波罗在中国度过了 17 个春秋。马可·波罗聪明好学，很快掌握了蒙古语和汉语，熟悉了中国的典章制度，得到了朝野上下的好感。他被任命为扬州总督[2]，到过中国的许多地方，也出使过南洋、越南、爪哇[3]、苏门答腊[4]等地，看到了当时中国一些城市和乡村风貌。

在杭州城内，他看到这里的风景犹如威尼斯，有 1.2 万座桥梁，城中还有一个美丽的大湖。杭州城的人们的住房清洁富丽，与欧洲的贵族无异。听说杭州城每一天消耗的胡椒达 43 担（每一担重 123 磅），他非常吃惊，从中推算出每天要消费掉多少其他香料，也推算出这里每天所需的全部生活必需品是多么的巨大。

在成都，他看到发源于远山的河水围绕和穿过这座平川大城，大河宽深，清澈见底，有的桥上经营着各种生意。桥既是沟通彼岸的通道，又成了人们交易的场所，同时又是官府收纳通行税的关口，可谓一举三得。在城外，马可·波罗惊叹这里的人们以务农为主，还经营许多制造业作坊，尤其是能纺织精美漂亮的丝绸。

进入云南后，他看到人们用小麦和稻米酿造美酒，感到非常奇怪。他认为酒只能用葡萄酿制，而粮食酒，是使人们驱风寒、鼓勇气的上等饮料。在保山地区，马可·波罗对人们的装饰很感诧异，这里有一种用金片镶牙的习俗，无论男女老少的牙齿都以金做套，一言一笑，金光满口，闪亮夺目。昂贵的黄金用来装饰，是一种爱美的追求。

公元 1290 年，马可·波罗结束了在元朝政府 17 年的仕宦生活，回到威尼斯。不久，他参加了对热那亚城的海战，兵败被俘入狱。他在狱中口述其在东方的见闻，由同狱难友为之笔录，这就是举世闻名

的《马可·波罗游记》。它的问世，轰动了西方世界，东方中国给欧洲人带来了一个新天地，中国的西南边地也成了欧洲人钦慕和渴望涉足的地方。

词语注释

【1】忽必烈：元世祖（公元 1215 年 ~ 1294 年），姓孛儿只斤氏，蒙古族，元朝的开国皇帝。公元 1260 ~ 1294 年在位。公元 1271 年，忽必烈改国号为大元，正式即位为皇帝，并开始南下攻打南宋的计划。公元 1279 年，南宋亡，忽必烈统治中国。忽必烈确立中央集权政治，恢复正常的统治秩序，采取有利于农业和手工业生产的措施，使社会经济逐步恢复和发展，边疆地区得到开发。

【2】总督：专管某地区事务的政府官员。

【3】爪哇：古国名。即今南洋群岛的爪哇岛。

【4】苏门答腊：印度尼西亚西部大岛，东北隔马六甲海峡同马来半岛相望，东南临南海和爪哇海，西南临印度洋。面积 43.4 万平方千米。

四、郑和下西洋

在中外文化交流史中，有一位伟大的航海家名叫郑和。从公元 1405 年到 1433 年，他率领庞大的船队七次抵达西洋，不仅是世界航行史上的壮举，而且有力地促进了中国人民与东南亚及非洲人民的友谊和往来。

郑 和

郑和（公元 1371 年 ~ 1435 年），本姓马，小字三保，云南昆阳（今晋宁）人，回族。大约 14 世纪末明朝军队占领云南后，少年郑和被迫去做了宦官。他办事干练勤快，又有胆识，得到明成祖的信任。明成祖为燕王时，赐其姓郑。而民间叫惯了他的小名，一直把他叫做“三保太监”。

公元 1405 年 6 月，明成祖正式派郑和为使者，带一支船队出使“西洋”。那时，人们叫的“西洋”，并不是指欧洲大陆，而是指中国南海以西的海和沿海各地。郑和带的船队规模很大，一共有 28 000 多人，除了兵士和水手，还有技术人员、翻译、医生、铁匠、木船匠等。他们乘坐 62 艘大船，这种船长近 150 米，宽约 60 米，在当时是少见的。船队从苏州刘家河（今江苏太仓浏河）出发，经过福建沿海，浩浩荡荡，扬帆南下。船上设有航海图，满载着金银绸缎和瓷器等珍贵的货物。

郑和第一次下西洋先到了占城（在今越南南方），接着又到爪哇、旧港（在今印度尼西亚苏门答腊岛东南岸）、苏门答腊、满剌加[1]（马六甲）、锡兰（斯里兰卡）等国家。他带着大批金银财物，每到一个国家，先把明成祖的信递交国王，并且把带去的礼物送给当地人，希望同他们友好交往。许多国家见郑和带了那么大的船队，态度友好，并不是来威吓他们，都热情

郑和下西洋路线图

地接待他。公元1407年10月，船队满载着象牙、胡椒、香料和药材返航，圆满地完成了首次航行的任务，受到了明成祖的褒奖。从此以后，郑和又六次率领船队出使西洋。他先后到过20余个国家，最远航程到达非洲东海岸和红海沿岸。

公元1431年，郑和最后一次下西洋时已是61岁的高龄，两年后回国，不久就去世了。郑和的七次航行，表现了中国古代人民顽强的探索精神，也说明当时中国航海技术已经有了很高的水平。郑和下西洋，加深了中国与各国人民的友好交往，至今在一些国家和地区还流传着郑和的故事和传说。为了纪念郑和，泰国建有三宝港、三宝庙和三宝塔；印尼有三宝城、三宝洞；马来西亚有三宝城、三宝井等。郑和的大规模远航，早于欧洲航海家们半个多世纪。公元1492年，哥伦布发现了美洲新大陆，公元1497年，达·伽马沿着非洲西岸绕过好望角，到达了印度海岸。他们的船队也无法和郑和相比。郑和不愧是一位伟大的航海家，中外文化交流的友好使者。

词语注释

【1】满剌加：即马六甲，马来西亚古城，马六甲州首府。地处马六甲河东西两岸冲积平原，马六甲海峡东岸南段。居民多为华人。约建于公元1400年，公元1405年成为马六甲王国都城。一度是东南亚的国际贸易中心。公元1511年沦为葡萄牙殖民地。公元1641年为荷兰占据。公元1826年成为英国海峡殖民地一部分。先后有华人、印度人、阿拉伯人、暹罗人、爪哇人来此居住。后因马六甲河口的淤塞和槟城、新加坡的兴起，城市地位下降。

编 后 语

《中华文化概览》（书 + DVD-ROM）为国家出版基金项目，从选材、编写、编译到制作，历经多次修改，终于面世了，我们感到十分欣慰。这部作品，是《中华文化概览》编委会遵循传承文明、积累文化、服务当代、繁荣出版的原则，为弘扬中华文化、促进中外文化交流向中外读者倾力奉献的一部双语普及型读本。

为保证精品力作，质量第一，编委会邀请了中外多位专家学者参与《中华文化概览》的编译和审校工作，集中大家的智慧，做到了中文选材简要精当、外文编译准确流畅，整部作品文脉清晰、重点突出。其中，中文由中国古代文化和文学造诣较深、著述颇多的天津外国语大学郑铁生教授主持编写；英文版由曾多次完成国际性重大会议文件翻译工作的天津外国语大学优秀教师团队完成；原天津古籍出版社社长杨钟贤教授对中文稿件进行了认真审阅；英、日、韩多位专家学者对外文版进行了仔细的审校。

本作品在申报国家出版基金项目的过程中，得到了中国比较文学教学研究会副会长孟昭毅教授的鼎力支持与推荐。在此，特向孟昭毅、杨钟贤先生以及为该书出版作出贡献的外籍专家致以诚挚的谢意。天津外国语大学科研处对本书的出版也给予了极大支持。另外，本作品的部分照片与资料从有关书籍中选取，我们也诚挚地向原作者致谢，相关版权问题，已委托中华版权代理公司代为处理，特此说明。

《中华文化概览》编委会

2010 年 8 月

Understanding the "Dragon":
A Panorama of Chinese Culture

Zheng Tiesheng (Chinese)
Chen Fachun (English)

Preface

Culture enjoys multiplicity. Great differences between Eastern and Western cultures have never been erased over thousands of years. Any attempt to enlarge the differences or to widen the gap between cultures will likely create cultural barriers or even conflicts. It is therefore natural, in the rapid process of economic globalization and world integration, for people all over the world to reach this common understanding that every nation should learn about and from other cultures, promote its own culture and strengthen cultural exchanges with other nations.

With the expansion of China's opening up and its rapid social and economic development, China desires and makes efforts to learn more about western culture. Likewise, China's rich culture, especially its long history and uniqueness appeals to an increasing number of people from other countries.

Understanding "the Dragon": A Panorama of Chinese Culture, jointly published by Tianjin Foreign Language Audio-Visual Publishing House and Tianjin Education Press, provides an insight for foreign friends into the splendid Chinese culture.

The book covers many typical and unique aspects of Chinese culture, such as ancient cultural heritage, far-reaching schools of thoughts including Confucianism, Taoism and Buddhism; Chinese medicine, martial arts and drama; currency, science and technology, crafts, food, arts, folk arts and exchanges with other countries.

This book (with DVD-ROM) is bilingual in Chinese and English versions, Chinese and Japanese versions, and Chinese and Korean versions. Each chapter is followed by notes which can help learners of Chinese better understand the Chinese language and culture. In addition, the book provides detailed explanations about terms, historical and geographical locations and Chinese philosophy, which are very helpful for English learners in China to gain an in-depth understanding of their own traditional culture.

Language is the carrier and symbol of culture. This book aims not only as a medium for cultural exchange, but also as a good reader for language learners–both foreigners interested in Chinese culture and Chinese engaged in cross-cultural communication.

At present, integration between the East and the West is becoming a trend as cultures created by different nations are considered to be part of the treasure house of world civilization shared by people of the world over. It is my hope that this book will play a positive role in the process of this cultural integration.

Xiu Gang
President of Tianjin Foreign Studies University
May, 2010

(Translated by Wang Huiyun)

Foreword

In the present great era when China is engaged in dialogue with the rest of the world, there is an increasing urgency to promote Chinese culture to other nations. On the other hand, popularizing the splendid Chinese culture in a systematic and comprehensive way will also help Chinese people to have a deeper understanding about their own culture, boost national pride, national cohesion and patriotism.

A timely publication, *Understanding "the Dragon": A Panorama of Chinese Culture*, caters not only to non-native speakers of medium and advanced levels but also to native Chinese readers.

There are two reasons to compile a bilingual version of *Understanding "the Dragon": A Panorama of Chinese Culture*:

First, with the expansion of China's opening up, more and more people of other nations continue to be attracted by the uniqueness of Chinese culture. However, many overseas students say that the most difficult part of learning Chinese is understanding Chinese culture. Therefore, the first reason to write this book is to help overseas students to have a quick but comprehensive understanding of Chinese culture while, at the same time, learning the Chinese language.

Second, many Chinese people, whether they are foreign language learners and teachers, or scholars, officials and businessmen, realize the need to improve their knowledge about Chinese culture and also find it difficult to explain it in another language. So besides being a rich resource of Chinese culture, this bilingual work can also be used as a reference by the above mentioned people when communicating with those of other cultures.

Chinese culture is extensive and profound. We have tried to make this book comprehensive but brief. Being comprehensive means the book should cover as widely and systematically as possible the rich Chinese culture. The 18 chapters of this book include almost all the aspects of Chinese culture. Being brief means that the book focuses on the most essential and characteristic aspects of Chinese culture.

We have followed three principles while compiling the book: first, to be systematic and comprehensive; second, to be specific; and third, to be easy to understand.

This book can help you better understand Chinese culture when you travel in China, visiting historic sites, museums, galleries, craft workshops, theatres and restaurants, and we hope you will be more fascinated by Chinese culture after reading it.

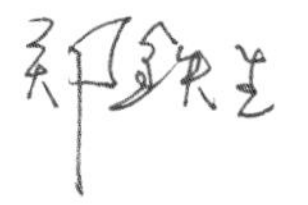

Zheng Tiesheng
May, 2010

(Translated by Wang Huiyun)

Chapter One The Origin of the Dragon

DRAGON CULTURE

As the symbol of Chinese culture, the image of the dragon originated from totems of different tribes in ancient China. Whether it be the Chinese character "龙" (dragon) seen on Oracle Bones or those carved into bronze vessels and jade, dragons are typically portrayed as long, scaled, serpentine creatures with horns and claws.

The dragon was created by and has evolved from people's imagination, but for the Chinese it is revered as a supernatural creature with great powers and has been worshipped by Chinese people for thousands of years. Legend has it that the dragon can fly among the clouds or hide in water, control winds and water, turn into various forms, has powers of thunder, and is as beautiful as a rainbow. According to *The Origins of Chinese Characters*[1], "Dragons can form clouds, turn into water or fire, become invisible or glow in the dark."

The image of the dragon that we know today was formed in the Han (206 BC-AD220) and Wei (220-265) Dynasties and this image changed little after the Sui (581-618) and Tang (618-907) Dynasties. But as an emblem to be worshiped for its auspicious powers, we can say that China is the birthplace of the dragon.

The Nine Dragon Wall (detail)

For centuries, dragon culture has been deeply rooted in Chinese culture and Chinese people claim themselves to be the "Descendants of the Dragon".

Over a long period of time in

ancient China, it was believed that "the dragon reveals itself when an emperor is on the throne". The dragon was symbolic of the great power of the emperor who was regarded as "the son of the dragon". Therefore, emperors of all dynasties wore dragon-robes, and their chairs and carriages were also decorated with dragons. But the image of the dragon and its cultural connotations has evolved and become diversified with history.

The dragon was also venerated by ordinary people who believed that it could generate rain. Ancient China was an agricultural society and people hoped for ample rainfall and good weather, which would guarantee a good harvest. Therefore, the dragon symbolized good fortune. People worshipped the dragon and prayed to the dragon for rain. They also held dragon boat races and dragon dances to celebrate their harvest. We can say that the emblem of the Chinese dragon developed through thousands of years of agricultural civilization.

Today, dragon culture can be seen in all aspects of Chinese culture such as arts and crafts, historical architecture, music and movies, holidays, weddings and funerals as well as clothing. As a dominant cultural element, the dragon either spirals or soars up in the clouds embodying the profundity of dragon culture. People read books about dragons, give performances about dragon stories, plant bonsai plants with dragon ornamentation and name their children with the Chinese character for the dragon "龙". People talk about dragons, write about dragons, paint dragons, carve dragons, appreciate dragons and aspire to be dragons (meaning to be successful and powerful), and hope that their children can be dragons too. Even today, people still have great interest in the dragon. Grand occasions such as the Chinese New Year, the Tomb Sweeping Day, and the Mid-autumn Festival, are often accompanied by dragon dances.

The dragon is the symbol of China, Chinese people and Chinese culture. The image of the dragon is ingrained in the soul of every Chinese.

Notes:

[1] *The Origins of Chinese Characters*: the first dictionary in China compiled by Xu Shen in 100, the twelfth year of Eastern Han Emperor He (r. 88-105), collecting 9,353 characters. It started an era for comprehensive explanations of the ideographs, phonology, and semantics of Chinese characters. The structures of the characters are analyzed with seal scripts and are categorized into 514 components. It marked the beginning of lexicography in China.

EMPEROR HUANGDI — THE LEGENDARY CHINESE ANCESTOR

Huangdi, literally meaning Yellow Emperor, lived in China at the end of the Neolithic Age about 5,000 years ago. His family name was Gongsun and his courtesy names were Xuanyuan and Youxiong. He lived in the area of Loess Plateau of northern Shaanxi Province, so his name is associated with the color of the earth. Later his tribe moved to an area near Zhuolu[1] in Hebei Province and started to be engaged in stockbreeding and agriculture.

Legend has it that many tribes and clans lived in the areas of the Yangtze River and Yellow River, but Huangdi was the most well-known ruler.

The ruler of another tribe who lived during the same period as Huangdi was Yandi, whose family name was Jiang and courtesy name Shennong. He improved agricultural tools, taught people to farm on land and tasted different kinds of herbs for their nutritious and medi-

Emperor Huangdi

cal effects, recording their qualities and usages. He also started free markets where people could exchange things for what they needed.

Yandi at first lived near Jiangshui[2] in northwest China. Later, however, Yandi's tribe clashed with Huangdi's and they went to war with each other at Banquan[3].

During this time, a tribe named Jiuli[4] under the leadership of Chiyou[5] who was said to have magical powers often invaded and stole from other tribes. Huangdi united his neighboring tribes and fought fiercely with Chiyou at Zhuolu. In the end, Chiyou was defeated and Huangdi joined all the tribes in this area, creating a tribe union, and therefore, gained their allegiance. Huangdi became the leader of the tribe union.

After unifying those tribes, Huangdi and his tribe settled in Qiaoshan[6] and also the areas surrounding the Loess Plateau in northern Shaanxi Province. He has been credited with inventing Chinese characters and calendars, making vehicles, breeding silkworms and the craft of weaving. He also made great achievements in arithmetic.

Legend says that the emperors during the periods of Yao[7], Shun[8] as well as Xia, Shang and Zhou Dynasties were all descendants of Huangdi. In *Shiji*, Sima Qian chose to begin Chinese history with Huangdi, who unified the tribes and ethnic groups in the Yellow River valley, hence promoting the cultural integration of the area which is considered to be the origin of China's prehistoric civilization. Therefore, Chinese people claim that they are the descendants of Huangdi.

Since Yandi was a close relative of Huangdi, both were later worshipped and Chinese people began to consider themselves the descendants of Yandi and Huangdi.

Notes:

[1] Zhuolu: located south of present-day Zhuolu County in Hebei Province.

[2] Jiangshui: located in the present-day city of Baoji in Shaanxi Province.

[3] Banquan: located southeast of present-day Zhuolu County in Hebei Province.

[4] Jiuli: an ancient tribe in Chinese mythology.

[5] Chiyou: the legendary leader of the Jiuli tribe who fought with Huangdi at Zhuolu and was killed after his defeat.

[6] Qiaoshan: located in present-day Huangling County in Shaanxi Province.

[7] Yao: a legendary king in ancient China.

[8] Shun: a legendary king in ancient China.

THE ORACLE BONE INSCRIPTION —THE EARLIEST CHINESE WRITING SCRIPT

The Oracle Bone Inscription, a type of writing script, is one of the oldest in the world and is the earliest Chinese writing script. Wang Yirong, who was born in Fushan, Shandong Province and an official in Peking in later Qing Dynasty (1616-1911), was the first to discover oracle bone inscriptions and discovered the site where the inscriptions were unearthed—Anyang.

Oracle Bone Inscriptions were carved on tortoise shells and ox scapulas, hence the name. Most of them were unearthed in Anyang, the site of the capital during the Shang Dynasty (1600-1046 BC), and recorded on the oracle bones were divinations.

The Oracle Bone Inscription

The Shang Dynasty was also called Yin or Yinshang Epoch, and therefore, these scripts are also called Yinxu divinations[1].

Divinations were typically performed for rulers of the Shang Dynasty for different purposes. After a divination was carried out, the time, the person's name, event and the answer of the divination as well as what really happened were later all carved on oracle bones. These divinations are concise but descriptive.

About 4,000-5,000 oracle bones have been discovered so far, among which over 1,000 are recognizable after study and analysis by philologists and archeologists. Most of the oracle bones are glyphs, which are considered to be well-developed characters including nouns, adjectives and numerals. There is also a basic sentence structure, i.e. subject-predicate-object, and some complex sentences. Besides glyphs, ideographs and phonograms can be found on the oracle bones. The Oracle Bone Inscriptions of the Western Zhou Dynasty (1046-771 BC) have been found in Qishan and Fufeng, Shaanxi Province in 1977.

Oracle Bone Inscriptions marked the beginning of recorded Chinese history through which we can learn about the social system, rituals and calendars of the Shang Dynasty. Other civilizations also used scripts about 4,500 years ago, but those scripts were lost and therefore were not inherited in the scripts that were used later.

The Oracle Bone Inscription was the only script in the world that was well-developed and widely used in ancient times (the Shang Dynasty) and well inherited in the bronze vessel inscriptions of the Zhou Dynasty (1046-256 BC), characters written on bamboo slips and silk cloth in the Qin (221-206 BC) and Han Dynasties, and stone inscriptions of the Wei (220-265) and Jin (265-420) Dynasties. So, Oracle Bone Inscriptions developed over time and have become an integral part of traditional Chinese culture. They are the oldest Chinese characters and writings that can be traced and the study of these writings are considered as an academic discipline.

Notes:

[1] Yinxu divinations: divinations practiced in the Shang Dynasty with people's name, topic, date and answer of the divination carved on tortoise shells or animal bones, and sometimes with a brief description.

I CHING—THE BOOK OF CHANGES

I Ching, *The Book of Changes*, is one of the oldest Chinese classic texts. Some people think that it is the best Chinese classic, but for others, it is nothing but a book of divination.

The mythical Fuxi is credited with creating the Eight Trigrams (Bagua[1]), which were developed into 64 hexagrams by King Wen of the Zhou Dynasty. During the Spring and Autumn Period (770-476 BC), Confucius wrote the *Shi Yi* (Ten Wings), a group of commentaries on the *I Ching*. So *I Ching* developed over one thousand years, covers a wide range of areas including sorcery, math and history, and is a mosaic of Chinese culture. Both Taoism and Buddhism have been impacted by *I Ching*.

The Eight Trigrams

The creation of this book experienced three stages: the cognition of Yin and Yang, the creation of the Eight Trigrams, and Guaci and Yaoci. *I Ching* consists of two parts. Part one is *Ching* which refers to *I* (change), including 64 hexagrams, the form, name, statement of hexagrams, 384 strokes and explanations of those strokes. Part two is *Zhuan* which includes seven topics such as Tuan[2], Xiang, Xici, Wenyan, Shuogua (interpretation of Gua), Xugua and Zagua, and ten commentaries. Guaci and Yaoci are categorized into three kinds. The first kind is about changes in nature; the second is about ups and downs in people's lives; and the third kind contains descriptions of good and bad luck. Though this practice is mystic, there is something reasonable and meaningful.

Certain Chinese philosophies have been derived from *I Ching*, for example, the concept of Yin and Yang, and the theory of seemingly disjunctive or opposing forces that are interconnected and interdependent in the natural world, giving rise to each other in turn. Yi means change and that's why this classic work is translated into English as *The Book of Changes*.

The central part of *I Ching* is eight trigrams of Yin and Yang (Bagua literally means "eight symbols"). It is a trigram representing heaven, earth and man. They are interconnected, complementary to and opposing each other. This idea is the basis of Chinese philosophy. Yin, Yang and Bagua further developed into 64 hexagrams with 384 strokes based on which the official of prediction could make divinations.

I Ching has had a great impact on Chinese culture and has been a great inspiration for traditional Chinese medicine. The Yin and Yang theory was not well developed until after the publication of *I Ching*, in such classics as *Huangdi Neijing*, *The Yellow Emperor's Classic about Medicine*.

Notes:

[1] Bagua: eight diagrams, the combination of "—" representing Yang and "- -"representing Yin. It symbolizes eight natural phenomena such as heaven, earth, thunder, wind, water, fire, mountains and rivers. Each combination may symbolize different things. The 64 hexagrams of *I Ching* all pertain to the combinations of "—"Yang and "- -"Yin.

[2] Tuan: texts about Gua interpretations in *I Ching*. It is also called Guaci (hexagram statement).

SIMA QIAN AND *SHIJI*

Shiji, formerly called *Records of the Grand Historian*, was written by Sima Qian who was also known as Zichang. He was born and grew up in Xiayang, which is present-day Hancheng in Shaanxi Province. He was the greatest historian and litterateur in China.

Shiji

His father, Sima Tan, served as Prefect of the Grand Scribes[1] for Emperor Wu (r. 141-87 BC) of the Han Dynasty. At the age of ten, Sima Qian went with his father to Chang'an, the capital. He was already well versed in history books at an early age. In order to collect historical records and broaden his vision, Sima Qian began a journey throughout the country, conducting surveys and collecting legendary stories. In 108 BC, he inherited his father's position and served as Prefect of the Grand Scribes. In 104 BC, together with other scholars, he created the calendar "Taichuli". After that, he began to compile history. In 99 BC, Li Ling, a military officer, led a campaign against the Xiongnu[2] in the north but was defeated and taken captive. Sima Qian defended Li Ling but enraged the emperor. He was put into prison and castrated. Later he was released from prison upon being granted amnesty and was employed as a palace eunuch[3]. Despite being disgraced, he continued to compile history. After more than a dozen years of hard work, the book *Records of the Grand Historian*, which was later called *Shiji*, was completed. Unfortunately, he died shortly after the book had been finished. When *Shiji* was completed, "one copy was hidden in the mountain and the other kept in the palace". It was impossible for ordinary people to read it. At the beginning of the Western Han Dynasty (206 BC-AD 25), Yang Yunzhi, Sima Qian's grandson, began to study this work in great admiration. The book has been widely read and studied since then.

Shiji is the origin of China's biographical history. It covers a history of more than 3,000 years ranging from Emperor Huangdi to Emperor Wu of the Han Dynasty. The book has 130 chapters; ten volumes of Biao or "Tables", chronology of events; eight volumes of Shu or "Treatises" on economics and other topics of the time; 30 volumes of Shijia or "Biographies of the Feudal Houses and Eminent Persons", including biographies of notable rulers, nobility and bureaucrats mostly from the Spring and Autumn and Warring States (475-221 BC) periods; 70 volumes of Liezhuan or "Biographies and Collective Biographies" containing biographies of important individual figures including Laozi, Mozi, Sunzi, and Jingke.

The book has a total of 520,000 Chinese characters. *Shiji* was based on plenty of sources including *Zuozhuan* (*Chronicle of Zuo*), *Guoyu*, a classical Chinese history book that is a collection of historical records of numerous states from the Western Zhou to 453 BC, *Zhan Guo Ce*, literally *Strategies of the Warring States*, *Chu Han Chunqiu* as well as various schools of thoughts and their exponents during the period from Pre-Qin times to the early years of the Han Dynasty. In addition to these sources, he added the materials of his own findings. There were historical works of different styles before the Han Dynasty, but they were no match with *Shiji* in terms of the history recorded, accuracy, comprehensiveness and organization of the materials.

In the development of Chinese historiography, *Shiji* was undoubtedly China's first comprehensive and systematic historical work. It was the first of 24 historical writings that presented history in a series of biographies. This writing style was followed by the later dynasties and therefore is regarded as a milestone in China's historiography.

Shiji is not only a faithful documentation of history but also possesses high literary value. In order to make it easy to read, Sima Qian simplified the abstruse language that was commonly used in older documents. Using strong artistic appeal, he depicted the subjects concretely, giving readers vivid images. As biographical literature, *Shiji* plays an important role in the history of Chinese literature and has been very influential to ensuing literary works.

Notes:

[1] Prefect of the Grand Scribes: an official in ancient China, who looked after historical writings, astrology, calendars and royal book collections.

[2] Xiongnu: a northern nomadic tribe in the Qin and Han Dynasties; the people of this tribe were also called the Huns.

[3] Palace eunuch: the head of officials responsible for drafting documents and announcing the emperor's orders.

(English Author: Wang Huiyun)

Chapter Two Confucius and Confucianism

CONFUCIUS AND *THE ANALECTS OF CONFUCIUS*

Cai Shangsi, a contemporary scholar, contends in *Confucius Thoughts*, "No one who intends to understand the development of Chinese thoughts can afford to pass by Confucius ideas." Confucius, or Kongzi, meaning "Master Kong", is the honorific name for Kong Qiu (551-479 BC), whose courtesy name was Zhongni. In ancient China, it was a custom to add "Zi" (Master) to a person's family name to show people's respect, for example, Laozi, Zhuangzi, Mengzi (Mencius) etc. Confucius, founder of Confucianism, was a statesman, thinker and educator at the end of the Spring and Autumn Period (770-476 BC). Confucius served as a lower-ranking official in his youth. He once worked as a funeral eulogist for noble families. He set up a private school in his middle age and started his teachings. He taught his students according to their aptitude and was never tired of teaching. He was known to have "3,000 disciples and 70 of whom sages". At the age of 50, he went into politics in State Lu and made great achievements. Later, he had to leave his country because of his dissidence against the king and the ministers. He traveled to different states hoping to fulfill his political ambitions but failed. He returned to Lu and devoted himself to education and edited old scriptures such as *The Book of Songs* and *The Book of History*. He died at the age 73.

Confucius

After Confucius's death, his disciples put his teachings and conversations with his students together and compiled a book entitled *The Analects of Confucius*. It was considered a classical work in China's feudal society and was worshiped as a holy book, just like the *Bible* in the West. Zhao Pu, a politician in Northern Song Dynasty (960-1127), once said when exchanging political views with Emperor Taizong, "A ruler can govern the country well with good understanding of half of *The Analects of Confucius*." The influence of this book in China is unprecedented.

Confucius spent a large part of his life and focused much of his thoughts on the learning, practice and teaching of ritual forms and rules of propriety, which were explicitly conveyed in *The Analects of Confucius*. As recorded in this book, Duke Ai of State Lu once asked Confucius what could make his people willing to obey. Confucius said that his people would obey if virtuous and talented men got promoted to higher positions than the wicked but not the other way round. He strongly believed that rulers should be men of virtues and this was very important in running a country and bringing benefits to people. In other words, only virtuous rulers could enlighten people. Confucius advocated an ideal society about people's relationship, e.g. Father and Son—There should be kindness in the father, and filial piety in the son; Husband and Wife—There should be righteous behavior in the husband and obedience in the wife; Elder and Junior—There should be consideration among the elders and deference among the juniors; Ruler and Subject—There should be benevolence among the rulers and loyalty among the subjects; Friends—There should be trust and faithfulness among friends.

The Analects of Confucius covers a variety of topics including personal values and ethics, attitude, methods and purpose of learning, and governmental moralities. It also deals with other things in life such as reading, music, travel and making friends etc.

The language of *The Analects of Confucius* is vivid, inspirational, and philosophical. It has a lot of aphorisms which are brief but meaningful and cover every aspect of life. Those aphorisms have been passed down generation after generation and often quoted by people, for example, "He who gives no thoughts to the future is sure to be beset by worries much closer at hand"; "Reviewing what you have learned and learning anew"; "Artful words are the root of being non-virtuous. Intolerance in small matters would lead to failure in big plans"; "At fifteen, I aspired to learn; At thirty, I became independent; At forty, I was free from delusion; At fifty, I knew my destiny; At sixty, I knew truth in all I heard; At seventy, I could follow my heart's desire without overstepping the line"; "In a group of three people, there is always something I can learn from", etc.

Confucius doctrine didn't become the mainstream until during the reign of Emperor Wu (r.141-87 BC) of the Han Dynasty when China was already a powerful and centralized nation. For the benefit of this centralized regime, Dong Zhongshu, a Han Dynasty scholar, proposed that "Anything other than Confucianism be banned". Since then, Confucianism became the official ideology which has influenced China for more than 2,000 years.

CONFUCIUS AND CONFUCIANISM

In 484 BC, 68-year-old Confucius returned to State Lu from the State Wei and thus drew an end to his 14-year-trip around the states. After returning to Lu, he dedicated himself to compiling the classical works and teaching.

Confucius taught his disciples with the books of poetry, history, ritual and music. These classical scriptures were passed down in bamboo slips and silks which were hard to select for teaching purposes without proper compilation. What was worse, as rituals and education were not respected at that time, many scriptures had been lost. In order to preserve these classical works, Confucius spent almost all his late years editing these manuscripts. He selected six categories from those scriptures which were the most important and typical and turned them into six books: *The Book of Songs*, *The Book of History*, *The Book of Rites*, *The*

The Spring and Autumn Annals

The Analects of Confucius

Book of Music, *The Book of Changes* and *The Spring and Autumn Annals*. These books cover ritual forms, music and culture since legendary Chinese ancestors of Yao and Shun and were used as classical textbooks for Confucius disciples and the later generations.

These six books used to be known as "the Six Arts" and later "the Six Classics". They are the most important classics and source of ideology of Confucianism. *Shih Ching* or *The Book of Songs*, containing 305 poems, is divided into folk songs, festal songs, hymns and eulogies. It was used as a good textbook integrating poetry with literature, politics and ethics. *Shu*, also known as *The Book of History*, is a collection of documents and speeches alleged to have been written by rulers and officials of and before the early Zhou Dynasty (1046-256 BC). *Li*, or *The Book of Rites* described the social norms, governmental systems, and ancient/ceremonial rites. *Yue*, also known as *The Book of Music*, covers the knowledge and skills of playing various musical instruments. *Yi* is also known as *The Book of Changes*. *Chunqiu* or *Spring and Autumn Annals* is the official chronicle of the State of Lu, covering a period of 242 years. It is the earliest surviving Chinese historical text to be arranged on annalistic principles. The language is terse and it only has 18,000 Chinese characters. It started a new writing style by which the author implied instead of speaking straightforwardly his political views and personal beliefs in life. This style was followed by later generations and was called "Spring and Autumn Writing Style".

Confucius edited the Six Classics because he believed that these books would play an important role in a society. He envisioned an ordered society with "virtues". He advocated "ren" which means benevolence and "li" which means ritual propriety. He suggested that "ren" and "li" were the best solutions to all kinds of problems in a society and that the Six Classics explicitly embodied "ren" and "li". Hence Confucianism was established emphasizing personal and governmental morality and it has had great influence not only in China but also in the world.

QUFU AND CONFUCIAN MANSION, TEMPLE AND CEMETERY

Qufu is the hometown of Confucius, founder of Confucianism, a great thinker and educator in ancient China. Confucius' descendants have lived here and were conferred noble titles. They were neither affected by the political turmoil nor the change of dynasties. Qufu hosts the largest complex of Confucius (Kong) Temple, Confucius Family Mansion and Confucius Cemetery (popularly known as the three "Kong") in China.

The biggest building of the complex, the Temple of Confucius, also the largest temple of China, is a historical site to offer sacrifice to Confucius. In 478 BC, the second year after his death, the Confucian residence was turned into a temple at the order of Duke Ai of the State Lu in which the utensils, such as clothes, hats,

The Dacheng Hall in the Confucius Temple

the chime stone, the carriage and books once used by Confucius were preserved. A ceremony was held each year to offer sacrifice and commemorate Confucius' birthday. After Western Han Dynasty (1046-771BC), Confucianism became the official ideology of China and the Temple of Confucius was expanded repeatedly during the reign of several emperors and turned out to be a large building complex. In the early 18th century, Emperor Yongzheng (1722-1735) of the Qing Dynasty ordered that the Temple of Confucius be renovated and expanded again to the extent of what it is like today.

Dacheng Hall, or the Great Perfection Hall, is the architectural center of the Temple complex. It is the highest building of the Temple as well as one of the three largest ancient halls in China. The Temple of Confucius consists of nine halls and nine courtyards, and Dacheng Hall consists of nine rooms. In the China's feudal society, the number nine could only be used for emperors, and those who broke the rule would receive capital punishment. However, the Temple of Confucius was an exception. Besides, there are five gates in front of the main hall of the Temple, which again according to the feudal rule, was the privilege of royal architecture. For example, the Forbidden City has five gates.

More than 1,100 stele inscriptions in the Temple were preserved since the Han dynasty. They are not only art treasures but can also be used for the study of the politics, economy and culture in China's feudal society. Over the past 2,000 years, the Temple of Confucius has undergone 15 major renovations, 31 large repairs, and numerous minor fixes.

The Confucius Mansion, also known as Official Residence of the Sage Confucius Family, is located on the east of the Temple. It was the residence and office of the direct descendants of Confucius. The Confucius Mansion was first built in 1038. Through complete renovations and expansions during the Ming (1368-1644) and Qing (1616-1911) Dynasties, it was not only the largest feudal noble mansion next to the Forbidden City, but also the most typical private estate in China, combining official buildings with a residence and a garden. Generation after generation of "Duke

Yansheng", noble title for the Confucius descendants, strictly followed the family teaching of "respect for poetry and ritual propriety" and collected about 80,000 ritual objects used in different dynasties. In addition, the most famous collection of the Mansion is the archives of the Ming and Qing Dynasties. These archives record the activities held at the Confucius Temple and Mansion over a period of 400 years. There are about 6,000 collections of its kind which are regarded as the biggest and oldest family archives.

Confucius Cemetery, formerly called "Forest of the Exalted Sage", is the graveyard of Confucius and his descendants. It is the largest family cemetery in the world with the longest line of descendants. Confucius died in 479 BC and was buried by the Sishui River[1] in the north of Qufu. His descendants were also buried here. There are about 10,000 tombs in the Forest. Starting from the Han Dynasty (206 BC-AD 220), the descendants of Confucius began to erect tomb tablets and there are altogether 3,600 tablets covering the periods of the Song, Yuan, Ming and Qing Dynasties. So Confucius Forest is actually a stele forest, which is very valuable for the study of Chinese calligraphy of different dynasties. Confucius Forest is also a grand artificial garden. After the death of Confucius, his disciples planted rare trees from all over China. From the first trees planted by Zigong, one of Confucius disciples, by the Confucius tomb, there have grown 10,000 old trees in the Forest. Since the Han dynasty, the Forest has been renovated and expanded for 13 times to the present-day scale covering an area of 2,000,000 m^2.

An annual worship ceremony is held at the Temple of Confucius. The Temple, the Cemetery and Family Mansion of Confucius in Qufu are world famous for their long history, cultural and historical relics, grand scale and artistic value. In 1994, the "Three Kongs" were listed as world cultural heritage. They play an indispensable role in the study of politics, economy and culture of different dynasties as well as the evolution of funeral rituals in China.

Notes:

[1] Sishui River: a river in Shandong province.

(English Author: Wang Huiyun)

Chapter Three Laozi and Taoism

LAOZI

Laozi, an honorific title (literally Laozi means "Old (lao) Master (zi)") for Laodan, was a thinker during the Spring and Autumn Period (770-476 BC). He is also regarded as the founder of Taoism[1]. According to *Shiji* by Sima Qian, Laozi's surname was Li, his given name Er, and courtesy name Dan. He was born in Ku Prefecture of the state of Chu (present-day Lu Yi County in Henan Province).

Laozi

Legend has it that Laozi was very tall, with long earlobes, big eyes, broad forehead and thick lips. He once served as an archivist for the royal court of Zhou. At that time, he was revered as a wise man. As he witnessed the decline of the State of Zhou, he resigned and left the capital Luoyi to live as a hermit.

During his lifetime, Laozi read many ancient classics that were preserved in Zhou's royal court. He also began to study natural science, most notably, astronomy and the lunar calendar. He meditated on the universe, life and politics, and turned them into *Laozi*, a classic Chinese text.

Laozi, also called *Tao Te Ching*, consists of two parts, *Tao* (the Way) and *Te* (Virtue). The text, totaling 5,000 characters, is terse in style but profoundly insightful. From his own perspective, Laozi explored a range of philosophical and political problems such as the formation of the universe, the origin of the world, and the governance of the country. The book puts forward such philosophical concepts as Taoism, naturalness and non-action and functions as the cornerstone of Chinese philosophy.

Laozi considered Tao (the Way) as the mythical source

and ideal of all existence. According to Laozi, Tao goes beyond nature, human society, supernatural beings as well as heaven and earth, and is the root of the universe. With simple dialectic thoughts, he pointed out that all things have oppositional aspects, for instance: beautiful and ugly, good and evil, existent and non-existent, difficult and easy, long and short, high and low, hard and soft, strong and weak, black and white, and light and darkness. Laozi contended that the oppositional aspects are all interdependent and interconnected, that everything transforms to its oppositional aspect in the process of change, and that this transformation is unconditional, absolute and unaffected by human will. He held the same attitude towards life, which is the pursuit of "Tao Fa Zi Ran", meaning that people should follow the way of nature. It suggests that people should "lay low" and avoid competition, or in other words, practice "Non-contention". This philosophy is reasonable in that it instructs people not to reach what is beyond their grasp and not be self-conceited. However, its negative aspects are obvious as well. Indeed, competition helps a society develop and without competition society would be static and life boring.

As a Taoism classic, *Laozi* has had a far-reaching impact. In fact, Laozi himself was revered as a deity. During the Tang Dynasty (618-907), he was granted the title "Emperor Taishang Xuanyuan", meaning "Supreme Mysterious and Primordial Emperor", and during the Song Dynasty (960-1279) he was respected as "Taishang Laojun", meaning "Supreme Lord".

In religious Taoism, Laozi is considered the founder, and is revered as "Taishang Laojun, or Taote Tianzun". Religious Taoist scriptures tell the story that Laozi has transformed numerous times since the ancient times before transcending into the human world to spread his teachings.

Notes:

[1] Taoism: the central concept of Laozi's theory. Tao or the Way in *Laozi* contains three meanings. First, things that are inherent in nature, called "Heng Tao"; second, reflection of nature called "Lun Tao"; and third, the correct interpretation of Tao.

TAOISM

Taoism is a religion that originated in China, and it has had a significant impact on Chinese history and culture. Taoism is so named because Tao (the Way) is considered to be the highest religious pursuit. It was believed that people could become immortal by practicing austerities.

In Taoism, Laozi is worshipped as a deity. Laozi's *Tao Te Ching* and Zhuangzi's *Nan Hua Ching*[1] are regarded as classic works of Taoism.

Taoism involves the Yin-yang school of thought[2], Mohism[3], a celestial geomancy starting from the Warring States Period (475-221 BC), Huang-Lao during the Qin (221-206 BC) and Han (206 BC-AD 220) Dynasties and Chen-Wei[4] superstitions during the Han Dynasty.

Taoism came into being during the mid Eastern Han Dynasty (25-220). It is generally believed that it was founded by Zhang Daoling on Mount Heming (Dayi County in present-day Sichuan Province). In the beginning, it consisted of two sects, one being the "five dou of rice". It was so named because believers were required to contribute five dou of rice to the sect they joined in. In this sect, Laozi was respected as hierarch, and Zhang Ling as Celestial Master. After Zhang Ling's death, his son, Zhang Heng and his grandson, Zhang Lu continued teaching, and therefore, it was called "Three Zhang Taoism". Zhang Sheng, son of Zhang Lu, migrated from Sichuan Province to Jiangxi Province. He went on teaching and passed down his knowledge to later generations.

The other sect is Taiping Taoism. Zhang Jiao and his

A Taoist Temple on Mount Zhenwu

two younger brothers from Pingxiang in Hebei Province called themselves "best solon" and created Taiping Taoism. Within ten years, its followers reached several hundred thousand. Later, the Zhang Jiao brothers launched an uprising known as Yellow Turban Rebellion[5]. Taiping Taoism began to decline after the Rebellion was suppressed. Meanwhile, "five dou of rice" Taoism (later called Tianshi Tao, or Zhengyi Tao) started to prosper.

After many reforms, early Taoism began to mature in the establishment of its classics, teachings, commandments, rituals and organizations, and around the 7th Century, with promotion by several emperors of the Tang and Song Dynasties, Taoism entered a period of great prosperity.

After the 12th century, Taoism was divided into Quanzhen Tao[6] (Complete Reality) and Zhengyi Tao[7] (Orthodox). Quanzhen Tao emphasized the discipline of internal and external alchemy. The former focused on the cultivation of Jing (vitality), Qi (energy) and Shen (spirit). The latter referred to a method of making edible pellets with lead, mercury and certain medicine. Originally, Quanzhen Tao had four basic commandments for professional practitioners: 1) They should not marry; 2) They should not eat meat; 3) They should always wear Taoist clothing; and 4) Their hair should be tied and they should wear a beard. Professional Taoists live in a Taoist temple.

Zhengyi practitioners, however, practiced demon exorcism and fortune telling. They were allowed to marry and eat meat. On occasions other than the worship and services in the temple, they could wear secular-style clothing. They didn't have to wear a beard and could have normal hairstyles.

Quanzhen Tao advocated residence in the temple to discipline oneself. Quanzhen Tao temples were mostly modeled after Buddhist temples, and gradually evolved into two schools: the Temple of Descendents and Shifang Jungle. In the first case, the master of the temple, namely the abbot, taught disciples or Taoist children. In Shifang Jungle, however, the abbot had no disciples of his own and only held initiation ceremonies for junior Taoists recommended by small temples. In both cases, there were rigid doctrines and strict rules regarding wealth management.

Over the past 2,000 years, Taoism has had a profound impact on Chinese culture. The concepts of immortality, naturalness, non-action and freedom have greatly inspired Chinese literati, and many Taoist allusions have become the sources of Chinese literature. The worship services of Taoism are closely related to Chinese people's daily life. Also, Taoist alchemy made great contributions to the development of ancient Chinese chemistry and pharmacology.

To sum up, Taoism has had various influences on different aspects of society, particularly the social psychology, customs and people's way of thinking. It is an integral part of ancient China's cultural heritage and plays a vital role in China's traditional culture.

Notes:

[1] *Nan Hua Ching*: namely *Zhuangzi*.

[2] Yin-yang school of thought: a school of thought that promoted the five-element theory during the Warring States Period. Led by Zou Yan, this school of thought taught that the development of human society is dominated by five elements, namely water, fire, wood, metal and earth. It also put forward the theory of "five cyclic virtues" and "five transforming virtues" to demonstrate the transformation of history and the change of dynasties, and therefore, the cyclic theory of history was established for idealism.

[3] Mohism: a very important school which advocated "universal love" and "non-aggression" in the early Pre-Qin Dynasty. It was founded by Mozi. Mohism, which had a vital impact at that time, was seen as a major rival to Confucianism. Mohism had strict disciplines, and its disciples were always ready to die for their beliefs. Mohism in its later practice eliminated religious superstitions, making contributions to logic, optics, geometry and mechanics.

[4] Chen Wei: a theological superstition during the Han Dynasty. "Chen" means argots or prophecies that were created by wizards or alchemists during the Qin and Han Dynasties. "Wei" means works that draw a far-fetched comparison to Confucianism classics; they were edited by alchemist scholars.

[5] Yellow Turban Rebellion: a large-scale peasant uprising led by Zhang Jiao at the end of the Eastern Han Dynasty. Zhang Jiao founded Taiping Tao and launched the uprising in 184 AD. The rebels were wearing yellow turbans, hence the name. After the rebellion failed, the remaining rebels continued to fight for more than 20 years, which was a heavy blow to the reign of the Eastern Han.

[6] Quanzhen Tao: a Complete Reality school of thought founded by Wang Chongyang in Ninghai (present-day Mouping), Shandong Province while teaching in the temple. It advocated the combination of Taoism, Buddhism and Confucianism. It regarded "a clear and focused mind, and conserving qi (energy)" as the only true power; it proposed "helping the poor, thinking of others before self and selfless giving" as true practice. Quanzhen Tao practitioners only practiced internal alchemy. They were required to live in Taoist temples and were not allowed to marry or eat meat.

[7] Zhengyi Tao: also known as "five dou of rice" Taoism founded by Zhang Daoling. Between 307 – 313, the fourth-generation grandson of Zhang Daoling migrated to Longhu Mountain in Jiangxi Province, and established "Zhengyi Bema", honoring Zhang Daoling as "Zhengyi Celestial Master". This school of thought has become famously known as the "Celestial Master school of thought". Zhengyi Taoists are allowed to live both at home or dwell in mountains, are able to marry, and on non-fasting days can eat meat and drink liquor.

TAOISM REGIMEN

Chinese people have long believed in immortality. The fairy tale of the Moon Goddess[1] is a typical example. During the Spring and Autumn Period (770-476 BC) and the Warring States Period (475-221 BC), legend had it that there stood three mountain deities in coastal areas, namely Penglai[2], Fangzhang and Yingzhou[3] where immortal beings lived and panaceas for immortality could be found. Therefore, many people went to seek panaceas for immortality.

Taoism carried on the concept of immortality and caused people to believe that immortality could be achieved by practicing austerities. According to Taoism, regimen can join human beings with deities. Furthermore, longevity is the precondition of immortality, which calls for regimen. One should follow regimens to stay healthy, both mentally and physically. In the process of pursuing immortal life and with the development of Taoism, Taoists created health science and body building techniques which are extensive, profound and extremely valuable. They can be categorized as external alchemy, internal alchemy, medication, coition, etc.

External alchemy is useful in manufacturing elixirs (also called golden elixirs or cure-all medicine) by calcining mineralized medicines with a furnace and ding (three-legged bronze caldron). The First Emperor of Qin (r. 246-210 BC) and the Han Emperor Wu (r. 141-87 BC) strongly believed in this method to gain immortality, and therefore, made this practice very famous. Taoism was tainted with mystery after being associated with rites such as protective talisman, Yin-yang and the five elements. Though experiments on elixirs failed, this practice promoted the development of smelting and chemistry as well as the invention of gunpowder.

Internal alchemy is the most typical regimen for Taoism. Internal alchemy is a general term for promoting the circulation of Qi, guiding Qi, breathing and meditation. The human body becomes a laboratory in which the Three Treasures of Jing, Qi, and Shen are cultivated for the purpose of improving physical, emotional and mental health, and ultimately merging with the Tao, i.e. becoming an Immortal. Internal alchemy, in terms of breathing, emphasizes training the body and mind, so as to balance Yin and Yang and improve the circulation of Qi. Although it is impossible to achieve immortality, internal alchemy can keep one healthy. Influenced by the art of breathing, the meditative practice of Qigong has been passed on from generation to generation. It remains China's traditional regimen and is still popular today.

People also ate herbs in order to achieve immortality. In Taoist books, there exist many records about medicated liquor and tea, Taoist foods and medicated diets[4]. In addition, they made wine with herbs, naming it celestial wine. The wines included: Chinese Fox-Glove Root[5] wine, benne wine, turpentine wine and asparagus wine. Many good Taoist recipes have been introduced to secular society, handed down and developed by later generations. These recipes, used for either helping people stay healthy or for medical treatment, were used by both emperors and common people, and were recorded in traditional Chinese medi-

Taking Elixirs

cine books.

The Taoists, many of whom were brilliant doctors, made great contributions to pathology and pharmacology. At that time, it was said that nine of ten Taoists were doctors. Some of the Taoists were even revered as medicine kings (the Chinese Aesculapius), and people offered sacrifices to them.

Though not all Taoist medical practices are scientific, undermined by concepts of deity and immortality, they are closely related to medical science. These practices have also played an important role in the history of traditional Chinese medicine as well as world medicine. Over the last few decades, Taoist regimen, with the vantage of modern science and technology, has proved to be very effective in helping people maintain health and prolong life.

Notes:

[1] Moon Goddess: Chang'e, who is said to be the wife of Houyi, stole the pill of immortality and floated to the moon. She is called the "fairy of the moon".

[2] Penglai: one of the legendary fairy mountains in the sea. Penglai usually refers to a kind of wonderland.

[3] Yingzhou: a legendary fairy mountain in the sea.

[4] Medicated diet: dishes blended with traditional Chinese medicine, for instance, stewed chicken with ginseng and astragalus, stewed duck with aweto and white fungus broth, etc.

[5] Chinese Fox-Glove Root: a perennial herb which is used as traditional Chinese medicine.

CAVE HEAVEN AND BLESSED REGION

Taoism emphasizes the notion of immortality, and more specifically, the hope of becoming immortal beings who live in a wonderland. The wonderland that Taoists pursue is a place filled with colorful clouds, pavilions, heavenly palaces of the gods as well as Dong Tian Fu Di, meaning "cave heaven and blessed region" or residence for celestial beings.

Dong Tian Fu Di is related both to the tradition of mountain dwelling in ancient China and to the religious pursuits of Taoism. Taoism reveres mountains not only because of their serenity, mystery and the convenience of collecting herbs that promote the circulation of Qi, but also because of the large variety of mountain plants that epitomize naturalness. In describing Taoism, Laozi enjoyed talking about "mountains (valleys) and water", which in his view symbolize peacefulness, tolerance, effeminacy and nourishment. With the conviction that celestial beings live in mountains, Taoists choose to live in mountains to practice internal and external alchemy and become immortal beings. Ultimately, "Dong Tian" means a cavern leading to heaven that connects all mountains.

Therefore, mountains play a more important role in Taoism than in any other religion in the world. As the ancient Chinese saying goes, "Taoists and monks mostly dwell in famous mountains." For thousands of years, Taoists lived as hermits in deep mountains, especially famous mountains, and devoted themselves to Taoist practices. There are many legends about the mountains where well-known Taoists used to practice, and these stories have made these mountains more mysterious. In some places, one can see Taoist temples, which make these locations ideal earthly wonderlands. As the old saying goes, "Any mountain can be famous with the presence of an immortal".

Taoism spread far and wide with the expansion of the local temples, and Taoist mountains came to be known as "famous Taoist mountains". In Chinese history, famous Taoist mountains include: Ten Big Grotto Heavens, Thirty-six Small Grotto Heavens, and Seventy-two Fairylands. Intellectuals of different dynasties also

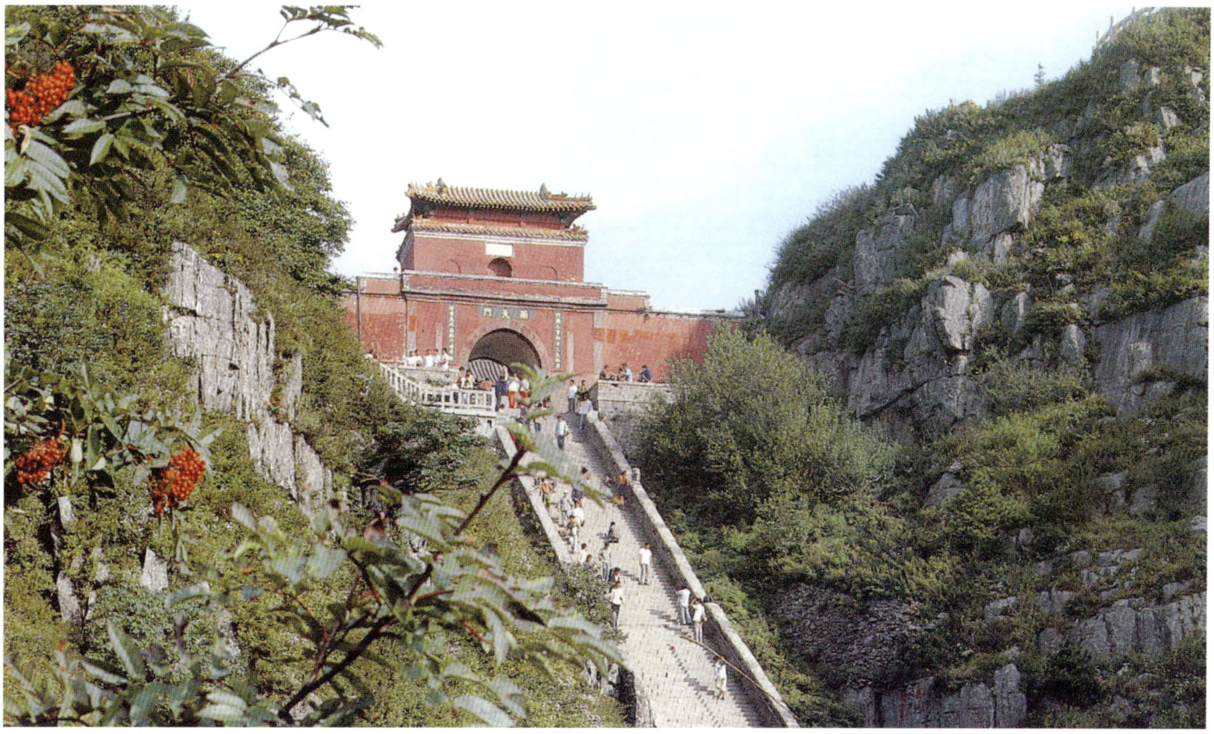

Nan Tian Men on Mount Tai

went to these famous mountains to relax and enjoy themselves, composing many poems in the process.

The 14 most influential Taoist mountains are: Mount Tai in Shandong Province, Mount Heng in Hunan Province, Mount Hua in Shaanxi Province, Mount Heng in Shanxi Province, Mount Song in Henan Province, Mount Longhu in Jiangxi Province, Mount Gezao in Jiangxi Province, Mount Mao in Jiangsu Province, Mount Qingcheng in Sichuan Province, Mount Luofu in Guangdong Province, Mount Zhongnan in Shaanxi Province, Mount Wudang in Hubei Province, Mount Lao in Shandong Province and Mount Weibao in Yunnan Province.

(English Author: Wang Huiyun)

Chapter Four Buddhism in China

XUAN ZANG'S PILGRIM TO INDIA

Xuan Zang

The story of Xuan Zang, a monk known for his journey to India in order to introduce Buddhist scriptures to the Chinese, has been popular in China since the Tang Dynasty (618-907).

Though the novel *Journey to the West* is fiction, the prototype of Xuan Zang and his arduous journey truly existed. Xuan Zang (602-664), named Chen Hui before he became a monk, was born in Yanshi, Henan Province. He was the youngest of the five children in his family. Under the influence of his brothers and father as well as the social environment, Xuan Zang developed an interest in academic research and he particularly favored the study of Buddhism, a subject popular at that time. Xuan Zang became a monk at age 13 and began to travel around the country to learn from well-known Buddhist scholars about many important Buddhist classics. Yearning for more knowledge about Buddhism, Xuan Zang decided to visit India in order to further his study. At that time, no other means of transportation than human powered and animal powered ones were available for this long trip. Furthermore, he had to travel through China's Gansu and Xinjiang, ascend the Pamir highland and pass through the middle and western parts of Asia before he could reach India. In August 627, Xuan Zang began his journey from Chang'an, now the city of Xi'an, and traveled westward among businessmen returning to Xinjiang and the countries of Central Asia. He survived the

800 miles of desert and the snow-capped Bedal Pass[1]. It took him nearly a year to cover the haphazard and arduous distance before he reached India.

While in Nalanda, the most renowned Buddhism institute in India at that time, Xuan Zang studied for five years and later, with the entrustment of Master Jie Xian, a well-known Indian Buddhist scholar, chaired the temple's study sessions.

In the spring of 643, Xuan Zang took 657 Buddhist scriptures with him on his homebound journey.

On January 24, 645 of the Chinese lunar calendar, Xuan Zang arrived in Chang'an, a city he had left 18 years ago. The emperor himself gave Xuan Zang a reception ceremony at the palace in Luoyang. Later, he began to translate the Buddhist scriptures, directing the translation efforts in Hongfu[2] and Da Cien Temples[3]. Da Yan Tower was constructed in Ci'en Temple in order to preserve the scriptures. Nineteen years after returning to China, Xuan Zang had translated 75 Buddhist scriptures of 1,335 volumes, and altogether 13 million words.

Great Tang Records on the Western Regions, a book dictated by Xuan Zang and recorded by his disciples, was memoir of his journey and description of various aspects of the 11 countries he had visited and the 28 other countries he had learned about. Some of these countries and regions included: the present Xinjiang of China, Afghanistan, Pakistan, India, Bangladesh, Nepal, and Sri Lanka. The book was translated into various languages and is considered a masterpiece today.

Despite the fact that Buddhism originated in India and was part of the Indian culture, Xuan Zang and other Buddhist scholars brought Buddhist scriptures to China, translated them into the Chinese language and helped the Chinese understand the religion by combining it with Chinese philosophy. His efforts not only saved a large number of Buddhist books and records but also created a Chinese version of Buddhism. Later on, when most of the Buddhist books and records were lost and Buddhism fell into obscurity in India, their Chinese versions still existed and Buddhism flourished in China.

Notes:

[1] Bedal Pass: a pass that must be crossed in order to access the countries of Central Asia.

[2] Hongfu Temple: a famous Buddhist temple in the Northwest of Xiude Fang in Chang'an of Tang Dynasty, near the present-day West Railway Station of Xi'an, Shaanxi. It was established in 634.

[3] Ci'en Temple: a temple established in 648 during the Tang Dynasty.

FOUR REPUTED GROTTOES

Thanks to the popularity of Buddhism in China, grottoes that combined traditional Chinese paintings and carvings quickly developed around the 3rd century. These grottoes of various sizes, known as "Artistic Treasure Houses" in the East, can be found across China, among which, the Mogao Grottoes in Dunhuang, Yungang Grottoes, Longmen Grottoes, and Maijishan Grottoes are the most famous. Together they are known as the four great grottoes in China and the first three are listed as UNESCO World Heritage Sites.

• Mogao Grottoes

The Mogao Grottoes, also known as "the Cave of One Thousand Buddha Statues", are located in Gansu Province's Western Hexi Corridor, 25 kilometers southeast of Dunhuang City. Standing on a 50-meter cliff east of Mingsha Mountain, the grottoes have five floors and are about 1,600 meters long. As the largest grottoes with the richest collection among the four reputed grottoes in China, they represent the essence of

Buddha Statues in Mogao Grottoes

Chinese stone carving, which has a history of nearly one thousand years. They compose the largest yet most intact Buddhist heritage site in the world. The first grotto was carved by an enlightened monk named Le Zun in 366, the second year of Jianyuan Era of the Former Qin State[1]. The story goes that he saw a magnificent light on Mingsha Mountain which caused him to believe that this mountain was a divine place for Buddha. After construction efforts during later dynasties, the number of grottoes in Mogao reached more than 1,000 in the 7th century during the Tang Dynasty. Currently, more than 490 grottoes completed during the Northern Liang Kingdom (401-439) and the Yuan Dynasty (1206-1368) have been preserved.

In the construction of the grottoes, generations of people carved large numbers of Buddha statues and painted numerous frescoes on the grotto walls. The Buddha statues of various poses and carving skills reflect features of different dynasties. The most distinctive frescoes feature Buddhist-related subjects such as Buddha, Bodhisattva and Vessavana, depictions from Buddhist scriptures, legendary Buddhist figures as well as historical figures from China, Central Asia and India. Frescoes of different time periods also reflect the social life, dress, architectural structure, music and dance of various ethnic minorities as well as history of exchanges with foreigners. As a result, western scholars refer to the frescoes in Dunhuang as a "library on the wall". The existing frescoes occupy 45,000 square meters and boast 2,400 colored sculptures. These frescoes, if connected one by one, could fill a 30-kilometer gallery.

On May 26, 1900, the 26th year of Qing Emperor Guangxu's reign (r. 1875-1908), Wang Yuanlu, a visiting Taoist, inadvertently discovered that a section of the grottoes' walls was hollow; a secret chamber was discovered and branded grotto No.17, also known as "the scripture grotto", in which more than 40,000 books and paintings from the 4-11th century were stored, including old hemp paper scrolls in Chinese and many other languages, paintings on hemp, silk or paper, numerous damaged figurines of Buddhas, and other Buddhist paraphernalia, covering Buddhist canonical works, original commentaries, apocryphal works, workbooks, books of prayers, Confucian works, Taoist works, Nestorian Christian works, works from the Chinese government, administrative documents, anthologies, glossaries, dictionaries, and calligraphic exercises. However, most of these priceless items were taken and smuggled into a dozen countries by foreign treasure hunters.

Positioned along the Silk Road, which connected China with western countries, the Mogao Grottoes is a place where eastern and western religions, cultures and knowledge were blended. For this reason, the grottoes have become a place of historical, artistic and scientific value. They not only serve as precious cultural heritage for Chinese people, but for people all over the world.

• Yungang Grottoes

The Yungang Grottoes are situated on the southern side of Mount Wuzhou, 16 kilometers west of Datong City in Shanxi Province. Construction work on the Yungang Grottoes began in 453, during the Northern Wei Dynasty (386-534). The grotto complex extends about one kilometer in Mount Wuzhou, witnessing magnificent and amazing carving skills to make a renowned and artistic treasure house.

Five grottoes were carved under the instruction of Tan Yao, a well-known monk during the Northern Wei Dynasty. All the five grottoes have domed ceilings and oval-shaped rooms.

Among the surviving 53 grottoes, the largest one is the 25-meter-tall grotto No. 3, which was carved during the Northern Wei Emperor Xiao Wen's reign (r. 467-499). The grotto's dome supported by a 60-square-meter-wide column is elaborately decorated with Buddha

Yungang Grottoes

statues of various sizes.

There are 51,000 vividly created statues and statuettes of Buddha, Buddhisattva, warriors and flying Apsaras in the grotto, with the largest one standing 17 meters tall and the smallest only several centimeters. The Buddha statues feature thick lips, high noses, long eyes, broad shoulders and a masculine look, all typical ethnic minority characteristics. It is worth mentioning that the size of the statues in the grottoes varies according to the rank of the subject in the Buddhist system, with the Buddha statue the most gigantic, majestic and dominant, and all others getting smaller and smaller to foil the importance of Buddha.

In addition to the exquisitely carved columns, the grotto's ceiling and other support columns are covered with various skin patterns of mythical animals. Upon entering the grotto, one may feel surrounded by a mythical world. In his book *Commentary to the River Classic*, Li Daoyuan, a well-known geologist during the Northern Wei Dynasty, thus depicted the magnificence of the Yungang Grottoes: "carved out of cliffs, vivid, grand and rarely seen elsewhere; mountain shrines and waterside palaces in perfect harmony".

• Longmen Grottoes

At the end of the 5th century, Emperor Xiaowen of the Northern Wei Dynasty moved the capital to Luoyang, Henan Province. Then another group of gigantic grottoes was carved into Mount Longmen along the Yishui River. The Longmen Grottoes gradually replaced the Yungang Grottoes as the mecca of Buddhist study. Later generations carved more than 2,000 grottoes into Mount Longmen. These grottoes are home to more than 100,000 Buddha statues and statuettes. Compared with the Buddha statues in the Yungang Grottoes, those inside the Longmen Grottoes are more artistic in terms of Chinese characteristics.

Most (60%) of the grottoes at Longmen were constructed during the Tang Dynasty, and among which most were completed during the reign of Wu Zetian, the only female emperor in Chinese history, coinciding with her long residence in Luoyang.

Fengxian Temple is the most representative grotto of the Tang Dynasty. Standing atop the peak of Mount Xishan, the temple enshrined a 16-meter Vairocana Buddha featuring plump face, long eyebrows and

Longmen Grottoes

Maijishan Grottoes

eyes and a mouth with down-turned corners, a sign of his concern about the human world and wisdom. The Buddha is flanked by his two disciples and a group of guards and warriors. Constructed at the order of Wu Zetian, the Buddha statue was consecrated in the presence of the emperor, who sponsored the construction herself. Legend has it that the Buddha's face was carved to resemble the features of Wu Zetian's face and, as a result, the Buddha's face has some feminine characteristics.

Tablet inscriptions in the Longmen Grottoes amount to more than 3,000 pieces, constituting a rare collection of calligraphy.

• Maijishan Grottoes

Thirty-five kilometers southeast of Tianshui City in Gansu Province, the Maijishan Grottoes are situated in Mount Xiaolong, along the western side of Mount Qinling. For its haystack-like shape, the mountain is called Maijishan (Haystack Mountain). Densely covered with trees and always canopied in clouds and mist, the mountain's natural scenery is breathtaking and most beautiful among the four reputed grottoes.

Beginning from the 4th century, more than 200 grottoes were constructed, all of which were dug into steep cliffs and connected with narrow plank roads. The existing 30-or-so grottoes were constructed in the Northern Wei, Western Wei (535-556) and Northern Zhou (557-581) Dynasties. Since Maijishan's rock is not suitable for carving, most of the Buddha statues in the grottoes are made of clay. Though they have lived through more than 1,000 years, these statues still remain intact with an air of gracefulness, indicating a high artistic level.

Today, the Maijishan Grottoes contain more than 7,000 statues, some frescoes and exquisite stone-carved Buddha statues.

Compared with the Mogao Grottoes, those at Maijishan are closer to China's Central Plain and, therefore, the influence of Han culture on Buddhist arts can be clearly felt. The statues in the Maijishan Grottoes feature strong national awareness and secularization. Most of the statues in the grottoes are looking toward the ground, which makes them appear gentle and kind. The statues' physical appearance and clothing bear Han characteristics. One statue of a monk in grotto No. 44 features common monk clothing, graceful and tranquil appearance and gentle smile, and is called "Venus in the East".

Notes:

[1] Former Qin: (351-394) a state of the Sixteen Kingdoms (304-439) in China.

FOUR SACRED MOUNTAINS OF BUDDHISM

The four major iconic Bodhisattva figures in Chinese Buddhism are Wenshu, or Manjusri, Bodhisattva of wisdom; Guanyin, or Avalokitesvara, Bodhisattva of mercy; Dizang, or Ksitigarbha, Bodhisattva Savior of Beings in Hell; and Puxian, or Samantabhadra, the Bodhisattva of truth. The four bodhisattvas all work to bring all beings to enlightenment and to save people from their sufferings, but each takes a different abode or place of practice, known in Chinese as Daochang and in Sanskrit as Bodhimanda. Manjusri's place of practice is located at Mount Wutai in Shanxi Province, Samantabhadra at Emei Mountain in Sichuan Province, Avalokitesvara at Putuo Mountain in Zhejiang Province and Ksitigarbha at Jiuhua Mountain in Anhui Province. The places of practice of the four bodhisattvas together are called the Four Sacred Mountains of Buddhism.

- **Mount Wutai**

Located northeast of Wutai County in Shanxi Province, Mount Wutai derives its name from its five flat-topped peaks. Also known as Mount Qingliang for its chilly atmosphere, the mountain is a well-known Buddhist sanctuary and ranks the first among the Four Sacred Mountains of Buddhism.

Mount Wutai's Buddhist tradition started during the Han Dynasty (206 BC-AD 220). In 58-75, two Indian monks came to China to preach the Buddhist doctrine and, with the approval of the emperor, they first established the Baima (White Horse) Temple in Luoyang, and then Lingjiu Temple on Mount Wutai. From then on, the mountain became a center for Buddhist practice and study.

After generations of construction, the mountain's five

Mount Wutai

peaks became dotted with monasteries and temples. In its most prosperous period, the number of monasteries and temples reached 360, with almost 10,000 practicing monks and nuns. Therefore, it is safe to say that Mount Wutai boasts the largest temple complex in China.

Mount Wutai hosts a large number of precious cultural relics. The landmark building on Mount Wutai is a white Lama tower in Tayuan Temple. The tower, also known as "Great White Tower", derives its name from its chalky-white outer appearance. Standing 56.4 meters in height, the tower has three halls in its middle part. Three bodhisattva bronze statues (Avalokitesvara, Manjusri and Samantabhadra), a porcelain statue of the legendary monk Jigong and a wooden statue of Liu Hai (a popular charm figure) playing with the Golden Toad are enshrined in the halls. The tower is the greatest structure in terms of construction difficulty and scale.

Foguang Temple's front sanctuary is one of the two existing wood-structured buildings completed during the Tang Dynasty, and the first to be completed in China.

As the greatest Buddhist Mountain, Mount Wutai combines diverse cultural elements including Indian, Tibetan and Han Buddhism, Confucianism, Taoism and Shanxi folk culture. It is not only a place of worship for monks of various nationalities, but also a sanctuary for tourists and Buddhists across the world. Each year, on April 4, the birthday of the Manjusri, a grand ceremony will be organized on Mount Wutai for numerous pilgrims from both home and abroad.

• Mount Emei

Located in the southwest part of Sichuan Province and 130 kilometers from Chengdu, capital of the province, Mount Emei is known for its breathtaking natural scenery and mythical Buddhist culture. As one of the Four Great Buddhist Mountains, Mount Emei is reputed for its natural beauty.

Golden Summit

Construction of temples at Mount Emei began at the end of the Han Dynasty and reached its peak during the Tang Dynasty and Song Dynasty (960-1279). By the end of the Qing Dynasty (1616-1911), more than 150 temples had been constructed. The development of Buddhism over 2,000 years in China has bestowed rich cultural heritage upon Mount Emei, making the mountain a Buddhist sanctuary and a major source of influence both home and abroad.

Mount Emei boasts of abundant cultural relics among which are a 6.8-meter, 62-ton bronze statue of Puxian, or Samantabhadra, the Bodhisattva of truth, made during the Song Dynasty, and a 14-level and 5.8-meter Hua Yan bronze tower, which was exquisitely carved and decorated with 4,700 smaller statues and the Buddhist scripture Avatamsaka Sutra.

The main peak of Mount Emei is Jin Ding (Golden Summit) and its peak, Wanfo Ding, rises up to 3,079 meters, which enjoys great reputation for its four wonders: cloud sea, sunrise, Buddha light and divine lamps. In the 16th century, a bronze sanctuary was constructed and was called "Golden Summit" because of its gilded roof. Both the bronze sanctuary and Huazang Temple were destroyed in a fire; the current two buildings were built in 1986-1989 according to the original design.

The golden Buddha on Jin Ding is a 48-meter, 660-ton

gilded statue consisting of pedestal and ten-direction statue of Puxian, or Samantabhadra. The height of 48 meters stands for 48 wishes of Amitable Buddha. "Ten-direction" means ten practices and wishes of Puxian.

The Golden Summit is the best place to enjoy Mount Emei's breathtaking scenery. Extending 1,200 meters and covering an area of 16,505 square meters, the Golden Summit consists of Jingang Zui, Sheshen Rock, Duguang Tai and Xiuxin Tai. Standing 2,079 meters above sea level, it looks like a rock fell from the sky, with an accommodation capacity of several thousand sightseers. From this vantage point, one gets a good view of the Golden Summit, gilded Buddha, Buddha light, divine lamps, sunrise, cloud sea and rolling peaks.

• Mount Putuo

Surrounded by the ocean on the eastern side of Zhoushan Islands, Mount Putuo faces Shenjiamen, the third largest fishing port in the world, and covers an area of 12.5 square kilometers. Blessed by picturesque scenery such as extensive golden sand beaches, fascinating rocks, marine-made caves, rhythms of the wave sound, surreal scenes and beautiful sunset clouds, the mountain is known as a fairyland and, according to a Buddhist legend, the residence of Guanyin, or Avalokitesvara, Bodhisattva of mercy (a place which was called the South Sea and now called the East China Sea). Different from other well-known Buddhism mountains, Mount Putuo is the only national island tourist attraction in China with a Buddhist focus.

▸▸ Mount Putuo

Religious activities on the mountain date back to the Qin Dynasty (221-206 BC). After the Guanyin sanctuary was established during the Tang Dynasty (618-907), numerous temples were established. During the peak construction period, in addition to the three major temples, 88 nunneries and 128 reclusive abodes were built on the mountain and accommodated 4,000 nuns and monks, making the mountain China's No.1 Buddhist Mountain.

The three largest temples on the mountain: Puji Temple, Fayu Temple and Huiji Temple, are the most noteworthy of the existing temples. As the largest temple on the mountain, Puji Temple is extravagantly decorated and equipped with eight gates, giving the whole structure a regal look. Built along the mountain, Fayu Temple has six halls, and at the lowest level, Jiulong Hall, which was built with materials that were removed from the Ming Palace in Nanjing. Huiji Temple is the most difficult to reach on Mount Putuo, with more than 1,000 steps to ascend.

Mount Putuo is also endowed with rocks of various shapes, the most well-known being Pantuo rock and scripture-listening turtle rock. Mount Putuo's sea caverns are also worth mentioning, namely Chaoyin and Fanyin caverns.

At the end of the 20th century, a new Guanyin bronze statue standing 33 meters and weighing over 70 tons was constructed. The gilded and elegant statue has since become the landmark of Mount Putuo.

• Mount Jiuhua

Situated in Chizhou, a city on the southern bank of the Yangtze River in Anhui province, Mount Jiuhua covers an area of 100 square kilometers and is known for its lofty peaks, lush vegetation, cascading waterfalls and gurgling springs. Blessed with a mild climate and distinctive four seasons, the mountain is also consid-

Mount Jiuhua

ered the No.1 Mountain in Southeast China.

The mountain, which was originally known as Mount Jiuzi, was renamed as Mount Jiuhua thanks to a poem by Li Bai, a renowned poet in the Tang Dynasty. In the poem, he describes the mountain as more than 3,000 meters in height, with nine lotus-shaped peaks.

Legend has it that in 653, Kim Qiaoque, a relative of the king of Xin Luo (in today's South Korea) came to Mount Jiuhua and practiced Buddhism for 75 years. He achieved parinirvana at age 99 with the same countenance as he was alive. His disciples believed that he was the incarnation of the Di Zang, or Ksitigarbha, Bodhisattva Savior of Beings in Hell, and built a three-level stone tower to serve as his resting place and sanctuary. A large number of temples were built after his death and, thanks to the construction efforts during the Song, Yuan, Ming and Qing Dynasties, the number of temples reached 150, with more than 3,000-4,000 monks dwelling there. Today, remain on the mountain are 99 monasteries and temples, more than 10,000 Buddha statues, 2,000 cultural relics, and 700 monks and nuns.

Mount Jiuhua is known as the cradle for reputed Buddhist practitioners. From the Tang Dynasty, a dozen bodhisattva mummies were preserved, with five available for public viewing. The mummies, which remain preserved for so many years in such a humid climate, make Mount Jiuhua even more mysterious to tourists and Buddhist pilgrims.

June 30 on the Chinese lunar calendar is both the day of birth and death for Di Zang, or Ksitigarbha, the Bodhisattva Savior. To commemorate this sacred day, temples on Mount Jiuhua host grand Buddhist activities.

TIBETAN BUDDHISM AND LAMA TEMPLES

Tibetan Buddhism is also known as Lamaism.

Songtsen Gampo was the first Tibetan leader to introduce Buddhism into Tibet. After he unified Tibet, Songtsen Gampo adopted a peaceful coexistence policy with the neighboring Tang Dynasty and Nepal Kingdom by marrying princesses of the two royal courts in the mid-7th century. The two princesses both traveled to Tibet with their respective Buddhist statues, classics, religious articles and monks. As a result, the Dazhao (Jokhang) and Xiaozhao (Ramoche) Temples were established to enshrine the Buddha statues they brought to Tibet. Furthermore, Songtsen Gampo invited monks from India, Nepal and the Tang Dynasty to translate the Buddhist scriptures and build temples.

After 400 years of struggle, Buddhism finally took root in Tibet during the 12th century. By interacting with and borrowing elements from the Tibetan Bonism, many branches of Tibetan Buddhism were formed such as Nyingma, Sakya, Kagyu and Gelug, of which the Gelug branch, created by Tsongkhapa after he reformed the religion in the early 15th century, had the most influence. This branch later was divided into two sub-branches: the Dalai and Panchen Lama systems.

Tibetan Buddhism is popular in China's Tibet, Inner Mongolia, areas inhabited by Zang, Meng, Tu, Yugu

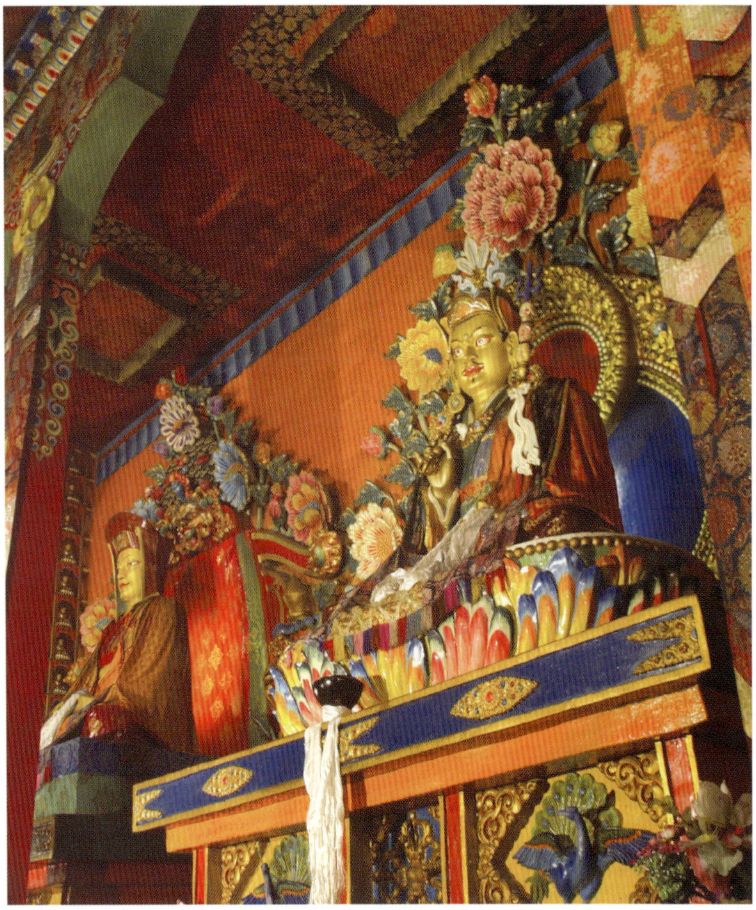

Tibetan Buddhist Statues

refined artistic skills. The Potala Palace is listed as a UNESCO World Heritage Site.

Following the peaks and valleys of the mountain and covering an area of 41 hectares, Potala Palace is a complex consisting of grand scripture halls, prayer rooms and Lama Temples. The main hall, in particular, is lofty and grand. The 6 pagodas covered with roofs of different kinds, bronze tiles and overhanging eaves, are beautifully decorated. Surrounded by gilded stone columns and colorful wish banners, the pagodas are both appealing and awe-inspiring in their radiating glory. The interior of Potala Palace serves as an art gallery and houses rich historical relics. Tens of thousands of sculptures, murals, silver and gold musical instruments, scriptures, imperial edicts and jade seals can be found in the palace, making it a cultural and artistic treasure house.

and Naxi ethnic minorities, Bhutan, Sikkim, Nepal, the People's Republic of Mongolia and Buryatia, Russia.

Most of the monasteries in Tibet bear strong Tibetan features such as tall Buddha statues, thick exterior walls, small windows and structures built against mountains. The most well-known Tibetan-style monasteries are the Potala Palace in Lhasa, Tashihunpo Monastery in Shigatse and Eight Outer Temples in Chengde, Hebei Province. All the monasteries feature magnificent buildings and beautifully decorated beams and columns.

Monasteries in Tibet boast of Buddhist statues which are so vividly carved, inscribed, casted and molded, that they are almost true to life. Large statues such as the 26-meter Maitreya statue in Tashihunpo Monastery and the 18-meter Maitreya statue (made of wood) in Beijing's Yonghe Lama Temple, reflect exquisite and

The Sakya Temple is also a world-class treasure that is home to ancient cultural relics, and it enjoys the reputation of being the second Dunhuang. It is also one of the first key historical and cultural relics put under government protection in 1961. Housing a large number of Buddhist scriptures and various astronomical, historical, literary, medical and geological books and records, the Sakya Palace has become a collection center for cultural relics. What makes the palace more impressive is the fact that it contains a large collection of pattra-leaf scriptures, which are of very high historical value. Among the large number of Yuan Dynasty murals, sculptures, embroidery and religious artifacts, the palace also holds more than 10,000 pieces of porcelain, most of which were produced during the Song and Yuan Dynasties and which are also known for their high quality. Therefore, it is fair to call the palace a small-scale porcelain museum.

Tibetan monasteries attach high importance to color contrast. Walls are painted red, while white and brown colors are used for the purpose of decoration. Towers and scripture halls are painted white, while window frames are painted black. This contrast of different colors adds a kind of mysteriousness to Tibetan Buddhism.

The layout of a Tibetan monastery is different from that of a Han Buddhist temple. A Tibetan monastery is equipped with a Buddha sanctuary, a Buddha tower to keep bodies of Lamas, a Buddha educational institute, a monastery leader's office, a scripture debating center, Lama living quarters, storages, kitchens, management rooms and a scripture reciting lobby. Among the above-mentioned buildings, the scripture reciting lobby, Buddha sanctuary and Buddha educational institute are the most important in the monastery. Situated along the axis of the monastery, these three buildings are surrounded by other structures such as numerous Lama living quarters, which give the overall layout of the monastery a clear look.

Tibetan monasteries generally are built against a mountain and various buildings in a monastery can be freely arranged, a clear difference from symmetrical Han temples. Under the influence of the Han, in terms of traditional architectural style, monasteries in Central China and Inner and Outer Mongolia gradually became symmetrical after the Yuan Dynasty. In addition, Tibetan monasteries are known to have several scripture reciting halls that are capable of accommodating several thousand Lamas, a feature not found in Han temples.

(English Author: Fan Tao)

The Potala Palace

Chapter Five Ancient Education

PUBLIC AND PRIVATE SCHOOLS

The origin of the ancient Chinese education system can be traced back to the Xia Dynasty (2070-1600 BC) and was developed into a modern system during the late Qing Dynasty (1616-1901) with the emergence of modern schools between 1870s and 1890s. Schools in ancient China fell into two categories: public and private.

The public school, as the name suggests, was organized by the central government and local governments with the aim of preparing students for public service. During the Han Dynasty (206 BC-AD 220), a relatively mature public educational system was established. Since then, central as well as local public schools have played a significant role in education, research and cultural promotion. Public school was called national school during the Western Zhou Dynasty (1046-771 BC), imperial school during the Han Dynasty, Hong-Wen Academy and Chong-Wen Academy during the Tang Dynasty and Guo Zi Jian during the Song Dynasty (960-1279).

During the Tang Dynasty, a complete school system was established, which was mostly followed during the later dynasties. Strict enrollment requirements regarding students' age, years of schooling and social rank in particular denied lower-class children from public schools. In the system, the top imperial schools only accepted students from the highest-ranking officials' families, and second-class imperial schools accepted children from middle-ranking and local officials' families. This practice was mostly followed during the later dynasties. According to the Qing Dynasty law, the children of prostitutes, opera singers, servants, soldiers and manual laborers were denied entrance into public schools. Only students from royal and noble families, after receiving elementary education, could receive instruction from government-appointed teachers in public schools organized by the central and local governments.

The curriculum in the public schools covered the Five Classics (*The Book of Songs*, *The Book of History*, *The Book of Rites*, *The Book of Changes*, and *The Spring and Autumn Annals*), *The Analects of Confucius* and *The Book on Filial Piety*.

Self-learning was the chief means of study, supplemented by lectures from teachers and outstanding students. Students were required to hold teachers in high regard and master at least one of the Five Classics. Outstanding students who excelled on exams were granted official titles.

During the Qing Dynasty, the central government hosted a hierarchy of royal clan schools, Giro clan schools and the Eight Banner schools, while the local governments hosted provincial and county public schools.

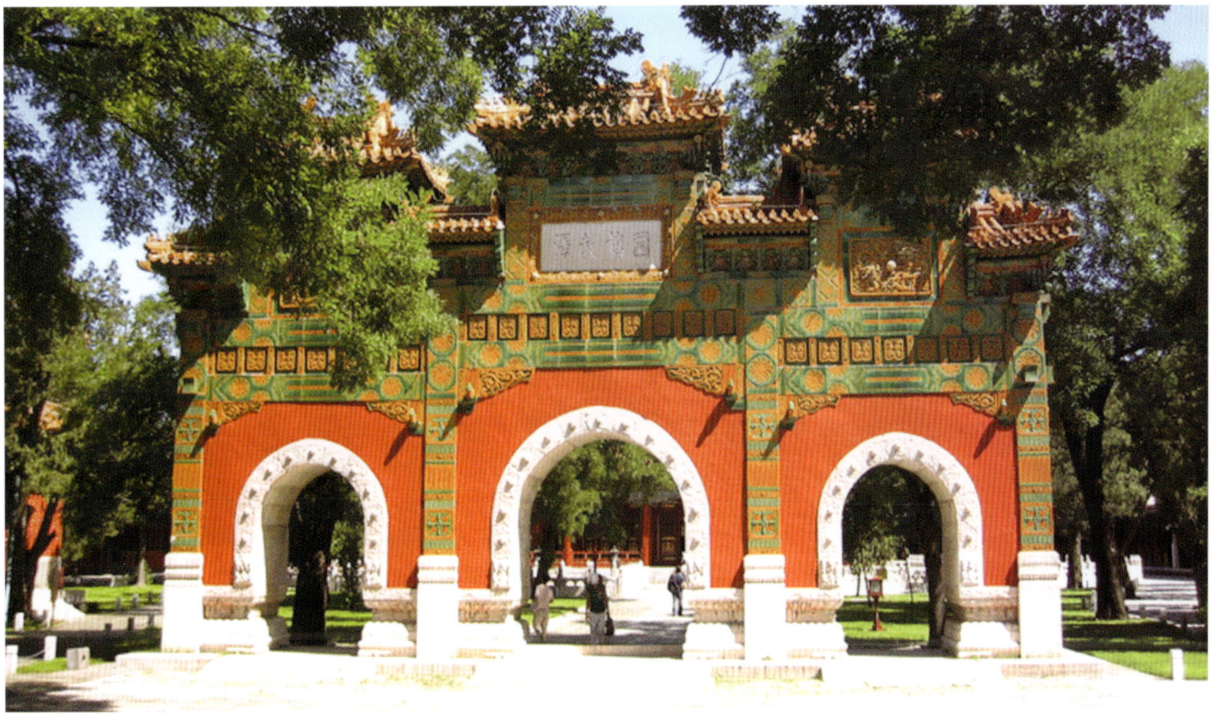

Beijing Guo Zi Jian

Since the curriculum was designed to prepare students for the Imperial Civil Examination, these schools were known as institutions where pupils were groomed to be government officials.

Private schools came into existence after public schools. During the Spring and Autumn Period (770-476 BC), Confucius was a pioneer of the private school. As the major role of the public schools was to prepare students for the Civil Examination, the private schools, responsible for most of the elementary education, became an indispensable part of the feudal education system beginning in the Han Dynasty.

Many related textbooks for elementary education were in wide use since the Song and Yuan Dynasties (1206-1368), such as *The Hundred Family Surnames*, *Thousand-character Classic*, *Three-character Scripture*, and *Poems of One Thousand Masters*.

During the Qing Dynasty, private education took place in family schools (where wealthy families employed teachers to instruct their children), old-style private schools (where teachers gave lectures in their own houses), and free private schools as well (where wealthy people employed teachers to give public lectures in temples or ancestral halls).

These private schools fell into two categories according to the content of teaching: elementary schools that taught literacy, and at a higher level, schools of Confucian classics.

Apart from government officials, most professional private school teachers were hermit scholars and government retirees/resignees.

Compared with public schools, private schools, for quite a long time in history, were larger in number and wider in fields of study than public schools, to the extent that they not only complemented public schools but predominated the school system. In the more than 2000 years of history, private schools made great contributions in reserving non-official ideas and studies, in including, in addition to the Confucian classics such fields as Taoism, feudal laws, celestial phenomenon, and medicine in their curriculum, in providing children from ordinary families opportunities for education, and in transmitting knowledge and culture.

THE CLASSICAL ACADEMY

Classical academies were distinctive ancient Chinese teaching and research institutes, and first appeared during the Tang Dynasty from 723 to 725. These academies served as places for storing and proofreading classics as well as self-study. They began to perform the functions of a school during the Five Dynasty Period (907-960). During this period of time, many officials withdrew from government affairs and built classical academies in order to study and teach independently.

The development of such academies was not smooth. The early Northern Song Dynasty (960-1127) witnessed the thriving of these institutions and the late Northern Song Dynasty saw their decline. However, during the Southern Song Dynasty (1127-1279), classical academies experienced a boom in terms of number and size.

Altogether, 37 academies were set up during the Northern Song Dynasty, and 136 during the Southern Song Dynasty, totaling 173 academies, including the four most renowned, namely, Yuelu Academy at the foot of Yuelu Mountain in present-day Hunan Province, Bailudong Academy, at the foot of Lushan Mountain in present-day Jiangxi Province, Songyang Academy, at the foot of Songshan Mountain in present-day Henan Province, and Yingtian Academy in present-day Henan Province.

Prosperity of academies in the Song Dynasty owed much to Zhu Xi, whose Neo-Confucian studies became a major part of the curriculum in the complementary development between academies and Neo-Confucian studies.

Academies experienced a revival during the Yuan Dynasty at the advocation of the rulers. However, the trend did not continue during the early Ming Dynasty (1368-1644) due to people's blind faith in the Imperial Civil Examination and public schools. It was not until during the period from 1465 to 1487 that academies began to thrive again. Unfortunately, due to involvement in satirical criticism against the government by scholars in the Donglin Academy, academies suffered four rounds of ban and burning.

The classical academy gained a short revival during the Qing Dynasty; however, it became more and more

Yuelu Academy

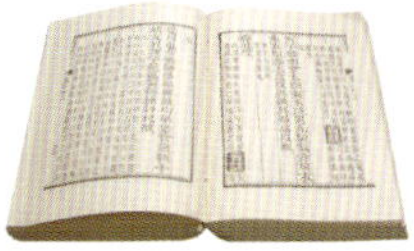

assimilated into the public school system. Finally, as this way of teaching became outdated, in 1901, the Qing Government put an end to the classical academy.

From its boom during the early Song Dynasty until its disappearance in the late Qing Dynasty, the classical academy played a crucial role in preparing students for government affairs and sustaining the Chinese culture. Its approach to education, organizational system and teaching methods all had an enormous impact on ancient education.

The classical academy distinguished itself from public and private schools in the following ways:

- Self-teaching under the guidance of the teachers was the rule of thumb. Out of respect for their teachers, students traveled long distances to the academy to seek their guidance. The teacher gave students reading lists and advice on independent reading.
- The classical academy incorporated academic research in its curriculum. Since the academy originally served the function of storing books, proofreading books and private reading, its owners and lecturers were distinguished scholars. The lectures, therefore, were mostly about their academic findings. The integration of teaching and research set a good example for later generations.
- The academy was open to all students and scholars regardless of academic stand and background. Zhu Xi[1], the orthodox Neo-Confucianist, for example, invited Lu Jiuyuan[2], an Ideal-Confucianist, to lecture in his Bailudong Academy, attended Lu's lectures himself, took down notes and had them engraved in the stone at the gate of the academy. This inclusiveness greatly enhanced academic exchange and broadened students' horizons.

The classical academy was customarily located in a pleasant environment, with the focus on nature and peace. The scenic spots on academy grounds were all given poetic names. In addition, the rich cultural atmosphere and serene environment was ideal for sharpening the senses. Thus, the rise of the classical academy must be mentioned in the same breath with the flourishing of exquisite scholars' gardens.

Notes:

[1] Zhu Xi: a Song Dynasty Confucian scholar who became the leading figure of the School of Principle and the most influential rationalist Neo-Confucian in China. His teachings were considered to be unorthodox at that time. He maintained that all things are brought into being by the union of two universal aspects of reality: qi, sometimes translated as vital (or physical, material) force; and li, sometimes translated as rational principle (or law).

[2] Lu Jiuyuan: a Chinese scholar and philosopher who founded the school of the universal mind, the second most influential Neo-Confucian school. He was a contemporary and the main rival of Zhu Xi. The unity of mind expressed in the work of Lu means the unity of the mind of humanity and the mind of the Way (Tao), or heaven. This statement was in direct opposition to Zhu Xi who claimed that the mind of the Way and the mind of Humanity were separate and different.

THE IMPERIAL CIVIL EXAMINATION SYSTEM

The Chinese Imperial Examination System lasted for 1,300 years, from its founding during the Sui Dynasty (581-618), through improvements in the Tang Dynasty (618-907), such legislative measures against cheating in the Northern Song Dynasty as sealing the examinee's name on the examination paper, duplication of the examinee's answers and the withdrawal system, and to its boom in the Ming and Qing Dynasties. It determined who among the population would be permitted to enter the bureaucracy, hence exerting huge influence on politics, economy, education and social life of ancient China.

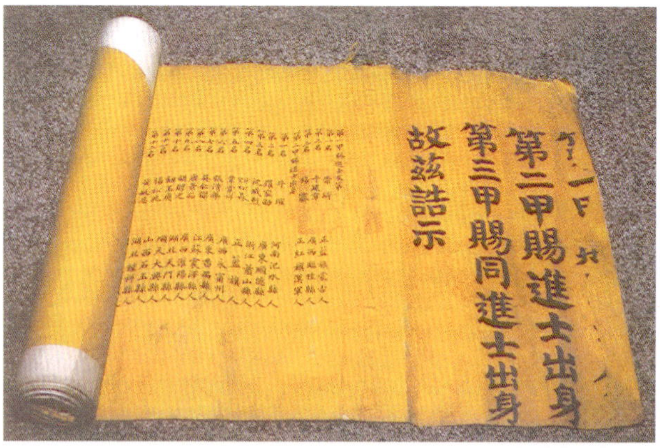

"Golden Paper" List in Qing Dynasty

During the Ming and Qing Dynasties, the examination system, with all its rigidity and complication, reached its maturity in a three-level hierarchy: the local examination, the provincial level examination and national level examination. To obtain qualifications for such exams, the examinees had to take two preliminary exams: a county-level exam hosted by the county magistrate and a regional exam chaired by the local governor. Those who passed the exams were called "Tongsheng", meaning a pupil, and qualified for the local examination set by the Governor of Education.

The local examination was administered in two rounds at the county or provincial capital. Those who pass the examinations were called "Yuansheng", popularly known as "Xiucai" , scholars who were recognized as licentiates to receive financial support from the government to attend provincial public schools in preparation for the provincial level examination.

The provincial level examination was held every three years in the capital of the province and occasionally in the capital of the country. Examinees did not become eligible until after three rounds of tests. Successful examinees, entitled "Juren", or "recommended man", became provincial graduates and were qualified to take the national level examination.

The national level examination was administered in the capital every three years. Successful examinees were called "Gongshi", or national "tribute personnel", popularly known as "Jinshi" or "presented scholar". The first national examination was held in 1371 during the Ming Dynasty in Nanjing at the Confucius Temple. Beginning in 1411, all national exams were held in Beijing.

National "tribute personnel" were also required to take part in the final imperial examination chaired by the Emperor himself. They were put into first class, second class and third class based on their examination performance. The top three examinees belonged to the first class category and won the titles of Zhuangyuan (the first rank examinee), Bangyan (the second rank examinee), and Tanhua (the third rank examinee). Several other examinees were accepted for the second class and third class categories and were duly entitled.

Achieving first place on the county-level, provincial level, and national level exams was the supreme honor for an examinee. Names of the examinees who passed the final imperial examination would be announced at the Imperial Palace and the name list would be displayed on Chang'an Street (in the capital) for three days, which was regarded as a great honor. Since the name list was written on golden paper, "to be listed in the golden paper" became the dream of every student. The imperial exam graduates were then appointed as government officials.

The late Qing Dynasty witnessed the corruption and decline of the imperial civil examination system. What's worse was that the introduction of eight-section essay seriously restrained the examinees' creativity. Eventually, in 1901, the eight-section essay requirement was revoked, and in 1905, the imperial civil examination was abolished.

The Civil Examination System, which originated from and enriched the Chinese culture, was the fairest means to select qualified personnel for the government in feudal society. It gave middle-class and lower-class citizens chances to serve as government officials. Since the Tang Dynasty, most statesmen, great thinkers, literary giants and historians experienced upward social mobility through such exams and then made great contributions to the Chinese political institution, economic system and cultural development. The system has not only influenced Chinese society, but also continues to be used by other countries as an examination model.

HUNDRED FAMILY SURNAMES, THOUSAND-CHARACTER CLASSIC AND THREE-CHARACTER SCRIPTURE

Traditionally, *Baijiaxing* (*Hundred Family Surnames*), *Qianziwen* (*Thousand-character Classic*) and *Sanzijing* (*Three-character Scripture*) served as the primers for elementary education. Since the birth of private schools at Confucius time of more than 2,500 years ago, great importance was attached to elementary education through all the dynasties. Among the great variety of elementary school primers, the three mentioned above were the most popular and influential.

Hundred Family Surnames was written by a Hangzhou scholar during the early Northern Song Dynasty. The 411 surnames were later extended to 504, including 444 single-character and 60 two-character surnames.

Wang Mingqing, a scholar during the Southern Song Dynasty, found evidence that the sequence of the first four surnames was thoughtfully arranged, while that of the others was arranged according to the frequency of its appearance.

Zhao, the surname of the Song Dynasty emperors, is considered most important and is followed by Qian, the surname of Qian Chu, King of Wu-yue during the Five Dynasties and Ten Kingdoms (907-960), Sun, the surname of the wife of Qian Chu, and Li, the surname of the Southern Tang emperors. The book, which listed all the known Chinese surnames in use at that time, is regarded as very useful though the arrangement of every four surnames in one sequence makes little sense.

Thousand-character Classic came into being during the reign of Liang Emperor Wu (464-549) of Southern Dynasties. It was said that he was an ardent lover of Wang Xizhi's calligraphy. In order to imitate and learn from Wang's calligraphy, he had 1,000 perfectly-written and commonly used characters selected from Wang's works. Since these characters were chosen at random, he then asked Zhou Xingsi, a famous writer, to compose a rhymed essay with them. A whole night's efforts turned Zhou's hair grey and gave birth to this great book. It took the form of a four-character rhymed prose that was extraordinarily structured in 250

Three-character Scripture, Hundred Family Surnames, Thousand-character Classic

chunks, promoting Confucian teachings and covering a wide range of knowledge related to nature, history, geography, military affairs, ethics, and education.

Three-character Scripture, the representative traditional primer, was said to be written by Wang Yinglin (1228-1296) during the Southern Song Dynasty. Compared with the poetically-written *Thousand-character Classic*, it was more easily understood and accepted by the common people. With the aim of encouraging children to be well-informed and upright, the more than 1,000-character primer touches upon the topics of ethics, morality, history, and common sense.

Written in rhymed patterns, the three primers are all easy to read and memorize, and hence ideal reading materials for children.

Hundred Family Surnames is a four-character rhymed text, fluent and easy to remember. *Three-character Scripture*, a three-character rhymed text, is smooth and expressive and easily accepted. It even became a popular style of writing, used by many texts, such as *Standards for Students* and *Bible for Girls*. *Thousand-character Classic* is well written and has won great popularity as a text as well as a calligraphy copybook. Many accomplished calligraphists coped the book, including Ouyang Xun, monk Huai Su, Zhao Ji of the Song Dynasty, Xian Yushu and Zhao Mengfu of the Yuan Dynasty and Wen Zhengming of the Ming Dynasty.

(English Author: Zhou Wei)

Chapter Six Ancient Technologies

THE FOUR GREAT INVENTIONS

Over the long course of history, the Chinese people have created resplendent civilizations. Besides the textile and silk products, porcelain and tea, papermaking, printing, gunpowder and the compass are four great inventions that represent ancient China's outstanding contribution to world science and technology.

• The Compass

The compass is a dial-based magnetic directional indicator, whose invention played a decisive role in the development of human civilizations.

Chinese people learned about magnetism in very early times. In *Guan Zi*, we find the words "Where there is a magnet, there is metal." This is proof that before 300 BC, the Chinese were aware of the magnetism of metals such as iron. It is recorded that as early as the Warring States Period (475-221 BC), the Chinese created the world's first device that pointed to the magnetic south, at that time named "Si Nan"; it was a piece of lodestone carved in the shape of a soup or wine ladle, whose handle would point to the south when it was placed on a smooth, flat divination plate.

Then during the Han Dynasty (206 BC-AD 220), the Chinese made the plate carved with 24 scales[1] around it in aiding the "Si Nan" to indicate direction – an invention that greatly improved the function of the compass.

"Si Nan", however, was not widely used because of its weak magnetism and great frictional resistance when coming into contact with the plate. In later times, people employed magnetization to come up with a better model – the iron-leaf compass; it was a fish-shaped device made from a thin piece of iron, which was then magnetized and placed on the surface of water to serve as a directional guide.

Not long after the invention of the fish-shaped compass, people tried magnetizing iron by rubbing a steel needle on a magnet – the first such effort ever made –

Si Nan

thus making a magnetized needle a genuine compass. During the Northern Song Dynasty (960-1127), water-floating type and suspension-type compasses, among others, were invented.

During the Southern Song Dynasty (1127-1279), the circular "heavenly plate" featuring the Heavenly Stems[2], and the square "earthly plate" featuring the Earthly Branches[3] were created. Exclusively used for determining direction, these compasses were made to function in a simple manner. Each of the characters on the circular card represents a particular direction tantamount to 30 degrees in our current use. A magnetic needle fixed in the center of the plate could easily spin, and when resting, would always point to the south – an improvement that ensured greater stability of the compass in terms of indicating direction.

After its invention in China, the compass was used in navigation, and after the 12th century, was introduced to other parts of the world. Today, compasses of this type are still widely used across the world.

• Gunpowder

Gunpowder originated from the ancient Chinese practice of alchemy. Alchemy was a kind of pill-making technology that the ancient people employed in their efforts to find the key to immortality. It was the forerunner of modern chemistry. In their alchemical experiments, people discovered the explosive properties of charcoal, niter and sulphur, and on this basis, they invented gunpowder in the early Tang Dynasty (618-907).

Recognizing its explosive properties, people during the late Tang Dynasty launched "rockets" made of gunpowder. They tied gunpowder to arrows, lighting it and then shooting the arrows in an attempt to burn down the barracks of the enemy. Later, they put gunpowder into spherical containers, and thus created the world's first cannonball.

With the reality of frequent wars during the Song Dynasty (960-1279), people invented explosive firearms – paper-tubes half-loaded with gunpowder and half-loaded with lime, and when lit, a tremendous boom ejected the lime powder with enough force to wound and kill the enemy. Then, during the Southern Song Dynasty, tube-shaped firearms were invented – bamboo tubes loaded with gun powder, which were used as weapons to kill the enemy on the battlefield. Later, the "fire gun" was invented.

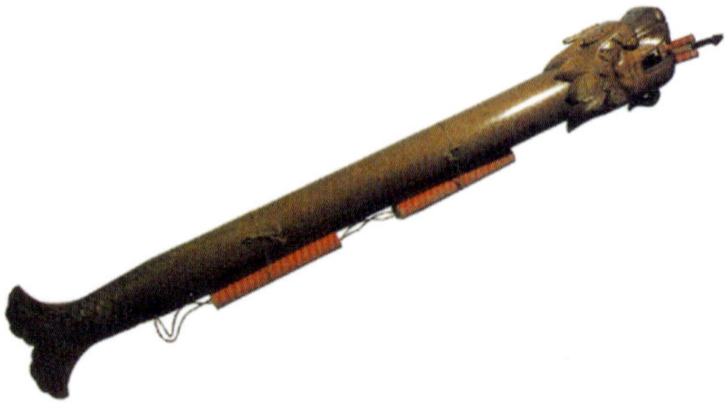

"Rocket" in Tang Dynasty

During the Yuan Dynasty (1271-1368), metals like copper and iron were used to cast cannons with bores so that it could hold more gunpowder, and therefore, achieve a greater firing range and killing power.

Aside from its application for military purposes, gunpowder was used to make fireworks for recreation and entertainment. According to historical records, during the Southern Song Dynasty, there was once a display of more than 100 fireworks set off in the royal courtyard that created a dazzling brilliance and splendor so bright as to light up the entire sky at night. Fireworks/firecracker-making technology was further developed after the Song Dynasty and setting off fireworks and firecrackers became a standard practice in recreation and in celebrating Chinese festivals.

Gunpowder was introduced to India in the 13th century and then to Europe in the 14th century via Arab countries. With the rapid invention and application of new explosives and dynamite during the period from the late 18th century to the 19th century, gunpowder began to be extensively used in the building industries, playing a major role in the further development of coalmining, road-and-house building, and water conservancy projects.

• Papermaking and Printing

Before the invention of paper, Chinese people wrote on bones, tortoise shells, bronze, stone tablets, bamboo and silk. During the late Zhou Dynasty (1046-256 BC), characters were mostly written on bamboo slips. A book of this kind would usually weigh dozens of kilograms and a cart could only carry just a few volumes. Confucius and Mozi are both believed to have had their pupils pull or push carts filled with their books while touring various kingdoms. It is said that after the unification of China, Qin Shi Huang, or the First Emperor (r. 247-210 BC) of the Qin Dynasty, would review the memorials presented to the throne every night, and he had to finish reading a whole basket of such memorials in every night. In those paperless days, writing and reading were tiring jobs indeed.

During the early Western Han Dynasty (206 BC-AD 25), people wrote on silk, which was fairly expensive. Later, they began to make paper from the fibers of hemp. In Xinjiang and Shaanxi, archeologists have discovered remnants of this type of paper. Its coarse texture made writing difficult, and therefore, was in no position to completely replace bamboo slips and silk. Dedicated efforts were made in searching for new writing materials during this period, and the emergence of new and improved papermaking techniques was only a matter of time. According to historical records, during the reign of Emperor He (r. 88-105) of the Eastern Han Dynasty, a eunuch named Cai Lun did much to improve the quality of paper.

Cai Lun, courtesy name Jingzhong, was born in Guiyang (now Chenzhou in Hunan Province) during the Eastern Han Dynasty (25-220). A man of talent and learning, Cai was appointed minister to take charge of consecration and lead artisans from all over the country in producing articles of everyday use for the royal family.

Concerned with the new techniques and production procedures, Cai Lun took a great interest in the use of raw materials and technology in regard to papermaking. As a matter of fact, he himself tried using bark, rags, used fish nets and other materials to make paper. First, he steeped the chosen raw material in water so that it would be completely saturated. Then, he took it out of the water and minced it. After rinsing it in clean water to remove the impurities, he put the thinner fiber in clean water again so as to make pulp. Lastly, he spread this pulp evenly on a sieve, which would become a piece of paper after fully dried.

Extraordinarily creative thinking and boldness in exploring new materials made it possible for Cai Lun and his workmen to make inexpensive paper good for writing, in the year 105, out of vegetable fiber, and paper in the real sense was thus invented. This advance provided a tremendous boost to the growth of the post-Cai Lun paper-making industry. In recognition of his achievement, Cai was conferred the title of "Marquis Longting"[4], and the paper that he invented was called the "Paper of Marquis Cai". With its lower cost, this paper found extensive application. It was not until after Cai Lun's improvements on paper-making techniques that paper began to be used widely for writing and painting.

Procesure of Papermaking

In much of the rest of the world people were still writing on sheepskin, bark and leaves long after the invention of fine paper in China. Chinese papermaking technology was introduced to Korea and Japan in the early 7th century, and arrived in Arab countries after another century had passed. Then, the Arabs spread this technology to Europe and other parts of the world. The art of Chinese paper-making was a great contribution to the civilizations of the world.

The widespread use of paper obviously encouraged more writings as well as the diffusion of science and culture. It also provided momentum regarding the development of printing techniques.

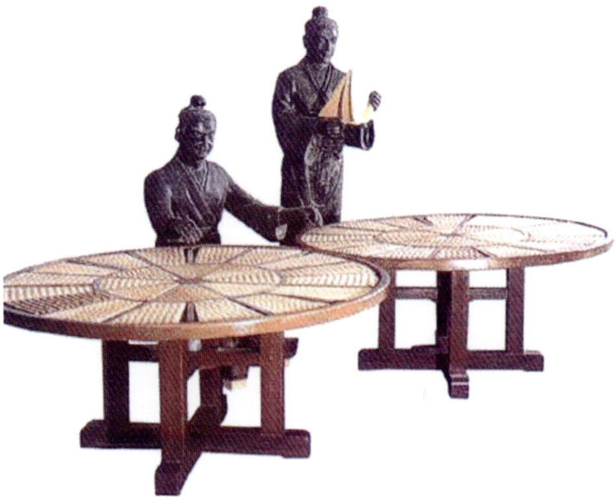

Movable-type Printing

Printing originated from ancient Chinese character-engraving techniques. As early as the Yin Epoch, the later period of the Shang Dynasty (1600-1046 BC), people carved characters on bones and tortoise shells. This was followed by increasingly improved engraving techniques that were utilized in lithoglyph (stone cutting/inscription) wood engraving, brick carving and seal cutting.

Around the 4th century, people spread paper on a stone tablet and, using ink, made rubbings from inscriptions on it. Drawing inspiration from seal cutting and ink-based inscription-rubbing techniques, people in the period between the late 6th century and the early 7th century invented lithographic printing (also called the lithographic process).

Lithographic printing involved affixing a piece of paper to a plate, then using a knife to carve the written characters into their antimorphs in raised type or in relief, thus a (cut) woodblock for printing was made. For printing, it involved sticking the paper on the woodblock, then using a brush to rub it gently and evenly, so that the characters would be printed on the paper. Diamond Sutra[5], which was printed in China in 868, is believed to be the earliest woodblock work in the world.

During the Five Dynasties (907-960), complete volumes could be printed using woodblock-cutting techniques. During the Song Dynasty woodblock printing industries experienced further development and whole volumes of books were printed. The development continued to the Song Dynasty as witnessed by books that were neat in script/typeface and superbly bound.

In the mid-11th century, during the reign of the Northern Song Dynasty, an engraver named Bi Sheng invented movable-type printing, which at that time was an unprecedented accomplishment. This type of printing method used clay in carving individual characters to create a matrix as thin as iron coin and then the matrix was baked in a fire to get hardened. For type setting, Bi Sheng firstly placed a mixture of rosin, wax and paper ash on an iron plate, and then affixed the matrixes on the mixture. Next, he heated the matrixes on a fire until the mixture under them melted. Finally, he used a flat plate, applying pressure to the surface of the matrixes in order to make the characters level and smooth enough for printing. After individual characters were made and baked, they were placed in proper order and were then ready for printing. After one printing, the characters could be arranged in a different order for a new printing. In this way, one woodblock could be used for multiple printing processes.

China's well-known movable-type print utilized a printing technique that not only saved manpower and raw materials, but also shortened printing time.

Around 1298, during the reign of the Yuan Dynasty, a man named Wang Zhen[6] invented the movable wooden matrix, and a composing stick/plate that could spin, which saved the trouble of selecting/sorting characters and type-setting, thus elevating movable-type printing techniques to a higher level.

China's printing methods were introduced to Korea, Japan and Vietnam in the mid-8th century and to Europe and other parts of the world thereafter.

Notes:

[1] 24 scales: In ancient China, people used the "Heavenly Stems" and the "Earthly Branches", together with the "gan", "kun", "xun" and "gen" from the Eight Diagrams (eight combinations of three whole or broken lines formerly used in divination) to indicate the 24 directions.

[2] the Heavenly Stems: jia, yi, bing, ding, wu, ji, geng, xin, ren, gui.

[3] the Earthly Branches: zi, chou, yin, mao, chen, si, wu, wei, shen, you, xu, hai.

[4] Marquis: second of the five ranks/titles of nobility in feudal China.

[5] *Diamond-sutra*: *Vajracchedika-sutra* in full, are Scriptures of the Great Vehicle, or of Mahayana. It is thus named as it used "Jin Gang", or Buddha's warrior or attendant, to denote intellect, with the function to rid one of worry and trouble. The Southern School of the Chan sect, or Dhynan, or simply Zen, based its religious doctrines on this canonical classic.

[6] Wang Zhen: a famed agronomist of the Yuan Dynasty, also known as Boshan, lived in Dongping, Shandong. While serving as magistrate of a prefecture, he showed great concern for agriculture. He compiled *On Agronomy* on the basis of available documents and farm work experience. What's more, he demonstrated his creativity by applying moveable type printing techniques to his book, which helped spread this new printing method.

ZU CHONGZHI AND HIS π

Zu Chongzhi was the first man in the world to have calculated the Ratio of the Circumference of a Circle to its Diameter (π) [1] to its 7th digit after the decimal point, a result that was more than 1,000 years ahead of Europe's mathematicians. Accordingly in 1967, a lunar crater and an asteroid (permanently numbered 1888) were named after Zu Chongzhi in commemoration of his great contribution to China's as well as the world's mathematical sciences.

Zu Chongzhi

Zu Chongzhi (429-500), courtesy name Wenyuan, with ancestors from Qiuxian County of Fanyang (north of what is now Laishui County in Hebei Province), was born in Jiankang (the present Nanjing of Jiangsu Province) of the Northern and Southern Dynasties (420-589). The Zu's family moved to south of the Yangtze River to escape the chaos of wars that plagued the country during the later years of the Western Jin Dynasty (265-317).

For generations, Zu's family had been put in charge of the royal court's calendar affairs. Zu Lü, Zu Chongzhi's grandfather, had once served as a minister of architecture. Therefore, during his childhood, Zu Chongzhi had numerous opportunities to interact with science and technology. This experience enabled him to create a precision calendar known as the Daming Calendar[2], when he was still fairly young.

In 464, Zu Chongzhi, then 35 years old, began his π calculations.

At that time, Chinese people already knew that a circle's circumference was three times longer than its diameter. Using his cyclotomic method[3], a mathematician named Liu Hui, who lived before Zu Chongzhi's time, had calculated a ratio to a figure that was approximating 3.1416.

Pressing on with his endeavor and after repeated calculations, Zu Chongzhi continued to make progress, obtaining a figure at the 7th digit after the decimal point (a figure between 3.1415926 and 3.1415927). He also determined the approximate value of the ratio's fractionation. Although there is no way to know how he achieved this result, it can be said that his successful findings must have been the fruit of painstaking efforts and an input of all his energies, considering that he lived in a time without calculators. Hence, his calculations were all done by hand, and the value of π that he determined was accurate to one millionth of 1/10.

Zu Chongzhi's achievement epitomizes what ancient Chinese mathematicians had accomplished. Up until the 14th century, China was recognized as one of the world leaders in mathematics. The Pythagorean theorem, for example, was expounded in *The Arithmetical Classic of the Gnomon* and *The Circular Paths of Heaven* in 200 BC; the concepts of negative numbers and the addition and subtraction of positive and negative numbers were first proposed in *The Nine Chapters on the Mathematical Art* in 100 and the deca-equation was solved in China as early as in the 13th century, while the Europeans had to wait until the 16th century to even find a method of solving their cubic problem.

It is sad that Zu's Official Calendar, rejected by crafty sycophants like Dai Faxing, was not adopted before his death at the age of 72 in 500. And what is more unfortunate is the loss of his text called *Method of Interpolation* as early as the Song Dynasty.

Notes:

[1] The Ratio of the Circumference of a Circle to its Diameter: a constant with π used as its symbol. Liu Hui calculated the value of π as $\pi \approx 3.14$, which is called the "Hui Ratio". Zu Chongzhi's calculated result was $3.1415926 < \pi < 3.1415927$, with 227 as the approximate ratio, and 355113 as the accurate ratio.

[2] The Daming Calendar: invented by Zu Chongzhi in 462, with a tropical year set at 365.2488 days. The calendar was characterized by its improvement on the intercalary to accord with astronomical or celestial phenomena, and its consideration of the procession of the equinoxes in calendar-making, with only a one degree error made in one hundred years.

[3] Cyclotomic method: Liu Hui's method for calculating π, in which he used the perimeter of an inpolygon to infinitely approach the circumference of a circle. Liu Hui started with a regular hexagon and continued calculations until arriving at a 192-sided polygon. In this way, he determined the ratio as approximating 3.14.

GUO SHOUJING AND HIS IMPROVED CALENDAR

Guo Shoujing (1231-1316), courtesy name Ruosi, from Xingtai (now in Hebei Province), was a renowned astronomer, mathematician and an expert in water conservancy and instrument-making during the Yuan Dynasty. Though his father died young, Guo Shoujing learned from his grandfather about astronomy, arithmetic and water conservancy. When still a boy, he developed an eager interest in science.

Guo Shoujing's major achievements were in astronomy and calendar-making. With the Yuan Dynasty having conquered the regions south of the Yangtze River, there was a time when different calendars were used simultaneously, which caused inconveniences that even made it difficult to accurately calculate the 24 Solar Terms (a Solar Term is a day marking one of the 24 divisions of the solar year on the traditional Chinese calendar; the 24 Solar Terms have often been used for agricultural purposes). In 1276, the rulers of the Yuan Dynasty decreed that their calendars be adjusted, so as to be more accurate. Guo Shoujing was asked to head the project.

He knew that the famous Armillary Sphere, a large instrument for observing celestial bodies and astronomical phenomena, was worn-out and obsolete, which meant it couldn't be expected to obtain reliable data. In adjusting the old calendars, Guo Shoujing first made improvements on the more than ten astronomical instruments that were in existence, including the abridged armillary and the celestial globe. Then, equipped with these improved instruments, he and 14 professionally-competent officials whom he had selected, formed groups and then embarked on journeys around the country to observe celestial phenomena.

Altogether, they set up 27 star observatory stations throughout the country, which sent all obtained data to Dadu, the capital of the Yuan Dynasty (now Beijing). Based on the data collected, Guo engaged himself in meticulous calculations. In 1280, he created a new calendar, which was named "Shoushi Calendar[1]" by Kublai, the 5th emperor of the Yuan Dynasty. In the following year, this new calendar was adopted by the whole country.

Setting the number of days in a year at 365.2424, Guo's calendar was much more accurate than its predecessors. What's more, it was basically the same as the Gregorian Calendar (the calendar used by most of the world), but Guo's calendar came into being 300 years earlier than the latter, being acclaimed as China's most accurate and finest calendar during the Yuan Dynasty as well as the most advanced in the world at that time.

Guo Shoujing blessed the world with 105 volumes in 14 categories in the fields of astronomy and calendar-making. He was the first person in the world to use the concept of sea level elevation as a measurement tool; this was 560 years before the mean sea level concept was proposed by Gauss, a German mathematician. His abridged armillary was the first equatorial telescope ever made in the world, more than 300 years ahead of the invention of similar instruments by Tycho Brahe, an astronomer from Denmark. And his latitude determination preceded such effort in the West by 620 years.

Guo Shoujing Commemorative Stamp

In the 1960s, China's Ministry of Posts and Telecommunications issued two commemorative stamps. The International Astronomical Union, as well as other organizations, named a crater on the moon and an asteroid in the Solar System after him in honor of his contributions in astronomy.

Notes:

[1] Shoushi Calendar: a calendar produced under the auspices of Guo Shoujing. Guo contended that "The fundamental function of a calendar is for observation, while an instrument is of first importance for observational purposes." He invented more than ten astronomical instruments and had 27 towers erected for measurement of the sun's shadow. It took him five years to successfully complete his calendar.

LI BING AND HIS DUJIANG WEIR

At the foot of Mount Yulei on the east bank of the Minjiang River in Sichuan Province, there stands an "Erwang Temple". It was built in memory of the river-taming feat achieved by Li Bing and his son Erlang.

There are few available records of Li Bing's life and his Dujiang Weir project. All that is known is that he served as Prefect of the Sichuan area in early 251 BC during the Warring States period. It was then that Li and his son led the construction efforts of the huge Dujiang Weir.

The stories of Li Bing building the Dujiang Weir are very popular among the Chinese people. Li Bing was a local official who understood and sympathized with people who lived in poverty and misery. He was also a prominent scientist. During his term as Prefect, he saw frequent rainstorms and heavy floods that destroyed embankments on the Minjiang River, inundated farmland and threatened the lives of inhabitants.

Li was determined to harness the Minjiang River, so as to save people from affliction and suffering. Across

Dujiang Weir

hills and rivers, he and his son Erlang walked hundreds of miles to inspect the water regimen and the topography. Considering the western Sichuan Plain is high in the northwest and low in the southeast, Li Bing focused on these geographical features in his endeavor to tame the river. He mobilized the local people to join him in putting up a huge dam on the Minjiang River, and it took them eight long years of hard labor to finish this gigantic water conservancy project.

The Dujiang Weir is located in Dujiangyan, Sichuan Province, consisting of three major projects, namely the V-shaped water-dividing dike, the Feishayan Spillway (for desilting and flood discharge) and the Baopingkou Water Inlet. This long dike cuts the Minjiang River into two separate parts, the inner river (a manmade watercourse for irrigation) and the outer river (for flood discharge).

The gigantic weir has a flat top, which is shaped like a fish mouth, and constitutes the most important part in dividing the water. At the end of the long dike is the 200-meter-wide dam called Feishayan, which serves the purpose of flood discharge; when the inflow into the inner river is small, Feishayan diverts water into the inner river, while in cases of an inflow spilling over the dam face, it is able to drain off the silt, sediment and pebbles from floods. Close to the Feishayan Spillway is the newly-dug narrows named Baopingkou, whose top section connects the inner river, and whose bottom part is divided into four trunk canals for outflows from Baopingkou into the western Sichuan Plain. So, these three projects are supplementary to each other, facilitating diversion, flow and flood control and discharge.

With the important role it played in ensuring an ample water supply for irrigation and in preventing and alleviating the menace of floods, the Dujiang Weir has been hailed as ancient China's greatest water control project.

The Dujiang Weir Project has withstood countless severe floods over the past 2,200 years. And with the removal of inundation fears, the western Sichuan Plain has become the "Land of Abundance". The local people enshrined Li Bing and his son as "Master of Sichuan" and "King of Bashu", commemorating their meritorious deeds. They even had these two men mythologized: Erlang became a dagger-wielding, three-eyed hero known as God Erlang[1].

With his great feat, Li Bing has remained immortal in people's memory. A stone statue of him with inscription of date discovered in 1974 proves that people paid homage to him some 1,800 years ago.

Notes:

[1] God Erlang: legend has it that Li Bing, while serving as Prefect of the Sichuan area, had his second son Erlang travel to a place called Guankou to fight the flood dragon (a mythical creature capable of invoking storms and floods) so as to rid the people of evil. Later people enshrined Erlang in temples as God Erlang.

THE GRAND CANAL —THE LONGEST AND OLDEST IN THE WORLD

People in ancient China dug numerous canals to spur economy and facilitate transportation. The Beijing-Hangzhou Grand Canal was the most famous and the largest of its kind, which, together with the Great Wall, claims to be one of the four greatest engineering feats in the world. And like the Great Wall, the Grand Canal is a symbol of China and the Chinese nation, widely recognized for its role in helping drive the country's economy, social progress and cultural prosperity, as well as for having nourished the towns and cities along its banks.

The digging of the Grand Canal began in 486 BC and was completed in 1,779 consecutive years of work. Navigable in 1293, the canal starts from Beijing and ends in Hangzhou. Flowing 1,794 kilometers through Tianjin, Hebei, Shandong, Jiangsu and Zhejiang, it is linked with all five water systems of the country, namely, the Hai River, the Yellow River, the Huai River, the Yangtze River and the Qiantang River.

The canal project went through three major stages of construction. The first was during the Spring and Autumn and Warring States periods (770-221 BC). Vying for supremacy, the various kingdoms started digging a number of canals. The second stage was in 589. The imperial rulers of the Sui Dynasty (581-618), after having reunified the whole country, engaged in a massive digging project that was later called the South-North Grand Canal, which started from Zhuojun[1] in the north and ended in Hangzhou, with Luoyang and Kaifeng as the center.

When Beijing became the capital, the rulers of the Yuan Dynasty endeavored to renovate this canal. In 1283 and 1289, the digging of the Jizhou Canal and the Huitong Canal was completed. The Tonghui Canal, beginning in Tongzhou and ending in Beijing, was also made navigable during the Yuan Dynasty. And transformation projects made it possible to reach Hangzhou from Beijing by ship. Also made possible was the non-stop transport of tribute rice and goods to the capital city from the south. Compared with the Sui Dynasty canal, the Yuan Dynasty canal shortened the voyage by 900 kilometers.

Flowing from north to south, the Grand Canal is comprised of eight individual canals: the Tonghui Canal (from Beijing to Tongzhou), the North Canal (from Tongzhou to Tianjin), the South Canal (also called

The Beijing-Hangzhou Grand Canal (Hangzhou Section)

the Wei River, from Tianjin to Linqing in Shandong Province), the Huitong Canal (from Linqing to Dongping), the Jizhou Canal (from Dongping to Jining), the Middle Canal (also called the Taierzhuang Canal, from Taierzhuang in the city of Zaozhuang, Shangdong Province to Xuzhou of Jiangsu Province), the Li Canal (also called Shanyangdu, from Huai'an to Yangzhou of Jiangsu Province), and the Jiangnan Canal (also called Jiangnan River, from Zhenjiang to Hangzhou).

Accompanying the completion of the Grand Canal was the emergence of towns and cities, trading ports and commercial and transportation centers along its banks, like Dezhou, Linqing, Jinan, Yangzhou, Zhenjiang and Hangzhou. Connecting the major river systems in the whole eastern half of the country, the Grand Canal contributed considerably to south-north transportation at a time when railroads, highways and developed maritime transport did not exist.

Notes:

[1] Zhuojun: a prefecture set up during the Han Dynasty, the area south of what is now Fangshan County of Beijing, east of Qingyuan, and Yixian County of Hebei Province, north of Anping and Hejian of Hebei Province, and west of Baxian and Renqiu of Hebei Province.

(English Author: Liu Guoqiang)

Chapter Seven Ancient Architecture

GARDEN ARCHITECTURE

Garden architectures have enjoyed an age-old tradition in China. As early as during the Zhou Dynasty (1046-256 BC), there appeared the first palatial gardens. Garden architectures in ancient China fall into three categories. There are the grand, majestic imperial gardens, like the Beihai Park and the Summer Palace in Beijing and the Mountain Resort and its Outlying Temples in Chengde, Hebei Province. There are those elegant, exquisite-designed private gardens, like the Shihuyuan Garden in Weifang, Shandong Province, the Jingyuan Garden in Yuci, Shanxi Province, and the Shizilin (Lion Grove) and Zhuozhengyuan (the Humble Administrators Garden) in Suzhou, Jiangsu Province. And there are the monastery gardens, like Hu Pao (the Tiger Running Spring Park) in Hangzhou and Du Fu Thatched Cottage in Chengdu, Sichuan Province.

Garden architectures are recognized for three distinguishing features, as follows:

- Practicality. Airy pavilions, waterside pavilions and marble boats are where people stay for rest or

West Bank of Kunming Lake in Summer Palace

enjoy the landscape around them. Pavilions, which might be square, round or polygonal in shape, are often combined with hills, water and plants to create beauty. Waterside pavilions are typically lined with railings where tourists can sit at the benches or French windows to rest and look into the distance for enjoyment of the scenery. Marble boats are actually garden-like, boat-shaped structures erected on water, and people on board would find themselves embraced amid the waterscape as if they were on the boat while enjoying themselves in drinking and delicacies.

- Uniqueness. With their vantage location and unique design, garden architectures are beautiful landscape paintings, dynamic or static. There are verandas, walls and paths leading to or separating from these architectures. Verandas are roofed galleries or independent covered corridors. As passageways linking the architectural structures inside and outside, verandas constitute an integral part of the garden structures, and they also serve as sunshade and shelter. Verandas can be direct galleries or winding corridors, and they might be built on the hills, over water, or above a bridge. The gardens are also embellished with bridges, whose aesthetic value overrides their functional role. There are the footbridges, arch bridges, pavilion bridges, lounge bridges, and others. Walls are put up to demarcate the different parts of gardens and ornament the landscape. According to their type of building material and structures there are the board framed walls, rubble retaining walls and white powder walls. Courtyards are mostly partitioned by white powder walls with grey tiles on the top. Serving as a foil to the hills and stones and the flowers and trees, the white powder walls convey an artistic conception, and they are like pieces of white paper on which the most beautiful landscape is painted. Portals, hole windows, leaking windows and latticed bricks and tiles are usually added to the walls, creating what is called "view borrowing", a traditional practice in ancient China to break from spatial limitations and enrich the gardens by borrowing scenes from outside the gardens.

- Artistic conceptions. Ingenious designing and distribution of hills and water scenery, flowers and plants, courtyards, veranda bridges, as well as couplets and horizontal-inscribed boards – these all give limitless vigor and vitality to the hills, the stones and the running water. China's garden architectures are of three levels or thematic concerns: Peace and Prosperity, the Fairyland, and Naturalness.

From Peace and Prosperity is seen the profound influence of the orthodox thought of Confucianism on architectural designs in feudal China. In the gardens, one sees the pavilion, the hall, the mansion, the veranda, the study, while these mostly serve as a medium, in cultural or customary terms, for communicating with "Heaven and Earth" and with the "ancestors". The designing of the palaces in the gardens manifests the ideal of harmony between man and nature, while highlighting the "Heavenly mandate", "the will of the Heaven", or the "Pre-Ordinance", and assuming an air of self-importance.

Peace and Prosperity as a theme of architecture is the very reflection of such ideology. In terms of architectural layout, the designers prefer to follow the guide of axis and bilateral symmetry in their pursuit of overall unity for the gardens. Everything must be done in strict compliance with the law and discipline rites, from structure and sequence to make-up. Most architectural structures are in the shape of a square or a rectangle, with the important ones arranged to be built along the vertical axis and the ones of less importance on the horizontal axis. And there are the walls and galleries to make the gardens an enclosed unity, and thus give them an impression of dignity and orderliness. These all demonstrate the pursuit of proportional and symmetrical beauty in garden architectural design, an aesthetic ideology and values advocated in Confucianism.

The Fairyland vision attaches more values to the Taoist thought of seeking freedom from wants and needs, and self-cultivation. Examples of this category of structures include the Immortal Abode on Penglai Island in Yuanmingyuan Palace, the Guchang Taoist

Temple on Mount Qingcheng in Sichuan Province, and the Nanyan Taoist Abbey on Mount Wudang. And a characteristic of these structures is the mystique in seeking immortality.

The periods of the Jin and the South and North Dynasties (420-589) marked a turning point in the history of garden architecture of China. In their way of detaching themselves from political upheaval, most men of letters and literati developed an interest in metaphysics and found pleasure in the beauty of the natural landscape. The hills and rivers became where they chose to live for good, to stay temporarily, or simply to enjoy themselves. The hills, water, flowers and trees in their gardens were meant to be a means of pursing the Fairyland vision and transcending the earthly world through self-cultivation.

The Naturalness level is one that stresses on freedom and relaxation for expressing sentiments. Naturalness as a thematic concern of architecture can be seen in the gardens of men of letters, like Su Shunqin's Gentle Waves Pavilion and Sima Guang's Dule Garden in the Song Dynasty (960-1279).

The gardens of the man of letters during the Tang (618-907) and Song Dynasties feature an addition of poems and paintings to the architecture itself. The perfect combination of natural beauty and architectural beauty brought about poetic and picturesque scenes everywhere in the gardens. Garden architecture as an art got further developed in this period; the scenes were no longer that simple putting-together of lines, colors and texture; they gave psychological suggestions and abounded in symbolism and ambiguity, whether in their designations, shapes or arrangement, inspiring thoughts and imagination, such as the imagination of vast expense of water in the form of a pool or ranges of mountain in a pile of rocks.

PALATIAL ARCHITECTURE – THE IMPERIAL PALACE

Looking southward into the distance from atop Jingshan in Beijing, one can see an ancient architectural complex embraced by green trees—layers upon layers of palaces and towers, so well-tiered, imperious, majestic and magnificent. That is the world-renowned Imperial Palace of Beijing. Along with Château de Versailles of France, the Buckingham Palace of the UK, the White House of the United States and the Kremlin of the Russian Republic, it is reputed to be one of the five greatest palaces in the world, and is included in UNESCO's World Heritage List.

Also referred to as the "Forbidden City", the Imperial Palace was the royal palace of the dynasties of Ming (1368-1644) and Qing (1616-1911). Twenty-four emperors (14 of the Ming Dynasty and ten of the Qing Dynasty) had lived and ruled their empire here, with a combined span of 491 years. It has an area of some 720,000 square meters (960 meters long and 750 meters wide), including a floor space of nearly 160,000 square meters with more than 9,000 rooms, claiming to be the largest and best preserved of all ancient royal palatial complexes in the world.

A visit to the Imperial Palace usually starts from the Gate of Heavenly Peace[1], where a straight broad thoroughfare leads to a front gate. A slab-paved "Emperor's Road" connects the front gate to the main entrance of the Imperial Palace – the Meridian Gate.

Inside the Meridian Gate, the major architectural structures are divided into the two categories of the Outer Court and the Inner Court.

The Outer Court centers on the halls of Supreme Harmony, Central Harmony and Preserving Harmony. These are flanked by the halls of Literary Glory and Military Eminence. It was here that the emperor issued decrees and held their grand ceremonies.

On the north of the three grand halls is the Inner Court, lined with the Palace of Heavenly Purity[2], the Hall of Union[3] and the Palace of Earthly Tranquility[4], which are surrounded by the Six Palaces of the East and the West and the Imperial Garden. East of the Six Eastern Palaces are the Hall of Imperial Splendor, the Hall of Tranquil Longevity, and west of the Six Western Palaces are the Palace of Benevolent Tranquility and others. These were the residences of the emperor and his empress, the empress dowager, consorts, concubines, princes and princesses.

These palatial architectural structures impress the visitors with their majesty and magnificence. Especially worthy of note are the halls of Supreme Harmony, Central Harmony and Preserving Harmony. These are built on three 8-meter-high white-marble steps, supported by three levels of platforms. Each of the platforms is encircled by white jadestone railings at the edges and carved with cloud, dragon and phoenix designs. The edges of each level of the platforms are decorated with more than 100 white jadestone dragon heads, with a built-in water outlet in the mouth functioning as the drainage pipe; in case of torrential rain, water would flow out from within the mouths of the dragons all at the same time, both impressive and practically useful. All these demonstrate vividly the perfect combination of the classical architectural science and art in ancient China.

Perfect plane layout and three-dimensional contouring, as well as the grandeur and imperiousness, make the Imperial Palace an unmatched masterpiece of ancient Chinese architecture, a symbol of old China, and a representative of all architectural marvels made realistic by the Chinese some 500 years ago.

The creation of the Imperial Palace started side by side with the reconstruction of the city of Beijing during the Ming and Qing Dynasties. That the city was built with the royal palaces at the center typifies the architectural layout of a capital city in feudal China. Beijing at that time consisted of three parts—the Forbidden City in the center, the surrounding Royal City and the outer Capital City. The well-known Gate of Heavenly Peace and Gate of Earthly Peace were originally the official entrances to the Royal City from the south and north. Inside the Royal City were sacrificial altars to the gods of grains and the land, the Imperial Ancestral Temple, Buddhist temples and Taoist abbeys, government offices and other structures related to the royal household. Imperial gardens, like the Beihai Park, the

The Palace of Heavenly Purity

Zhongnanhai and the Jingshan Park, are also situated inside the Royal City.

The Imperial Palace has city walls and moats around it for protection. The walls are over ten meters high and the moats, over 50 meters wide, making the Palace a "city inside a city". Also, there is built an exquisitely-designed watchtower high above each of the four corners of the city walls, which represents a style unique to the Chinese ancient architecture. The Capital City was separated from the Royal City with a wall surrounding it. With an Outer City created to the south of the Capital City in the mid Ming Dynasty, the Forbidden City was protected by three walls, an obvious indication of the prominence of imperial authority.

Notes:

[1] The Gate of Heavenly Peace: located in the center of the city of Beijing, originally the main entrance of the Forbidden City during the Ming and Qing Dynasties.

[2] The Palace of Heavenly Purity: a palace where the emperors handled their daily affairs.

[3] The Hall of Union: a palace with its name meaning the "union of Heaven and Earth"; The emperors had their privy seal stowed in here.

[4] The Palace of Earthly Tranquility: consisting of two separate palaces called *nuandian* (one in the east and one in the west), it was the residence of the empresses of the Ming Dynasty and the bridal chamber of the emperors of the Qing Dynasty.

TOMBS AND MAUSOLEUMS

Ancient Chinese followed the custom of burying the deceased under the ground, for it was their belief that a person after death would live a life similar to their earthly existence, and therefore the deceased should be treated as they were living. This could explain why the architectural structures above and under ground served as part of the ancient tombs and mausoleums, and why the funerary objects were modeled on their counterparts in the earthly world. A number of the huge graves unearthed in the Yin Ruins Palace ancestor temple area in Anyang of Henan Province had in them lots of slaves, vehicles and horses as part of the burial articles.

Tombs and mausoleums constitute an important integral part of ancient Chinese architecture. According to *Shiji* (*The Records of the Grand Historian*), there were two imperial tombs in the early Qin Dynasty, one was the Mausoleum of Emperor Huangdi in Shaanxi Province, and the other, the Da Yu Mausoleum in Shaoxing, Zhejiang Province. And the Mausoleum of Qin Shi Huang, the First Emperor of the Qin Dynasty, was undoubtedly the largest of its kind in China and even in the world, both in size and in grandeur.

In the long dynastic history of China, tomb/mausoleum-building as an art witnessed great strides forward, accompanied by an increasingly obvious integration of the natural landscape with various art forms, like architecture, sculpture and painting.

In terms of architectural layout, the imperial tombs and mausoleums can be classified into three types:

- The layout with the mausoleum at the center. One example is the impressive Mausoleum of Qin Shi Huang, which was built against the Lishan Mountain, with walls surrounding it.

- The axis layout. One example is the Qian Mausoleum for Emperor Gaozong of the Tang Dynasty (r. 649-683), which was located against hills, with its majesty created by the watchtowers, stone animals, human figures, inscribed tablets and ornamental columns erected in front of the mausoleum.

- The complex layout. The tombs and mausoleums of the Ming and Qing Dynasties were well-arranged at an enclosed area surrounded by high hills. The erection of honorific arches, the main entrance and

The Ming Tombs

tablet-housing pavilions along the Divine Passageway bring about harmony between constructions and the natural environment, and an atmosphere of dominant imperial power.

The imperial tombs complex built during the Ming and Qing Dynasties are the best preserved of their kind in China. Thirteen emperors of the Ming Dynasty had their tombs built together, collectively referred to as the Ming Tombs. Construction of the tombs started in 1409 and was completed in 1644, the year marking the ruin of the Ming Dynasty, lasting more than 200 years.

Located on the hillside of a small basin encircled on three sides by a mountain named Tianshou and facing an open land to the south, the tombs are well-tiered and spaced, occupying an area of some 40 square kilometers. Different as they are from each other in form, these tombs have a lot in common. Each and every tomb was referred to as "Palace", and surrounded by a red wall. Inside the gate of the "Palace" was the Leng En Hall, a place where sacrificial rites were held, and behind the Leng En Hall there were the places of burial for the thirteen emperors, twenty three empresses and a great number of imperial concubines, princes and princesses.

The Ming Tombs are the most complete and most concentrated complexes of their kind. The largest of these are the Changling (Chang Tomb) for Emperor Shenzong (Zhu Di, r. 1402-1424) and the Dingling Tombs for Emperor Chengzu (Zhu Yijun, r. 1573-1620). Excavations have found that the underground palaces of the Dingling (Ding Tomb) have strong stone arches and good drainage facilities, with no serious water logging and no subsidence – this is proof of the superb skills of the Chinese in building underground structures.

The grandest and most intact of all existing imperial burial places in China are the East Imperial Tombs of the Qing Dynasty built at a place called Ma Lan Yu in Zunhua County, Hebei Province. The 78-square-kilometer mausoleum, majestic and imposing, is the burial place of five emperors and Empress Dowager Cixi. The grandest tombs here are Yuling for Emperor Qianlong (1736-1799) and Dingdongling for Empress Dowager Cixi.

Known as an "underground Buddha worshipping hall", Yuling had its four stone gates, walls and ceilings carved with Buddhist scriptures. Dingdongling for Empress Dowager Cixi was made all the more beautiful with some 24,000 golden dragons painted on the walls and coiling dragons on the 64 pillars supporting the palace; the beams were all of rose wood, and the flight of steps leading to the palace hall was sculptured with dragon and phoenix designs in high relief, so vivid and full of life, and instead of the traditional expression with the dragon and phoenix placed in parallel, it was a breakthrough with the dragon flying somewhat below the dancing phoenix.

Official acknowledgement of the unique charm and high historical, artistic and scientific value of the East Imperial Tombs of the Qing Dynasty came on November 30, 2000, when it was included in UNESCO's World Heritage List.

THE GREAT WALL

The Great Wall of China represents a rare ancient military defense system in the world history of architecture. With its magnificence, grandeur and long history, it has been included in the World Heritage List by UNESCO and is widely described as one of the "Eight Wonders of the World".

The slightest mention of the Great Wall would remind you of Qin Shi Huang, the First Emperor of the Qin Dynasty. Indeed, the building of the Great Wall was a key military strategy he adopted after he unified China in 221 BC. Construction of the Great Wall, however, began long before his time. Far back in the Spring and Autumn and Warring States periods (770-221 BC), the various kingdoms, and the states of Yan, Zhao and Qin in particular, put up huge walls to defend against each other, or to fend off the intrusions and harassment from Xiongnu, or the Hun, and Donghu[1], two powerful nationalities in the north.

The state of Qin, after bringing the six other states under its sway, began to build a thousand-li great wall on the basis of the existing ones, making much of what we see now. From Qin and onward, rulers of the imperial dynasties had the walls further built and extended. During the Ming Dynasty, the part of earth-filled wall was replaced by brick-and-stone structures to defend against the assaults from the Mongolians and Nuchen, also a powerful nationality in the north.

The Great Wall that we see now dates back to the Ming Dynasty. It started from the Shanhaiguan Pass in the east and ended at the Jiayuguan Pass[2] in Gansu Province, traversing Hebei, Tianjin, Beijing, Shanxi, Inner Mongolia, Shaanxi, Ningxia and Gansu, meandering to extend a total length of 6,700 kilometers.

Quite a number of beacon towers were built on the Great Wall, some on high hills and some connected with the walls, used for transmitting military messages and sending alarms and warnings to secure border defense. Were the enemy to come to attack, the soldiers on guard at the nearest beacon tower would set a fire to give out smoke in daytime and flame at night as a signal of warning. Seeing the smoke or flame, nearby beacon towers would follow suit. Through this coordinated relay, warning of danger could be sent to the capital within hours, even if it was ten thousand miles away.

There is a military pass every 7,500 meters apart along the Great Wall. Some are huge and some are small, depending on their topography and military importance. Famous passes include the Shanhaiguan Pass, the Jiayuguan Pass, the Pingxingguan Pass, the Yanmenguan Pass, the Juyongguan Pass[3] and the Badaling.

The Great Wall at Jiayuguan Pass

The Shanhaiguan Pass stands on the only way connecting the north and northeast of China, in a place of vital strategic importance, hence its reputation as "No. 1 Pass in the World". The Juyongguan Pass is about 60 kilometers away from Beijing. Here is a world of green beauty, with range upon range of hills covered with verdure. There were two gates in the front of the pass, the southern gate, and the northern gate—the Badaling.

Notes:

[1] Donghu: a minority nationality living in the north and northeast of the State of Yan (what is now the upper reaches of the Liaohe River), with animal husbandry as the main line of business supported by hunting.

[2] The Jiayuguan Pass: a pass known for its stone reliefs and painted murals of the Wei and Jin dynasties.

[3] The Juyongguan Pass: a vital pass on the Great Wall northwest of Beijing, located in a deep valley between two mountains with the surrounding terrain being of great strategic importance; A chief passageway linking Inner Mongolia, it has been a place contested by all military strategists.

ARCHITECTURE OF ANCIENT CAPITALS

• Xi'an

Xi'an is the oldest among the six imperial cities of China, serving as the dynastic ruling center for more than 1,000 years. Located west of what is now the Fengshui River in Chang'an County, Shaanxi Province, it was the capital of the Eastern Zhou Dynasty (770-256 BC) (then called Fengjing) during the reign of Emperor Wu, and capital of the Western Zhou Dynasty (1046-771 BC) (then called Fengjing). During the Qin Dynasty (221-206 BC) it was called Xianyang. Thirteen dynasties that followed also established their capital here, including Western Han, Western Jin, Former Zhao, Former Qin, Later Qin, Western Wei, Northern Zhou, Sui, and Tang.

The fossil cranium of the Lantian Man, excavated at Kung-wang-ling on the southern bank of the Ba River of Xi'an, is believed to be the Homo erectus of the early Paleolithic Age dating back to some 500,000 to 600,000 years ago. The sites of the Banpo and Jiangzhai Neolithic Villages discovered in the eastern suburbs of the city are remains of the well-known Yangshao Culture and the Longshan Culture of about 5,000 years ago. These are all evidence of Xi'an as an earliest cradle of the Chinese nation.

Xianyang extended from the northern bank of the Wei River (the largest tributary of the Yellow River) to west of what is now the city of Xi'an. The E-pang Palace[1], whose foundations still exist, represented the architectural art of the Qin Dynasty at its highest level. During the Tang Dynasty, Xianyang came to be called Chang'an, which is much larger than the current city of Xi'an. And with the erection of three palatial complexes, flourishing of culture and economy and increasing exchanges with the outside world facilitated by the "Silk Road", Chang'an entered its period of full bloom and reached the height of splendor in feudal China, witnessing its golden age in its history of evolution.

The Big Wild Goose Pagoda and the Small Wild Goose Pagoda are, unfortunately, the one and only one of the few architectural structures left from the Tang Dynasty. The Daming Palace has its ruins north of where the current railway station stands. The city walls, bell tower and drum tower in Xi'an are of the styles of the Ming Dynasty, with the city walls identified as the best preserved of their kind in China.

Lying round the city proper were the Qin Shi Huang Mausoleum, some 30 tombs of the Han Dynasty and the same number of tombs of the Tang Dynasty, making itself a most concentrated place of burial of deceased emperors, empresses, concubines and court officials. These ancient cemeteries occupied large areas, built with grand architectural structures and stone figures and images and tombstones above ground, and imposing palaces and a great variety of funerary

Ancient City Walls in Xi'an

The White Horse Temple

objects, with the Qin Shi Huang Mausoleum at Lishan and the Terracotta Army being best known in the world.

Xi'an also boasts China's largest and oldest collection of stone sculptures – the Forest of Steles; the earliest Chinese-style sacred shrine of Islam—the Great Mosque at Huajuexiang; and the country's best museum—the state-level Shaanxi Provincial Museum of History.

• Luoyang

Luoyang derived its name from its location on the northern bank of the Luoshui River (now called the Luo River, in Henan Province). Luoyang and its surrounding area emerged as a center of business and cultural activities in the Xia Dynasty (2070-1600 BC). The discovery of the Yangshao Culture in a village in northwestern Luoyang and the legendary "Hetuluoshu" have proved the long history and culture in the Heluo areas. Cities appeared here as far back as in the Western Zhou Dynasty, and then called Luoyi. Dozens of locations in Luoyang have so far been recognized to be the sites of the Erlitou Culture which flourished in the Xia and Shang (1600-1046 BC) Dynasties.

For a period of 950-plus years since 770 BC (next only to Xi'an), Luoyang had served as the imperial capital of different dynasties, including Eastern Zhou, Eastern Han (25-220), Kingdom of Wei (220-265), Western Jin (265-317), Northern Wei (368–534), Sui (581-907), Tang, and the Later Liang (947-950) and Later Tang (923-936) of the Five Dynasties (907-960). Widely referred to as "Nine-Dynasty Ancient Capital", it ranks prominently among the six imperial capital cities of China.

East of Luoyang is the White Horse Temple, which was first built in 68 during the Eastern Han Dynasty. It was once administered by two monks, Shemoteng and Zhufalan, and sutra translators from Tianzhu (India in ancient times), winning it the reputation as the first Buddhist temple in China, hence the name *Shiyuan* and *Zuting*.

In the south of the city is a place called "Guanlin", which is said to be where the head of Guan Yu, the legendary general during the Three Kingdoms (220-280), was buried. "Guanlin" was first built in the Tang Dynasty, and expanded during the Ming and Qing Dynasties.

Luoyang is also a concentration of tombs of monarchs

of dynastic empires. The dynasties of Eastern Zhou, Eastern Han and Northern Wei had relatively more tombs here, with many cultural relics and artifacts unearthed.

The famous Longmen Grottoes in Luoyang date back to the years 477-499 during the Northern Wei Dynasty, with their digging continued to last for more than 400 years running through many dynasties. Boasting more than 100,000 images of the Buddha, it is one of the "four largest ancient grottoes" in China.

Admiring its various cultural and historical relics, Sima Guang, the famous literati of the Song Dynasty, wrote in a poem, "If you want to know about the great many vicissitudes of the state, Luoyang is the only place you need to come to see and experience." Luoyang is a mirror on the ancient civilizations and long history of China.

• Beijing

Beijing, the capital of the People's Republic of China, is world-renowned for having served as capital of six dynastic empires and regimes running through more than 800 years. As the center of the political, economic and cultural life of China, it sends out its charm as an age-old capital city and modern dynamics as an international metropolis.

Beijing as we call it now dates back to the Ming Dynasty, with Ming Emperor Taizu (Zhu Yuanzhang) reigning in Nanjing (1368-1398), when Beijing, then called Shun Tian Fu, was territory under the control of his son, Prince Zhu Di. Ascending to the throne later on after a successful coup, Zhu Di renamed Shun Tian Fu as Beijing.

Beijing is a city of symmetry, with a central axis formed starting from the Yongding Men Gate all the way through Qianmen (literally "Front Gate", the colloquial name for Zhengyangmen), the Gate of Heavenly Peace, the Meridian Gate, Shen Wu Men (the Gate of Divine Might, Jingshan, the Gate of Earthly Peace and finishing at the Drum Tower. Dongsi, Xisi, and other thoroughfares stretching from the north to the south, interwined with hundreds of crisscross alleys (hutong), are alongside this central axis.

The ancient city proper of Beijing was convex-shaped, comprising the inner city and the outer city. The inner city in the northern section appeared first, built in the early years of the Ming Dynasty, on the basis of the remains of Da Du of the Yuan Dynasty (1206-1368) and following the models of Nanjing and Zhongdu (now Fengyang in Anhui Province). The outer city in the southern section was not built until the years of reign of Emperor Shizong (r. 1522-1566) in the late Ming Dynasty.

The Temple of Heaven

Outside of the inner city were the four sacrificial altars—the Temple of Heaven, the Temple of Earth, the Temple of the Sun and the Temple of the Moon – standing respectively in the four directions of south, north, east and west of the city.

The Temple of Heaven was where the emperors of the Ming and Qing Dynasties offered sacrifices to heaven on the Winter Solstice, prayed for a good harvest at the beginning of the first month of spring, and offered prayers for rain on the Summer Solstice. The Temple of Earth was where the Emperors offered sacrifices to the God of Earth. At the Temple of the Sun the Emperors prayed to the Sun God on the Spring Equinox, and at the Temple of the Moon, they offered sacrifices to the Goddess of the Moon on the Autumnal Equinox of each year. Offering thanksgiving sacrifices to gods has been a custom followed by all generations of the Chinese nation.

With its numerous remains of historical and cultural splendor, Beijing stands out prominently for its architectural structures of unique styles and radiance.

Its Forbidden City claims to be the largest and most intact imperial palace ever erected in the world. The Summer Palace, the largest imperial garden still in existence in China, features a perfect combination of the exquisiteness of the typical landscape of the regions south of the Yangtze River and the bold vigor of the gardens of the north; picturesque scenery entitles itself to a high repute in not only domestic but also world history of landscape architecture.

Another architectural wonder of the world, the gorgeous, imperious Temple of Heaven, represents an invaluable architectural legacy China has left to the world, and is living evidence of the glory and magnificence of old Beijing.

The Ming Tombs are the largest of their kind in Beijing, with the Dingling being the most impressive. The Badaling, the best preserved section of the Great Wall, boasts to be one of the eight greatest architectural wonders of the world.

Beijing is also known for its religious establishments, including the Buddhist Biyun Temple, the Taoist Baiyun Temple, the Lamaist Temple of Peace and Harmony[2], and the Islamic Mosque at Niujie, to name just a few.

The *Siheyuan*, or quadrangle, is characteristic of the local flavor of the residences of the Beijingers.

• Nanjing

Nanjing, another one of the four major capital cities during dynastic rules, is world renowned, also for its resplendent history and culture.

The city of Nanjing lies south of the Yangtze River and north of the Ningzhen hills, with a river called Qinhuai flowing down its southwest city walls into the Yangtze. "Coiling dragon and crouching tiger"[3] are the words ancient people used to describe its terrain of strategic importance, forbidding and difficult access.

Its emergence as a city dates from the Spring and Autumn period (770-476 BC) over 2,400 years ago. The long years from the 3rd century to the early 15th century saw the city serve as the capital of six dynasties, namely Kingdom of Wu (222-280), Eastern Jin (317-420), and Song (420-479), Qi (479-502), Liang (502-557) and Chen (557-589), hence "the six-dynasty ancient capital" as it is generally called. Following dynasties of Southern Tang (937-975), Ming in its early years, and the Taiping Heavenly Kingdom (1851–1864) also had their capital established in Nanjing.

Formerly called Jinling, Nanjing first got its name when for the first time it served as the capital of a wholly-unified country during the reign of Zhu Yuanzhang, the first emperor of the Ming Dynasty, for 43 consecutive years from 1378 to 1421. In the years before and after it was established as the capital city, Zhu Yuanzhang launched a massive consolidation campaign which made Nanjing a stronghold comparable to the best in the world.

The city was made up of three sections—the old city

proper, the imperial palaces, and the garrison district, with the first two sections being extensions from the early Ming Dynasty. The 33.68-km brick-and-stone wall now surrounding the three sections of the city, dates back to the Ming Dynasty and claims to be the longest of its kind in the world. The base of the wall was paved with stone slabs, its surface built of 10cm x 20cm bricks, and solidified within with earth. Entrance to the city was by the 13 gates along the wall, each with a tower erected on top. All these gates connected the main crisscross and neatly-laid-out streets of the city. The mighty city-gate towers are like warriors in armor standing guard at the entrances to their city. The most amazing of them is the southern gate (now called Zhonghua Gate). It is a "gate of tricks", as it has three jar-like caves, 27 hideouts and a lifting jack, which together make an impregnable fortress, or a "bastion of iron", so to speak.

East of Nanjing crouches the famous Mount Zhongshan (the Purple-Golden Mountain, so named owing to the purple color of the shaly bedding on the mountain). With its luxiriant vegetation cover, the mountain is an exceptional scenic spot bordering on the busy downtown area.

The Mount Zhongshan is dotted with sites of historical and cultural interest, mostly scattered at its southern foot, with the Sun Yat-sen Mausoleum in the middle, the Soul Valley Temple and the Tomb of Deng Yanda[4] in the east and the tombs of Emperor Zhu Yuanzhang, Liao Zhongkai[5] and He Xiangning[6] and the Zhongshan Botanical Garden in the west. On one of its peaks stand the ruined site of the Taiping Heavenly Kingdom and the world-renowned Purple-Golden Mountain Observatory. The western part of the mountain that connects the city proper is where stood the Royal Garden of the Six Dynasties (222–589), and to its north flows the Xuanwu Lake[7].

Notes:

[1] E-pang Palace: a palace of the Qin Dynasty, whose ruins are located five kilometers west of what is now the city of Xi'an; While the front palace was built in 212 BC, in the 35th year of reign of Qin Shi Huang, the palatial complex was not completed when the Qin Dynasty met its doom, when General Xiang Yu and his army marched past the Shanhaiguan Pass and committed the entire palace to the flames.

[2] The Lamaist Temple of Peace and Harmony: the largest Lamaist monastery in Beijing, located within the Andingmen Gate on the northeastern corner of the inner-city.

[3] "Coiling dragon and crouching tiger": a metaphor for describing the majesty and grandeur of Nanjing; Coming to see the city as an envoy to the Kingdom of Eastern Wu, Zhuge Liang of the Kingdom Shu exclaimed, "It's like a coiling dragon and crouching tiger! It bounds to be the place for the Monarch!"

[4] Deng Yanda (1895-1931): a leading Leftist within the Nationalist Party (the Kuomintang, or the KMT) of China, he was Director of the General Political Department of the National Revolutionary Army during the Northern Expedition (1926-1927), and a member of the Revolutionary Committee during the August 1 Nanchang Uprising (1927). He was killed by Chiang Kai-shek in 1931.

[5] Liao Zhongkai: (1877-1925), contemporary democratic revolutionary, once the Party Representative of the Whampoa Military Academy, Party General Representative of the National Revolutionary Army, member of the Standing Committee of the Central Executive Committee of the Nationalist Party (the KMT), and Minister of Workers and Peasants.

[6] He Xiangning: (1879-1972), woman revolutionary, a follower of Sun Yat-sen, like her husband Liao Zhongkai; served after the founding of New China as Vice Chair of the Chinese People's Political Consultative Conference (CPPCC), Vice Chair of the Standing Committee of the National People's Congress (NPC), Chair of the Revolutionary Committee of the Chinese Kuomintang, and Honorary Chair of All-China Women's Federation.

[7] The Xuanwu Lake: a lake outside the Xuanwu Gate, having its rise in the northern section of the Mount Zhongshan.

(English Author: Liu Guoqiang)

Chapter Eight Ancient Arts and Crafts

BRONZE ARTIFACTS

Bronze, an important invention in civilization, was first used in China thousands of years ago. In 1975, a bronze knife was excavated from the Majia Yao Culture Relics (dating back to about 3,000 years ago). To date, it remains the most ancient bronze artifact uncovered in China. The bronze industry hit its peak during the Shang (1600-1046 BC) and Western Zhou (1046-771 BC) Dynasties, also known as China's "Bronze Age".

Human-faced Bronze Square Ding

Not only did ancient China boast of the largest number of bronze artifacts, it also enjoyed the greatest variety, which included weapons, cooking pots, food containers, drinking vessels, water bottles, musical instruments and ornaments for carts and horses. Bronze artifacts varied from region to region, and from dynasty to dynasty. There were over 20 different kinds of drinking vessels, such as the Jue[1], Jiao[2], Zun[3], Hu and Square Yi[4].

The Simuwu Rectangle Ding[5] is known for its large size among existing bronze artifacts made during the Shang and Zhou (1046-256 BC) Dynasties. In ancient times, the Ding was used to boil, heat or contain food. Later it became a container of sacrifice, and was made in different forms to cater to different contents, as in the case of the Deer Ding, Cow Ding etc. The Simuwu Rectangle Ding was cast during the heyday of the Shang Dynasty and was excavated from Anyang City's (Henan Province) Yin Ruins. It is the largest of its kind ever discovered, 133 cm in height and 875 kg in weight. Moreover, it was designed to have a square body, big ears and four strong legs, all of which demonstrate invincible stability and gigantic power. The central parts of the Ding's four sides are smooth, without any decoration, but are wreathed with ornamental patterns, with a two-bodied gulosity (Taotie)[6] sitting on its top, and bull head patterns on each corner and joint. A total of 24 gulosities and bull heads are carved

Bronze Zun

on the Ding, which records the advanced bronze casting technique of the Shang Dynasty.

Chinese bronze artifacts, especially those from the Shang and Western Zhou Dynasties, feature intricate patterns such as the mysterious gulosity design which dominated that period. Sometimes, the face of the gulosity composed over almost half of the design, with round and large eyes, ears, mouth and nose all being very lifelike. While dragon and bird designs were commonly used, elephant, deer, cow, snake, turtle and cicada designs appeared occasionally. Moreover, geometrical patterns and drawings of hunting, battles and banquets also appeared on bronze artifacts.

Most bronze artifacts excavated in China are sacrificial vessels while those from other countries are mostly weapons such as spears, swords and arrows. This difference has clearly indicated the diverse cultural orientation of European and Chinese bronze cultures. Sacrificial vessels entail more advanced technology than weapons. In ancient China, ceremonies involving sacrifice served as an important part of people's life. Sacrificial vessels were used as drinking or washing vessels during various ceremonial occasions. Also, some were meant to be funerary pieces for tombs.

Chinese bronze artifacts, of which most are sacrificial vessels, feature inscriptions. Of all the bronze artifacts excavated in China, more than 10,000 bear inscriptions. This is a major difference between Chinese bronze artifacts and those excavated in other countries. In the mid Shang Dynasty, only one or two characters were inscribed on bronze artifacts, and these were referred to as "emblems". During the late Shang Dynasty, more characters were inscribed on bronze artifacts and the longest inscription was composed of 48 characters. Inscription reached its peak during the Western Zhou Dynasty. The Mao Gong Ding casted at this time bears the longest inscription of 487 characters. Written in different styles, these inscriptions, bold or elegant, are of great calligraphic value.

Notes:

[1] Jue: an ancient drinking vessel with three legs.

[2] Jiao: an ancient wine container similar to Jue, but with a cover.

[3] Zun: an ancient drinking vessel.

[4] Fang Yi: an ancient wine container; here it refers to sacrificial utensils in general.

[5] Simuwu Rectangle Ding: a sacrificial utensil used by the royal family during the late Shang Dynasty. Excavated in 1939, it is now housed in the Chinese History Museum.

[6] Gulosity (Taotie): according to legend, a greedy and fierce monster. In ancient times, its head was commonly used on bronze artifacts.

TERRACOTTA ARMY

The Mausoleum of the First Qin Emperor (Qin Shi Huang) was located at the foot of Lishan Mountain to the east of Xi'an's Lintong County, Shaanxi Province. The Terracotta Army, literally "soldier and horse funerary statues", represent Qin Shi Huang's Terracotta Warriors and Horses. These clay figures are a form of funerary art, which were buried with Qin Shi Huang to help him rule another empire in the afterlife. Three pits have been excavated. Pit No.1, the first to have been discovered, is rectangular in shape and flanked with two others, named Pit No. 2 and Pit No. 3.

The Terracotta Army were discovered in March, 1974 by some farmers while drilling a well near Xi'an. Some believed these clay fragments came from a brick kiln, while others argued they were temple statues. This discovery prompted archaeologists to investigate. After a whole year of painstaking work, they finally unearthed "the world's largest underground military museum".

According to historian Sima Qian's (145-90 BC) *Shiji* (*Shih Ching* or *The Records of the Grand Historian*), construction of this mausoleum began in 246 BC when Qin Shi Huang was only 13. The construction involved a total of 700,000 workers. Colossal wood materials were transported from Sichuan and Hubei. So were stone materials from the Zhong Mountain and Cuo'e Mountain. The whole project took 39 years and was completed one year after Qin Shi Huang's death.

Since 1974, a great number of relics have been excavated from the pits, amazing the entire world. The Terracotta Army was regarded as the epitome of the powerful Qin Army, which greatly contributed to Qin's unification success.

In 1977, the Qin Terracotta Army Museum was built on the site of Pit No.1. Over 6,000 life-like and life-sized figures were placed in this 14,620-square meter pit, demonstrating Qin Shi Huang's unprecedented power in the world. The weapons excavated were made of refined bronze, with some of them found in immaculate condition.

Apart from the clay figures and bronze weapons, two groups of bronze carts, horses and horsemen were excavated right beside the pit. These two-wheel carts are pulled by four horses, with a horseman on each cart. The 3.28-meter cart weighs 1,200 kilograms and stands 1.04 meters tall. The 1.2-meter horse stands 0.7 meter tall, half the height of a life-size horse. The cart, which was fashioned by casting, is comprised of over 3,000 parts.

The discovery of the Terracotta Army proved that the Qin Dynasty (221-206 BC) enjoyed a high level of technology. The Terracotta Army, which continues to attract the attention of scholars from home and abroad, is recognized as one of the Eight Wonders of the World. It has also proven that Chinese painted pottery was quite advanced during the Qin Dynasty, undermining the misconception that it was imported from India but became mature during the Southern and Northern Dynasty (420-589). In 1987, the Terracotta Army and the First Qin Emperor's Mausoleum were both listed as World Culture Heritage sites by UNESCO.

Crouching Archer of the Terracotta Army

TANG SANCAI GLAZED POTTERY

Tang Sancai Glazed Pottery was first discovered by two Chinese scholars, Luo Zhenyu and Wang Guowei in the early 1900s. In 1907, Luo Zhenyu came across two pieces of ancient pottery at Changsi in Beijing, and his collection of pottery kept growing for ten straight years. In 1916, Luo compiled *The Catalog of Ancient Pottery*, which consisted of four volumes; it records how he found every single piece of his entire collection. This brought a storm to the world of archeology and started a Tang Sancai Glazed Pottery purchasing craze. Therefore, more and more Tang Sancai Glazed Pottery flowed to Beijing. In the following decades, a large number of Tang Sancai works were excavated in Henan, Shaanxi and Jiangsu, which revealed a whole new world of art.

Sancai Heavenly King Figure

Tang Sancai Glazed Pottery is a special kind of painted earthenware which was made in China during the Tang Dynasty (618-907), hence the name Tang Sancai Glazed Pottery. "Sancai" literally means "tri-colored"; this is because the colors yellow, green, and white were widely used during the Tang Dynasty to make this earthenware, although some pieces were created using other colors such as sky blue, bistre, aubergine and maroon.

It took hundreds of years for Tang Sancai to fully mature as an art form. Single-colored glaze first appeared during the Han Dynasty (206 BC-AD 220). During the Northern Wei (386-534), double-colored glaze was created, and it was not until the early Tang Dynasty that Tang Sancai (triple-colored) appeared.

Up to now, Tang Sancai (triple-colored) has a history of over 1300 years. Having combined the characteristics of various traditional arts, it has developed into a unique art form boasting of bold lines, vibrant colors and intricate patterns.

The culturally rich Tang Dynasty faithfully recorded cultural exchanges between China and the rest of the world. Tang Sancai played an important role in this process. Elements of Indian culture, west Asian culture and Persian culture have been found on Tang Sancai figures. Therefore, Tang Sancai Glazed Pottery is popular with Indians, Japanese, Koreans, Iraqis, Iranians, Egyptians and Italians.

JINGDEZHEN — THE CHINA CAPITAL AND HOME OF THE FOUR ANCIENT KILNS

Jingdezhen is situated in the north-east of Jiangxi Province and neighbors Anhui Province. It was first known to the world during the Han and Tang Dynasties for its porcelain and was listed as one of the Song Dynasty (960-1279) "four famous towns". Jingdezhen got its name after Song Emperor Zhenzong (r. 968-1022) had "景德年制" (made during the Jingde reign) inscribed on the bottom of porcelain works to the palace. Jingdezhen was the center of China's porcelain industry during the Yuan (1206-1368), Ming (1368-1644) and Qing (1616-1911) Dynasties. Blue and white porcelain[1], underglazed red porcelain, decorative porcelain[2] and polychrome enamel décor[3] ware made in Jingdezhen have attracted buyers from Europe, America, northeast Asia, south Asia, west Asia and North Africa. For the past ten centuries, Jingdezhen has prospered mainly because of its ceramic industry.

Underglazed Red Bowl

Jingdezhen has made a great contribution in the history of Chinese ceramics and that of whole world as well. Its ceramics industry has thrived for over a thousand years, making it the only city relying on a single industry in the world. After the founding of New China, it was included in the first list of Chinese famous historic and cultural cities.

During the Song Dynasty, Chinese ceramics reached its peak. Kilns of different styles were set up throughout the country. The top five kilns at that time were Junyao, Geyao, Guanyao, Ruyao and Dingyao.

The Guan Kiln was first established in Kaifeng by the royal family and was later moved to Hangzhou. The Guan Kiln produced some exquisite work due to the use of sound techniques and quality materials. Because the Guan Kiln produced products with elegant shape and unique pattern, they were exclusively used by the royal family. The best materials were used and most skilled craftsmen were employed in manufacturing these products. Occasionally, products refused by the royal family were sold, and on some other occasions, bestowed upon officials.

The Ding Kiln got its name because it was established in Dingzhou (now Quyang County in Hebei Province) during the Song Dynasty. White porcelain was the main product of the Ding Kiln and its other products featured the use of green glaze, black glaze and blackish brown glaze. Known for its colorful patterns, porcelain from the Ding Kiln is regarded as the gem of ceramic arts.

As a large kiln with highly developed techniques, the Ding Kiln had a considerable impact on other kilns and enjoyed a rather high status in the history of Song Dynasty ceramics. Most Ding Kiln products were light, thin and translucent. Flowers, sea waves and fish were commonly used patterns.

The Ru Kiln was located in Ruzhou (today known as Linru in Henan Province), hence its name. Few Ru products have been found because Ru Kiln existed for only two decades. Porcelain from the Ru Kiln is famous among Chinese porcelain. During the late Song Dynasty, the Ru Kiln was exclusively meant for the royal family. Porcelain from the Ru Kiln was produced using fine materials and advanced techniques. Valuable agate was used and unique colors were generated; some say the color of the porcelain was like the sky after a heavy rain, and the surface as smooth as jade.

The Jun Kiln was situated in Henan Province's Yuxian County. It was thus named because Yuxian belonged to Junzhou during the Song Dynasty. The Jun Kiln experienced the most prosperity during the late Song Dynasty. The most interesting aspect of porcelain from the Jun Kiln is that it entered the kiln in one color, but after being fired with 1,350-degree heat, came out in various beautiful shades.

So far scholars are uncertain of Ge Kiln's site. Legends suggest that the kiln was named after the elder brother of the director of the kiln. Porcelain from the Ge Kiln prevailed during the Song and Yuan Dynasties and is distinguishable from other porcelain by its unique and multi-colored crack-like lines. Blood red, dark-blue and light yellow are the most common colors of Ge Kiln porcelain, and most are shaped like a net or plum blossoms.

Notes:

[1] Blue and white porcelain: a piece of porcelain with white patterns on a blue background.

[2] Decorative porcelain: a piece of porcelain bearing a five-colored pattern on a blue-and-white background or single color glaze.

[3] polychrome enamel décor: a kind of porcelain that was exclusive to the Qing Dynasty imperial family and outstanding officials.

FOUR FAMOUS VARIETIES OF INK STONES

Ink is one of the "four treasures of the study". For calligraphers and painters, a good ink stone is as important as the quality of the ink. An ink stone will affect the quality and texture of the ink that is ground upon it. Therefore, some literati have developed a keen interest in collecting inks, which last due to its incorruptibility.

Among the four treasures, the ink stone is considered most important by literati because it is solid and lasting. Most Chinese literati have a keen interest in ink stones, of which the best-known are the Duan Ink Stone from Guangdong, She Ink Stone from Anhui, Tao Ink Stone from Gansu and Chengni Ink Stone from Shanxi.

Those who have learned to master the brush, ink, ink stone and paper, are very passionate about their craft. Holding an antique ink stone, it is hard not to feel the power that emanated from the precedent painter or scholar owners of this stone. For this reason, ink stones are avidly collected and treasured by Chinese and some foreigners.

The Duan Ink Stone originated in Duanxi, Guangdong Province and is commonly a purple to purplish-red color. On these stones are various distinctive markings such as eyes, which have given them traditional value. A great variety of the stone was mined during the Song Dynasty.

The She Ink Stone features natural patterns and lines, which look like golden stars, eyebrows and sea waves. The "golden stars" are just like those that twinkle in the autumn night sky; "eyebrows" are of various shapes and "sea waves" are very lifelike. The carvings on the She Ink Stone are unique and plain because they were greatly influenced by Huizhou's tile and wood carvings.

She Ink Stone

Tao Ink Stone

The Tao Ink Stone is of great rarity because it was found on a steep cliff. This stone, which first appeared near the Tao River, gained great popularity during the Tang Dynasty. The stone is crystalline and jadelike, bearing distinct markings such as bands of varying shades. It is easily confused with the Duan Ink Stone of the green variety, but can be distinguished through careful observation of its crystalline nature.

Chengni Ink Stone is a ceramic-manufactured ink stone. The production of these stones commenced during the Tang Dynasty and is said to have originated in Jiangzhou, Shanxi Province.

At the early stage of inks, they were more practical but less beautiful. During the Ming and Qing Dynasties, more decorations were applied to ink stones, making them more like art pieces. Gradually, famous literati developed great interest in ink stones. Many started collecting various ink stones and spent their spare time enjoying ink stones in the study.

THE ART OF CHINESE SCULPTURE AND CARVINGS

Chinese sculpture includes tile carving, stone carving and woodcarving.

• Brick Carving

Brick carving[1] is a kind of ornamentation done on grey bricks. Qin and Han Dynasty patterned tiles are perhaps the earliest examples of tile carving. It originated during the Warring States Period (475-221 BC) and was widely used from royal palaces, temples and tombs to the screen walls, eaves, roofs and door lintels of civil dwellings. In the long history of architecture, tile carving played an important role. Myths, legends and drama stories were all themes illustrated on various tiles. These beautifully carved tiles added great charm to a building and were thought to have brought good fortune to its dwellers.

The brick carving was derived from ceramic crafts and stone carving. It involved various techniques and presented diverse styles in different periods. Most Han Dynasty and Wei Dynasty brick carvings were used to decorate tombs; it belongs to the initial stage of tile carving.

In recent years, about one thousand Han Dynasty tiles have been excavated in Nanyang, Henan Province. Skilled craftsmen of the time carved lifelike dancers and singers on the tiles, which today unfolds before our eyes a life scene from the Han Dynasty. Acrobats performing various nimble feats such as tightrope walking, Cuju[2], and handstands were also found on some tiles. All these carved bricks reveal that Han nobles dreamed of enjoying this kind of entertainment in the afterlife. Moreover, they represent the Han Dynasty's marvelous art achievements.

During the Tang Dynasty, the brick carving was still

Brick Carving

used to decorate tombs and pagodas, and additional carving techniques were used after the bricks had been molded. Multilayer carving appeared during the Song Dynasty but wasn't widely used in decorating civil dwellings until the Ming and Qing Dynasties. Due to its lower cost, the brick carving began to replace the wood carving.

Stories were often illustrated on the carved bricks that were used in civil dwellings. In terms of this unique artwork, bricks from the north featured advanced techniques and simple style, while those from the south involved more complicated techniques and elegance. At that time, Shanxi Province's flourishing business propelled the development of civil dwelling brick carving. Furthermore, booming business in Anhui benefited Huizhou brick carving.

• Woodcarving

Wood carving has a long history in China. As early as prehistoric times, simple wood carving began to appear. Three-dimensional carving was favored over intaglio and the simple patterns that were used during the Shang Dynasty. During the Qin and Han Dynasties, wood carving experienced great progress.

Various types of wood carving in China are classified into two categories: craft carving and art carving. Dongyang wood carving from Zhejiang, gold lacquered wood carving from Guangdong, boxwood carving from Wenzhou and Longyan wood carving from Fujian are considered the best types of carving in China. Craft carving is both pleasing to the eye and practical in everyday life. Many things of nature appear on the beautiful pieces including mountains, rivers, human figures, animals, birds, flowers and fish. They represent good fortune and people's love for life. The most frequently used patterns include dragon, phoenix, crane and magpie which denote safety, fortune, longevity and good harvest. Dragon and phoenix have played the most popular roles in Chinese wood carving. Also, folk tales, legends and fables have been illustrated through wood carving.

Traditional wood carving is an important type of architectural ornamentation. It appears on doors, windows, porches and columns outside buildings and halls, partition boards and screens inside buildings.

Architectural ornamentation of North and South China reflected different ethnic characteristics and tastes. Sophisticated techniques such as line cutting, bass-relief and appliqué carving, could be seen on northern

Woodcarving Brush-holder

buildings which included royal palaces and official dwellings. Ruyi[3], a traditional Chinese art ware, was frequently used to convey the wish for good fortune. In the north, most carvings were plain and not painted. Southern buildings, most of which were civil dwellings, featured various ornaments. As one of the most popular forms of decoration, carvings in the south were often delicate, elegant and interesting, carrying the artistic conception of Chinese paintings. Wood carving was widely used in Fujian and Zhejiang Provinces during the Ming and Qing Dynasties. Wood-carved boards and windows embody the essence of traditional Chinese architecture.

Wood-carved pendants, screens and tea tables add traditional elements to a household. This ornamentation causes simple furniture to appear elegant.

Wood carving also appears on things such as tables, chairs, cupboards and jewel cases. Regardless of color, they all reflect people's longing for a happy and healthy life.

In China, a great variety of woods have been used for carving. With different colors and quality, wood carving provides diverse effects. Take boxwood carving for example, it is as hard and beautiful as ivory and its color is long-lasting. Therefore, it was used to carve human figures, birds, animals and flowers, all of which involve many details. During the Tang Dynasty, boxwood was used to make wood pictures. Today, this technique is still in use.

- **Stone carving**

The history of stone carving dates back to the beginning of art. It is safe to say that stone carving is the most ancient and popular art form in the history of art. It originated in the Neolithic Period, became more mature during the Shang and Zhou Dynasties, and reached its peak during the Qin, Han and Tang Dynasties. Stone-carved masterpieces include delicate Buddha statues, robust horses and dragons carved on the Zhaozhou Bridge.

Stone carving has enjoyed a long history and a great number of carved pieces, which ranges from the Four Reputed Grottos to folk stone art crafts, and can be found in imperial gardens, temples and courtyards. According to the different techniques involved, stone carving is classified into four types: full relief, low relief, openwork carving and line engraving.

Wenling City in Zhejiang Province was known for its stone carving which commenced during the Song Dynasty and reached its peak during the Ming Dynasty. What's more, the title "Capital of Chinese Stone Carving" was conferred on Wenling City by the Ministry of Culture. Huian stone carving was regarded as a splendid flower in the world of carving, for it was successful in combining the culture of central China, Minyue culture and oceanic culture. *Shine Forever like the Sun and the Moon*, the large stone carving in Yuhuatai Memorial Hall, is a masterpiece attributed to Huian stone carving. In Qingtian, Zhejiang Province, stone carving appeared during the Shang Dynasty. In the early 1900's, at international fairs, it won gold silver awards, and continues to hold a high reputation. In 1995, the title "Hometown of Chinese Stone Carving" was conferred on Qingtian by the State Council.

Stone lions, robust horses and quiet giraffes lay on both sides of the four kilometer-long "carved road" in Quyang City, Hebei Province. Truly, one may mistake Quyang for a wildlife park.

The stone statues standing in front of the tomb of Huo Qubing (140-117 BC), a general of the Western Han Dynasty (1046-771 BC), are so far the best preserved and oldest large stone art crafts, which are also representative of Han Dynasty stone carving.

Deployed as a commander, Huo Qubing defeated Han's enemy Xiongnu twice, making great contribution to Han's unification. Huo Qubing died in 117 BC, at the early age of 24. To commemorate this valiant man, Emperor Wu (r. 141-87 BC) of the Han Dynasty had Huo Qubing's tomb built near his own tomb. With 16 carved stones standing there, Huo's tomb appeared magnificent. "Treading on Xiongnu", a stone statue

Stone Human Statue

measuring 168 cm in height and 190 cm in length, is the major piece among these 16 stone men and horses. Holding its head high, the horse is stepping on a struggling Xiongnu man who has a bow and knife in his hands. This vivid life-size statue is a monumental work in Chinese art history.

Chinese grottoes are known throughout the world. The Yungang Grottoes, one of the largest grottos in China, has been called the greatest museum of art carving in the world, which includes figures of Buddha, ornamental patterns and scenes of singing and dancing. Combining carving techniques of the Qin and Han Dynasties and absorbing the essence of religious art, the above mentioned pieces exemplify a unique style. Therefore, in the late 5th century, the Yungang Grottoes was chosen as an exhibition hall to display religious art carvings.

Architectural stone carving of the Ming and Qing Dynasties is the last phase of Chinese classical architectural stone carving. The most commonly used themes and patterns used on imperial buildings were the dragon, phoenix, lotus, cloud and flower. Dragon patterns, which represent the carving style of the Ming and Qing Dynasties, have been found on stone balustrade sideboards with a background composed of peony, chrysanthemum, lotus and camellia patterns. What's more, the huge dragons carved on the steps of the three great halls of the Imperial Palace are historically known as magnificent pieces of carved stone art due to their majestic beauty.

Notes:

[1] Brick carving: a kind of folk art used to decorate buildings by carving human figures, plants, birds and animals on tiles.

[2] Cuju: a sport like football played in ancient China.

[3] Ruyi: a traditional Chinese art ware frequently used to convey wishes of good fortune.

JADE CULTURE

The Chinese cherish jade as a token of purity, nobility, beauty and fidelity. For thousand of years, Chinese people have developed such a special affection for jade that today they admire, love and collect jade for exhibition. Some people even wear a piece of jade. Chinese people often say that precious gold has a price but that jade is priceless. Chinese people speak highly of jade's natural features, judging the character and virtue of a person according to these same features. The Chinese saying "a broken piece of jade is still better than a complete tile" is used to refer to a person with noble personality and uncompromising spirit, which is a clear glorification of jade's beauty. In traditional Chinese poems, jade was often used to describe people or things that are graceful and beautiful. For example, the Chinese character "Yu", jade, is used to depict an excellent face, a young and beautiful girl and the graceful presence of a female. The character is also often used in names, for example, Jia Baoyu and Lin Daiyu, two protagonists in the heartbreaking Chinese classic novel *A Dream of Red Mansions*, in which Cao Xueqin authored his ideal about life into a story about a piece of magical jade. Obviously, Chinese people's affection for jade is deeply rooted.

In ancient China, jade was a symbol of power, social status, wealth and divine right. Also, jade wares were routinely used as sacrificial vessels[1] in various ceremonies including those related to sacrifice, funerals and recruiting nobles. The emperor's seal was made of jade and was commonly called the Jade Seal[2]. As a result, wearing a piece of jade was not only a decoration but also a representation of social status and ethics. Jade occupied a special position in ancient Chinese people's cultural and spiritual lives.

5,500 years ago, North China was dominated by Hongshan culture, while Liangzhu culture was popular in the south. Jade played an important role in the political lives of both cultures. In Hongshan culture, the most representative jade ware featured a pig's head and a snake's body. Shang Dynasty inscriptions on the oracle bones revealed that during this time wars took place over jade resources. The manner in which jade was collected was recorded on one oracle bone, while the war over the jade resources was inscribed on another.

Chinese people's favor toward jade is stronger than that of gold and other gemstones. For example, men in ancient China would not take off their personal jade ornaments unless it was really necessary to do so. [3] Gradually, Chinese people's ideas about jade took shape which led to the tradition of respecting, loving, wearing, admiring and appreciating jade.

Jade can be carved into different shapes to serve as decoration, coins, religious tools and gifts. It can also be carved into a cherished lucky charm animal. As a result, an intricate jade-processing procedure was developed to meet the demand. A series of processing steps such as material selection, pattern design, carving and polishing is followed before the jade finally emerges as various bracelets, pieces of jewelry and artifacts shaped like beautiful ladies, Buddha figures, plants and animals.

Nowadays, major jade manufacturing bases in China include Beijing, Shanghai, Guangzhou, Yangzhou and Xiuyan. Jade styles vary depending on the manufacturing base. Jade wares manufactured in Beijing are solid and elegant, while those manufactured in Shanghai demonstrate classic beauty by copying the style of bronze wares. Jade wares manufactured in Guangzhou, which are known for their Western elements, are popular because of their graceful and innovative designs, while those manufactured in Yangzhou are admired for their smooth lines, exquisite design and transpar-

Green Jade Cabbage

ency. Jade wares from different areas, by maintaining ancient traditions, continue to create unique styles of their own.

Notes:

[1] Sacrificial vessels: various instruments and tools such as tripods, vases and bells that were used in ancient sacrifices.

[2] Jade seal: the seal used by the emperor. This tradition began during the Qin Dynasty (221BC).

[3] Men in ancient China would not take off their jade unless it was really necessary to do so: in ancient China, people believed that a man of integrity showed his virtue by wearing a piece of jade. In order to prove his integrity, a man should wear a piece of jade except on some special occasions such as a funeral.

FOUR BRAND-NAME EMBROIDERY STYLES

As a well-known traditional Chinese art, embroidery occupies an important position in the country's art history. China was the first country to discover and use natural silk. Chinese people started to breed silkworms 4,000 to 5,000 years ago. Thanks to the evolution and development of weaving products and the use of natural silk, embroidery arts gradually developed. When it reached the Qing Dynasty, embroidery was developed into several branches with distinctive local features, among which Suzhou, Hunan, Sichuan and Guangdong embroideries were most famous because of their unique local features.

Suzhou embroidery is a name for all embroideries produced in and around the city of Suzhou in Jiangsu Province. Suzhou embroidery has a long history, and according to excavated embroideries, embroidery arts in this area reached a fairly high level as early as the Five Dynasties (907-960). During the Song Dynasty, the production scale of Suzhou embroidery developed a great deal and embroidery workshops specializing in the production of embroidered clothes, flower patterns and embroidery thread began to appear. During the Ming Dynasty, Suzhou embroidery developed its own unique style and influence. The development of Suzhou embroidery reached its peak during the Qing Dynasty and a great number of embroidery artists distinguished themselves. Most of the embroidery used by the royal family was produced by embroidery workers in Suzhou, which further enhanced the reputation of Suzhou embroidery both home and abroad.

Embroidery produced in Suzhou is known for its refined workmanship and elegant style featuring beautiful patterns, harmonious colors, flexible stitches and vivid pictures. Various traditional elements such as plants and animals, landscape scenes, Chinese characters and calligraphy were adopted to diversify embroidery patterns, and more than 40 kinds of stitches were developed.

Since the Qing Dynasty, local embroideries from Sichuan, Guangdong and Hunan have been heavily influenced by Suzhou embroidery.

Hunan embroidery is a name for all embroidery artifacts produced around Changsha, Hunan Province. This type of embroidery developed from folk embroidery in Hunan and has drawn on the merits of Suzhou and Guangdong embroidery. Hunan embroidery is known for its refined and true-to-life patterns made of velvet thread, earning itself another name, which is "fine wool embroidery". In terms of color arrangement, deep and light grey and black and white are well managed. Deep and light colors are appropriately contrasted so as to enhance the texture and three dimensional effect of the embroidery. The colors, properly arranged, give Hunan embroidery a landscape look. Tigers, lions and squirrels are common pictures that appear on Hunan embroidery, with the tiger being most popular.

Guangdong embroidery refers to embroidery manufactured in Guangdong Province. Legend has it that this

Guangdong Embroidery

type of embroidery was created by ethnic groups and gradually formed its unique features during the middle and latter Ming Dynasty. In addition to silk thread and knitting wool, peacock feathers and horse hair are also used as thread for this embroidery. Light color, sharp contrast and luxuriant effect and patterns outlined with golden thread are common features. The patterns of Guangdong embroidery are delicate and lively. Local subjects of interest such as a hundred birds paying homage to a phoenix[1], sea creatures and local fruits such as fingered citron[2] are often used as embroidery patterns. Different from embroidery made in other areas, Guangdong embroidery is made mostly by men.

Sichuan embroidery is a name referring to embroidery manufactured around Chengdu, Sichuan Province. Major Sichuan manufacturing bases are Chengdu, Chongqing and Wenjiang city. During the latter half of the Qing Dynasty, Sichuan embroidery gradually developed into an industry with its products mainly being official dress, gifts, ordinary colorful clothes, border print, dowry, colorful screen[3] and couplet screen[4]. Screen is the epitome of Sichuan embroidery and includes couplet screen, stand screen and hanging screen. Examples of these embroidered screens can be seen in the Great Hall of the People such as the gigantic stand screen featuring carp and lotus, the hanging screen featuring female musical instrument players in the palace[5] and the stand screen featuring aquatic float grass and carp in the Sichuan Hall; all of these are unique in terms of embroidery skill, and are manufactured with at least 100 delicate stitching techniques.

Embroidery in China today is exquisite and complicated. The cat, for example, is the epitome of Suzhou embroidery. Embroidery workers are capable of dividing an embroidery thread as thin as a human hair into 1/2, 1/4, 1/12, and even 1/48 of its original thickness, concealing thousands of thread ends and knots. Seen both from the front and the back, the embroidered cat is vivid. The cat's eyes are the trickiest part to embroider. Silk thread of 20 colors is used to breathe life into the cat's eyes.

Notes:

[1] A hundred birds paying homage to a phoenix: this sentence is used to refer to and also refers to a highly respected person.

[2] Fingered citron: an evergreen with ellipse leaves and white flowers. Its fruits are yellow colored with a crack at the bottom. Its fruit is fragrant and can be used as medicine.

[3] Colorful screen: in ancient times, a screen of various colors hanging over a bed rail. It can be used for decoration.

[4] Couplet screen: couplets hanging on a wall, mostly calligraphy and paintings.

[5] Female instrument player performing in the palace: a picture drawn by Tangyin, a Ming Dynasty artist.

CLAY FIGURINE ZHANG AND CLAY FIGURINE HUISHAN

During the Ming and Qing Dynasties, the painted clay figurine was admired by ordinary people. The two most popular types were Clay Figurine Zhang in Tianjin and Clay Figurine Huishan in Wuxi, Jiangsu Province.

• Clay Figurine Zhang

Clay Figurine Zhang is a type of North China folk art that dates back to the late Qing Dynasty. Its founder is Zhang Mingshan. Zhang was born into a poor family in Tianjin and helped support his family when he was young by working with his father, a clay figurine maker. Gifted with deft hands and creative imagination, he often observed people of various industries working in the market and spent much time in the theater, both of which gave him inspiration as he created his clay figurines. Zhang's work was praised for its vividness and the characters he created were true-to-life. He honored the tradition of the painted clay figurine by using elements from paintings, traditional operas and folk woodblock New Year paintings in his work. Inner character and instant movement are two important qualities seen in Zhang Clay Figurines, reflecting the feelings of ordinary people in their daily lives and embodying traditional Chinese culture. Zhang produced more than 10,000 figurines during his life, all of which were unique and domestically and internationally known.

Clay Figurines Zhang has won many prizes at international exhibitions. Furthermore, China's National Art Museum has an exhibit featuring nine Clay Figurine Zhang works, topping all other folk arts. Among the collection, the most famous work is *Zhong Kui's Sister's Wedding*, which is a 5-meter long work involving 40 figures with different characteristics, physical movements and vivid facial expressions.

• Clay Figurine Huishan

Clay Figurine Huishan, bearing its name from Mount Hui, has enjoyed 400 years of history. It is said that the clay figurine was made in Huishan as early as the Song Dynasty. During the Qing Dynasty, manufacturing and sale of the Clay Figurine Huishan in Wuxi, Jiangsu Province reached its peak. The Clay Figurine Huishan were made from clay excavated from the foot of Mount Hui. The clay, with fine texture and plasticity, was dried crack-free and could be bent without being broken.

The Clay Figurine Huishan can be divided into the following categories: opera figurines, Peking opera masks, human beings, animals and toys. The Clay Figurine Huishan features simple shapes, vivid facial expressions and exaggerated big heads. Today, craftsmen of Huishan figurines continue to attach great importance to hand painting and color arrangement, often using original colors such as red, green, golden and grey to create sharp contrast, bearing distinctive local flavor of South China. Most notably, the contrast of green and red against a refined, light background color is one unique characteristic of the Clay Figurine Huishan.

The essence of the Clay Figurine Huishan can be found in a boy and a girl clay figurine that is also known as big A Fu. It depicts two smiling and innocent children who hold two divine beasts in their hands.

In terms of clay figurine A Fu, legend has it that Huishan once was occupied by four beasts (poisonous dragon, fierce tiger, smelly turtle and treacherous horse) which wreaked havoc for human beings and destroyed their livestock and crops. Later, a twin sister and brother named A Fu went into the mountain and

A Fu

fought a fierce battle against the beasts. The beasts were eliminated but the twins were mortally wounded. Local people made figurines of the twins, commemorating their heroic feat, and today, after generations of artistic creation, big A Fu has evolved into the current happy and healthy images.

In 1992, Huishan big A Fu was selected as the symbol for China International Tourist Year, and big A Fu not only traveled to America but also became popular with families across the globe. A Fu zest, for a time, swept the world and various products such as snacks, daily necessities and restaurants were named after it.

BANDHNU

Bandhnu is a traditional Bai nationality folk art. In producing the Bandhnu, plain white cloth with folds are dyed repeatedly before being taken out and dried. The final product features white patterns against a blue background. Blue and white give bandhnu a peaceful look. The colors not only create a simple and unsophisticated feeling, but also give one a feeling that he is admiring elegant porcelain with blue and white patterns. Ancestors of the Bai nationality did not chose the color blue by coincidence since their world was enveloped by Mount Cang and Erhai Lake, both of which feature blue and serene sky, sea and mountains.

Bandhnu

Today, Zhoucheng, the largest Bai community in Dali, Yunnan Province, continues to keep Bandhnu culture alive, with the women of each family making a living as Bandhnu-dye workers. Each family in Zhoucheng has a dye vat for Bandhnu production, earning the area an undisputed reputation as the hometown of Bandhnu.

Bandhnu could be found in China as early as the Han and Tang Dynasties and reached its peak in Wei (220-265) and Jin (265-420) Dynasties. To this day, Bandhnu is part of the national culture. With an increasing market demand for Bandhnu, Bandhnu patterns have become more sophisticated and diversified, with the number totalling more than 100. Patterns of various sizes are available and are often used in making bags, hats, skirts and other clothing. Local scenery and objects such as colorful clouds, Mount Cang, legends, ethnic lifestyle, plants and animals provide endless possibilities for Bandhnu patterns. The patterns, elegant, simple and natural, are extremely vivid.

Bandhnu carries the ethnic ideal and sentiment of the Bai nationality and serves as a window to this ethic group. From this perspective, Bandhnu is no longer a commodity in the general sense, but a special product that embodies cultural and national values.

(English Author: Wang Lihua)

Chapter Nine Ancient Literature

THE BOOK OF SONGS AND "SONGS OF CHU"

Poetry is the most highly regarded literary genre in China. Its development over thousands of years has given birth to numerous poems and songs and left a unique legacy to world literature.

Shih Ching (*The Book of Songs*) and "Songs of Chu" represent the peak achievements of Pre-Qin literature.

The Book of Songs is the earliest collection of Chinese poems. It is comprised of 305 poems, dating back to the Western Zhou Dynasty (1046-771 BC) and the Mid Spring and Autumn Period (770-476 BC). The collection is divided into three parts according to their genres, namely *feng* (folk songs), *ya* (festal songs) and *song* (sacrificial songs).

Feng (folk songs) includes folk songs from 15 areas along the Yellow River. The 160 poems in Feng predominate *The Book of Songs* and are more realistic in that they faithfully present the life and emotions of the local people. *The Seventh Month*, for instance, describes in detail rural life; *Woodcutting and the Big Rat* implicate greedy rulers; *Broken Axe* and *Banging the Drum* mirror the bitterness of warfare and forced labor; and *The Reeds and Rushes* and *A Simple Fellow* show people's longing for love and attitude towards marriage.

Ya (festal songs) is further divided into minor festal songs traditionally sung at court festivities and major festal songs sung at more solemn court ceremonies. The 105 narrative poems and lyrics either sing praise for heroes or condemn social evils.

Song (sacrificial songs) includes 40 poems that eulogize ancestors, gods, and the heavens.

With its contents, employment of rhetorical devices and well-organized structure, *The Book of Songs* has exerted profound influences on the art of Chinese poetry.

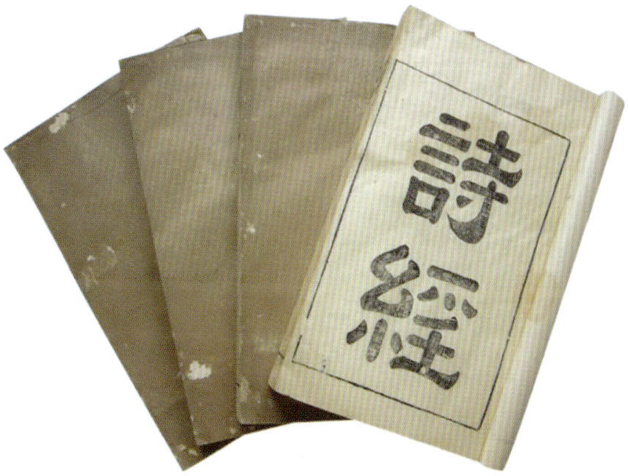

Shih Ching

The collection was originally called *Shi* (*Songs*) and *Shi Sanbai* (*Three Hundred Poems*). It was the Confucians of the Han Dynasty (206 BC-AD 220) who gave it the name *Shih Ching* (*The Book of Songs*). Confucius once commented that there was not even a trace of evil thought in this collection. Furthermore, it has been frequently quoted in literary works of later generations.

The Book of Songs, together with *The Book of History*, *The Book of Rites*, *The Book of Changes*, and *The Spring and Autumn Annals*, forms the Five Classics of Confucianism.

The Book of Songs, a masterpiece representing the Yellow River culture, is perfectly matched by "Songs of Chu", a masterpiece of the Yangtze River culture.

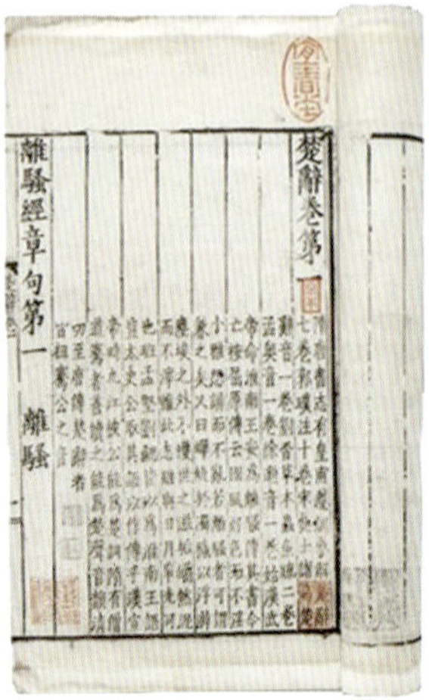

Songs of Chu

During the late Warring States Period, Qu Yuan (340-278 BC) in the State of Lu, is the first great poet in Chinese literature. He initiated the creation of Chuci (Songs of Chu), a new style of poetry. Inheriting the traditions of Chu's local folklores, the songs break the bonds of four-character rhymed lines, adopt flexible sentence structures and repeatedly employ the character Xi.

Besides Qu Yuan, Song Yu, Tang Le, and Jing Cha are also renowned Chuci poets. Though most of their poems have been lost, some of Song Yu's works still exist, bearing witness to the charm of this poetic style; some of these include: *The Nine Debates*, *On Deng Tu-zi's Lubricity*, and *Ode to the Wind.*

Born to a noble family in the State of Chu, Qu Yuan had an extraordinary aptitude for literature and politics. His ability won him the trust of Chu's King and an important position in the government. Yet his political viewpoints on fighting the State of Qin offended conservatives and brought about their slander. He thus lost the favor of the King and was exiled. Later, he was called back to the court and then exiled again. On the fifth day of the fifth lunar month in 278 BC, when the Chu capital was taken by the Qin army, he committed suicide by drowning himself in the Miluo River, leaving to the later generations his masterpieces: *Li Sao* (*On Encountering Trouble*), *Jiu Zhang* (*Nine Pieces*), *Tian Wen* (*Heavenly Questions*) and *Jiu Ge* (*Nine Songs*).

TANG POETRY

The Tang Dynasty (618-907) witnessed the high tide of Chinese classical poetry. The greatest poems from the Tang Dynasty, a brilliant diamond in world literature, still enjoy great popularity as an irreplaceable literary legacy.

The general peace and prosperity of the Tang Dynasty gave birth to many world-renowned poets. Besides the three greatest poets Li Bai, Du Fu, and Bai Juyi, there are also the Four Heroes of Early Tang (Wang Bo, Luo Binwang, Yang Jiong, and Lu Zhaolin), pastoral poets (Wang Wei and Meng Haoran), frontier poets (Gao Shi, Cen Shen, and Wang Changling), the Middle Tang poets (Bai Juyi, Yuan Zhen, Liu Zongyuan and Han Yu) and the Late Tang poets (Dumu, Wen Tingyun, and Weizhuang).

A total of 48,900 poems written by 2,300 poets can be found in *The Complete Poetry of the Tang Dynasty*. Covering almost every aspect of society, their poetry condemns social evils, demonstrates patriotism, depicts the beauty of the country, and expresses their personal emotions. It is safe to say that nature, politics, social customs and delicate affections are all well presented either realistically or romantically in Tang poetry.

The development of Tang poetry is generally divided

into four periods, namely, Early Tang, Flourishing Tang, Middle Tang and Late Tang.

The Early Tang witnessed the poets' initial efforts to abandon the ornate and flowery style of Southern Qi and Southern Liang, and to write pastoral poems in five-character lines. Then emerged the Four Heroes of Early Tang, a name which refers to four great poets — Wang Bo, Yang Jiong, Lu Zhaolin, and Luo Binwang. They enjoyed the same literary aptitude and all led a hard life. Their challenge against the old and lifeless court style and endeavor to involve more themes in poems injected new life into poetry. Even today, their poems still enjoy great reputation, such as *Sending off a Friend* by Wang Bo and *Joining the Army* by Yang Jiong.

Chen Zi'ang, who was in favor of hard-hitting, authentic poetry, was another advocate of poetry reform. His poems, such as *Ascending Youzhou Terrace*, brought fresh air to Early Tang poetry.

The greatest achievement in poetry during this period lies in the establishment of five-character-regular-verse and the development of seven-character-verse.

The Flourishing Tang is regarded as the Golden Age of poetry and gave rise to many famous poets, such as the greatest poets, Li Bai and Du Fu, after Qu Yuan. Meng Haoran was adept at writing five-character-verse in presenting landscape and countryside life. His *A Morning in Spring* and *A Visit to a Friend* are well received by readers.

Li Bai

In his day, Wang Wei was credited as being an art genius, who integrated music, calligraphy, painting, and poetry in the most intricate ways. His poems, like *Zhongnan Mountain*, and *Birds Chirping over the Hill Creek*, either portray grand natural scenery or convey his Buddhist thought.

Pastoral poetry was not the only favored style during the High Tang; frontier poetry also occupied an important place during this period. Gao Shi's frontier poems express in-depth emotions such as *A Farewell Poem to Dong Da*, while Cen Shen's poems provide an exotic view of wild frontier scenes such as *Snow for Chief of Secretarial Staff Wu*.

Du Fu

Li Bai and Du Fu are undoubtedly the greatest Flourishing Tang poets. Their poems represent the highest achievement of ancient Chinese poetry.

Li Bai is renowned for his wild imagination and unrestrained style, and therefore, ushered in the climax of romantic poetry. His works, such as *Drink Your Fill!*, *Seeing off Fellow Poet Meng Haoran* and *The Road to Shu is Hard*, fully reveal the conflict between his noble ambition and the cruel reality, his pursuit of freedom and rebellion against the authorities. The artistic value of Li Bai's works is highly complimented by Du Fu.

Du Fu is famous for his realistic poems, which mirror the catastrophic events of the An Shi Rebellion and the hard life of the common people. Using the writing techniques of *The Book of Songs* and the Han Dynasty's Yue-fu poems, and borrowing some of the writing nuances from previous dynasties, he is known as a master of the seven-character-regular-verse. His verses surpass those of his contemporaries not only in quantity, but also in artistic value and depth of emotion. Through his efforts, realistic poetry reached its height during the Flourishing Tang.

The An Shi Rebellion put an end to the thriving Tang.

Bai Juyi

Though the Middle Tang does not enjoy the same social prosperity as the Flourishing Tang, it does see a great diversity of poetry. The most notable poems come off as somewhat angry and can be characterized as speaking-truth-to-power, which are written during the New Yue Fu Movement led by Bai Juyi. He is known as the pioneer of the long narrative poem, with good examples being his *Song of Sorrow* and *The Pipa Tune*.

Poets Han Yu and Meng Jiao shared a common interest in experimental exploration of the relationship of poetry to words. Han Yu's works are witty and satirical and were well inherited by Song Dynasty poets, while Meng Jiao's five-character-regular-verses are extremely well-composed and well-rhymed.

During the Middle Tang, several eminent poets stand out as being too individualistic to be considered a group. For instance, Liu Changqing and Wei Yingwu produced numerous pastoral poems. Li Duan, Lu Lun and Qian Qi created poems by imitating Flourishing Tang poetry. Liu Yuxi was in favor of folklore and therefore wrote poems in plain yet poetic language. His contemporary Liu Zongyuan showed his concern for the lower-class and conveyed his personal emotions in a realistic manner. Li He was another famed poet during this period, who expressed his emotions through ornate language, melancholy style and wild imagination in such masterpieces as *The Song to the Guards in Yanmen*, *A Dream of Heaven* and *A Bronze Immortal Takes Leave of Han*.

The Late Tang enjoyed a short period of glory and was represented by poets Li Shangyin and Du Mu. Li Shangyin, a master of the seven-character-regular-verse, impresses readers with his unique romantic imagery and his love poems, like *A Letter Sent North about These Nightly Rains*. Du Mu, a master of the seven-character-quatrain, integrates scenery with emotion and produced many popular poems, such as *Overnight Stay on Qinhuai River*.

Tang poetry is unrivaled in terms of diversity. For instance, the ancient poetry of this period is divided into five-character-ancient-verse and seven-character-ancient-verse. It is not strict in regard to number of the lines and change of rhymes.

However, Tang Dynasty "modern style" poetry lays down rigid requirements for tonal patterns and rhyme schemes and thus is called metrical poetry; it falls into five-character-quatrain, seven-character-quatrain, five-character-regular-verse, and seven-character-regular-verse.

Inheriting the traditions of folklore and poems of previous dynasties, Tang poetry is rich in style and metrical pattern. Its contribution lies not only in using ancient style poems as carriers of complicated narratives, but also in the creation of metrical poems. The appearance and development of Tang Dynasty "modern style" poetry is of enormous significance, for it perfectly utilizes the lyrics by giving them the best expression through refined rhythm. However, its rigid rhythmical patterns choke spontaneous outflow of emotion, which hindered its future development.

SONG POETRY

Song poetry occupies a unique place in ancient Chinese literature with its unparalleled variety. Song poetry (also called Ci during the Song Dynasty) is originally defined as Song lyrics popular among common

Xin Qiji

people.

Different styles of music require different kinds of lyrics. In the early 20th century, music scores and lyrics of the Tang Dynasty, the earliest collection of such kind discovered so far, were discovered in Gansu Province's Mogao Grottoes. The popular lyrics of the Tang Dynasty were then refined by literati during the Five Dynasties Period and became Song poetry. This important literature genre in China is generally divided into two schools: that of graceful and restrained, and that of bold and unconstrained. The former is represented by Liu Yong, Qin Guan, Zhou Bangyan, Jiang Xie and Li Qingzhao, while the latter by Su Shi, Xin Qiji, Yue Fei and Chen Liang.

During its early stages, Ci mainly centered on the topic of love affairs and was popular among the lower class. It is flamboyant and excessively ornamented. The Five Dynasties Period's *Collection of Huajian School* is an example of such expressions.

However, during the Late Tang and Five Dynasties (907-960), Ci was greatly developed. Wen Tingjun, a master of metrics, set up writing rules pertaining to Ci. The Five Dynasties saw more and more poets dabble in Ci. Those composing Ci in Sichuan formed the famous Huajian School, while those composing it during the Southern Tang (937-975) also achieved great success. Li Yu, the last ruler of the Southern Tang, for instance, conveyed his sadness over the split of the country in a touching manner and left great masterpieces, like *To the Tune of Yu Mei Ren*.

Song poetry is divided into the poetry of the Northern Song (960-1127) and Southern Song (1127-1279). During the early Northern Song, Yan Shu and Ouyang Xiu followed previous styles, employing ornate diction, so as to convey subtle sentiments. It was Liu Yong who brought a real breakthrough to poetry writing. Liu Yong, who lived in frustration and despondency all his life and tried to find escape in all kinds of low class amusements, was able to blend elements from the lower class in his poetry. It was said that Liu Yong's poetry could be heard in every corner of the city. His exposure to lower class life and aptitude for writing lyrics enabled him to involve numerous poetic themes in his work as well as create many narrative poems for slow music.

Thanks to the efforts of many poets, Song poetry became increasingly meaningful and multi-faceted. Fan Zhongyan, for example, wrote frontier poems to music, which significantly changed Song poetry. Later, Su Shi initiated a bold and unconstrained school of poetry writing and greatly extended topics beyond tender sentiment. Therefore, Song poetry became a serious carrier of bureaucratic thought and its reflection on life and society fully showcases the spirit of that time. Su Shi's poems are diverse in style, which can be seen in *To the Tune of Shui Diao Ge Tou*, and *To the Tune of Nian Nu Jiao*. Moreover, Huang Tingjian, Qin Guan, He Zhu and Zhou Bangyan also enriched Northern Song poetry.

The most renowned Southern Song poet is Li Qingzhao. Her Yi An style poems present deep emotions in a natural and graceful manner. After the northern Song capital fell to the Jurchens and Li Qingzhao's family fled to the south, her poems, like *To the Tune of Sheng Sheng Man*, conveyed her sadness over the nation's fall and the loss of her

Li Qingzhao

home.

Another poet similar to Li Qingzhao in terms of artistic achievement is Xin Qiji, whose works boldly and freely demonstrate his patriotism. His poems, such as *To the Tune of Shui Long Yin*, and *To the Tune of Yong Yu Le*, portray the life during warfare and exemplify his heroism and great passion.

Yue Fei, Lu You, Chen Liang and Wen Tianxiang also wrote poems to express their hatred toward invaders as well as the love they had for their country.

NOVELS OF THE MING AND QING DYNASTIES

The novel boomed during the Ming (1368-1644) and Qing (1616-1911) Dynasties. Its social influence and artistic value earned it a position in Ming Dynasty mainstream literature. During the Qing Dynasty, the novel matured and underwent a modern transition.

The development of the novel was preceded and accompanied by the prosperity of city life. During the Song Dynasty, the thriving handicraft and commerce industries provided the ideal conditions for the development of folk culture, which further promoted people's need for cultural entertainment.

It was under these circumstances that Hua-pen came into existence. Hua-pen is a story-telling script that helped Qing Dynasty folk artists tell stories concerning history, unofficial history, legal cases, and ghost spirits. Later, Hua-pen was influential in novel writing.

With the steady refinement and advance of typography, the novel finally developed into a mature genre of literature during the mid-Qing Dynasty.

An Illustration in *Strange Tales of a Lonely Studio*

Ming Dynasty novels fall into the categories of long and short. The former, well represented by *The Romance of the Three Kingdoms*, *Heroes of the Marshes*, *Journey to the West*, and *The Forbidden Legend*, in terms of subject matter, can be further divided into: historical novels, ghost novels, secular novels and legal case novels.

The historical novel is the first kind of long novel. One such example is *The Romance of the Three Kingdoms* by Luo Guanzhong, which presents the political and military interaction among the States of Wei, Shu and Wu from the end of Eastern Han Dynasty to the Jin Dynasty. Reviving the stories of ancient heroes (Cao Cao, Liu Bei, Sun Quan and Zhuge Liang), the novel, in simple language and plain style, conveys the author's longing for benevolent governance. Throughout many generations, the novel has been well received and has made such heroic stories very popular.

Heroes of the Marshes gives life to many heroes in simple yet expressive language. It was also followed by such novels as *Legend of Yue Fei* and *Legend of Warriors of Yang Family*.

Journey to the West is about four Buddhists' pilgrimage to seek Buddhist scriptures. The legendary setting is a reflection of the social life at the time, and its witty language and satire embodies the author's philosophical understanding of society.

The Forbidden Legend, from its very birth, brought about massive controversy. Some condemn the book as tremendously obscene, while others value it as one of the most realistic novels.

Short stories also attained a high level of sophistication during the Ming Dynasty, which were best expressed in the three collections of short stories compiled by famous novelist Feng Menglong. The collections incorporate 120 story-telling scripts of the Song, Yuan and Ming Dynasties, which are based on unofficial history and legends. After Feng's artistic fine-tuning, the stories more vividly portrayed the lifestyle, thoughts and habits of the common people at that time, which have notably influenced modern novels and plays.

The impact of these three collections is paralleled by that of two collections of amazing tales compiled by Ming novelist Ling Mengchu.

During the Qing Dynasty, novels were greatly influenced by conflicts among different classes, ethnic groups and ideologies. The development of novels in terms of quality, quantity, form and style, lasted from the early Qing Dynasty to Qian Long's reign (r. 1736-1799).

Qing Dynasty novels, though drawing inspiration from historical and folk stories, were literati's serious efforts to present their view of life as well as their personal reflection on society. Truly, novels during this period underwent extraordinary development in regard to structure, narrative technique and the depiction of characters.

Furthermore, *The Scholars*, *Strange Tales of a Lonely Studio* and *A Dream of Red Mansions* pushed the creation of classical Chinese novels and vernacular novels to a new level.

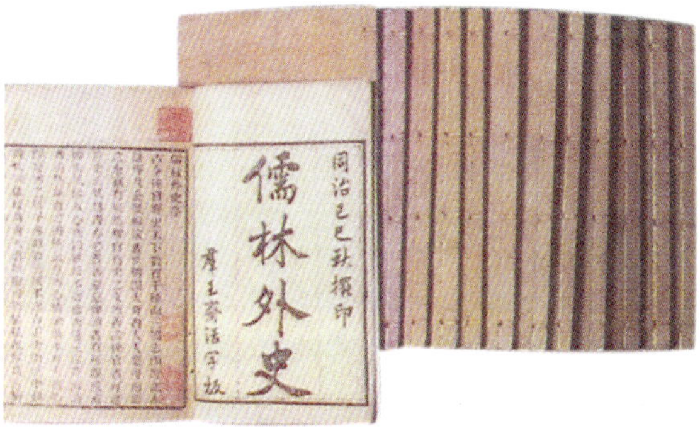

▸▸ *The Scholars*

A Dream of Red Mansions is one of the greatest masterpieces in world literature because it is unrivalled in terms of artistic fineness. The main plot, which depicts the decline of the Jia Family, mirrors the decline of feudal society. Its subtlety and depth in portraying feudal society is beyond comparison. And its language sets a model for literature during the May Fourth Movement of the early twentieth century.

Novels of Ming and Qing Dynasties mirror every minute detail of social life with great depth, and thus dominated the literature scene of the day. Without any doubt, the vernacular novels of the Ming and Qing Dynasties continue to have a far-reaching influence on modern Chinese literature as well as other forms of modern Chinese art. The literature of Japan, Korea and Vietnam has also been influenced. Having been translated into dozens of languages, Ming and Qing Dynasty literature has made a significant contribution to world culture.

(English Author: Zhou Wei)

Chapter Ten Chinese Painting, Calligraphy and Seal Cutting

CHINESE PAINTING

Chinese painting, also known as "National painting", refers to ink and wash paintings, light color and strong color paintings, and baimiao[1] painted on a piece of Xuan paper[2] or silk with a writing brush that has been soaked in black ink or colored pigments. As a unique system in the art world, Chinese painting, the quintessence of the dialectic thinking in images of the Chinese people, is considered one of the three pillars (the other two being martial arts and traditional Chinese medicine) of the Chinese culture, which is based on Chinese philosophy.

Using line and ink as the major expression, Chinese painting has distinctive national features in form and style. After thousands of years of development, Chinese painting now falls into three categories, namely, landscape, figure and bird-and-flower paintings. In contrast, Western painting can be classified into portrait, landscape, and still life paintings.

All three categories of Chinese painting attach great importance to the spirit and artistic conceptions expressed in the form. Chinese painters are adept at choosing subjects for their works. For example, billows in the sea and giant trees on the plateau are used for great momentum. Sparse bamboo forest and a small bridge over a brook are usually used to show that the painter is free from worldly care. Pine, bamboo, plum blossom and chrysanthemum are symbols of lofty qualities, and peony and phoenix stand for wealth and happiness.

The ultimate goal pursued by the Chinese artists is "yijing" (artistic conception), that is, the emotional appeal, artistic style and philosophical thinking expressed with a few strokes. In terms of color, Western painting focuses on ambient color of the object (light and shadow, dimness and brightness, reflection, etc.), while Chinese painting emphasizes natural color and depiction of the essence of the object, the so-called principle of "color of the object".

In Western painting, space is expressed through color gradation as well as subtle variation of color in the light and air. In Chinese painting on white paper, only black color accounts, and in painting on black paper, only white color accounts. The blank—in white on white paper and in black on black paper—is to be filled with the imagination and association of the audience, and the distance is expressed with the thickness of the ink. Unlike Western painting, which adopts focus perspective, Chinese painting uses scattered focus which presents a different time or space on the same painting.

Cognitive ability is crucial in the appreciation of Chinese painting in which white is colorless and formless, while black is colored and takes a form. The colors of Mother Nature are expressed with the density and gradation of ink. Take *Huangshan Mountains* for example. With wild imagination, one can see exuberance in summer, bleakness in winter, and colorful clouds at sunrise and vast blur in the misty rain.

Wanghui of the Qing Dynasty Painting Landscape

To create a painting with "spirit resonance", "vivid and lively in both form and spirit", Chinese painters should have a good mastery of traditional culture, a high aesthetic perspective, and apply calligraphy and seal in the painting.

Western painting (mainly oil painting) is a pure visual art, whereas Chinese painting (literati painting) emphasizes the unity of poetry, calligraphy, painting and seal to make a complete art work. Western painting uses dots, lines and surfaces to create the body of the object itself, while Chinese painting stresses on "bone method"[3] and "calligraphy in painting". The painters must be skillful in calligraphy so as to draw lines with strength and rhythm that have a special aesthetic value of appreciation.

The history of the development of Chinese painting is like a long river surging with waves of inspiration, comprehension, creativity and conception of generations of artists. At the beginning of the 20th century, inspired by oriental wisdom, the modernist painters of the West broke the pre-19th century purist painting concepts. Chinese painting has also been enriched with new concepts, scientific techniques and innovated art forms borrowed from Western painting.

Notes:

[1] Baimiao: in Chinese painting, a brush technique that produces a finely controlled, supple ink outlined drawing without any color or wash embellishment.

[2] Xuan Paper: produced in Xuancheng and Jingxian, Anhui Province, it is renowned for its softness, fine-texture, tensile strength, resistance to creases, and evenness in absorbing ink; it has been favored by the Chinese painters for centuries.

[3] The bone method: originally referring to the profile of a person, "bone" is now used in a much broader sense, meaning the outline of any object in a painting. "Method" refers to the way of using the brush. This method stresses the proper way of using the brush to depict not only the form but also the spirit of an object.

FIGURE PAINTING

• Gu Kaizhi

A native of Wuxi, Jinling (now Jiangsu Province), Gu Kaizhi (c. 345-406), courtesy name Changkang, and nickname Hutou, was a great writer and painter during the Eastern Jin Dynasty (317-420). His legacy can be found in his techniques, which have been handed down to numerous generations of Chinese painters. Born into an elite family, he was talented, intelligent and well educated. Perfect in poetry, calligraphy, and painting, he was called by his contemporaries "unrivalled talent" and "peerless painter".

When he was young, Gu learnt painting from Wei Xie, a great master of painting, under whose instruction the talented and hard working Gu soon became an outstanding painter. Gu was a multi-faceted artist adept at landscape, flower, and figure paintings. His figure paintings, in particular, were very famous for their vividness in terms of the subjects' deep and subtle emotions.

In theory, Gu was the first to advocate the principle of "depicting the spirit through the form", stressing the importance of the elaboration of the eyes in conveying the spirit of the subject. He took full advantage of the writing brush, and his ink line was like endless silk thread, a wandering cloud or running water. Unlike his Han and Wei Dynasty predecessors, who first painted in color and then drew the outline with ink, he drew the outline before adding color. During the Eastern Jin Dynasty, spiritual resonance was given priority over form and color, and Gu is an excellent representative.

None of Gu's original work exists today. The best-known copies of his paintings are *The Admonitions of the Instructress to Court Ladies* and *Nymph of the Luo River*.

The Admonitions of the Instructress to Court Ladies (detail)

The Admonitions of the Instructress to the Court Ladies illustrates a political satire written by Zhang Hua (c. 232-300) of the Western Jin Dynasty (265-317). Taking a moralizing tone, the satire sings praise to the virtuous women in history, attacking the excessive behavior of Empress Jia Nanfeng. In total, twelve scenes, with the text of the satire, are depicted on this scroll. The spirit of the figures is vividly presented in a fine linear style. Take the story of Feng Zhaoyi for example. To save the Han Emperor Yuan (r. 48-33 BC), Feng courageously stands in the way of a bear. Calm and brave, Feng is in sharp contrast to the horror-stricken Emperor Yuan. With long and dense lines, the painter presents a figure both gentle and tough.

Nymph of the Luo River illustrates a prose-poem written by Prince Cao Zhi (192-232) of the Three Kingdoms (220-280) and is dedicated to his deceased love whom he met by the Luo River in his dream.

Gu depicted the literary masterpiece in the form of a hand scroll. On the first part of the scroll, accompanied by his servants, Prince Cao Zhi, distressed and gloomy, walks to the riverbank, meeting the nymph in the water. Then the nymph starts dancing in the air and forest for Cao Zhi. In the end, the nymph departs in a chariot drawn by dragons, while Cao Zhi sees her off in a boat. The immortality of this beautiful painting rests not only in a romantic story between Cao Zhi and the nymph, but also in Gu's creative application of landscape background to figure painting.

As a master artist, Gu Kaizhi's work has influenced his contemporaries and later generations of painters.

- **Wu Daozi**

A native of Yangzhai, (now Yuzhou, Henan Province), Wu Daozi (c. 685-758), also known as Daoxuan, is the most famous painter during the most prosperous part of the Tang Dynasty (618-907).

Wu lost both his parents when he was young and lived a hard life in his early years. He learned from folk artists and sculptors. Because he studied hard and was talented in art, he earned himself a good reputation as a painter by the time he was about 20 years old. He used to serve as an assistant for a county magistrate. But before long, he resigned and moved to Luoyang where many temples were built as a result of the prevalence of Buddhism. Wu began painting in the temples and won instant fame for his brilliant artistic talent. Actually, he was so famous that Tang Emperor Xuanzong (r. 712-756) invited him to Chang'an, the capital, to be a court painter.

Court life turned out to be the most artistic period of creation for Wu. He painted more than 300 murals and many hand scrolls in Luoyang and Chang'an alone.

One of Wu's most famous murals is *The Hell Scene Painting*. The artistic appeal of the work is overwhelming. Legend has it that after looking at the painting, butchers and fishermen in Chang'an all felt remorse for their sins and switched to other professions.

The Hell Scene Painting

Wu was also famous for painting very quickly. Once Emperor Xuanzong took him to Sichuan and asked him to draw some sketches of the Jialing River. Several months later, however, he returned to Chang'an empty-handed. The Emperor was very disappointed and annoyed by his carelessness. "The beautiful scenes along the Jialing River," Wu replied calmly, "are all in my mind." Without any hesitation, he started painting in the Datong Hall. In just one day, a great mural of the breathtaking scenes from the 150-kilometer Jialin River appeared before the eyes of the Emperor and his court officials. Emperor Xuanzong exclaimed in admiration to his astonished officials, "We all know that Li Sixun[1] is a great painter. He used to paint in the same place on the same topic. But it took him several months to complete the work. Today Wu Daozi finished the whole painting in just one day!"

Through years of artistic creation, Wu learned extensively from the strong points of his predecessors and created a unique style of his own. His ink line had reached the acme of perfection, and was unparalleled in history. Using his brush in a calligraphic manner, Wu's strokes, no matter light or heavy, slow or quick, coherent or broken, were always full of change and vigor. On the whole, his style is harmonious and his figures are vivid and dynamic, with their straps fluttering in the wind; this is the reason why people use the term "straps fluttering in the wind" to describe his unique style.

Wu's style exerted great influence on Chinese painting after the climax of the Tang Dynasty, and his baimiao became the model for painters of later generations.

Unfortunately, most of Wu's works cannot be found today. We can only appreciate the marvelous works of the Sage of Painting from the copies of his *Presentation of Buddha*[2] and *Daozi Sketchbook*.

• ***A Riverside Scene at Qingming Festival***

Born in Dongwu (present-day Zhucheng in Shandong Province), Zhang Zeduan, courtesy name Zhengdao, was a court painter during Northern Song Emperor Huizong's reign (r. 1100-1125). As a child, he went to Bianliang, the capital, (present-day Kaifeng in Henan Province) to study painting. He liked painting boats, carts, bridges and cities, becoming a prominent painter with a unique style. His masterpiece, *A Riverside Scene at Qingming Festival*, was revered as a divine work by Chinese painters.

A Riverside Scene at Qingming Festival, 248 cm wide and 528.7 cm long, is housed in Beijing Palace Museum. The panoramic painting captures the prosperity of Bianliang as well as the natural scenery along the Bian River during the Qingming Festival. The long scroll features magnificent and complex scenes with a rigorous structure, which can be divided into three parts: scenes of the suburbs, the Bian River and city streets.

The first part is the prelude of the scroll. In the quiet suburbs of Bianliang during the Qingming Festival, a road leading to the capital winds its way through a willow woods. On the road, two porters drive five donkeys loaded with charcoal. Sitting in a sedan chair decorated with tender green willow twigs and wild flowers, a noble woman is returning after paying homage to the grave of her deceased family members, followed by porters and men on horseback.

In the second part, the Bian River scene is the most magnificent. During the Northern Song Dynasty (960-1127), the Bian River was an artery for shipping and transportation. In this part of the painting many figures are engaged in various activities, drinking tea, dining, fortune telling, etc. There are many boats on the river. Some are propelled with oars, some are sailing against the current, loaded with cargo, and some are anchored and being unloaded. An arched bridge made of wood, exquisite and graceful, stands like a rainbow over the river. A big boat is about to pass under the bridge. Everybody in the boat is busy working for its safe passage. The men on another boat nearby seem to be very anxious, pointing and shouting at the boat. The boat also attracts the attention of many onlookers on the bridge.

The third part captures bustling scenes on the city streets. Around the tall gate tower are rows of houses.

A Riverside Scene at Qingming Festival (detail)

The streets are lined with government mansions, temples, teahouses, wine shops, hotels, butcher shops, barber shops and various other shops dealing in silk and satin, jewelry and perfume, incense, medicine, wagon repairing and fortune telling. The streets are packed with people of all walks of life, men and women, old and young, merchants doing business, officials riding on horses, peddlers hawking their wares, noble women in sedan chairs, wandering monks, lost tourists, children listening to stories, drunkards in the wine shop, and disabled beggars asking for help. Vehicles of various kinds, sedan chairs, camels, oxcarts, wagons, rickshaws, and other carts are also vividly presented in the painting.

On the five-meter scroll, there are over 550 human figures of all walks of life, some 60 animals, 20 wooden boats, about 20 vehicles of various kinds, and numerous houses, pavilions, gate towers and other buildings with unique Song Dynasty features.

As a masterpiece of realistic painting depicting the life of Bianliang in the Northern Song Dynasty, Zhang Zeduan's *A Riverside Scene at Qingming Festival* enjoys high historical and artistic value.

Notes:

[1] Li Sixun: also known as Jian, he was a native of Chengji (present-day Qin'an, Gansu Province), and a descendant of the royal family. He was a prominent painter during the Tang Dynasty, and was also famous for his military exploits as a general.

[2] *Presentation of Buddha*: the most representative work of Wu Daozi. It depicts the story of the birth of Shakyamuni Buddha, the son of King Shuddhadana.

LANDSCAPE PAINTING

• Zhan Ziqian and His *Sightseeing in Spring*

A native of Bohai (present-day Hejian, Hebei Province), Zhan Ziqian was a great painter during the Sui Dynasty (581-618), and was as well-known as Gu Kaizhi, Lu Tanwei, and Zhang Senyao. Active from 550-604, he lived through three dynasties (from North Qi through North Zhou to Sui) and served as a high-ranking official in Sui Emperor Wen (r. 581-604)'s court and army. It is said that without Zhan' works,

Sightseeing in Spring

one could not be called a real art collector.

Zhan was a versatile and creative painter whose subjects ranged from horse-chariots and human figures, to landscape. His landscape paintings, in particular, are distinguished for their grand capacity and overwhelming momentum.

Of all artwork preserved in China, his *Sightseeing in Spring* is believed to be the earliest and most complete landscape painting scroll. It presents a panoramic view of the spring, in which the sun is shining, trees and flowers are blooming, water is flowing in the far distance between the green mountains, and nobles and beautiful ladies are either riding horses or rowing boats, enjoying the spring beauty. The essence of the ancient saying "the benevolent enjoy the mountains, the wise enjoy the waters" was superbly interpreted on this beautiful scroll.

Unlike previous landscape paintings, in which human figures are always the subject and landscape only serves as the background, *Sightseeing in Spring* takes the landscape as the main body in which the figures, reduced in proportion, become just an ornament. Zhan's creative work gives landscape the predominant position in the painting, putting an end to the phenomenon of "figure is larger than mountain" and spacing out the distance between close and distant views.

This dramatic change marked the birth of landscape painting as an independent art form and brought about a number of innovations in Chinese painting techniques. The first innovation was from line drawing to drawing of various forms. The second was the proper adjustment of perspective in panoramic paintings—things close at hand were painted larger than distant objects. The third was made in the application of colors. Zhan's landscape paintings are predominately blue and green, embellished with red, white and other colors. Moreover, the application of gold powder makes the paintings glorious and magnificent. These innovations made in painting techniques directly influenced the blue-green and green-gold landscape paintings of Li Sixun and Li Shaodao during the Tang Dynasty. Hence Zhan Ziqian is also adored as "Father of Tang Dynasty Paintings".

As a masterpiece, Zhan's *Sightseeing in Spring* heralded the maturity of Chinese landscape painting. It established a norm of painting that conformed to the Chinese culture and drew a blueprint for Chinese painting in terms of composition, brush usage, application of ink as well as colors. Both the Southern and Northern Chinese painting techniques originated from this masterpiece.

BIRD-AND-FLOWER PAINTING

Bird-and-flower painting is a unique art form of Chinese painting depicting flowers, birds, fish and insects. It originated during the Tang Dynasty, further developed during the Five Dynasties (907-960), matured during the Song Dynasty (960-1279), and flourished during the Ming (1368-1644) and Qing (1616-1911) Dynasties.

Bird-and-flower paintings feature Chinese people's appreciation of nature. They are characterized by strong emotional appeals and the diversity of highly developed techniques. According to these techniques, bird-and-flower paintings fall into three categories, namely, fine-brush, freehand style, and fine-brush with freehand style. Freehand style can be further divided into great freehand and slight freehand. In light of the difference in the application of ink and water, bird-and-flower paintings are classified into ink-and-water, splash-ink, baimiao, mogu[1] and colored.

In the long course of development, Chinese bird-and-flower painting has evolved into a symbolic and metaphoric art form based on sketches from life so as to cater to Chinese people's aesthetic appreciation. Bird-and-flower painting is not the duplication of nature. Animals and plants are not depicted for their own sake. Rather they are painted in human terms, expressing the relationship between the experiences, ideas and emotions of the human beings and the appearances and characteristics of other living beings in nature. Truth is pursued only for the sake of beauty and virtue. The primary function is to cultivate one's temperament.

Finches and Bamboos by Northern Song Emperor Huizong

Bird-and-flower paintings help the painter express his ideas and ambitions, and the appreciation of such paintings is a way to cultivate one's temperament and refine the interest, sentiments, and spiritual life of the people.

Chinese bird-and-flower painters do not pursue mere resemblance in form, but rather something between similarity and dissimilarity, or even similarity from dissimilarity, which expresses their sentiments and ideas through the depiction of the objects.

In terms of arrangement, bird-and-flower painting highlights the subject, stressing the contrast between the real and the virtual, the harmony and coherence of the whole painting. With a poem or theme statement written in appropriate calligraphic style conforming to the topic of the painting and a seal affixed to the scroll, bird-and-flower painting, especially the freehand type, is a comprehensive art encompassing painting, poetry, calligraphy and seal cutting.

In technique, bird-and-flower painting, comparatively speaking, is more concrete and detailed than landscape painting and more diversified than figure painting. The application of colors using the fine-brush is realistic and ornamental, while the use of ink in the freehand is concise, programmable but irreversible.

The most prominent figures in the creation and development of bird-and-flower painting are Huang Quan (903-968) of Shu and Xu Xi (937-975) of Southern Tang during the Five Dynasties, who brought to maturity the techniques and main style of bird-and-flower painting.

During the Northern and Southern Song Dynasties (960-1279), thanks to the imperial painting Academy, bird-and-flower painting experienced a significant change in style. Emperor Huizong (r. 1100-1125) of the Song Dynasty was so obsessed about painting and calligraphy that he neglected state affairs. He held examinations to select painters nationwide, and personally took charge of the imperial painting academy where painting masters around China worked together. They created a new style, which was exquisite, extravagant and elegant, representing the aesthetic tastes of the court. The imperial academy style, which was characterized by fine-brush and bright colors, soon became the painting arena's mainstream style.

After the Yuan Dynasty (1206-1368), the pine tree, bamboo, plum blossom and chrysanthemum became the main subjects of bird-and-flower painting. Wang Mian (1287-1359) was a master painter of the plum blossom. Xu Wei, a great painter during the Ming Dynasty, fully utilized the unique effects of brush, ink and paper, and created great freehand ink and wash paintings. He was a genius painter but led an unsuccessful life. His painting, which represented the emerging artistic trend of the times, heralded a new era for the development of bird-and-flower painting. After Xu Wei, great masters of bird-and-flower paintings include Zheng Banqiao (1693-1765), Yun Shouping (1633-1690), Wu Changshuo (1844-1927) and Qi Baishi (1863-1957).

Notes:

[1] Mogu: a technique in Chinese painting where the subject is painted directly with color and without an ink line outline.

CHINESE CALLIGRAPHY

As an ancient and unique art form, Chinese calligraphy is an indispensable part of excellent Chinese cultural heritage and a symbol of the Chinese people.

Although Chinese calligraphy, in the real sense, came into being at the end of the Eastern Han Dynasty (25-220), the art of writing Chinese characters is as old as the Chinese civilization. The evolution of Chinese characters has experienced a long period of time. It is generally accepted in the academic field that the earliest Chinese writing scripts are inscriptions on the Oracle Bone Inscriptions (Jiagu Wen) and the Bronze Inscriptions (Jin Wen) of the middle and late Shang Dynasty (1600-1046 BC).

Appreciated from the perspective of calligraphy, these antique inscriptions have very high artistic value. They possess nearly all the elements of calligraphy's formal beauty—beautiful lines, symmetric shapes, symmetrical composition and various styles.

What fascinates people most about the Oracle Bone Inscriptions is the composition of the scripts—some of them are big, some small; some circular, some square; some slender, some flat, in graceful disorder and perfect harmony.

The stone drum inscription is known for its artistic value in calligraphy. The work of Qin during the Warring States Period (475-221 BC) was engraved on ten drum-shaped granite blocks, each with a four-character verse. Known as "Father of Small Seal Script", the inscription is a typical example of the transition from greater seal script to lesser seal script[1]. Its strokes become even in thickness but are still drawn by a brisk hand; its characters are, by and large, regularly built and evenly sized, and its style is plain and natural.

From the late Shang Dynasty to the unification of China by the Qin Dynasty in 221 BC, simplification, both in form and style, was the general trend of the evolution of Chinese characters. The simplified lines of the Bronze Inscriptions in the late Western Zhou Dynasty (1046-771 BC) and the transition from seal script to clerical script in the unofficial writings during the Warring States Period was the evidence of Chinese characters' weakening pictographic features. However, the artistic value of calligraphy was greatly enhanced by the evolution of Chinese characters.

The lesser seal script by Li Si, prime minister during the Qin Dynasty (221-206 BC), is highly appraised for its balanced structure and smooth and vigorous style. His handwriting, neat and well-spaced, was the model during the Qin Dynasty.

The Han Dynasty (206 BC-AD 220) stele is another treasure of Chinese calligraphy. There are over 100 famous steles engraved with characters in Han Dynasty clerical script such as Huashan Temple Stele, known as "No. 1 Han Stele", Zhang Qian Stele, the agglomeration of Han steles, Shi Chen Stele and Cao Quan Stele, all of which are famous for their beauty and elegance.

What exactly is calligraphy? The birth and development of Chinese calligraphy is closely related to the evolution of Chinese characters. Therefore, it should be defined from its nature, aesthetic characteristics, origin, and unique methods of expression. Calligraphy is the art of writing Chinese characters with a writing brush. As an art of abstract signs with four-dimensional characteristics, it expresses the law of the unity of opposites as well as a person's spirit, temperament,

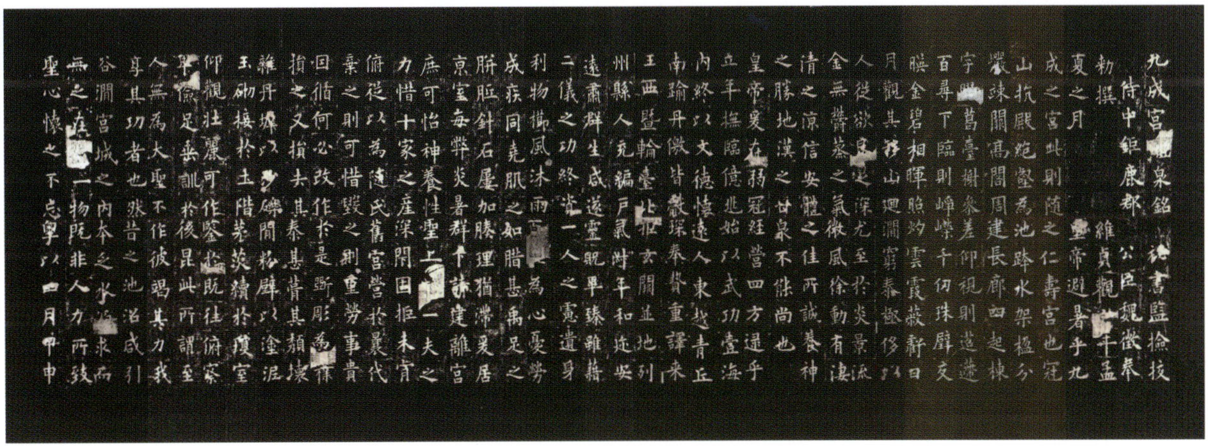

A copy of running script by Ouyang Xun

education and accomplishments in self-cultivation.

Li Zehou, a famous Chinese aesthetician once pointed out in his *The Journey to Beauty*, that calligraphy is the condensation and purification of the art of lines unique to China. It came into being, in the real sense, during the Wei (220-265) and Jin (265-420) Dynasties when the Han Dynasty clerical script was replaced with cursive, running and regular scripts, and at a time when the work of the lower class became the fashion of the upper class.

Calligraphy evolved into an independent art form and entered a new era during the Wei and Jin Dynasties when cursive hand, running hand and regular script took the place of seal and clerical scripts to become the preferred form. The appearance of Wang Xizhi, the greatest calligrapher of all times, was a unique phenomenon of that period, whose artistic achievements were highly appreciated during the Tang Dynasty. Emperor Taizong of the Tang Dynasty revered Wang Xizhi so much that he offered a huge sum of money to buy Wang's works, ordered his crown prince to copy Wang's handwritings, and even made calligraphy one of the major requirements for candidate officials.

The Tang Dynasty also witnessed a great number of prominent calligraphers of diversified styles, such as Yu Shinan, Ouyang Xun, Chu Suiliang, Yan Zhenqing, Liu Gongquan, masters of regular script, as well as Zhang Xu and Huai Su, who were famous for their cursive script.

The four great calligraphers during the Song Dynasty were Su Shi, Huang Tingjian, Mi Fu and Cai Xiang. Zhao Mengfu, Dong Qichang and Deng Shiru were famous calligraphers during the Yuan and Ming Dynasties. After the inheritance and development through the Song, Yuan, Ming and Qing Dynasties, today calligraphy has become a symbol of the Chinese culture with great and everlasting charm.

Notes:

[1] Lesser Seal Script: a style of Chinese calligraphy that evolved from the scripts on Qin state bronze ware and stones during the Eastern Zhou Dynasty (770-256 BC), with reference to the scripts of other states. It is the first uniform script in China popularized by Emperor Shihuang during the Qin Dynasty after his unification of China, and plays a crucial role in the history of Chinese calligraphy.

CHINESE SEAL CUTTING

Chinese seal cutting is a combination of calligraphy and cutting. It was addressed as one of the four skills required of an ancient scholar, the other three being calligraphy, painting and poetry.

A very unique phenomenon in seal cutting is that since ancient times seal script has always been the script for cutting, while other scripts such as clerical or regular scripts have seldom been used. Besides stone which is the most common material for the seal, other materials used to make seals include gold, silver, copper, iron, jade, stone, bone and wood.

Though modern seal cutting did not appear until the Ming Dynasty, ancient seal-cutting as an art came into being about 2,000 year ago, as early as the Spring and Autumn Period and the Warring States Period.

Before the Qin Dynasty, the seal was called "xi"[1] and used as the symbol of corresponding power or tokens of credibility. After the unification of China by the First Emperor of the Qin Dynasty, only the royal seal could be called "xi"; other seals were referred to as "yin" or "zhang".

Chinese seal cutting has a long history and a great variety of styles. There have been two climaxes in the development of seal cutting, one during the Han Dynasty and the other during the Ming and Qing Dynasties. The seals of the Han Dynasty, mostly with in-

Four Works of the Seal Cutting

tagliated seal script and a touch of clerical script were characterized by square strokes, balanced composition and imposing and elegant style. They are excellent models for learners of seal cutting.

By the mid-Ming Dynasty, seals had evolved from a practical utility and an accessory to calligraphy and painting to an independent art form. The appearance of different schools and numerous master cutters brought ancient seal cutting into its heyday from the mid-Ming Dynasty to the late Qing Dynasty. Seal cutting schools were usually named after surname, birthplace, workplace, or master-disciple relationship. For example, Wen Peng, the eldest son of Wen Zhengming, a well-known painter and calligrapher during the Ming Dynasty, benefited a lot from a family tradition that was centered on the study of poetry, calligraphy and painting. He was so good at seal cutting that in China he was known as the "Father of Seal Cutting".

With the excavation of bronze and stone relics, epigraphy flourished during the Qing Dynasty. Many scholars were dedicated to the collection and study of the inscriptions on ancient bronze ware and stone tablets. The achievements of their studies broadened the vision of seal cutters and gave birth to an unprecedented number of master cutters of various schools, such as Deng Shiru, Zhao Zhiqian and Wu Changshuo.

Seal cutting is a varied and colorful art performed within limited space. Generally speaking, seal writing precedes seal cutting. The former is the foundation of the latter, while the latter is an expression of the former. From an artistic point of view, calligraphy and seal cutting are sisterly arts from the same origin. To be a good cutter, one must be a good calligrapher first, especially a good calligrapher of seal script. Although calligraphy and seal cutting both stress line, structure and pattern arrangement, they differ in terms of instrumentation use. One is writing with a brush on paper, while the other is cutting with a knife on stone.

The relationship between seal cutting and painting is even closer. The affixed seal on a painting serves not only as a certificate for authenticity but also enrichment to the artistic appeal of the work.

No longer an insignificant skill for idlers, seal cutting has developed into a unique art for appreciation. Mastery of the art requires knowledge, skill as well as self-cultivation.

Notes:

[1] Xi and yin: before the Qin Dynasty, all seals (royal, official and private) were called "xi". After the unification of China during the Qin Dynasty, only the royal seal could be called "xi"; other seals were referred to as "yin". The seal originated from scripts carved on bones and shells during the Shang Dynasty, bronze ware during the Zhou Dynasty, and stones during the Qin Dynasty. All scripts carved on metal, jade, stone and other materials are called "metal-stone script", including the seals.

(English Author: Wang Chunbo)

Chapter Eleven Chinese Folk Art

CHINESE MUSICAL INSTRUMENT

Chinese musical instrument is a general term for traditional musical instruments found in China. As early as the Pre-Qin Period the instruments were divided into eight categories, namely, silk, bamboo, wood, stone, metal, clay, gourd and hide. Yet nowadays they fall into four major categories—wind, drawing, stringed, and percussion instruments[1]. The order in which these instruments were invented is percussion, wind[2], stringed and pulled string.

Chinese musical instruments have a long history and are various in kind. The most well-known Chinese musical instruments have been handed down since ancient times, and one must not forget about the significance of exotic and folk instruments.

Musical instruments and inscriptions on bones and tortoise shells unearthed in the Yin Ruin in Henan Province prove that more than 3000 years ago, at least 10 types of Chinese musical instruments were already played, such as the bell, Qing[3], Xun[4] and bronze drum.

Up to the Western Zhou Dynasty (1046-771 BC), there were records of more than 70 kinds of musical instruments, along with a more developed music culture. In May 1978, with the exploration of a tomb in present Hubei Province, which was established at the beginning of the Warring States Period (475-221 BC), a complete musical band with 124 pieces of valuable musical bells and drums were found. In particular, among them, was a set of bronze bells of 2.73 meters in height, which had 64 chimes and an 11.83-metre-long shelf. The chimes were different in size, and could produce 12 melodic tones.

As governors of the Han (206 BC-AD 220) and Tang

Chime Bells

(618-907) Dynasties were quite open-minded, music and musical instruments from the Islamic world and India began to flood into China. Therefore, flute, tartar pipe, Chinese lute and huqin were accepted by Chinese people.

The art of singing and dancing reached its apex during the Tang Dynasty with the arrival of multiethnic music as well as the introduction of music from Japan, India, Korea, and Southeast Asia, which greatly enriched China's music culture.

Folk and court music both experienced unprecedented favor, especially in terms of stringed instruments. The Mogao Grottoes in Dunhuang provide a perfect example with its frescoes and sculptures. In the frescoes one can see many figures flying in the sky while holding the Pipa[5], which indicates that the Pipa was already a leading instrument at that time. Historical records show that there were approximately 300 kinds of musical instruments in the Tang Dynasty.

In the Song (960-1279) and Yuan (1206-1368) Dynasties, the rise of opera music brought about the development of instrumental musical arts. The creation of new musical instruments such as the Sanxian[6], Erhu[7] and Jinghu[8], led to the establishment of traditional Chinese musical instruments of the time. Accordingly, four major categories of traditional Chinese musical instruments were formed – wind, drawing, string and percussion.

In the Ming (1368-1644) and Qing (1616-1911) Dynasties, Western music and musical instruments flooded into China, such as brass instruments[9], the piano, violin and trumpet, as well as symphony music, which were harmonized with Chinese folk instruments, and therefore expanded the field and vision of these instruments.

After the founding of the People's Republic of China, the government attached great importance to the cultural heritage of ethnic musical instruments and saved many that were on the verge of extinction, such as the Hulusi[10], Taoxun[11], Yangqin[12] and Koudi[13], making them an important part of flourishing Chinese culture.

Notes:

[1] Percussion instrument: any object which produces a sound when hit with an implement, shaken, rubbed, scraped, or by any other action which sets the object into vibration.

[2] Wind: a musical instrument that contains some type of resonator, in which a column of air is set into vibration by the player blowing into (or over) a mouthpiece set at the end of the resonator.

[3] Qing: an ancient percussion instrument, made of jade or stone.

[4] Xun: a kind of ancient wind instrument made of fired clay, which is oval in shape and contains six holes.

[5] Pipa: a string instrument made of wood with four strings, the lower part of which is composed of a melon-shaped plate and upper part a long handle.

[6] Sanxian: also known as Xianzi, is a traditional Chinese plucked string instrument with a long handle, square-shaped speaker box, skin covered sides and three strings, which, when played, is held in the arms. The sound is rough, and is played alone and in ensembles, or accompanies folk or opera music.

[7] Erhu: also known as Nanhu, is a kind of Huqin larger than Jinghu, with a wooden box, skin covered sides and two strings. It produces low tones.

[8] Jinghu: also known as Huqin, is a pull string instrument.

[9] Brass instrument: a musical instrument whose tone is produced by vibration of the lips as the player blows into a mouth piece.

[10] Hulusi: an instrument that looks like a combination of a gourd and a flute, which produces unique, simple, soft and elegant sounds. It is the primary musical instrument of ethnic minorities in Yunnan, and most popular among the people of the Dai Nationality in Yunnan's Dianxi area.

[11] Taoxun: a kind of ancient wind instrument made of fired clay, which is oval in shape and with six holes.

[12] Yangqin: also known as "dulcimer" and "Butterfly Guoqin" or "Shanmianqin", is a stringed instrument.

It was created by the ancient Assyrian in Western Asia and Persia, and was introduced to China around the late Ming Dynasty.

[13] Koudi: a type of whistle.

FOLK SONGS

Folk songs can be considered as "songs of the common people".

Folk songs are created and performed by working people in their daily life and labor and are passed down orally. In the process of circulation, folk songs experienced endless selection, transformation, enrichment and refinement.

Different types of folk songs include: the "holler"[1] when doing labor, love songs, popular ethnic children's songs, songs for drinking and amusement, elegies to commemorate friends, songs for leisure time and popular folk songs sung in mountainous regions.

Folk songs are distinctively ethnic in character and contain a special local color. Chinese folk songs are further divided into those of Hebei, Northern Shaanxi, the Northeast, Jiangsu and Zhejiang, Hunan, Xinjiang and Qinghai. Because China has a long history, vast lands, large population and a variety of nationalities, it boasts a variety of folk songs. According to statistics, today, more than 300,000 folk songs have been collected. These songs have a strong flavor of life, simple style and are interesting lyric. Many of them are already well-known, and the representative pieces

Old Men of the Yi Nationality Singing Folk Songs

include *Jasmine*, *Xiaobaicai* (literally *The Little Cabbage*), *Xikou Progress* and *Little Cowherd*.

Jasmine, a folk song of the Han Nationality, is a very popular Xiaoqu[2], dating back to the Qing Dynasty. It is not only well-known in most parts of China, but also in various parts of Europe, the United States and Asia since the 18th century. As a typical representative of Chinese folk songs, it is well accepted in other countries, often found in the collection of "world folk songs". In countries with a large Chinese population, *Jasmine* can even be regarded as local folk music.

Xiaobaicai is a popular folk song in Hebei Province, which tells the story of a devastated young orphan girl and her sadness over missing her late mother. As for the construction of the song, each line contains three words and each stanza four lines, with one note written for each word. A smooth melody and lamented chanting for "Mom, mom" in the last two stanzas highlight the girl's grievance and sweet memory of her mother. This song was once used as the theme music of the movie *White-haired Girl*[3], and was entitled *The North Wind*, which won great popularity.

Xikou Progress is a well-known folk song in China's northwestern Shaanxi Province. It tells the story of a newly-wed couple. Under the pressures of life, the husband had to leave his wife right after the wedding ceremony in order to travel to a far away land to make a living. The song, a depiction of the touching scene of their parting, actually reflects the real life experience of the local people.

Little Cowherd is a folk song-and-dance in northeastern China. It is a pattern of questions and answers between a village shepherd boy and a country girl. In the song, the girl asks the boy for directions, but the shepherd boy deliberately raises difficult questions before giving any direction. When performed as a dance, the questions and answers are sung in step. The song's flexible, crisp tone and rich expression, coupled with a vividly witty form of dance, demonstrate the wisdom of the working people and their optimistic, cheerful personality.

Folk songs include monophonic songs and counterpoint songs and most Chinese folk songs are monophonic songs. Over 20 nationalities in China, namely, Zhuang Nationality, Dong Nationality, Gelao Nationality, Buyi Nationality, Yao Nationality, Gaoshan Nationality, Lisu Nationality, She Nationality and Qiang Nationality possess a precious heritage of monophonic songs.

In the history of Chinese literature, folk songs have been an important source for Chinese literature and Chinese folk music. In fact, a variety of Chinese poems and local operas originated from folk songs. For example, basic tunes of "Er Ren Zhuan", a song-and-dance duet popular in the Northeast of China, and huagu opera, are both derived from folk songs.

Notes:

[1] Holler: a type of folk song sung during labor-work.

[2] Xiaoqu: oral singing (ballad).

[3] *White-haired Girl*: an opera script written in the Yan'an Lu Xun Art Academy in 1945 by He Jingzhi and Ding Yi, with Ma Ke as the composer. In the story, a reactionary landlord, Huang Shiren, drove his tenant Yang Bailao to commit suicide and raped his daughter Xi'er. When he planned to sell Xi'er, the girl escaped and hid herself in the mountains for many years, during which her hair turned completely white. After the Eighth Route Army arrived at her hometown and removed the landlords, she was rescued.

FOLK DANCE

China is an extended family of 56 ethnic groups. In its long history, each nationality has its own unique artistic style, represented by rich and colorful folk dances.

Folk dance can be found in many facets of daily life including: courtship, weddings, mourning and other activities. As a form of entertainment that has garnered more attention from Chinese society, folk dance patterns have become simpler and more flexible. It is important to note that singing often accompanies folk dance.

Folk dance has been deeply rooted in the people since its birth. Its various forms and rich contents provide professional dances with an indispensable source of creation. Boasting a long histroy and beautiful elements, Chinese folk dance is a smooth combination of culture, art and aesthetics.

Ethnic groups all have their own cultural style of folk dance. Folk dances in the north are expressive, vigorous, bold and rhythmic, while those in the south are delicate, graceful and lyrical in nature. Dances from the west are deeply rooted in nomadic life with vigorous and intense rhythm. Agricultural groups from the eastern part of the country prefer a soft, slow-paced dance.

Tibetan, Mongolian, Uighur, and Korean folk dances are most frequently seen on the stage.

Mongolian folk dance is vibrant, bold and outstretching. It is rich in shoulder movement – up and down, back and forth. When dancing, men often demonstrate the spirit of the cavalier, while women's movements are nimble and lively. The most popular Mongolian folk dances are the "chopsticks dance"[1] and the "cup and bowl dance"[2], which are popular in western Inner Mongolia. The music accompanying these dances is often local folk songs played on the Sihu[3], Matouqin[4], flute and Yangqin.

Xinjiang folk dance is unique, as Xinjiang played an important role on the Silk Road and has a mixed culture of the Central Plains, Persia, India and Arabia among other regions. It has a colorful and splendid style of dance. Uygur dance, as the representative, is specialized in the employment of head movement, neck shifting, head shaking and a rich variety of wrist action, and is characterized by an erect head, chest, and waist. In conveying emotion and sentiment, the eyes also play a major part in Uygur dance. Uygur dancers usually follow a circular floor pattern, and for this reason, the dance is considered gentle and graceful. .

Tibetan folk dance demonstrates the characteristics of Tibetan clothing to the utmost – the swing of long sleeves is the most prominent feature. In terms of upper body movement, there are strict rules for male dancers: regardless of hand-held props, "upper body movement should imitate a lion". The male dancer should embody a mighty, majestic and giant figure, on whom a powerful faith from the heavens is bestowed; a faith that can overcome all difficulties and obstacles. The female dancer should adhere to subtle and elegant upper body movement, conveying the feeling of health and beauty. Tibetan dance is rich in vivid hand movement, which reflects the abundance of body language. For differences in geography, climate, dialect, dress and religious belief, subsections of Tibetan folk dance also exist, including a dance for the upper classes of society, one for religious services as well as various Tibetan Operas[5].

Korean (ethnic group) folk dance features a fine mixture of elegance and passion. Take the famous "Long Tassel Dance" for instance. It is performed with a special headdress that has a long tassel, which swings

The Korean Folk Dance

The Dai Folk Dance

around the head. Sometimes, dancers also make a variety of movements to express the optimistic spirit of the common worker. The dance is often beautifully and cheerfully carried out by female performers, who fasten the tassel in front of their headdress, beat the drum with the left hand and hold a mallet in the right.

"Peacock Dance" is an ancient folk dance of the Dai Nationality. A favorite of the Dai people, it is performed during every grand festival, such as "Songkran"[6] and other important gatherings when dancing is a must. Dai people love and respect the peacock for its beauty, and because it is a symbol of good luck, happiness and prosperity. Therefore, they dance as a proud people, expressing their ideals and aspirations. During the dance, performers imitate peacocks that strut down mountains, walk through forests and drink and frolic in water. The peacock's wings and tail are also important parts of the dance.

Miao folk dance greatly emphasizes the use of costumes and props. In "Lusheng Dance" and "Encouraging Steps", female performers wear silver ornaments and silver-collared, multi-colored clothing. Swinging their body, they wave their silver-decorated skirts and make special vocalizations accompanied by the Lusheng, drums and singing. Folk dance is an integral part of the Miao lifestyle and culture.

In China, some ethnic groups have preserved an ancient dance – the Nuo dance or the "Exorcism Dance"[7]. It is an ancient Chinese ritual dance. The dancers, who wear frightening masks, represent spirits and ghosts, portraying the story of God. Today, the Nuo dance has developed into a folk dance and drama, which is widespread in the provinces of Jiangxi, Hunan, Hubei, Guizhou, Anhui and Shandong.

Notes:

[1] Chopsticks Dance: one of the representative forms of traditional folk dance of the Yikeshaomeng people. A performer holds the thinner ends of the chopsticks in each hand while hitting the thicker ends together. The Mongolian chopstick dance embodies people's love for life and wisdom to make life better. It is an important part of Mongolian spiritual life.

[2] Cup and Bowl Dance: a popular folk dance of the Jumeng people of Inner Mongolia, as well as the "top

bowl dance" and "small handless wine cup dance". Originally, it was improvised for festivals, receptions and feasts.

[3] Sihu: an instrument shaped like the Erhu and named for its four strings. The first and third strings share an identical tone, as do the second and fourth strings. It is played with the accompaniment of the drum, and is commonly used in folk art.

[4] Matouqin: a Chinese Mongolian pull- string instrument, also known as the "chaor", with a wooden body and about one meter in length. It has two trapezoidal resonance boxes and two strings, and is masked with horse skin.

[5] Tibetan Opera: an important part of Tibetan socio-cultural life, known in the Tibetan language as "akilam". It is popular in Tibet, Sichuan, Qinghai, Yunnan and other Tibetan-populated areas, and closely related to Tibetan Buddhism.

[6] Songkran: originally derived from India and once a religious ceremony of Brahmanism. It was later absorbed by Buddhism and was spread to the Yunnan Dai Nationality area via Burma. On the Dai Calendar, Songkran is the celebration of the New Year, which generally falls between April 13 to 15 on the solar calendar, when people go to Buddhist temples, dancing and splashing each other with water to express sincere wishes. Laughter is heard everywhere in this festive and happy atmosphere.

[7] Exorcism Dance: also known as "Da Nuo" or "Tiao Nuo" (literally "ghost opera"), was derived from the ancient faith clan totem. It gradually developed into an original witch ceremony with seasonal rituals. Generally speaking, there are two forms of the dance: one with four performers and the other with 12. In the former, shouting performers are masked, dressed in animal skins and equipped with shields. In the latter, performers dye their hair red and hold a long whip, shouting as if they would devour all kinds of evil beasts. The dance is usually accompanied by music.

YANGKO

Yangko is one of the most popular rural folk dances of the Han Nationality in the north of China. Lively and flexible, Yangko always creates a hilarious scene whenever and wherever people perform it.

Yangko appeared quite early, and Song Dynasty reliefs unearthed in Shaanxi Province were found to have Yangko portraits on them. The costumes and facial expressions, as well as the poses and dance dynamics of the figures in the portraits are similar to the Yangko in Northern Shaanxi. This shows that Yangko was actually a popular folk dance as early as 800 years ago during the Southern Song Dynasty (1127-1279).

Yangko is popular throughout China. In the south, it is called "lantern dance." In the north, various styles of Yangko are practiced, and each has its unique local flavor, such as Shaanbei Yangko, Northeast Yangko, Hebei Yangko, Jiaozhou (in Shandong Province) Yangko and Marine Yangko.

In some places Stilts[1] (Gaoqiao) is also known as Yangko. This form of folk dance is usually performed by a female character with facial make-up with the company of clowns. The dance is usually performed in the streets, with one person taking the lead and holding an umbrella (a symbol of favorable weather) and the rest following her holding fans, handkerchiefs, hand-held drums, sticks and colored silk. With the accompaniment of gongs and drums of unified beat, the dance is performed in the city square. It begins with "Guochang"[2], and then changes to a variety of formations and patterns, finally composing an organized group dance. During this period, there are two or three individual performances in between. The dance is lively and interesting.

Hebei Yangko "Paolü" (literally "running donkey") is a favorite local tradition. The dance tells the story of a young couple's visit to the wife's parents. The farmer's wife rides a donkey and carries an infant in her arms.

Yangko

chest, and the occasional shaking of the head with pride, which conveys a strong sense of rawness and simplicity. A typical example is "Ansai Waist Drum". In the Ansai area in Northern Shaanxi, the "Drum" is played in various ways, and the most common is a fierce skills competition between two Drum teams. The jumping and shouting of the dancers carry great momentum and symbolize their strong will.

The husband drives the donkey with a small whip. On their happy way, the donkey becomes stuck in mud, and the child starts crying. After pulling and pushing with every effort, the two finally get the donkey out of the mud. The dance is full of daily life sensibility and comedic style.

Shaanbei Yangko features sound and appropriate pace while twisting the body, flinging arms, swelling the

Notes:

[1] Stilts: a folk dance, also known as "wooden stilts".

[2] Guochang: ① the activity of passing and leaving the stage between scenes of a performance; ② a short and brief performance that connects the plots of a drama.

LION DANCE

The lion dance is a form of traditional dance in Chinese culture, in which performers mimic a lion's movements in a lion costume. Basic lion dance movements can be found in most Chinese martial arts.

In Chinese towns and cities during every Spring and Lantern Festival, lion dances will be performed. The custom began in the Three Kingdoms (220-280), prospered during the South and North Dynasties (420-589), and has therefore enjoyed a history of more than one thousand years. Bai Juyi, a famous poet of the Tang Dynasty, gives a vivid description of the mask, wooden head, gilded eyes, silver teeth and swift movements of lion dance in his poem *Xiliang Show*.

Northern-style "Lion"

The Chinese hold the lion in great reverence as a totem

of bravery, a symbol of majesty, power and auspiciousness, next only to the dragon. Therefore, in the front of temples and courts and on the railings of various stone architectures, lion sculptures are abundant. Different forms of lion dance are also popular across the country, which is mainly reserved for festive occasions.

The styles of Chinese lion dance are divided into North and South, and the most famous performance in the north (Hebei Province) is the "Double Lion Dance". The design of the special costume resembles a real lion, and the performers (one or two) hide themselves inside the "lion clothes", with the lower part of the body covered with similarly colored pants and boots. The "lion tamer", holding a hydrangea, pretends to be a warrior, as he "tames" the lion to the beat of drums and percussion gongs.

Basic dance moves include ups-and-downs, rolling, jumping, itching, stepping on balls and climbing chairs. The lion dance is characterized by lively, swift and happy footwork.

In the north, the lion dance embodies the strong sentiment of the common people, and is a representation of soft and colorful folk dance art.

In Southern China, lion dance is most famous in Guangdong Province. In the south, the lion is smaller than its northern counterpart with a focus on head design. Southern style "lions" have a smaller head and are painted with brighter colors. Also, a mirror and an embroidery ball appear on the lion's forehead. The placement of glass bead eyes emphasizes great power. The lion's fur is composed of a piece of patterned cloth with lines of beads. Performers stand on the ground and hold their heads high. Two dancers in one lion are responsible for the movements of head and tail respectively. They cooperate with each other when performing different movements and maneuvers related to martial arts.

Southern-style "Lion"

In Guangdong, lion dance has become a custom during the Lunar Chinese New Year. A group of lion dancers will cooperate with one another to finish a performance and obtain a bonus in an envelope that is placed at the centre of the stage and surrounded by all kinds of obstacles.

Lion dance in the south features the mimicking of the lion's actions such as walking and playing in water.

(English Author: Xia Zhi)

Chapter Twelve Chinese Opera

THE ART OF BEIJING OPERA

Beijing Opera, also called "Peking Opera", is the most influential and representative of Chinese operas and has a history of about 160 years. Although formed in Beijing, it is not native-born.

A local opera troupe from Anhui Province came to Beijing in 1790, to celebrate the 80th birthday of Emperor Qianlong, and brought its "Hui Tune" (which originated in Anhui Province) to the capital, which soon became popular. Later, it partly drew and adopted repertoire, tune and manner of performance from Kunqu[1] and Shaanxi Opera as well as folk tunes, gradually developing into what we now call Beijing Opera.

Beijing, as the political and cultural center of China, has facilitated the popularity of Beijing Opera, which has become popular all over the country and has also spread to other countries. Beijing Opera, as a fairly contemporary art, has surpassed its predecessors, and has come to be known as the "National Opera", a symbol of Chinese culture.

Beijing Opera is a scenic art integrating Chinese folklore, music, dance and the fine arts and infusing four categories of skills—singing, chanting, acting and acrobatic fighting.

Beijing Opera is a comprehensive performing art that aesthetically combines music, fine arts (including makeup, facial makeup, stage design and setting), lighting, costume (embroidery craft) and stage property (art and craft manufacture). Hence an actor

The Drunken Concubine

or actress in Beijing Opera has to meet more requirements than those in other forms of performing art. The performers should blend singing, dancing, chanting, pantomime, arias, acrobatics and martial arts in performances. Becoming an outstanding performer requires a long and arduous apprenticeship beginning from an early age.

In Beijing Opera, the actor's roles are divided under four main headings, *sheng*, *dan*, *jing*, and *chou*.

Sheng roles are divided into three subtypes, *laosheng*, *xiaosheng* and *wusheng*; *Dan* roles, five, *laodan*, *zhengdan*, *huadan*, *guimendan* and *daomadan*; *Jing* roles, three, *dahualian*, *erhualian* and *wuhualian*. *Jing*, also known as *hualian*, usually represents a man of virile, rough or evil character. *Dahualian*, with singing as its strength, usually plays characters like important royal officials, marshals or senior generals. *Erhualian*, known as *jiazihualian*, is characterized by acting and body movements and plays characters of humorous, bold and uninhibited nature. *Wuhualian* specializes in acrobatic-fighting and speaks few words.

Chou is a comic role, with the character's face painted with a small patch of white chalk around the nose and known as *xiaohualian*, or *sanhualian* (*hualian No.3*) after *dahualian* (*hualian No.1*) and *erhualian* (*hualian No.2*).

Chou roles can be divided into *wenchou*, civilian roles, and *wuchou*, minor military roles. *Chou* is feathered with short and scattered moustache to highlight the comic effect, and short sole boots representing low status.

Beijing Opera provides a set of standardized artistic rules in various aspects such as costume, makeup and performance. The roles have the natural features of age and gender, as well as social status, and are artificially exaggerated by makeup, costume and gestures.

The performance of Beijing Opera is symbolic and suggestive, rather than realistic. The performers have to portray and symbolize the characters, scene, time and place. For example, the performer sometimes should portray coming into or going out of a door though there is no door on the stage.

The stage symbolizes water, a battlefield or a study when actors hold an oar, a gun or a sword, and a book respectively. With the performers' movement and control of movement, the stage is used to complement spectators' virtual space by exploiting their life experience.

A character will sweep their hand in an arc from left to right in order to indicate an object on the right, which presents the principles of aesthetics.

Notes:

[1] Kunqu: one of the traditional Chinese theatres, also known as Kunju, which is popular in south Jiangsu (South Kunqu), Beijing and Hebei (North Kunqu)

FOUR FAMOUS *DANS* OF BEIJING OPERA

The *dan* refers to any female role in Beijing Opera, which was exclusively played by men in the feudal society as women were banned on the stage. Even at the beginning of the Republic of China (1912-1949), some female roles in drama were impersonated by male performers.

The *laosheng*[1] was the main role in Beijing Opera while *dan* the minor one before the Revolution of 1911 (the Chinese bourgeois democratic revolution led by Dr. Sun Yat-sen which overthrew the Qing Dynasty).

In the early 1920s, the situation was changed once and for all when four *dan* actors became stars: Mei Lanfang, Shang Xiaoyun, Cheng Yanqiu and Xun Huisheng who originally played *huadan* role in Bangzi Opera.

Mei Lanfang

At China's first Dan Master Selection Contest, held in Beijing in 1927, Mei Lanfang shared the honor of the Four Famous *Dans* with the other three. The four actors continued to make renovations and to improve their performance, and each had his own features and formed his original style: the grandiose Mei school, the majestic Shang school, the graceful Cheng school and the lively Xun school, which ensured the *dan* a very important place in Beijing Opera and contributed to the development of Beijing Opera.

The Mei school is charactered by a sweet voice, clear pronunciation, and exquisite performance of ordered steps, accurate rhythm and graceful posture.

The Shang school conveys power and strength through high-pitched voice and precise and pleasant pronunciation.

The Cheng school is soft and pleasing, firm but gentle.

The Xun school is best known for soft and gentle singing, mellow chanting, varied and rhythmic posture and, in particular, telling eyes.

Born in the family of famous Beijing Opera actors, Mei Lanfang (1894-1961) began to learn Chinese opera when he was eight years old, studied from famous *dan* Wu Lingxian at the age of nine, and made his stage debut at 10. At 20, he gave an exquisite, elegant and graceful performance with sweet voice in *Muke Village* in Shanghai, which created quite a stir there and won him great fame.

During his stage life, Mei Lanfang embellished the traditions of the past with his own creations and adapted them to a new stage.

Mei Lanfang's greatest contribution to Beijing Opera was changing the traditional opera which stresses singing rather than performance.

He enriched stage performance, blending singing and dancing by gathering together the best of the Kunqu and other local operas.

He created the new role of *huashan* by blending the features of *qingyi*[2], *huadan* and *daomadan*[3] with Wang Yaoqin, and improved on those inherited traditions by personalizing them with his own creations.

Along with his exquisite art and unique style, Mei Lanfang had the noble character of modesty and integrity. After the Japanese invaded China, Mei gave such performances as *Re-commanding the Army* and the *Distance between Life and Death* to inspire Chinese people to fight for their country. He refused to perform for the invaders and puppet regime, grew a full beard as a sign of protest, and made a living by selling his paintings. Mei didn't shave his beard and resume his stage career until the Chinese won the war against the Japanese, showcasing the patriotic national integrity of an artist.

Mei was the first artist to introduce Beijing Opera to other countries, and helped the people in the world to better understand traditional Chinese opera.

He performed Beijing Opera three times in Japan (1919, 1924 and 1956), which made the art known to all there.

Introduced by John Leighton Stuart, then president of Yanching University, Mei's troupe took their tour in America in 1930 at their own expense, which attracted much attention of the American education field and soon helped make Beijing Opera popular in America.

Mei's tour was a trumpeted media spectacle, hailed as a triumph of cultural exchange. Many professors and experts went to watch his performance to study oriental culture and Chinese classical arts. As they enjoyed the excellent performances, they wrote very positive press comments.

Mei toured abroad many times, which popularized the Chinese classical drama among foreign audiences, guiding them to a better appreciation of Chinese art and culture. Through his performances, Beijing Opera obtained world fame and in return exerted much influence to the foreign stage.

His representative works were *Drunken Beauty*, *King Xiang Yu Bids Farewell to His Beloved*, *The Distance between Life and Death* and *Mu Guiying Takes Command.*

Cheng Yanqiu (1904-1958), began to learn Beijing Opera at an early age and became famous at 18. He took Mei Lanfang as his tutor and was well known for playing parts of *qingyi*. The most prominent part of the Cheng style was its unique singing characterized by stretched voice, varying tones, changing rhythms, strict adherence to rhyme and perfect blend of rhythm and tones. This kind of novel and vivid singing blew a fresh wind in improving the Beijing Opera's *dan* singing.

Cheng Yanqiu

Furthermore, his unique acting best portrayed the personality of the character he played through his facial expressions, posture and lines. The water sleeve skills that he created greatly enriched the art of *dan* sleeve skills. His acting style was recognized as the Cheng school. He was good at tragedies and most of the roles he took were women with miserable fates in feudal society.

His representative works were *Lady Wens Return to the Han People*, *Tears on the Desolate Mountain*, and *The Snowfall in June.*

Shang Xiaoyun (1900-1976), began to learn Chinese opera at an early age, first *wusheng*[4] and afterwards *zhengdan*[5] and *daomadan*, and was known as "No. 1" among child actors when he was 14. He was famed for his good voice—loud and sonorous, sweet and mellow, and clear and melodious. The female heroes he played were unique artistic images and he was thus dubbed as the creator of the Shang school. His representative works were *Han Ming Imperial Concubine* and *Liang Hongyu.*

Shang Xiaoyun

Xun Huisheng (1900-1968), began to learn Hebei Bangzi Opera at an early age but switched to playing Beijing Opera's *huadan* and *daomadan* when he was 10. Later, he innovated Beijing Opera by combining the *huadan* role in Bangzi Opera to best suit himself, and was best known for his portrayal of vivacious and tender women. His performing style was highly regarded and dubbed the Xun school. His representative works were *Red Maid* and *Two You Sisters in the Red Mansion.*

Xun Huisheng

Notes:

[1] *Laosheng*: also known as *xusheng*, meaning bearded men, because the actors wear artificial beards which were called Rankou in Beijing Opera. And they are middle-aged or elderly men.

[2] Qingyi: young female characters, also known as *zhengdan*.

[3] *Daomadan*: one subtype of *dan* roles, playing young female warriors.

[4] *Wusheng*: a martial character for roles involving combat.

[5] *Zhengdan*: the leading female roles in Chinese opera.

THE ART OF FACIAL MAKEUP IN BEIJING OPERA

Colorful facial makeup in Beijing Opera is a pattern of put-on facial makeup of exaggerated lines and colors for the actors to portray dramatic roles in accordance with certain set norms to reflect the characters' identity, status, fate, personality and appearance and to intensify the artistic appeal on stage. The Chinese name for facial makeup is *lianpu* (patterns of faces).

The origin of facial makeup can be traced back to the Tang Dynasty (618-907), when actors used to wear masks. A mask can change the appearance and depict a fixed facial expression. Its only deficiency is its set design which cannot change along with the actors' facial expressions.

As the operatic arts developed, performers gradually took off their masks and instead painted colorful patterns on their faces so that people could better see their facial expressions.

During the reigns of Emperor Tongzhi (r. 1861-1875) and Emperor Guangxu (r. 1875-1908), with the emergence of Beijing Opera, the art of facial makeup was increasingly perfected and finalized.

Facial makeup is a special art in Chinese operas which distinctly shows the appearances of different roles as well as their dispositions and moral qualities in a greatly distorted and exaggerated way.

The basic colors employed on a face, which were originally black, red and white, gradually came to include blue, yellow and green, and then pink, purple, grey, gold and silver. Each color has a symbolic meaning.

The red face shows bravery, uprightness and loyalty. A typical "red face" is Guan Yu of the Three Kingdoms.

The black face indicates either a rough and bold character or an impartial and selfless personality. Typical of the former is General Zhang Fei (of *the Romance of the Three Kingdoms*), and of the latter is Bao Gong (alias Bao Zheng), the semi-legendary fearless and impartial judge of the Song Dynasty.

A yellow face depicts atrocity and cattiness

A blue or green face depicts surly stubbornness, impetuosity and a total lack of self-restraint.

A gold or silver face signifies mysterious or supernatural presences. A typical "golden face" is Sun Wukong, known as the Monkey King, the main character in *Journey to the West*.

Commonly seen on the stage is the white face for the powerful villain. It highlights all that is bad in human nature: cunningness, craftiness, treachery. Typical characters are Cao Cao, powerful and cruel prime minister, and Sima Yi, a famous strategist and statesman.

In Beijing Opera, the art of facial makeup is limited only to the roles of *jing* and *chou*.

There are a large variety of facial makeup patterns, namely, "whole face", "three-tile face" and "flowery face with broken patterns".

For the whole face, one should first apply the basic color to the entire face and then use another color to depict the brows such as red or white face with black brows, or black face with white ones. Typical characters for red face, white face and black face are respectively Guan Yu, Cao Cao and Bao Zheng.

The three-tile face is the basic form of Beijing Opera

▶▶ Whole Face

▶▶ Three-tile Face

▶▶ Facial Makeup for a *Chou* Role

facial design. First, a brush is used to delineate the eyebrows, the eye sockets and nostrils to divide the face into three empty parts, namely, the forehead and the left and right cheeks. Then, the empty spaces are filled with different colors to form the designs appropriate for the character.

Flowery face with broken patterns is also known as deformed face. Curved lines are generally applied to the forehead, the eyes and the eyebrows as well as the cheeks, to produce rich and varied patterns mainly used for those disfigured characters or bad characters.

The defining characteristic of a clown character's facial makeup is a small patch of white chalk in various shapes around the nose to differ from other roles. Usually, black is used to delineate the sense organs, then white is applied to the part between the eyes, and the nose and mouth, to form square or kidney shapes for different roles, hence the term *xiaohualian*.

BEIJING OPERA COSTUMES

Beijing opera costumes are based on every-day clothing that was worn in ancient times, imitating the Ming Dynasty (1368-1644) attire. The Song (960-1279), Yuan (1206-1368) and Qing (1616-1911) Dynasty attire is also used today. After refinement, recapitulation, beautification and decoration, the appropriative clothing of a certain pattern is then formed. The costumes are informally known as Xingtou, the general term used for clothing for all kinds of roles, including long gowns, short clothes, armor, casqued hats, boots and shoes.

Costumes function first to distinguish the rank of the character. The robe worn by Emperors and their families is called *mang*, or python robe. It is a costume suitable for the high rank of the character, featuring brilliant colors and rich embroidery, often in the design of a dragon.

On formal occasions, lower officials may wear the informal robe *pei*, a simple gown with patches of embroidery on both the front and back.

All other characters, and officials on informal occasions, wear the *xue*, a basic gown with varying levels of embroidery and without a jade girdle, which is typically worn to denote rank.

Minor characters of no rank wear simple clothing without embroidery.

Colors indicate different social status: bright yellow for the emperors or kings, dark yellow or apricot for the infantes or princes, red for majestic and noble characters, blue for upright men, white for young characters, and black for boorish and unconstrained roles. *Hualian* is often in black with black facial makeup.

The armor, or *kao* in Beijing Opera terms, is worn by actors impersonating high-ranking generals and military officials and is modeled on the ancient armor. A piece of armor with four triangle banners (also known as *kaoqi*) standing in a leather sheath lashed to the actor's back is called grand armor, also known as *dakao* or *yingkao*. *Kaoqi* is an ornamental accessory to showcase the official's power and prestige.

The color of the *kao*, related to the color of the painted face, reveals information about the character's identity, age and personality. For example, handsome young generals wear a white *kao*, while aggressive or rude characters wear the black *kao*.

There are many different kinds of hats in Chinese opera, among which, the gauze hat worn by prime ministers in ancient times is the most typical. It is a hat with two wings some 30 cm in length and 3 cm in width stretching out on both sides. The wings denote an actor's character or rank; peach-shaped wings are worn by corrupt and treacherous characters.

Different from the every-day boots, boots used in Beijing Opera have some 6-12 cm white soles to increase the height of the actors, and to be in line with the embellished costumes.

Baldrics, though apparently of little or no account as compared with such principal items as crowns and robes, may nevertheless function to bring about more dramatic effects on the stage. For instance, the jade belt worn by the officials hangs balanced at an angle that slopes down in the front as an accessory.

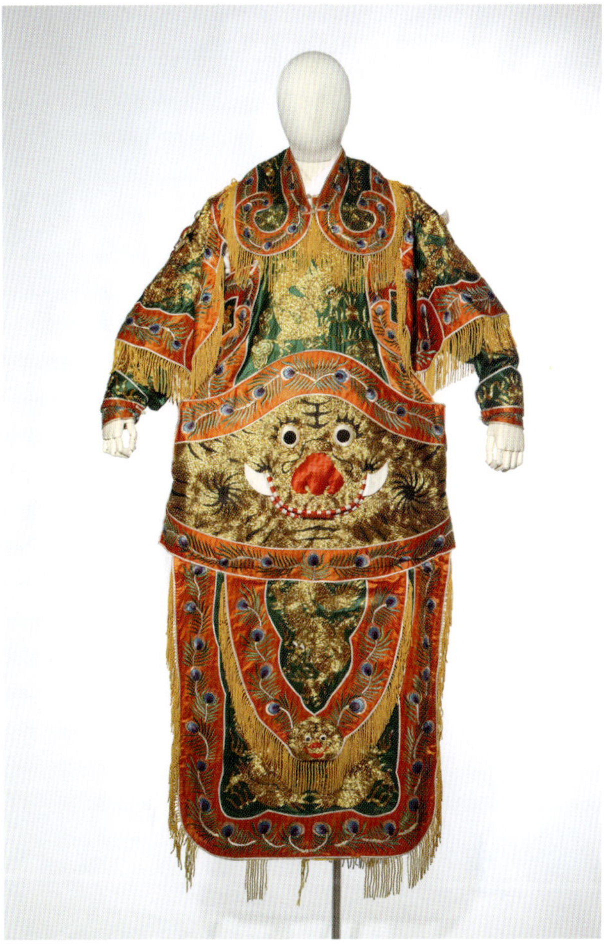

Kao

SHAANXI OPERA AND THE SHADOW PLAY

• Shaanxi Opera

Also dubbed Qin Opera or Qinqiang, Shaanxi Opera is a local Chinese opera that mainly thrives in northwest China's Shaanxi Province, as well as its neighboring northwestern regions, like Gansu Province and the Ningxia Hui and Xinjiang Uygur Autonomous Regions.

The genre uses the *bangzi* (date woodblock) as one of the accompanying instruments, from which it derives its other name—clapper opera, also known as Bangzi Opera.

Its repertoires usually feature such themes as historical events, daily life and love stories.

The roles in Shaanxi Opera cover *sheng*, *dan*, *jing* and

chou, and each has a unique style and numerous subtypes.

The performances are characterized by a simple, bold, exquisite, and penetrating, yet exaggerated style, and feature highly stylized movements from daily life. During the performances, there are some sideshows and stunts, among which are: horse riding, flame spitting, fire blow-out, fire stick performance, *lingzi* (peacock feathers attached to the hat) and *shuixiu* (long sleeves) performances, and *fan* performance.

Shaanxi Opera facial makeup follows a set of standardized methods of artistic expression, such as red to represent loyalty, black for righteousness and pink for treacherousness.

▸▸ *Sheng* in the Shaanxi Opera

It was said that a renowned Shaanxi Opera actor called Wei Changsheng went to Beijing and captivated audiences with his touching sound, impressive makeup and librettos in 1779. Shaanxi opera soon spread to Shanxi, Hebei, Henan, Shandong, Jiangsu, Zhejiang, Fujian, Sichuan, Yunnan, Guizhou and other provinces in China, and helped create such new operas as Four Big Shanxi Bangzi Operas and Hebei Bangzi Opera by integrating some other local operas.

- **The Shadow Play**

The Shadow play or shadow puppetry, with a history of 1,000 years, is a form of storytelling and entertainment using opaque figures moving on sticks in front of an illuminated backdrop. The Shadow Play prospered during the Tang and Song Dynasties and still exists today.

Characters and props for shadow puppet theatre are made from animal leather, treated to become translucent, then intricately carved and vividly painted, each with separate and movable parts.

A good shadow puppet requires as many as 24 procedures like scratching, rubbing, washing, carving and coloring, and more than 3,000 cuts.

Such traditional auspicious patterns created by virtue of homophony and trope as *Happiness, Wealth and Longevity*[1], *Five Boys Fighting for Top Prize*[2], *Kylin Bringing a Child*[3], and *Giving Birth to a Number of Children*[4] are adopted in the performance.

Lavish background pieces including architecture, furniture, vessels and auspicious patterns are featured in shadow puppet shows. Shadow puppet shows impress audiences with their vividness and refinement.

As the puppets and props are made of thin and lightweight materials, they will fit in one easy-to-carry box, ideal for a traveling vagrant performer.

Chinese shadow puppetry is unique also in the sense that it combines the rich tradition of Chinese folk art such as paper-cut with the indigenous theatre, capturing the basic elements of popular folk entertainment. It is the earliest form of motion picture screen art for entertainment, and also the embryonic form of cinematographic art.

Shadow puppetry has gained popularity in almost all

Shadow Play

parts of China. Over the centuries, different regions have all developed their own unique styles of puppet character design and performance techniques. Among which, donkey shadow play in Tangshan, Hebei Province, and cattle shadow play in Northwestern China are the most popular. Shadow puppetry in Tangshan wins the heart of an audience with its lingering music, exquisite sculpture, and lively performance.

Notes:

[1] *Happiness, Wealth and Longevity*: a picture composed of bat, deer and god of longevity, with a bat representing forthcoming happiness, a deer connoting a high official rank, and a god of longevity.

[2] *Five Boys Fighting for Top Prize*: a picture composed of five boys fighting for a helmet to show their virtuous personages, which depicts that the ancient people were eager for the children and grandchildren to glorify them.

[3] *Kylin Bringing a Child*: a picture that portrays a child riding on a kylin with a lotus in hand. Kylin, one of the "Four Divine Creatures", the other three being the phoenix, the turtle and the dragon, is regarded as a celestial animal, a benevolent animal and a symbol of auspiciousness. It is widely believed that the animal would convey the will of Heaven and therefore dictate the rise and fall of a dynasty, and that the child brought by the kylin would be a brilliantly talented person.

[4] *Giving Birth to a Number of Children*: a picture composed of lotus and osmanthus, or lotus, and a young child, implying "to give birth to a number of children".

(English Author: Liu Runzhi)

Chapter Thirteen Quyi and Acrobatics

XIANGSHENG

Xiangsheng, a popular comic performance characterized by humor and fun, and originated from North China's folk story-telling art, is made up of four skills—speaking, imitating, teasing, and singing. The language, rich in puns and allusions, is delivered in a rapid, bantering style.

"Speaking" refers to story-telling, ways of speaking and foreshadowing, including giving lantern riddles[1], reading duilian[2], making drinker's wager game[3], doing a word puzzle, speaking wordplay, doing tongue twisters[4], using language conversion, and telling jokes; "imitating" means to imitate the cries of birds, animals, singing tunes, dancing, and the expressions and words of different people; "teasing" means to make fun with jokes, arousing laughter, with one of the two players acting as the main speaker; finally, singing originally refers to a sort of Beijing folk song, named Tai Ping Ge Ci, which is a kind of Quyi (Chinese Folk Vocal Art) that appeared in the beginning of the Qing Dynasty (1616-1911) and gradually disappeared during the 1950s. Its tunes evolved from a Lotus Rhyme (Beggar's Song) popular in the downtown and suburbs of Beijing. Singing remains at the core of Xiangsheng, and is also a way of attracting audiences for the cross-talk comedian; it can also refer to folk melodies without accompaniment and local operas.

Xiangsheng can be performed in the form of a monologue, dialogue or a multi-player talk show.

The earliest form is performed by one person, and is called monologue Xiangsheng; it mostly involves telling jokes and humorous stories.

Xiangsheng

Dialogue Xiangsheng is performed by two actors, with one actor usually taking the lead as "Dougen" and the other playing the stooge as "Penggen". "Gen" refers to the words or expressions that bring laughter to the audience.

The third form of Xiangsheng performed by three or more people is called multi-player show, otherwise known as Qunkou (group performance) Xiangsheng.

It calls for one actor to say funny things, while others chime in and yet another makes them stray from the subject.

Of the three forms, dialogue Xiangsheng is the most popular and widespread.

"Baofu" is an important term used in Xiangsheng, which is the major element in a Xiangsheng piece that contributes to the comic effect of this art form. Therefore, we can say that there would be no Xiangsheng without baofu[5]. One or two instances of baofu in a joke are enough.

Xiangsheng art has made great advances in terms of content and skill, thanks to representative artists such as Liu Baorui, Ma Sanli and Hou Baolin.

Notes:

[1] Lantern riddle: a kind of riddle that is written on lanterns. It focuses on the literal meaning of a word, poem or object.

[2] Duilian: a Chinese couplet, also known as antithetical couplet, a pair of poetry lines that usually rhyme and may be written on paper, cloth, bamboo and wood.

[3] Drinker's wager game: a game which requires the loser to drink alcohol.

[4] Tongue twister: a kind of folk game, also called ji kou ling or rao kou ling in Chinese. A tongue twister is comprised of sentences and takes advantage of similar initial consonants, final sounds and tones to generate confusion.

[5] Baofu: literally meaning "package", it refers to the jokes arranged in a Xiangsheng or a rhythmic storytelling performance. In Xiangsheng jargon, the absurd and humorous showing of the punch line is called doubaofu.

KUAIBAN AND KUAIBANSHU

Kuaiban, once called shulaibao[1], shunkouliu or liukouzhe, is a variety of rhythmic talking and singing, or oral storytelling performance. It is one form of Chinese folk vocal art where storytellers accompany their own vocal performance with the rhythmic sound of bamboo clappers. Its stories are usually short, but are of a strong, rational and sentimental nature.

Kuaiban was originally performed by street entertainers, who made up semi-extemporaneous verses to make a living.

Drawing on their rich life experiences, shulaibao performers improvise their lyrics according to the things they see and the situations in which they find themselves, with some comparison between the present with the past, quoting the classics and adding comments to narration.

Over the years, numerous set lyrics and performance forms have been established. The stories performed by one actor or two, as well as those by three actors, are respectively called solo, cross-rhymed dialogue and group-rhymed dialogue. The form of cross-rhymed dialogue shares the original name of shulaibao. Different styles and dialects of Kuaiban exist in various places, so there are many kinds of tunes. Examples are Tianjin Kuaiban, Shangdong Kuaiban and Shaanxi

Zhuban, Bamboo Clappers Used in the Kuaiban Performance

Kuaiban.

Kuaiban has adopted the sentence structure of the seven-word antithetical couplet. Its script is rhythmical, easy and fluent.

Kuaibanshu was created in 1953 by Li Runjie, a famous Tianjin performer, by relating stories with complex plots and creating typical figures based on Kuaiban. He staged many excellent scripts, for example, *The Cock Crows at Midnight* tells the story of a sly and greedy landlord who imitated the crow of a cock at midnight to make the farmhands get to work earlier.

Notes:

[1] Shulaibao: a kind of quyi, which is popular in northern China, made by clacking bamboo clappers or ox hipbones. The basic sentence patterns of lyrics are characterized by a six-syllable first line and a seven-syllable second line, with the last characters of the two lines having the same tone and rhyming with each other.

GUQU

• **Dagu**

Dagu, literally meaning big drum, is a ballad singing art, usually accompanied by a drum and sometimes also a sanxian[1]. It is also called drum ballad, and is popular in the North and Northeast of China.

Dagu originated from the region of the Yellow River and prospered at the end of the Qing Dynasty (1616-1911). It evolved from a folk dance called Yangko originally performed by farmers and accompanied by a big drum at the beginning or end of a song.

Many genres of big drums exist such as: Xihe, Shandong, Jingyun, Laoting, Jingdong, Fengdiao, Dongbei, Anhui, Hubei, Guangxi, Jiaodong, Huainan, which are named after the geographical dialects. Categorized by materials of the instrument, big drum includes: tiepian dagu, muban dagu, meihua dagu, lihua dagu and qingyin dagu.

Dagu is usually performed by a standing performer, and its lyrics are mainly ten-character and seven-character lines; its subject matter varies a lot through such colorful contents as battle and love stories. Their tunes vary from region to region. The performances, which are characterized by highly expressive and variable gestures, cater to both nobility and commoners.

Guqu's golden age began during the Qing Dynasty and lasted until the 1940s.

Jingyun Dagu

From the 1930s to 1940s, guqu comprised three quarters of the programs on some of Beijing's private radio stations. Different special performances were put on to cater to audiences with different tastes, while Tianqiao (Bridge of Heaven) Bazaar, Gulou (Drum Tower) Bazaar and temple fairs in old Beijing took guqu as the main form. To celebrate an elderly person's birthday or babies' completion of their first month of life, people often held a tanghui of Dagu to entertain friends and relatives.

• **Tanci**

Tanci, also known as nanci (southern lyrics), literally means telling a story while playing an instrument and is mainly popular in southern China. Some storytellers perform solo (dandang) in dialects, playing the sanxian-banjo, while most performers have another storyteller to accompany them on the pipa[2]. Such duos are termed shuangdang.

Tanci

Suzhou Tanci shares the same style as that of Yangzhou Tanci.

There are a number of divisions in performance style that are recognized by the performers. These categories are basically divided into speaking, the narration of the prose part of the lyrics; biao, the narrative voices of the narrators; and bai, the dialogue of the characters; singing or tan, the seven-word antithetical verse sung to the tune of the sanxian and pipa; xue (laugh), the comical part of the lyrics; and playing, imitating or acting, the imitation of facial expressions, words, tones and actions of the characters.

At the beginning of the Qing Dynasty, the prosperous economy in Jiangsu Province facilitated the prevalence of Tanci in Yangzhou and Suzhou.

Tanci is popular in a relatively small area, exclusive to Jiaxing, Zhejiang Province to the south, Changzhou to the west, Changshu[3] to the north and Shanghai's Song River to the east. Tanci includes different genres featuring unique scripts, styles and performances to suit the tastes of different audiences.

Yang Zhenxiong and his brother Yang Zhenyan, born in a poor family, started their apprenticeships at an early age. For decades, due to their diligent study and good cooperation, they were able to create their own duo style, and gained their fame in Jiangsu Province, Zhejiang Province and Shanghai. Showcasing their artistic ability, they created *Wu Song* and *The Romance of West Chamber*, both of which contained great artistic effects, with the former rough and cadenced, and the latter soft in showcasing the fascination and charm of the female character.

From 1985 to 1988, Yang Zhenxiong and Yang Zhenyan accepted respectively an invitation from Shanghai University and the University of Toronto in Canada to give a forum on the characteristics of Tanci. Their interpretation of the language and other literary features of Tanci stunned students and artists home and abroad to awareness of the art form.

- **Danxian**

Danxian is one form of Chinese folk vocal art originated in northern China. It is accompanied by sanxian (a guitar-like three-stringed instrument) and an octagonal drum which is a kind of percussion instrument. It usually uses easy-to-understand popular songs.

Danxian

The easily understandable songs and lyrics of Danxian were collected from folk songs in the middle of the Qing Dynasty (1616-1911). During the reign of Emperor Qianlong (r. 1736-1799), soldiers who were Manchu by birth used Danxian to express their loneliness due to tedious life or the joy after a victory. After the unification of China in the Qing Dynasty, Danxian spread from the army into society. They were well received by the audiences from all circles. Later some amateur Danxian artists who were Manchu by birth became professional singers.

Danxian is a form of storytelling, especially the telling of traditional stories, such as *Baoyu Visiting Qingwen*,

Zhang Sheng Flirts with Yingying, and *Legend of White Snake*.

• Errenzhuan

Errenzhuan, originally an entertainment of farmers, usually consists of two people, a man and a woman, singing and dancing while the actor playing tricks with fans and the actress with red square handkerchiefs.

Also known as "Hop-Hop", Errenzhuan is a folk art with strong local flavor and features ballad singing and dancing. It is popular in Jilin, Liaoning and Heilongjiang Provinces. It combines local folk song, Yangge and dagu, and is funny and easy to understand. It is well received by the people of northeastern China, especially farmers. Its dance performance combines folk dance, acrobatics and fan and handkerchief skills.

Errenzhuan has some 200 years of history and is characterized by its humor and strong local northeastern Chinese accent. Originally, there were no female performers, and thus these female roles were played by men. Beginning in the 1950s, female performers began to appear in shows. Early topics included love stories, while in the last decade people's daily life has become popular theme.

Errenzhuan is one of the main genres of drama in northeastern China. Thanks to the contributions of Zhao Benshan, one of the most famous Chinese comedians, and his Liulaogen Local Opera Theater that enjoys great popularity in North China and other parts of the country, Errenzhuan has attracted more attention and is at the peak of development.

Notes:

[1] Sanxian: also known as Xianzi, is a traditional Chinese plucked string instrument with a long handle, square-shaped speaker, skin covered sides and three strings. It is widely used in solo performances, ensembles or as accompaniment in folk and opera music with rough sound, and is usually held in the arms when played.

[2] Pipa: a traditional Chinese plucked string instrument often used for solo performances and popular with Chinese people.

[3] Changshu: located in the southern part of Jiangsu Province, facing the Yangtze River on its north, is a famous city of Chinese history and culture.

PINGSHU

Pingshu is a folk form of oral storytelling in northern China, representative of non-music vocal art. It developed into an independent art form in the early years of the Qing Dynasty, originated from Beijing and popular in Hebei, Liaoning, Jilin and Heilongjiang Provinces as well as Tianjin.

Pingshu performers often sit behind a table, with a handkerchief, a folded fan and a small stick, the so called wakening-rod (xingmu in Chinese). With the xingmu, the storyteller grabs the audience's attention at the start and during intervals of the performance, in order to create tension or to strengthen the effect of the performance.

Pingshu is free from the limitation of setting, time and place, and depends on the impressive storytelling of the performers, so as to grab audiences' attention. Storytellers often add their own commentaries on the subjects and characters in their storytelling.

The repertoires of Pingshu can be classified into two types—one is not based on a script or scenario but focuses on traditional history; the other type is based on literary works such as *The Story of Yuefei*[1], *Generals of the Yang Family* and *Mu Guiying Takes Command*.

Most storytellers speak in mandarin, while a few use local dialects, as in cases of Sichuan Pingshu, Hubei Pingshu and Shandong Pingshu.

Lian Kuoru (1902-1971), a famous performing artist, established his own style. His method of storytelling, rhythmic, with a sonorous tone and a sense of humour, quickly made him popular. He was good at telling many repertoires such as *The Story of the Eastern Han Dynasty*[2] and *Romance of the Three Kingdoms*. After a local radio station broadcast his storytelling, Lian became a household name in Beijing.

Liu Lanfang, an outstanding female Pingshu artist from Anshan Quyi Troupe became famous because of *The Story of Yue Fei*. In it, she attaches great respect and passion for the patriotic national hero Yue Fei, and severely reprimands such treacherous court officials as Qin Hui[3]. As the original script contained much superstitious and feudal rubbish, she made bold cuts and edited it to retell the old tale with a fresh approach, which gives the audience a wonderful feeling and has a sensational effect. Undoubtedly, she is an innovative and unique performer.

Notes:

[1] Yue Fei: a famous patriotic general of the Southern Song Dynasty. He was a national hero who fought against the Jin Dynasty armies. In Chinese culture, he has evolved into the standard model of loyalty.

[2] *The Story of the Eastern Han Dynasty*: a historical novel written by Xie Zhao during the Ming Dynasty.

[3] Qin Hui: a Chancellor of the Song Dynasty, who is widely regarded as a traitor of the Han race for his part in the political execution of General Yue Fei. He has become one of the most important examples in Chinese history of an evil minister and is condemned by most people.

WUQIAO ACROBATICS

In China, Wuqiao County is known as the cradle of the circus and acrobatics.

Wuqiao acrobatics has a long history. The tomb murals of the Eastern Wei Dynasty (534-550) during the Southern and Northern Dynasties (420-589) unearthed from Xiaomachang Village, Wuqiao County in 1958, depict handstand, plate spinning and deft horsemanship performances.

Acrobatic art is deep-rooted in Wuqiao. There is a saying that goes like this, "Everyone, old or young, is good at acrobatics." However, it was after the Yuan Dynasty (1206-1368) that Wuqiao acrobatics prospered and gained a positive reputation.

It is recorded that most acrobats had to make a living by performing in the street or at a temple fair until a big stage was built in Wuqiao County 500 years ago. When lamps lit up the whole county of Wuqiao for three days during festivals, people set off firecrackers and performed acrobatics.

Acrobatics

Wuqiao acrobatics is composed of such items as animal training, stunt performances and aerial acrobatics, among which animal training is a traditional art covering: monkey, sheep, tiger, bear, horse and snake, with horsemanship performances being the most fascinating.

The horsemanship performance was first seen during the Tang Dynasty (618-907) and prospered during the latter part of the Qing Dynasty. Through many years of training, the tamers could exhibit many breathtaking skills while riding a horse such as handstands, standing and straddling and somersaults.

The stunts included plate spinning, vat pedaling, bowl flipping and trick-cycling. When performing vat pedaling, the acrobat freely rotates a vat of more than 120 kg in weight and one person sitting in, with a total weight of roughly 200 kg.

Aerial acrobatics included chair stacking handstand, wire-walking, and flying trapeze.

As the hometown of acrobatics, the sport is a lifestyle for the Wuqiao people. Both work tools and living appliances are used as props.

Today, the people of Wuqiao, both young and old, often possess astonishing acrobatic ability. It is no wonder that the county has produced many of the country's most famous acrobats. Wuqiao performers can be found in acrobatic troupes throughout China and across the world.

China Wuqiao International Circus Festival—CWICF, which is named after the famous birthplace of acrobatics—Wuqiao, Hebei in 1987, is a magnificent and comprehensive international meeting of "the circus".

Wuqiao has been honored one of the three magnificent and comprehensive international circus meeting places, following Paris and Monaco.

(English Author: Liu Runzhi)

Chapter Fourteen Chinese Medicine

YIN-YANG AND WU-HSING IN CHINESE MEDICAL THEORY

The theories of Yin-Yang and Wu-hsing came into being as early as the Pre-Qin Period and the most sophisticated forms were recorded in *Huangdi Neijing* (*The Yellow Emperor's Classic about Medicine*).

The theories of Yin-Yang and Wu-hsing are known as China's earliest materialistic dialectics as well as the basis of Chinese medicine.

Part of ancient Chinese philosophy, Yin and Yang are known as an opposing pair that depend on, restrain and balance one another. While Yin embodies dark, downward, cold, weak and passive, Yang connotes bright, upward, hot, strong and active.

The principle of Yin-Yang is applied to the Traditional Chinese Medicine (TCM) so as to interpret the complex correlations between parts of the body as well as between human life, nature and society. The balance between Yin and Yang is essential to the health and well-being of the body, while an imbalance would lead to diseases and abnormalities in human life.

Co-related with the philosophical concept of Yin-Yang is the theory of Wu-hsing (the Five Elements), known as the five basic phases that explain changes in the cosmos. Referring to earth, wood, metal, fire, and water, the five elements are believed to reinforce and constrain one another.

The Wu-hsing cycle serves as a principle in TCM that explains the functional correlations between the Five Zang Organs[1], the Six Fu Organs[2] and the etiopathology upon the Zang-Fu[3] imbalance. It also is useful in diagnosing and treating Zang-Fu diseases.

The concepts of Yin-Yang and Wu-hsing are put to use in TCM to explain the origin, physiology and pathological changes of human life and to guide clinical diagnosis and disease prevention. As a major component of China's medical theory, they have exerted profound impacts on the formation and development of TCM theoretical systems.

Notes:

[1] Five Zang Organs: heart, liver, spleen, lungs and kidneys.

[2] Six Fu Organs: large intestine, small intestine, stomach, gall bladder, urinary bladder and sanjiao (three areas of the body cavity).

[3] Zang-Fu: collective name in TCM for the internal organs of the human body.

HUANGDI NEIJING

Huangdi Neijing, or *The Yellow Emperor's Classic about Medicine*, a monumental classic in Chinese medicine, is attributed to the great Huang Di, the Yellow Emperor, who reigned during the middle of the third century BC and is canonized as forefather by the Chinese and Taoists.

Huangdi Neijing consists of two texts: the *Suwen*, "Questions of Organic and Fundamental Nature", and the *Lingshu*, also called the *Zhenjing*, "Classic of Acupuncture". Each is in the form of a dialog between Huangdi and his ministers. The *Suwen* expounds the changes of the natural world while the *Lingshu* elaborates the theories of Zang-Fu and Jing-Luo[1].

Huangdi Neijing highlights the relations between man and nature by taking the human body as an organic whole, while explaining the physiological and pathological phenomena to guide diagnosis and treatment.

▸▸ *Huangdi Neijing*

Huangdi Neijing has laid a primary foundation for the theories of Chinese medicine and its diagnostic methods such as the Jing, Qi, Shen[2], the relation between heaven and man as well as the theories of Yin-Yang and Wu-hsing.

A major component of *Huangdi Neijing*, the Yin-Yang theory elaborates physiology, pathology, disease and prevention, diagnosis and healthcare, integrating the exterior and the interior of the body by focusing on the system of the Five Zang and Six Fu. In the system, the Jing-Luo is the channel through which exterior and interior, and Zang and Fu are linked up, while the Jing, Qi, Shen are the mainstays that safeguard and dominate the whole system.

Huangdi Neijing detailed, for the first time in the history of Chinese medicine, the four diagnostic methods[3] of TCM. And it also catalogs various diseases especially fever, malaria, cough, gout and paralysis, whose etiology, pathology, clinical symptoms and therapies are discussed, many of which remain as guiding principles for clinical practice today.

Huangdi Neijing, which embodies dialectical materialism, has become a landmark in the history of Chinese medicine. Rich in medical theories, this time-honored therapy resource has functioned as part of mainstream clinical practice in Chinese medicine for more than two millennia.

Huangdi Neijing can also be appreciated as a literary classic as most of the writings in it present a good flavor of literature.

Notes:

[1] Jing-Luo (meridians and collaterals): in TCM, it refers to blood circulating inside one's body. A vertical line can be called Jing and a horizontal one, Luo.

[2] Jing, Qi, Shen (essence, vitality, spirit): often referred to as the Taoist Three Treasures in the human body, which are the essential energies sustaining human life.

[3] The four diagnostic methods: inspection, listening and smelling, inquiry, pulse taking and palpation.

HUA TUO—THE DIVINE DOCTOR

Hua Tuo

Hua Tuo (c.145-208) was born in Qiao County of Pei State (now Boxian, Anhui Province), and lived during the Eastern Han Dynasty (25-220). He is considered one of the most eminent personalities in the history of TCM, and an expert in several branches of medicine such as acupuncture, gynecology, pediatrics and surgery, earning himself the title of Shen Yi, meaning a divine doctor, and the "forefather of surgery".

At an early age, Hua Tuo studied and mastered many classical texts related to clinical and medical measures, astronomy, geography, philology, agriculture and astronomy. The deaths caused by famine and epidemics, and injuries from battles stimulated him to pursue a career in medicine. He traveled to many places in Anhui, Jiangsu, Shandong and Henan, collecting herbs and practicing medicine among the local people, reaping wide respect as a healer.

Hua Tuo was skilled in diagnosing by reading the patient's face. He would tell one man he came across that he shouldn't drink much, and help by prescribing a certain kind of medicine, and aid another getting rid of parasites that had gotten into his body. Once, he deliberately infuriated an official who had long suffered from depression, only to find the person getting well upon vomiting some dark blood.

In his later years, Hua Tuo was summoned by Cao Cao, chancellor of the Eastern Han Dynasty (25-220), to his court as Cao Cao was suffering from acute migraine attacks. Hua Tuo treated Cao Cao with acupuncture, and after that was asked to work as Cao Cao's private healer. But before long, Hua Tuo left for home with an excuse and refused to come back. Cao Cao became angry and ordered that Hua Tuo be jailed and executed.

To cherish the memory of this divine doctor, "Hua Tuo Temples" were built in many of the places where Hua Tuo practiced medicine during his lifetime.

Hua Tuo's biggest achievement was in surgery. He has been credited with inventing some anesthetic herbal formulas. One of them was a powder called Mafeisan, the basic ingredient of which was cannabis. This was administered with alcohol prior to operations. Hua Tuo was the first surgeon in China to use Mafeisan in his surgical operations.

Unfortunately, formula for Mafeisan was lost.

Hua Tuo devised a set of therapeutic Qigong exercises known as Wuqinxi, which was interpreted as the five animal (tiger, deer, bear, monkey and bird) movements. Throughout this set, actions of wild animals were imitated, in a group of physical and breathing exercises. This system was developed on ancient Chinese traditional physical exercises by following the theories and functions of the internal organs and meridians as well as the principles of the circulation of Qi and blood in the human body.

It was found that wild animals regularly perform certain exercises to build up their constitution and improve their skills. Indeed, regular exercises of this set demonstrated improvement of both physical and mental health to the practitioners.

ZHANG ZHONGJING AND *SHANGHANLUN*

Zhang Zhongjing

Zhang Zhongjing (c.150-219) was born in Nieyang of Nanyang (now Nanyang County, Henan Province). Living in the same period with Hua Tuo the "divine doctor", Zhang Zhongjing was laurelled as a "medical sage" in terms of his eminent contributions to TCM.

Zhang was an avid reader since his youth and developed a keen interest in medicine as he read about Bian Que, the earliest known Chinese physician (c. 500 BC), who advocated the four diagnostic methods. Later, he took on medicine by following Zhang Bozu, a well-known healer in his hometown, and reaped much both theoretically and practically, which contributed to his success as the most famous clinical physician of the time.

After decades of efforts as his clerical experiences increased, Zhang accomplished, between 200 and 210, his masterpiece *Shanghanzabinglun* (*Treatise on Exogenous Febrile and Miscellaneous Diseases*), the first medical monograph that integrated pathology, therapy, prescription and medicine in TCM and shaped the unique theory of differential diagnosis.

The book was lost through the chaos of war and was re-collected and edited by medical experts of later generations into two separate works—*Shanghanlun* (*Treatise on Exogenous Febrile Diseases*) and *Jinkuiyaolue* (*Essential Prescriptions of the Golden Coffer*). The first was dedicated to the dialectic analysis of typhoid and the second, internal injuries. The two books recorded altogether 397 prescriptions and 113 medicines with detailed descriptions of medicine processing, usage and dosage.

Zhang's work is recognized as the most influential on China's clinical medicine in the past two millennia and has remained as a TCM must-read for the medical students since the Song Dynasty.

In addition, medical researchers of later generations have contributed many writings explicating or interpreting this masterpiece by Zhang Zhongjing.

Memorial temples were built in different places of the country in honor of Zhang Zhongjing. The most famous one is the Medical Sage Temple in Nanyang, his hometown, which is now a historic site under provincial level protection.

LI SHIZHEN AND *BENCAOGANGMU*

Li Shizhen (1518–1593) lived during the Ming Dynasty (1368-1644). He was born in Qizhou (now Qichun County, Hubei Province). His grandfather was a healer, as was his father. In his youth, Li suffered from frequent illnesses and it was his father who saved him from chest tuberculosis. This generated in him a personal interest in becoming a healer. Available to him were the medical books his father used, and he often followed his father to the mountains to gather herbs and accompanied him on medical calls, helping to write out prescriptions as they were dictated to him.

During his childhood, Li became interested in medical classics and he kept consulting his father about miscellaneous diseases while practicing medicine himself.

Li Shizhen

Of all Chinese medical literature, those on Chinese herbal medicines are titled "Bencao" (medical material), which literally means plant roots and grasses as most Chinese herbal medicines are derived from plants. The most popular book on "Bencao" during Li's time was the *Shennongbencaojing* (*The Divine Farmer's Medical Material*), which came out during the Han Dynasty (206 BC-AD 220), as China's oldest medical material that recorded 365 kinds of herbs.

However, it became apparent to Li that the *Shennongbencaojing*, like other earlier *Bencao* literature, had failed to reflect the new developments of Chinese herbal medicine until the Ming Dynasty as there were errors, repetitions and omissions regarding identification and classification of herbal medicines. And moreover, available herbal medicines were on the increase and many more folk prescriptions and proven recipes were gaining popularity. Therefore, Li, in his early thirties, took on a massive project which was to become *Bencaogangmu* (*Compendium of Medical Material*).

Li consulted as many as 800 medical books. He visited woodsmen, fishermen, hunters and herb farmers, collecting folk prescriptions, and went to mountains and fields, gathering herb samples while growing medicinal herbs himself. Li's 30 years of painstaking efforts paid off as the encyclopedic *Bencaogangmu* was completed in 1578 when he was 60 years old.

The book was comprised of 52 volumes and presented 11,096 formulas, with 1,127 illustrations which helped identify the different types of medicinal herbs. It also detailed the nature, taste, places of origin, methods of cultivation and compatibility of different medicinal herbs which were then properly classified. The book was indeed a huge contribution to TCM.

Li found himself bedridden the following year after the printing of *Bencaogangmu* commenced. It was not until 1596, three years after Li's death, that the first edition of *Bencaogangmu* (the well-known Nanjing edition) was officially published. The book was soon spread across the world as it was translated into Japanese, English, German, French, Russian and Latin, being recognized as a masterpiece in the world's history of medicine.

THE FOUR DIAGNOSTIC METHODS

The TCM system includes four diagnostic methods: Inspection, Listening and Smelling, Inquiry, and Pulse-taking and Palpation.

The four diagnostic methods are based on the theory of integral treatment in TCM, which holds that as the human body is an organic entity, its partial pathological changes may tell the conditions of the whole body, and the pathological changes of the internal organs may manifest themselves on the body surface. By examining the symptoms through the four diagnostic methods, the doctor can find the possible cause, position, nature and internal relations of a particular disease, thus providing a foundation for dialectical treatment.

Pulse-taking

Though "the integration of the four diagnostic methods" is advocated by all practitioners, particular stress is placed on Inspection and Pulse-taking and Palpation in real practice.

Inspection means to observe the patient's outer appearance (especially the face) and his/her tongue, which are believed to reflect changes of the visceral functions in the human body so that a visceral disease can be detected.

Listening and Smelling involves two aspects: listening to the patient's voice in speaking, wheezing, coughing and vomiting to identify the pathological changes of the voice-related organs; smelling the patient's breath, and body odors (especially those of secretion and excrement) to diagnose diseases related to the internal organs, vital energy and blood, and body fluids.

Inquiry is to ask the patient or his/her company about the "when, where, why and how" of the disease, its history as well as the patient's lifestyle and diet. During the Ming Dynasty, Inquiry was extended to "10 Questions" about hot and cold, sweat, head and body, stools and urine, food and drink, chest, hearing, thirst, persistent diseases and their causes, so as to distinguish between Yin and Yang, the interior and the exterior, chills and fever, asthenia and asthenia, which are characteristic of TCM dialectical treatment.

Pulse-taking and Palpation refers to touching or pressing the patient's pulse points or certain parts of the body to learn about the pathological changes which are reflected by the flow of Qi and blood throughout the body. Therefore, in terms of TCM practice, Pulse-taking tops the list of the four diagnostic methods as the commonest.

Today, the four diagnostic TCM methods are still widely used, even as modern medical devices continue to be invented. Tongue Inspection and Pulse-taking, in particular, remain irreplaceable by any modern medical instruments.

THE BRONZE ACUPUNCTURE FIGURE

The two bronze acupuncture figures, the earliest of their kind in history, were cast in 1027 during the reign of Emperor Ren (1023-1031) of the Song Dynasty. They remain monumental in Chinese medical education and unprecedented in the world as a model in acupuncture teaching.

Wang Weiyi (987-1067), a famous acupuncturist who served the royal family, found while teaching acupuncture, that the acupuncture points mentioned in different medical books were inconsistent. To solve the problem, Wang, based on previous literature and his own teaching experience, drew a diagram of the human body, on which acupuncture points were marked. However, two-dimensional drawings like this were subject to damage and failed to show the acupuncture points exactly. Therefore, Wang finally decided to design and cast a three-dimensional bronze figure. His proposal was approved by the royal court.

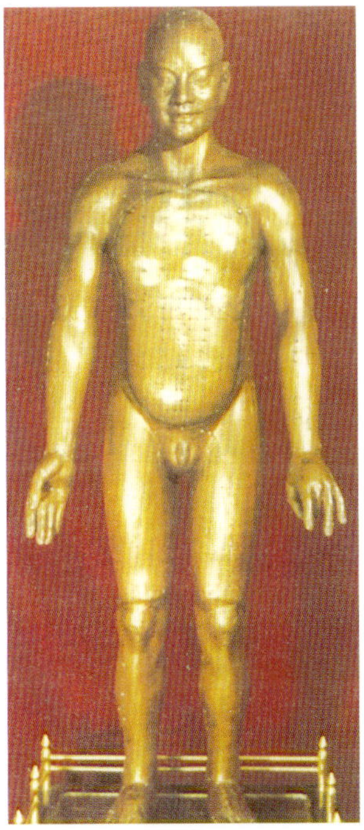

▸▸ Bronze figure

The bronze figure was designed into a full-size, hollow model with wooden internal organs set inside, and 354 acupuncture points exactly marked in small holes. This bronze figure, a 173 cm-tall strong young man, stood nude with removable pieces attached to the bronze framework.

The bronze figure functioned as not only a teaching model but also an examination tool. Yellow wax was applied all over the figure's body, hiding the acupuncture points. Furthermore, the inside of the bronze figure was filled with water or mercury. During the exam, students were required to prick the covered points. If they were not accurate in locating the points, the water or mercury inside would ooze out. The bronze figure was later used as a standard teaching aid in hospitals.

In addition to acupuncture, the bronze figure was also applied to anatomy teaching, which was some 800 years earlier than in the West.

In order to illustrate the bronze figure and specify acupuncture treatment, Wang worked out his monograph the *Illustrated Manual of the Bronze Figure and Acupuncture*, which was also known as a summary of the achievements in meridian acupuncture until the 11th century.

Wang had the *Illustrated Manual* which helped "read" the bronze figure carved on a dozen of stone tablets for long-term preservation.

The two bronze figures were kept in the Yiguanyuan (House of Medical Officials) and the Daxiangguo Temple respectively. They survived chaos and turbulence in 1126 when a rebellion broke out and Bianjing (now Kaifeng City, Henan Province), capital of the Northern Song Dynasty, fell to enemy occupation.

The bronze figure marked the biggest achievement in anatomy and acupuncture at the time. It was designated by the court as a "code" of meridian acupuncture for the medical circle, and the standards set with the bronze figure continued to be used during the following hundreds of years.

Since the creation of the Tiansheng Bronze Figure, many copies have been made. Also, historical records reveal that while used as a medical teaching aid, the bronze figure was appreciated and enshrined by medical doctors of the subsequent dynasties.

(English Author: Li Jing)

Chapter Fifteen The Culture of Money

SHELL MONEY, SPADE MONEY, KNIFE MONEY, SQUARE-HOLED COPPER MONEY AND COPPER COINS

Shell money, the earliest currency in China, appearing during the Xia (2070-1600 BC) and Shang (1600-1046 BC) Dynasties, was made of cowrie shells. Cowrie shells, which could be counted in pieces, were precious ornaments representing good luck. Moreover, they were solid, durable and easy to carry, so they could serve as money.

At the end of the Shang Dynasty and the beginning of the Zhou Dynasty (1046-256 BC), as the demand for currency was increasing, there appeared imitations in bone, stone, mussel, clay, clam, or gold, silver, bronze and gilded bronze.

Shell money was counted in the unit of "piece" or "peng".

Shell money was used until the last years of the Warring States Period (475-221 BC). In Yunnan Province, it was used until the early years of the Qing Dynasty (1616-1911). The influence of shell money on later generations can obviously be seen in Chinese characters. "贝" (shell), a character component, is used in characters concerning wealth, value and exchange, such as (买) 買 (buy), (卖) 賣 (sell), 财 (fortune), 货 (goods), 贵 (expensive), 贱 (cheap), 贩 (monger), 贾 (merchant), 赊 (credit), 赚 (gain), etc.

Copper coins had the edge over other coins thanks to their relatively uniform size, weight and value. The appearance of copper coins started the age of metal currency which was of great significance in the history of Chinese currency. As no copper coins had been found in use in any other countries at that time, Chinese copper coins are regarded as further proof of China's high-level civilization in ancient times.

Shell Money

Spade Money

Spade money, circulating during the Eastern Zhou Dynasty (770-256 BC) and Warring States Period, got this name from its shape. The coin evolved from bo, a spade-shaped farm tool used to hoe up weeds.

According to time and type, spade money was divided into hollow handled spade money and flat handled spade money. The former was used in the early years of the Spring and Autumn Period (770-476 BC). It was spade-shaped and retained the hollow socket by which a genuine tool could be attached to a handle. There were different shapes, such as pointed shoulder and pointed foot, square shoulder and arched foot, sloping shoulder, etc. Three lines existed on the reverse. Most of these coins were inscribed with characters, which could be a Chinese era[1], a number, or a place name.

Flat handled spade money was used in the Warring States Period. It had two feet, generally breaking away from the original shape of weeding tools. With flat top, there was no straight line on the coin. Place name and currency unit were inscribed on it. The coin was relatively light.

Just as its name implies, knife money is knife-shaped. It circulated in the Spring and Autumn Period in present Shandong Peninsula, Hebei and Shanxi Provinces. Knife money was first used in the eastern fishing and hunting areas and areas with a developed handicraft industry. It evolved from a tool called xiao. Earlier knife money was large and had a pointed tip. At the end of its handle, there was a ring through which thread could be strung. A crack existed on the handle. Later knife money was small, flat and blunt. Its tip was square or round.

Knife money could be divided into four types according to its size and place of origin. The first, Qi knives, were large knives attributed to the State of Qi. They were the most exquisitely minted currency during the Pre-Qin Period. The weight of each knife was over 40 grams. The second, pointed tip knives, were small knives minted and circulated in the State of Yan. They were light, and the end of the blade was sharp. The third type was Ming knives (also known as Yan knives), which could be found in the State of Yan. They were categorized into square clasp knives and round clasp knives according to the radian of blade. The last type was straight knives used in the State of Zhao. This small knife was straight and flat, with an approximate weight of 10 grams.

Square-holed copper money was a kind of coin minted during the Qin Dynasty (221-206 BC). After the unification by Qin Shi Huang, the first emperor of the Qin Dynasty, the economic contact between different areas became increasingly strong; however, it also brought great difficulty to the financial administration of the State. In order to change this situation, Qin Shi Huang abolished all other forms of local currency and introduced a national uniform copper coin. The square-holed round coin symbolized the understanding at that time: the heaven was round and the earth was square.

There were two categories—one was a gold coin counted in the unit of yi, equaling 20 liang, and the other was a square-holed round copper coin, called ban liang, with a diameter of 12 fen. The coin, with the inscription of "ban liang", circulated in China for over 2,000 years. It was the most influential coin in feudal society and was of great significance in the history of

Chinese currency.

The copper coin (Tongyuan), commonly known as "Tongban" or "Tongzier", was round and first cast during the Qing Dynasty. Its front bore four Chinese characters "光绪元宝" and the back was engraved with a dragon pattern. During the late years of Qing Guangxu reign (r. 1875-1908), "大清铜币" appeared on the back instead. During the early republican era, "中华民国" took the place of "光绪元宝" and "大清铜币" was replaced by the five-color flag and the eighteen-star flag. After the Japanese invaded China, they looted a large number of copper coins. Thereafter, the copper coin was rarely seen in circulation.

Notes:

[1] Chinese era: the Chinese ancients invented a form of measurement using two sets of signs: Heavenly Stems and Earthly Branches, in a certain sequence to calculate and record the chronological sequence of events. They matched "jia, bing, wu, geng, ren" of the Heavenly Stems with "zi, yin, chen, wu, shen, xu" of the Earthly Branches, "yi, bing, ding, ji, xin, gui" with "chou, mao, si, wei, you, hai" to form 60 pairs, circularly indicating the order of year, month and date. Heavenly Stems and Earthly Branches were originally used to record dates, and later were used to record years. Today, the Chinese lunar calendar is still recorded in this way.

GOLD AND SILVER COINS

A gold coin is money minted with gold according to certain shape, denomination, and weight. The history of minting gold coins is one that lasted for thousands of years in China. The earliest gold coin was "yuan jin"[1] used in the State of Chu. After unifying the currency, Qin Shi Huang minted two types of currency: a yellow gold coin, which was the currency of the higher class; and a bronze coin, which was the currency of the lower class. Thereafter, gold continually played an important role in the history of Chinese currency.

Silver Ingot

Silver coins, minted in the shape of a spade, first appeared in the State of Chu during the Warring States Period. During the reign of Emperor Wu of the Han Dynasty (r. 141-87 BC), silver coins called "bai xuan" were minted, but were soon abolished. In later generations, silver was cast into ingot, sycee and cake shapes. During 1573 to 1620, the western silver dollar was introduced into China. It was constantly copied by state enterprises and private enterprises during the Jiaqing Era (1796-1820) of the Qing Dynasty. In 1889, "Guangxu yuanbao" went into circulation, which was the earliest official silver yuan in China. Later, there were state founding commemorative coins with Sun Yat-sen's half-length portrait in profile in 1912, and the silver yuan with Yuan Shikai's head portrait in 1914.

In 1933, silver coins were forbidden by the Kuomintang government. When the PRC was established in 1949, the People's Bank of China issued Renminbi, the only lawful money in China. However, silver coins were still in use in some remote areas including Sichuan, Yunnan and Tibet. In 1951, when Tibet was peacefully liberated, the central government didn't stop the circulation of silver coins in Tibet out of the respect for Tibetan people's habits. On May 10th, 1962, silver coins were completely abolished by the

Tibet Autonomous Regional People's Government.

Notes:

[1] Yuan jin: the name of gold coins in the State of Chu. With a gold content of 95%, they were the earliest gold coins in China, circulating in Hubei, Anhui, Zhejiang, Jiangsu, Henan and Shandong

PAPER MONEY

The origin of paper money in China can be traced back to 119 BC when deer leather currency was officially issued. The deer leather currency already had the property of paper money. During the reign of Emperor Xianzong (r. 806-820) in the Tang Dynasty, there appeared da die[1] named "fei qian", similar to the present circulating bill.

Paper money began to circulate during the Northern Song Dynasty (960-1127). In 1024, the earliest paper money—jiaozi—came out. At first, jiaozi was a privately issued exchange certificate appearing in Sichuan. Jiaozi came from Sichuan dialect, which meant withdrawing money with two certificates. It was a handwritten finance bill like a receipt issued by some merchants; later, copperplate printed jiaozi was issued by 16 tycoons in association in Chengdu. Houses, trees, and people were printed on it; in order to prevent counterfeiting, it was signed and printed with secret marks. In 1023, the State issued official jiaozi, and limitedly circulated in the areas of Sichuan, Shaanxi and Hedong (present Shanxi). The jiaozi of the Northern Song Dynasty was the earliest form of paper money issued by the government in China and the first form of paper money in the world.

Official Paper Money of the Ministry of Revenue

During the Southern Song Dynasty (1127-1279), there were a variety of paper money, and huizi, which meant meeting, was the most widely used kind. It was a kind of paper money used as bill of exchange, which was first issued by merchants in a nongovernmental way and issued by the government later, circulating in the areas of Jiangsu, Zhejiang, Anhui and Hubei. Issuing organ and period (it would be changed after three years, namely one period) were printed on it. Huizi was rectangular-shaped and printed with copperplate in red, blue and black. Its denomination was fixed; at first, there was only a one-guan bill; later, 200, 300 and 500 wen bills were issued.

During much of the Yuan Dynasty (1206-1368), paper money was the only legal currency; all gold, silver and bronze coins were prohibited. In 1375 "bao currency of Great Ming" was issued, which was the only state paper money in Ming Dynasty. During the reign of Emperor Xianfeng of the Qing Dynasty (r. 1851-1861), "bao currency of Great Qing" and "official paper money of the Ministry of Revenue" were issued. In 1879, the first modern bank, Tongshang Bank of China, was established by the Qing Government, which marked the commencement of modern paper money emission.

Notes:

[1] Da die: commerce was developed during the Tang Dynasty. There was no paper money at that time, and it was very inconvenient to do business in other places with gold and silver; at the same time, silver coins were prohibited from leaving the country. Thus, the way of exchange came out, named "fei qian". Different departments of the army and government set liaison offices in the capital. If the merchant gave his money to the liaison offices and received a note,

he would withdraw the money in his local government department. This note was called "da die".

COMMEMORATIVE COIN

Commemorative coin is a kind of special coin issued to commemorate a major national or international event, outstanding figures, places of historical interest, rare animals or plants, and sports events.

Some commemorative coins are made of ordinary metal while others precious metal. Those made of ordinary metal are called ordinary commemorative coins while those made of precious metal are called precious metal commemorative coins. Ordinary commemorative coins can be used as common coins but can't be counted as circulating currency as they are made of gold, silver, platinum or palladium. In 2008, gold commemorative coins, silver commemorative coins and bronze commemorative coins were in honor of the Beijing Olympic Games. As they are delicately made and issued in limited edition, people kept them as expensive gifts or a kind of savings.

2008 Beijing Olympic Games Commemorative Coins

In China, the oldest commemorative coins, "Guangxutongbao", was issued in 1883 to welcome the establishment of Xinjiang Province in the following year.

In 1912, a series of commemorative coins were issued to mark the founding of the Republic of China by Nanjing Mint. During the early years, mints in Tianjin, Wuchang, Nanjing, Yunnan,etc. had issued a variety of commemorative coins bearing some politicians, which brought a climax in the history of commemorative coins. Those coins of different styles involved some special techniques which represent the highest level in China.

After the founding of new China, the Commemorative Coins on the Thirtieth Anniversary of the establishment of the People's Republic of China, the first of its kind in the history of New China, were issued in 1979. In the following years, more than ten different series were issued on various themes such as major events, outstanding figures, giant pandas and rare animals, the twelve animals of the Chinese horoscope, Chinese classics, inventions of ancient China, Chinese culture, religious activities, sport events, etc. Everything symbolizes the five thousand years history of China culture.

From 1984 to 1993, a series of commemorative coins were issued to commemorate those elites in different field such as medicine, military, science, geography, literature, water conservancy, etc. in Chinese history.

Each of the patterns was beautifully designed and vividly portrayed the characteristic of Chinese people-smart, wise, generous, composed, brave, industrious, persistent, etc. Even western sculpture skills were used on the coins, which are proved to be among the best of commemorative coins in modern China.

More special commemorative coins have been issued after China's reform and opening up policy was implemented. From 1997 to 1999, three groups of commemorative coins were issued for Macao's return to the motherland. The most surprising thing about these coins is that they bear three different languages, namely, Chinese, English and Portuguese. So far, it is the only of its kind in the world.

In 1980, when Commemorative Coins of the 13th Olympic Winter Games and Commemorative Coins of the Chinese Olympic Committee were issued, not a country's name but the nominal amount appeared on the front side. And the commemorative coins of the cock's year, the dog's year, the pig's year and the rat's year on Chinese lunar calendar issued in 1981, 1982, 1983 and 1984, and the commemorative coins of Chinese excavated bronze wares didn't bear the name of China either.

Commemorative coins issued in the special administrative regions constitute an important part of Chinese commemorative coins. In 2008, the year of rat on Chinese lunar calendar, Monetary Authority of Macao issued three types of commemorative coins of the rat's year, which is the first of its kind in the history. Designs of these coins are the same but the color is different. The figure of a rat is found on the front side while the back side bears A-Ma Temple, an ancient magical worship place in Macao.

(English Author: Wang Lihua)

Chapter Sixteen Cuisine

Chinese cuisine culture includes cooking skills, food and beverages, cooking and dining vessels, food customs, table rituals and deeper cultural connotations, wisdom and art. This chapter will cover a few representative cuisines such as Gong Ting Yu Shan, four different styles of cooking in China, flour food and snacks, traditional banquet, Chinese spirits culture and tea-relishing culture, in order to help the reader grasp the richness and profundity of Chinese cuisine culture.

GONG TING YU SHAN

Gong Ting Yu Shan, also known as "the food for the emperor", refers to various dishes prepared by government institutions responsible for providing food and beverage for the emperor, his wife and concubines in ancient times.

On such occasions as holidays, ceremonies, birthday celebrations for the senior imperial family members, memorial ceremonies, imperial tour inspections and award ceremonies, various banquets were thrown in the imperial palace or temporary residences. The royal cooks, therefore, had to rack their brain in order to satisfy the appetite of the emperor, nobles, ministers and concubines with their delicacies.

The exquisite and precious dining vessels, seat arrangement according to post ranks, solemn and elaborate dining rituals and warm atmosphere were all part of the imperial cuisine culture with Gong Ting Yu Shan at the core.

Gong Ting Yu Shan of various dynasties actually represented the top cooking style of that era.

As the best fruit of Chinese cuisine culture, imperial cuisine features quality materials, refined processing craft, eye-pleasing shapes and color and satisfying flavor.

The dishes, which can be boiled, roasted, fried and stir-fried, are extravagantly prepared and enjoyed following strict etiquette, a typical feature of imperial dishes during various dynasties. The imperial cuisine of the Qing Dynasty (1616-1911) especially bears this feature. Imperial Qing Dynasty kitchens had nine departments responsible for preparing different kinds of food such as dry nuts, fruit, snacks, gruel, staple food, food to go with sauce, soups, meat and vegetables; these departments composed a complete and huge system to prepare food for the emperor. Precious cooking materials were used and the style and shape of the dishes were given due consideration. The color, tex-

Manchu Eight Bowls

During the Qing Dynasty, cows and sheep were raised to exclusively supply milk, beef and mutton to the imperial family.

The grandest banquet during the Qing Dynasty was Manhan Quanxi, an extravagant meal that combined dishes of Man and Han nationalities. Historical records have it that this meal was usually prepared under such circumstances as triumphant return of the army and the death of an emperor, his wife or a favorite concubine.

ture, flavor and nutrients of the imperial dishes were carefully coordinated.

Imperial cuisine of the Qing Dynasty featured mainly Manchu, Shandong and Huaiyang cuisines.

The emperor's daily food list revealed that the number of dishes enjoyed by the emperor reached more than 1,000. Even a simple staple meat such as mutton can be cooked in more than 100 ways. The emperor's simplest meal had more than 20 dishes. Historical records show that the Qianlong emperor of the Qing Dynasty ate 76 dishes during only one day, without counting the snacks in between.

Each dish enjoyed by the emperor was carefully prepared. An example of this is Ba Zhen Gao (Eight Delicacy Cake), which was prepared for Empress Dowager Cixi. This cake was prepared with finely milled corn, millet, chestnut flour and eight differently flavored materials. The cake, small and delicate, has a light flavor and is easy to digest.

Furthermore, rice consumed by the emperor and his family fall into several categories such as yellow, white and red rice. Some of the rice was known as "tribute rice" and came from far-away parts of the country and some was harvested in the emperor's pilot field.

Among the diversified imperial banquets of the Qing Dynasty, Qiansouyan (One-thousand-men Banquet) was the grandest for its massive scale and expense. To showcase the generosity of the emperor, the imperial kitchen would mobilize all the tribute goods in preparing the meal. All the attendees of this grand occasion were formally dressed and directed by the person in charge of the imperial kitchen into two rows of seats arranged according to respective government ranks. The emperor would arrive with a fanfare of musical instruments and all officials would show their respect to the emperor by kneeling down three times and kowtowing nine times before various kinds of delicacies were served. By the end of the Qing Dynasty, the total number of dishes served at such kind of extravagant meal reached 200.

In addition to the delicious food and beverages, the beautifully shaped tableware, mostly made of gold, silver and jade, was of high artistic value.

Today, the imperial kitchen, along with the emperors associated with it, has become a historical record. What's more, Yu Shan has become a significant part of the rich Chinese cuisine culture.

FOUR MAJOR CHINESE CUISINES

Cooking in China is a culture, a science and an art. Traditionally there are four major cuisines in China, which refer to Shandong cuisine, Huaiyang cuisine, Sichuan cuisine and Guangdong cuisine. Different cuisines developed different local flavors according to their respective geographical location, climate, customs and specialties.

• Shandong cuisine

Shandong cuisine has enjoyed a long history. Description of cooking gurnard and carp caught from the Yellow River as food can be found in *Shih Ching* (*The Book of Songs*) and fried carp with sweet and sour sauce remains one of the most reputed Shandong dishes and is known for its special and tender flavor as well as refined preparation process.

Congshao Haishen (Scallion-flavored Sea Cucumbers), Shandong Cuisine

Shandong cuisine attaches great importance to deep boiling, braising, stirring and frying until the food is crispy. "Ta" is a unique cooking style from Shandong Province. In this cooking method, the main materials have to be preserved in condiments before they are covered with flour. The flour-covered materials are then fried until they achieve a yellow color. Another method calls for soup or condiments to be added into a pot and then the materials in the pot are braised with slow fire until the soup in the pot evaporates. Cooked this way, the main material of the dish can absorb and represent all the flavor of the condiments. Traditional and popular dishes include: Guota Doufu (Braised Bean Curd) and Guota Bocai (Braised Spinach).

Shandong cuisine features the flavor of green onion. Green onion slices are usually stirred in a pot before other materials are added. Even steamed, fried or roasted dishes such as Kaoya (Roast Duck), Kaoruzhu (Roast Suckling Pig), Guoshao Zhouzi (Fried Pork Joint) and Zhazhigai (Fried Mutton) often include green onion slices.

In terms of cooking materials, cooks in Shandong often choose freshwater fish, pork and vegetables. Various food resources are also available such as lotus root and common cattail from the Daming Lake, Jinan city; green onion in Zhangqiu city, carp from the Yellow River, bean curd from Taian city and vegetables from Beiyuan city.

Representative dishes of Shandong cuisine include Tangcu Huanghe Liyu (Sweet and Sour flavored Yellow River Carp) and Hongshao Zhouzi (Braized Pig Leg). Shandong Peninsula cuisine, a branch of Shandong cuisine, is well-known for its seafood dishes. All sea products such as sea cucumber, bird's nest, dried scallops, shrimp and crab can be cooked into various delicious dishes.

The representative dishes of Shandong Peninsula include Xiuqiu Haishen (Silk Ball Sea Cucumber), Hongshao Ganbei (Braised Dried Scallops) and Furong Xiaren (Shrimp with Scrambled Egg). The dishes of Shandong Peninsula are known for their unique cooking style in precious sea products. The local flatfish can be cooked into a dozen of delicacies with different cooking techniques. Sea food dishes such as Youbao Shuanghua (Sauteed Squid and Pig's Kidney), Hongshao Hailuo (Red Braised Conch) and Zhalihuang (Fried Oyster) are all unique and delicious.

Shandong cuisine refers to all dishes prepared according to Shandong style of cooking. In addition to Shandong Peninsula cuisine (featuring mainly seafood), there are also Jinan cuisine and Confucius Family cuisine. Confucius Family cuisine in Qufu features exquisite cooking material, fine cutting technique and strict cooking procedures. Characterized by tender, mild and original flavor, these exquisitely prepared dishes maintain a traditional flavor and are considered the top echelon of Shandong cuisine. The cuisine used to be consumed only within the Confucius Mansion and entered the dining market during the 1980s. Kong Shan Tang, a restaurant featuring Confucius Family cuisine, was established both in Jinan and Beijing.

• Sichuan cuisine

Known as the land of abundance, Sichuan prides itself upon unique natural conditions and time-honored Bashu folk customs. Since ancient times, the living habit of people in Sichuan has laid a solid foundation for the development of Sichuan cuisine. As an exquisite cuisine in the land of abundance and unique in Chinese cuisine, it easily outshines cuisines of other places in China. The name of the cuisine itself conjures up images of strong, hot, spicy and delicious dishes with diversified flavors.

Baochao Yaohua (Stir-fried Pork Kidney), Sichuan Cuisine

People in Sichuan have created various delicacies such as vinegar in Baoning city, mustard tuber in Fuling city, spicy sauce in Chongqing city, bean sauce in Pixian city and bean sprouts in Yibin city. With these condiments, cooks are able to prepare various simple yet delicious dishes with strong local flavor that are popular not only among Sichuan natives but also people across the country. Dishes like Mapo Doufu (Mapo's Bean Curd), Yuxiang Rou Si (Fish Flavored Pork Slices) and Gongbao Jiding (Spicy Diced Chicken with Peanuts) are inexpensive and delicious, making Sichuan cuisine the most popular cuisine among Chinese people.

In preparing Sichuan-style cuisine, various condiments such as salt, sugar and vinegar, pepper and sauces are often used to enrich flavors. The materials are often lightly fried and stirred within a short period of time with intense fire. The materials remain in a pot throughout the cooking process. Cooked in this way, dishes such as Stir-fried Pork Liver and Stir-fried Pork Kidney are often completed within one minute, which is all the time needed to render the dishes properly cooked and tender. According to the Sichuan-style cooking method, food and vegetables with long fibers such as beef, radish, bitter gourd and string beans are often deep-fried.

• Guangdong cuisine

Guangdong cuisine developed on the basis of Guangzhou, Chaozhou and Dongjiang cuisines (also known as Kejia cuisine). Guangdong Province, which is located in China's southern coastal region, enjoys mild temperature and abundant rainfall, and hosts of mountains, plains, rivers and lakes, all of which provide inexhaustible food resources.

Guangdong cuisine is different from other cuisines in China in terms of cooking materials, cooking method and the use of condiments. Thus "peculiarity" becomes the first and foremost feature of Guangdong cuisine. Guangdong cuisine cooking materials may include any living creature, and after being prepared and processed by the cook, become exotic delicacies on the dinner table.

The second characteristic of Guangdong cuisine lies in its precise use of materials, diversified use of condiments and extravagant decoration. Furthermore, it is very innovative. During the Well-known Dishes and

Delicacies Exhibition held in Guangzhou in 1965, more than 5,457 dishes were introduced.

Kao Ruzhu (Roast Suckling Pig), Guangdong Cuisine

The third characteristic of Guangdong cuisine is its strength of highlighting flavor and quality. The flavor of the cuisine changes according to the seasons. During summer, the cuisine takes on a light flavor while in winter the flavor of the dish becomes stronger, with the color of the dish changing accordingly. Guangdong dishes have a reputation for being tender, light and delicious while maintaining an inclusive flavor.

Well-known Guangdong dishes include: Kao Ruzhu (Roast Suckling Pig), Long Hu Dou (Dragon vs Tiger), Gourou Bao (Dog Meat Casserole) and Wucai Sherou (Colorful Snake Meat Slices). Restaurants like Beiyuan, Datong, Guangzhou, Dasan Yuan, Panxi, Taotao Ju and Snake Meat Restaurant are well-known restaurants in Guangzhou city specializing in Guangdong cuisine.

• Huaiyang cuisine

Huaiyang cuisine refers to the cuisine developed in Huaian (now Chuzhou city), Yangzhou and Zhenjiang, which are situated next to the Beijing-Hangzhou Grand Canal, and serve as transportation hubs that connect south and north and west and east.

Yangzhou, a transportation hub at the canal that connects the Hai River, Yellow River, Huai River, Yangtze River and Qiantang River, attracts cooking specialists from across China. One advantage is the availability of cooking ingredients: soy beans, wheat, coarse cereals and oils produced in north China and grains, tea, fruit, salt and seafood produced in south China. Another factor can be attributed to Emperor Yang (604-618) of the Sui Dynasty, who during his three visits to Jiangdu city, brought north China delicacies to the palace in Yangzhou city. Officials in other counties and cities prepared various delicacies as a tribute to the emperor, giving a chance for chefs in various places to demonstrate their skills.

After the Tang Dynasty (618-907), Yangzhou became home for wealthy businessmen, who attached great importance to the scale and style of their food. Most salt dealers had their own star chefs capable of preparing one or two top-class dishes. As a result, when a salt dealer threw a banquet, he often invited the chefs of other salt dealers to work for him in order to produce an extravagant banquet that was rarely seen. Huaiyang cuisine gradually developed as a result of the salt dealers' extravagant demands.

After the Ming (1368-1644) and Qing (1616-1911) Dynasties, Huai-style and Yang-style cuisines started to integrate. Finally, they merged to form a unified cuisine with both southern and northern flavor.

Huadiao Jiuniang Zheng Shiyu (Hilsa Herring Sauted with Huadiao and Fermented Rice Wine), Huaiyang Cuisine

Huaiyang cuisine is known for its slow-time cooking methods such as braising, covered boiling, boiling and steaming. This character is well reflected in well-known dishes such as Huotui Dun Jiayu (Ham boiled with Soft-shelled Turtle), Yan Xian Guiyu (Preserved Fresh Mandarin Fish), Huotui Dun Sun (Ham Boiled with Bamboo Shoot), Lizi Huangmen Ji (Chestnuts

Boiled with Chicken), Heye Zhengrou (Lotus Leaf Covered Meat) and Yangzhou Shizitou (Yangzhou Meatballs). For this reason, Huaiyang dishes attach great importance to soup and highlight the original flavor of the dishes. Complemented with other condiments and refined cutting skills, Huaiyang dishes appear elegant and imposing.

Yangzhou is also reputed for its production of various snacks featuring thin wraps, rich juice and fresh flavor. A common saying goes that Sichuan is known for its cuisine while Yangzhou is reputed for its snacks.

Huaiyang dishes have a slightly sweet flavor as a result of the use of both salt and sugar. This cooking method gives Huaiyang dishes a lasting and lingering taste. In addition, special attention is also paid to selecting fresh cooking materials, adopting fine cutting techniques, preserving original flavor of soup and materials and making the color and mold of dishes pleasing to the eye.

FLOUR-MADE FOOD AND SNACKS

With its diversified flavor and cooking method, flour-made food has enjoyed a long history in China, which dates back to the Neolithic Age when the millstone was developed to process wheat into flour. During the Spring and Autumn Period (770-476 BC) and the Warring States Period (475-221 BC), fried and steamed flour food had already appeared. Later, with the development of cooking utensils, ingredients, cooking methods and genre, flour-made food became more diversified. For example, dumplings, noodles, Lamian (Stretched Noodles), Jianbing (Thin Pancake made of Millet Flour) and Tangyuan (Glue Pudding) in North China and steamed Shaomai (Pork Dumplings), Chunjuan (Spring Rolls) and Youtiao (Deeply Fried Dough Sticks) in South China.

In addition, various snacks with strong local flavors evolved according to the products and customs of various places. For example: Jiaoquan, Mimahua, Wandouhuang and Aiwowo in Beijing; Xiekehuang and Nanxiang steamed bread in Shanghai; Erduoyan Zhagao (Fries of the Ear Alley), Goubuli steamed bun and Guifaxiang doughnut in Tianjin; Kaolaolao, Daoxiaomian (Sliced Noodles), Jiupian in Shanxi Province; pita bread soaked in mutton, beef soup and Guokui in Xi'an city; Lamian (Stretched Noodles), Youguokui in Lanzhou; Zaoguokui, Baitang Jiaobing, Jidan Budai in Henan Province; Kaonang in Xinjiang Uyghur Autonomous Region; Jianbao in Shandong Province; Congyou Huoshao and Xiehuang Shaomai in Jiangsu Province; Chongyang Ligao in Zhejiang Province; Yunmeng Chaoyumian, Reganmian and Dongpobing in Hubei Province; Longchaoshou, Dandanmian, Laitangyuan in Sichuan Province; and Guoqiao Mixian in Yunnan Province.

Shaomai (Steamed Pork Dumplings)

Flour snacks are more localized than cuisine and are closely related with the products, weather, geology and history of the local area. For example, Shaanxi Province is divided into three areas by the Qinling Mountains and the central plain stretches 400 km. Since the Han Dynasty (206 BC-AD 220), wheat has been a major produce on the plain and, as a result, a majority of the snacks here are made of flour. Shizimo, a snack dating back to the Neolithic Age and currently popular in central Shaanxi Province, was baked by ancient people in between heated rocks after human beings started to eat cooked food. The snack, crisp, appetizing, digestible and nutritious, is a good gift to give to friends and relatives. Other grains include rice (rice, sticky rice, millet and black rice), beans (soy bean, mung bean, pea, red bean, cow pea and hyacinth bean), coarse cereals (corn, buckwheat, broom corn millet and unhusked rice) and yams (potato and sweet potato).

In terms of cooking style, flour food can be boiled, steamed, fried, roasted, braised, soaked and baked. In terms of preparation, the food can be wrapped, cut, kneaded, rolled, sliced, stirred and stretched.

The number of flour-made snacks totals more than 1,000.

Among the flour-made snacks in north China, those made in Shanxi Province are reputed for their diversity, quality and influence. Dao Xiao Mian (Sliced Noodles), for example, is the most popular flour-made food in Shanxi Province and has enjoyed a history of more than 100 years. In the traditional way of cooking, the chef cuts a piece of dough resting on the hand. The cut noodles then fall directly into a pot containing boiled water. In cutting the noodles, the knife never leaves the surface of the dough which rests securely on one hand. The chef fully stretches his hand and arm. The noodles can be flat and triangle shaped according to different manipulation of the knife. During a noodle-cutting technique contest held in Shanxi in 1985, a competent cook cut the dough 118 times in one minute and technically could cut 25 kg of flour dough in one hour.

The sliced noodle is palatable and unique. The noodles taste even better if combined with Aged Shanxi Vinegar.

In addition, various unique snacks have been developed according to the local produce and customs. For example, most of the flour-made snacks in Beijing are derived from imperial dishes. Lizimian Wotou (Cornflour Steamed Bread) is one of the snacks once enjoyed by the Empress Dowager Cixi during the Qing Dynasty. Made with the best corn and soybean flours, the bread is steamed with sweet osmanthus flower and white sugar. One gram of flour can produce 100 pieces of delicious steamed bread.

Lizimian Wotou (Corn-flour Steamed Bread)

Yundou Juan (Kidney Bean Roll) used to be a local snack and legend has it that, on a hot summer day during the reign of Emperor Guangxu (r. 1875-1908) of the Qing Dynasty, the Empress Dowager Cixi heard someone hawking outside the walls of the Forbidden City and found out that the hawking had come from a kidney bean roll seller. Interested, she demanded to taste the kidney bean roll which immensely satisfied her taste buds. Thus, the kidney bean roll became a snack enjoyed by imperial family members.

Of all the flour-made food in South China, Shanghai-style snacks were recorded in history as early as the Southern Song Dynasty (1127-1279). After the Qing Dynasty, when Shanghai became a port city open to foreign trade, Shanghai's local snacks drew elements from other snacks made in different parts of the country and gradually developed into snacks with unique features. Snacks made of rice and flour became diversified and formed their own characteristics. For example, Xiekehuang (Yellow Crab Shell) is a flaky pastry made of fermented oil dough. It derives its name from the shape and color of the pastry; after being cooked, it looks like a boiled crab shell. During early times, all of the tea houses in Shanghai were equipped with a vertical roasting cylinder and a flat pot which were used to make Xiekehuang and Shengjian Mantou (Fried Steam Bread Slices), two snacks popular among tea house visitors. In the late 1930s, stores specializing in making the two snacks such as Huangjiasha, Dahuchun and Wuyuan prospered.

TRADITIONAL YAN XI

Yan Xi, banquet in English, was an occasion to host guests with food and wine. Before the Sui (581-618) and Tang Dynasties, people didn't use a table during the banquet. Yan, a kind of woven product made of thick material, was laid on the floor on which Xi, the smaller pieces of woven products made of thin materials were laid. During the banquet, people drank while sitting on Xi and the food and drinks were laid on Yan. Later, tables and chairs were used for the banquet and the food and drinks were moved to the dining table. Though round tables and square tables were adopted in the Ming and Qing Dynasties, the name Yan Xi was kept for the banquet and the seats around the table were still called Xi.

Traditional banquet has developed a complete catering culture and the delicacies on the dining table not only are prepared with pleasing color, taste and shape but are also named according to the occasions that they represent with the hope of blessings and good luck. A traditional Yan Xi has a complete set of dishes including wine, appetizers, dishes, main food, and beverages. The dishes should be served in a certain order.

In China, banquets generally are held on occasions such as wedding ceremonies and funerals. Due importance is given to style and serving order of dishes. Cold dishes should be served before hot dishes, while salty dishes should be served before sweet dishes. Expensive dishes should be served before general dishes. The first hot dish is the main and most expensive dish of the banquet and the last hot dish should be served together with the principal food. Soup should be served last in North China. The guests will know that all the dishes have been served when the soup arrives. Certain etiquette should be followed at the table. Since the Yan Xi itself is a process full of rituals and etiquette, social status, posts and age are given due consideration in entertaining guests so as to meet public expectations.

Yan Xi

Chinese people have a tradition of using square tables to accommodate eight people for a banquet. The seat facing the door is the seat of honor and should be reserved for the most important guest or the most respected person. The host should sit facing the most important guest. According to Chinese dining etiquette, the left seat ranks higher than the right. The upper seat ranks higher than the lower. The middle seat ranks higher than the side seats.

Currently, the tables used by various restaurants in cities are round and the number of people sitting around the table is also adjustable. In enjoying the meal, courtesies are often exchanged between the guests.

According to Chinese banquet tradition, the host should propose a toast to each guest sitting around the table round after round, while the guests should humbly decline the drink. Chinese people believe that only by entertaining guests in this way can the warmth and sincerity of the host be properly represented. In addition, a happy and jubilant atmosphere is often encouraged in throwing a banquet. The very scale and the atmosphere of the banquet, in most cases, are impressive.

The casual way of hosting guests is to invite several friends to the host's home and the hostess will prepare several dishes to be served with a beverage. Under this circumstance, dining etiquette and seat order are not important. A harmonious atmosphere, the host's warmth and a pleasant chat between the host and guests are the most important factors. In recent years, western style receptions such as cocktail parties and buffet dinners have been introduced to China. However, these kinds of receptions remain popular only in activities organized by the government and companies and are rarely adopted by the common citizens.

CHINESE WINE CULTURE

China is a country known for its production of spirits of various genres, colors and flavors. Reputed for their love of spirits, Chinese people, regardless of birthplace, age and nationality, are proud of the country's 1000-year spirit-drinking tradition. Drinking spirits was so popular among both the nobles and common citizens that they became drunk during ceremonial events, banquets, memorial ceremonies, wedding ceremonies, farewell banquets and festivals.

Since ancient times, men of letters in China have tended to compose poems while drinking. In his poem Duan Ge Xing, Cao Cao, a military strategist, statesman and writer during the Three Kingdoms Period (220-280), hailed Dukang spirits as capable of alleviating one's depression. Li Bai, a renowned poet during the Tang Dynasty, praised the flavor of Lanling spirits in one of his best poems, while Du Fu, another prominent poet during the Tang Dynasty, also sang high praises of Xinghua Cun Spirits in his poetry. Even prisoners facing execution would drink three bowls of spirits before being executed. These examples are living proof of the omnipresence of spirits in the life of Chinese people.

On many occasions, spirits serve as a cultural symbol and a cultural consumption. It also represents etiquette, atmosphere and mood. Unique Chinese spirits culture gradually took shape as history developed.

Spirits also play a significant role in traditional Chinese painting and calligraphy. Rumor has it that Zheng Banqiao, a well-known calligrapher and artist, was reluctant to paint for anyone. However, if one treated him with good spirits and dog meat and asked him to paint while he was slightly drunk, he would agree. Wang Xizhi, a reputed calligrapher known as the Sage of Calligraphy, wrote the powerful and unique *Lan Ting Xu* (*Preface to the Lanting Pavilion Collection*), when he was drunk. He wrote a dozen more copies after waking up but none could match the original.

Chinese people continue to attach great importance to drinking etiquette which has evolved over one thousand years. Drinking etiquette can be summarized as follows:

- Some spirits should be poured on the ground before drinking. In worshiping Gods, ancestors, mountains and rivers, the worshiper should hold the cup in hand and pray. A small amount of spirits should be poured on the ground three times before the rest in the cup is poured on the ground in a semi-circle. The wine is poured in a way to form the Chinese character 心 (heart), representing the true heart of the worshiper.

Proposing a Toast

- People should propose a toast to each other to show their respect. The man proposing the toast should drink first. Those who do not follow the etiquette will be subject to extra drinking. In addition, seniors and superiors should be served first. When the host is proposing a toast to the guest, the guest should hold the glass with two hands. When a toast is proposed by elders or superiors, the one receiving the toast should bow slightly while holding the glass with two hands. In clinking glass with other guests, one should lower his glass slightly to show his respect.

- Wager games are played during drinking as a form of recreation. These games were invented in China in order to enhance the communication between people. Jokes, puzzles, dice and finger guessing games are played so as to add fun to a banquet.

CHINESE TEA CULTURE

As the birth place of tea, China has thousands of years of tea-producing and tea-drinking tradition. Though tea has many names in history such as Ming, it was officially called Cha (tea) during the Tang Dynasty. However, people still called tea Ming when they treat tea-drinking as an art. Consisting of such procedures as tea set, tea water test, water-pouring, water boiling, tea brewing and tea relishing, the tea ceremony, together with tea-drinking and tea relishing, formed the tea culture in ancient times.

Originating in China, tea is prepared with boiled water and tasted to savor its natural flavor. Even the tea of the same quality can produce different flavor if the water, the tea set or the preparing techniques are different. Chinese people have attached great importance to tea set, tea water and tea brewing since ancient times and, as a result, rich experience has been accumulated. To make the best flavored tea, one must know the characteristics of the tea and master the scientific tea-making technique so as to fully showcase the inherent quality of the tea.

Tea drinking is an art, not so much to quench one's thirst as to enjoy the flavor and process. The latter is more important because, since ancient times, tea was tasted not only to distinguish its quality but also to savor the carefree lifestyle and set the mind free. When it comes to relishing tea, enjoying color, flavor, fragrance and shape often are more important than quenching thirst.

In modern society, people live a busy life. Sitting down and tasting a cup of tea amid all the business is a great way to relax and refresh oneself.

Entertaining guests with tea is a time-honored tradition in China. Many well-known men of letters in ancient China enjoyed sipping tea. Tea parties were often organized among them in order to make new acquaintances and compose poems. This practice has developed further since the Tang Dynasty. Lu You, a patriotic poet during the Song Dynasty (960-1127), loved drinking tea very much. About 320 poems and verses in his *Jiannan Collection of Poems* are about tea, making him the ultimate "tea poet."

Tea Set

During the Ming and Qing Dynasties, tea was not only enjoyed by upper class people but also popular among common citizens. Teahouses could be found in large numbers along the city street and the number could even match that of the taverns.

Serving tea is a must when hosting guests at home. Tea can also be given as a gift to friends and relatives. According to folk culture in some parts of China, tea-drinking is closely related with engagement and marriage. Many areas have the tradition of "engagement by drinking tea together." Acceptance of betrothal gifts given by the girl's family is called "Chi Cha (drinking tea)" and newlyweds should present elders with a cup of tea during the wedding ceremony to show their respect. The gift given by the elders to the newlyweds is called "Cha Bao (Tea Bag)". For example, in *A Dream of Red Mansions*, Wang Xifeng asked Lin Daiyu: "Why don't you marry Baoyu after drinking our family's tea?"

The points mentioned above show the close relationship between tea and Chinese people's daily life.

(English Author: Fan Tao)

Chapter Seventeen Wushu —Chinese Martial Arts

Wushu, or Chinese martial arts when referring to the entire spectrum of styles and systems, boasts a long history. A gem of the Chinese culture, Wushu embodies well-knit philosophical thinking and an integrated system of skills that help miraculously in protecting the body from diseases while nourishing the mind with peace and tranquility. It has close ties with the military, religion, education, medicine, and art and recreation, featuring intelligence and wisdom as well as aesthetic temperament of the Chinese people.

CHINESE BOXING

Among the most popular styles of Wushu is Chinese boxing, which was embraced by the folks after the Song Dynasty (960-1279) and prevailed in the Ming (1368-1644) and Qing (1616-1911) Dynasties. It is an art of attack and defense that mainly features kicking and striking.

Chinese boxing is generally classified into the Southern and Northern styles on a geographical basis.

Southern styles are distinguished by strikes and punches. Physically speaking, for the southerners, strength is generally derived from the fists, while the Northern styles are well known for their high and rapid kicks; thus, strength is developed mostly in the legs, hence the phrase "Nanquan Beitui" (Southern fist and Northern leg). Both styles feature rapid motion movement shifts.

In addition to this Southern-Northern classification, Chinese boxing throughout its long history has also fallen into several major systems on a regional basis. They are, among others, the Shaolin around Henan, Hebei and Shandong on the Yellow River downstream; the Southern around Fujian and Guangdong; the Emei around Sichuan; the Wudang around Hubei, Jiangsu and Sichuan, the Tai Chi around Henan and Beijing, and the Pa Kua Chang around Beijing.

The Shaolin system, the earliest and best-known, is said to originate from the famed Shaolin Temple on Henan Province's Mount Songshan, which was built during the Southern and Northern Dynasties (420-589).

The Buddhist monk Bodhidharma from South India was credited as influencing the Shaolin system. In 525, Bodhidharma came to the Shaolin temple to teach Buddhism, where he saw that the monks were vulnerable to fatigue because of long-time meditation and the attacks of venomous serpents and wild beasts. So

Tai Chi

to promote health and self-defense, he developed a series of exercises based on animal movements, dubbed "Bodhidharma 18 Hands", thereby initiating the practice of martial arts for fitness at the Shaolin Temple.

The Shaolin Temple became known for the practice of martial arts during the end of Sui (581-618) and early Tang (618-907) period. One day, Li Shimin (599-649), then titled Duke of Qin, was besieged in Baigezhuang Village. Thirteen Shaolin monks, all highly skilled in martial arts, came to his rescue. Later when Li became Emperor of Tang, as a reward, he entitled the Shaolin Temple as the "No. 1 Temple under Heaven", and the Shaolin Temple was authorized to keep monk soldiers. The Shaolin system has thereupon established its reputation as a unique representative of Chinese martial arts.

The Shaolin style, known specifically as Shaolin Kung Fu, originated from the "Shaolin Five Animal Fists": the Shaolin Dragon, which nourishes the mind; the Shaolin Tiger, which strengthens the bones; the Shaolin Panther, which requires strength; the Shaolin Snake, which grants energy; the Shaolin Crane, which tests vital essence. When well versed in these five Fists, one can develop mental and physical agility and defeat opponents with only a minimum effort.

The Wudang style, which is classified as Taoist internal art, focuses on awareness of the spirit, mind, energy and the use of relaxed leverage rather than muscular tension. It is a style of elegance, ease, serenity and flexibility.

What is noteworthy is the distinction between the Shaolin and the Wudang as two major groups of Wushu: the external and the internal, which, in the final analysis, represent the two different religious thoughts of Buddhism and Taoism.

The term "Tai Chi" presented itself in the *Tai Chi Treatise*, authored by Wang Zongyue, a legendary Taoist monk credited with devising Tai Chi, in 1852. In agreement with the philosophical thinking of Taoism, Tai Chi is practiced for both defense training and health benefits with particular attention paid to the incoming and outgoing breaths. Featuring soft and slow movement plus meditation, Tai Chi distinguishes itself from other martial arts with non-violent techniques.

WUSHU FOR HEALTH PRESERVATION

A major function of Wushu lies in health preservation. People practice Wushu not only for self-defense but for health and longevity.

Wushu in its evolution has been influenced by and integrated with the traditional Chinese regimen until establishing itself as a set of body building exercises and a type of therapy. In this sense, Wushu advocates activating the meridians, circulating vigor and blood and balancing Yin and Yang under the principles of integration between hardness and softness, motion and stillness, falseness and trueness, and openness and closeness, in an effort to enhance health of the human body.

The traditional medical concepts of Jing Qi Shen and Jing-Luo help enrich the essence of Wushu: "to practice spirit and soul internally and muscles and bones externally", so to speak. Wushu as a health regimen attaches importance to guiding for limb movements and balance between the motional and the still, between the internal and the external, between the form and the spirit as well as between practicing and meditating and recuperating. All this makes Wushu an art that integrates attack-defense and health preservation, and a major component of Chinese Wushu culture with the following main features:

- Balancing between the form and the spirit. According to Chinese medical theories, Qi, or vitality, is the vital basis of human life. Yin and Yang as two forms of Qi, keep flowing and moving inside and outside the human body, and the balance and harmony between Yin and Yang in the human body is a general indication of health and a basic requirement for health preservation and longevity. Hence Wushu advocates balance between the form and the spirit. The form refers to the body while the spirit, the mind, disposition, consciousness and thoughts which are outward manifestations of Qi. Balancing between the form and the spirit means maintaining a healthy body while conserving mental energy for the harmony between Yin and Yang and the development of life potential in the human body.

- Exercising for the benefit of internal organs. In the practice of Wushu as a health regimen, internal functions of the human body such as thoughts, breaths, Zang-Fu, Jing-Luo and blood vessels are emphasized with a view to ensuring internal strength of the human body. A representative of this is Internal Boxing which includes, among others, Hsing Yi, Tai Chi, Pa Kua and Yi, with the exercise's effects laid on the strength and comfort of the internal organs rather than development of the muscles. In terms of skill, Chinese Boxing is broken down into External Style and Internal Style. External Style, originating from the Shaolin Boxing, advocates powerful strikes, agility and fast moves, focusing on strong arm and leg muscles, from which strength is derived. In addition to Shaolin, Southern Boxing is also a typical of External Style. Internal Style emphasizes breathing techniques, softness, balance and control, with strength developing mostly in the torso and legs. The best-known form of the Internal Style is Tai Chi Boxing, which concentrates on the use of Qi, the internal strength. While External Boxing is more suitable for young practitioners and sports competitions, Internal Boxing, which incorporates physical training, medical treatment and artistry, is more helpful as a course of therapy.

Wuqinxi

- Guiding for limb movement. This therapy which goes with that of "exhaling the stale and inhaling the fresh" boasts a long history. In the *Map of Guiding Therapy*, a silk painting unearthed in 1973 from Tomb No. 3 of Mawangdui, an archaeological site in Changsha, Hunan Province, 44 movement gestures of different figures can be seen, some of them with while others without implements in hand. In the map are also a number of imitated motions of animals. Till the Wei and Jin Dynasties (220-420), the guiding therapy had incorporated limb movement, exhaling-inhaling and inner meditation, as well as massage and saliva swallowing. Hua Tuo's Wuqinxi, for example, is good for blood flow, mental vigor and physical agility and fitness, while Internal Tai Chi, which focuses on the tapping of "energy within" through meditating and breathing, helps build muscular strength and dispel diseases.

Thanks to its value in terms of health preservation, Wushu has been widely acknowledged as a physical culture as well as a major oriental school of physical fitness.

From the Song Dynasty through the Ming and Qing Dynasties, the guiding therapy was getting more pragmatic and simple. The most typical were the Eight Trigrams Boxing of the Song Dynasty, the Twelve Trigrams Boxing, the Sixteen Trigrams Boxing and Nine Massage Therapies of the Qing Dynasty, as well as Tai Chi Boxing which features "guiding the Qi for harmony and the body for softness"— a cardinal principle of the traditional guiding therapy.

WUSHU AND THE ART OF WAR

Sun Tzu

Ancient China saw frequent wars which brought forth many military strategists and their writings on the art of war. Quite a number of terms popular with the Chinese are derived from these writings which remain second to none in the world for their substantial contents. *Hanshu • Yiwenzhi*, China's earliest book on bibliography, for example, covers 790 pieces of writing on 53 different schools of strategics. These books, rooted in the fertile soil of traditional Chinese culture, integrate the art of attack and defense in Wushu with the military strategies and tactics and have helped turn out great generals such as Yue Fei and Qi Jiguang. As the old proverb goes, he who practices Wushu must know the art of war; he who knows no art of war must never practice Wushu—an indication of the close ties between Wushu and the art of war.

The close ties between Wushu and the art of war were witnessed as early as in the Pre-Qin Period. *Chuang Tsu: Swordsmanship* covers tactics like luring the enemy, meeting an emergency and no striking until the opponent does so.

The best known among the books on military strategies and tactics is *The Art of War*, written by Sun Tzu, a military strategist, during the Spring and Autumn Period (722-476 BC).

The Art of War which is loaded with military and philosophical sayings such as "Know thy self, know thy enemy. A thousand battles, a thousand victories," "If he is secure at all points, be prepared for him; If he is in superior strength, evade him," and "Attack him where he is unprepared, appear where you are not expected". These sayings have exerted great influence on the theories of attack and defense in Wushu and have been well received as cardinal principles for Wushu practice.

Also influencial on Wushu are such statements as "There is no instance of a country having benefited from prolonged warfare", and "A war brings great loss to both the loser and the winner".

In ancient China, strategists believed that only when in a certain formation or battle array could an army fight with effectiveness. Troops were arrayed in certain patterns according to their positions and strengths as well as those of their opponents in order to facilitate hand-to-hand combat with short weapons, unified command and coordinated movement.

Among the well-known battle arrays were the Pa Kua Array[1], the Star Array[2] and the Yuanyang Array[3].

According to the *Romance of the Three Kingdoms*, when Liu Bei and his troops from the Shu State were pursued by the Wu troops, Zhuge Liang's "Pa Kua Array" came to his rescue. Zhuge arranged for the enemy to be trapped in his "Pa Kua Array". The Wu troops of hundreds of thousands of soldiers found themselves lost in flying stones, and it took them quite some time before they were directed and found their way out.

Notes:

[1] The Pa Kua Array: also called the "Eight Arrays", devised by Sun Tsu during the Warring States Period (475-221 BC). A general was positioned in the middle, with a squad of regular soldiers on each of the four sides and four squads of mobile soldiers between those of the regular soldiers, forming "Eight Arrays" which could be assembled into one or split into 64 arrays.

[2] The Star Array: adopted by Yue Fei, a general during the Southern Song Dynasty (1127-1279). The soldiers were arrayed like stars, which meant they would scatter to let the enemy come away empty-handed. And as soon as the enemy troops retreated, they gathered together for a surprise attack.

[3] The Yuanyang Array: created by Qi Jiguang, a general who fought against Japanese pirates along the east coast of China during the Ming Dynasty (1368-1644). Soldiers were arrayed into three groups. When the enemy was 100 steps away, the first group used firearms; when the enemy was 60 steps away, the second group shot arrows; when the enemy was 10 steps away, the third group charged with swords and spears.

THE 18 TYPES OF WEAPONS

The term "18 Types of Weapons" has prevailed in Chinese martial arts circles since ancient times. The 18 types of weapons commonly identified in the Wushu arsenal are dao, shuo, qiang, jian, ji, fu, yue, gou, cha, bian, jian, chui, shu, tang, gun, bang, zhua, and liuxing.

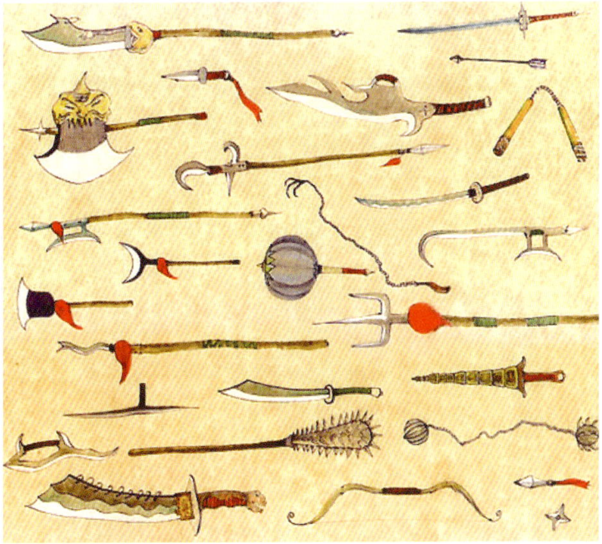

18 Types of Weapons

It was in 107 BC of the Western Han Dynasty (206 BC-AD 220) that the 18 types of weapons were sorted out and authorized by Emperor Wu. And during the Three Kingdoms Period (220-280), they were renamed and ranked into "nine long" (dao, mao, ji, shuo, tang, yue, gun, qiang, cha) and "nine short" (fu, ge , dun , jian, bian, jian, jian, chui, zhua).

Roughly speaking, the 18 types of weapons fall into five groups in terms of form: the saber-like, the spear-like, the sword-like, the axe-like, and the staff-like. Some of them are hidden weapons of two kinds: short and small types and soft and rope types.

According to their different features and functions these weapons were used by different people. In Chinese martial arts novels, delicate female figures and gentle male figures are seen with the sword which is light and flexible, while men with a strong build and rough character are equipped with heavy weapons such as the saber or mace.

In classical Chinese novels, particular weapons symbolize particular figures: the falchion stands for Guan Yu, the halberd for Lü Bu and the golden cudgel for Sun Wukong the Monkey King, all known to each and every Chinese household.

The 18 types of weapons have, throughout history, witnessed survival or elimination as a result of warfare. Some of them have been exclusively used by guards of honor, while others have been reserved for common folk. However, the use of these weapons has become a special art that remains on the Chinese drama and acrobatics stage, and some weapon skills have been handed down to this day for popular sporting events.

The use of weapons in Wushu is totally different from that in war. In battlefield fighting, weapons are used in a very real sense, but in Wushu which advocates precise swordsmanship for every single movement of the two individual opponents, weapons can be used on a real-and-false basis.

THE 18 TYPES OF FEAT

The "18 Types of Feat" is a technical term in Chinese Wushu, which is commonly seen in classical Chinese operas and novels and folk performances such as storytelling, in which "be well-versed in 18 types of feat" is a compliment for military officers with superb skills. Like the term "having eight dou (decalitres) of talent" which figuratively describes a man of great learning, "be well-versed in 18 types of feat" is now used to address a man of great ability.

Literally, the "18 Types of Feat" refers to the skills in using the 18 types of weapons. Like the "18 Arhats" and the "108 Outlaw Heroes", the "18 Types of Feat" also has its exaggerated and emphatic use in addition to its literal use. It implies "numerous", as in Chinese tradition, "nine" is taken as the maximum number, and "nine" together with its multiples indicates a large number of things.

In classical Chinese novels, outlaw heroes are depicted as proficient in using each and every weapon of the 18 types. Those in the *Heroes of the Marshes* (*Shuihu Zhuan*), for instance, are a typical example.

Another example is the well-known Generals of the Yang family during the Song Dynasty (1127-1279).

The 18 Types of Feat is also embodied in the martial arts of Shaolin Zen Buddhism directly handed down by Bodhidharma.

Dharma Master Hai Deng (1902-1989) of the Shaolin Temple was well-versed in the 18 types of feat. Beginning in the 1950s, he gained recognition, especially for his skills in using the sword, three-section cudgel, free fighting and Qigong, thanks to which he remained physically fit even into his eighties

Strictly speaking, an ancient hero tends to be skilled in using one or two types of weapons only, each, however, is uniquely categorized. The spear, for example, is comprised of dozens of forms such as long spear and short spear.

As for spear skills, a large variety exists. The most famous are, among others, those of Zhao Yun, Yue Fei and Generals of the Yang Family. Li Kui, in the *Heroes of the Marshes*, is known for his adept use of the broad axe.

In addition, many of the outlaw heroes in Water Margin are nicknamed in association with weapons that mark their identity and personality.

(English Author: Li Jing)

Chapter Eighteen Cultural Exchanges with the World

In history, three major instances of cultural exchange between China and the West have been recorded.

The first of these came during the Han Dynasty (206 BC-AD 220), beginning with Zhang Qian's historic creation of the "Silk Road" to link China with Central Asia and Europe, with China's silk products, smelting foundry and water conservancy technology introduced to Central Asia, Korea and Europe; Chinese characters to Korea, and the Confucian scriptures to Japan. At the same time, Buddhism, ivory, perfume, jewelry and plant species were introduced to China.

The second instance was seen during the Tang (618-907), Song (960-1279) and Yuan (1206-1368) Dynasties, when paper-making and printing techniques, textiles, the compass and gunpowder were all introduced to Korea, Japan, India, the Arab countries and Europe, while sugar-refinery techniques, astronomy, medicine, music, dance and Buddhism were brought to China.

The late Ming (1368-1644) and early Qing (1616-1911) Dynasties, with the influx of foreign missionaries, experienced yet another surge of cultural and trade exchanges between China and the outside world. *Bencaogangmu* (*Compendium of Medical Material*, compiled by Li Shizhen) and *Exploitation of the Works of Nature* (compiled by Song Yingxing) were translated into different languages, advanced technology and culture were introduced to the Malay Archipelago, the Malay Peninsula and Indonesia—Southeast Asia, while the potato, sweet potato, corn and tobacco, which were native to America, were introduced to China.

National strength constitutes a prerequisite of international exchange, whereas exchanges between countries and regions are indications of the development of human civilization. The afore-mentioned examples are but a few among many in an attempt to present the vastness and grandeur of Sino-foreign exchanges in history.

JIANZHEN AND HIS VOYAGES TO JAPAN

Jianzhen was born in 688 in what is now the city of Yangzhou, Jiangsu Province. His father was a merchant and a pious believer in Buddhism. Influenced by his father, Jianzhen developed an eager interest in Buddhism. When he was 14 years old, he became a monk at the Dayun Temple in Yangzhou. At 21, he went to Chang'an and Luoyang to study the Buddhist Scriptures, and was officially initiated into monkhood

Jianzhen

a year later at a temple in Chang'an. At 26, he returned to Yangzhou to become a Great Master at the Daming Temple (now called Fajing Temple[1]). A man of great learning and lofty virtues, he became widely known at the age of 45, and then initiated more than 40,000 people into monkhood.

The periods of the Sui (581-618) and Tang Dynasties registered increasing exchanges between the people of China and Japan. Starting from 630.until 894 during the Tang Dynasty, Japan sent a total of 12 envoy missions to China, with each envoy including more than 100 members, and on one occasion, 650 members. Many of these envoys came to study at the Imperial College, the institution of highest learning during the Tang Dynasty. They lived in China for more than 20 years, while some stayed permanantly to become officials within the dynastic government.

Influenced by China, Japan made a great effort to advocate and spread Buddhism among its people. They built Buddhist temples, dispatched monks to China to study Buddhism, and invited Chinese eminent monks to Japan to impart precepts. Entrusted by the Mikado, the emperor of Japan, two Japanese monks, Rongrui and Puzhao, who were then studying in China, made a special trip to the Daming Temple in Yangzhou in 742 to invite Jianzhen to come to disseminate the Buddhist scriptures in Japan.

The 54-year-old Jianzhen happily accepted the invitation. But one of his pupils, named Xiangyan, was not as confident about this mission: "Japan is at the other end of the sea. Few could survive such a dangerous journey," he expressed his fear. But Jianzhen was determined, saying, "A person's life is less important than spreading Buddhism. You have your worries, but I've made up my mind to go!" Encouraged by Jianzhen's firmness of will, his pupils all promised to follow their master.

Though very confident, Jianzhen failed in five attempts to make a voyage to Japan. However, he was not discouraged by this, nor by the deaths of Rongrui, his capable assistant, and Xiangyan, one of his favorite disciples. Five years later, when he was already 66 years old and blind in both eyes, Jianzhen decided to make yet another attempt. This time, he had four ships. In spite of the sinking of one of the ships midway through the voyage, he didn't stop, and after a long hard voyage, landed somewhere south of Kyushu (what is now Kagoshima, Japan) in 754.

The 12 years of unremitted efforts to journey to Japan were filled with repeated failures and setbacks, and 36 people lost their lives. Jianzhen, however, was undaunted. At the age of 68, he landed on Japanese soil without eyesight, but with his lifetime wish fulfilled.

Upon his arrival in Kyoto and Nara, Jianzhen, as well as his entourage, was met with a warm welcome by the Mikado and the local people, an event that created a sensation throughout Japan. During his 10-year stay, he and his followers preached and spread Buddhism among the Japanese.

They introduced the Chinese culture to Japan as well. The 50-odd calligraphic works by Wang Xizhi (303-361 or 321-379, well-known calligrapher of the Eastern Jin Dynasty (317-420), venerated as "Sage of Calligraphy") and by his son, Wang Xianzhi[2] that they brought along helped popularize calligraphic art in Japan. A Wang-styled horizontal board with the two words "Toshodaiji Monastery" was inscribed by the Empress Kōken; it can still be seen in Japan today. In fact, the Japanese royal court still treasures the calligraphic copybooks in Wang Xizhi's style of writing donated by Jianzhen.

What's more, Jianzhen brought medical science, medicinal materials and empirical prescriptions to Japan. He personally treated ailments for the Japanese emperor and empress dowager. He was also entrusted to taste and smell the medicines there in order to discern the false from the genuine.

Also, he brought the Chinese bean-curd-making techniques, which were then popular among the temples in Yangzhou; Jianzhen is in fact enshrined in Japan as father of bean products.

Furthermore, his introductions of Chinese architecture and sculpture helped enhance the cultural exchanges between the two countries.

Jianzhen, the great Buddhist monk, experienced Parinirvana[3] in 763 In his honor, a seated figure of him, 90 centimeters tall, was enshrined and worshipped in Japan's Toshodaiji Monastery, whose very creation was credited to this Chinese monk. The statue, now a national treasure in Japan, maintains his pre-death posture: facing the west, he sat in meditation – cross-legged, with his hands clasped before him in a prayerful attitude – and eyes and lips shut, wearing a smile. In 1980, the 81st abbot of the Toshodaiji Monastery escorted the return of the statue to China. It is in recognition of Jianzhen's outstanding contributions to bilateral relations and cultural exchange that the people of China and Japan continue to fervently cherish his memory, even after 1,200 years.

Notes:

[1] Fajing Temple: also called Zhongtianzhu, located on what is now Tianzhu Rd. in Hangzhou; Dating back to 597, during the reign of the Sui Dynasty, legend has it that in the early Southern Song Dynasty (1127-1279), the 16th goddess of the 20 Buddhism-defending gods had her epiphany, and so was venerated by the imperial court, which gave the temple its reputation.

[2] Wang Xianzhi: (344-386), 7th son of Wang Xizhi, who lived in Guiji (what is now Shaoxing, Zhejiang.

[3] Parinirvana: death of a Buddhist monk or nun.

THE SILK ROAD

The Silk Road refers to the land trade route that linked ancient China via Middle Asia with south and west Asia, Europe and north Africa. Chinese natural silk and silk fabrics were transported westward along the route, hence the name "Silk Road" or "Silk Route".

Silk was first made in China. When introduced to northwestern regions of the Eurasian Grassland via the normadic tribes as early as during the Warring States Period (475-221 BC), fine Chinese silk was well received by the people there. But the "Silk Road" was not fully opened until the reign of Emperor Wu (141-87 BC) of the Western Han Dynasty, who dispatched Zhang Qian to visit the Western Regions (the areas west of Yumenguan, including what is now Xinjiang and parts of Central Asia) as an envoy. From then on, group after group of Chinese envoys and merchants, with full loads of silk fabrics, journeyed to the Western Regions starting from their capital city of Chang'an.

The southern "Silk Road" led to as far as modern-day Afghanistan, Uzbekistan, Iran and Egypt's Alexandria.

Another route covered Pakistan and Afghanistan's Kabul to reach the end of the Persian Gulf. Southward from Kabul, it could reach what is now Carachi of Pakistan and then Persia and Rome by ship. The Chinese silk fabrics are said to have enjoyed great popularity among the nobles in Rome, who fell over each other in their eagerness to buy it; the silk was rendered as valuable as gold.

Zhang Qian Visiting the Western Regions, a Mural in No. 323 Cave, Mogao Grottoes

The "Silk Road" made possible the availability of Chinese silk in a steady stream to the Western Regions. At the same time, it facilitated the introduction of highly valued materials, items and traditions from western and middle Asia to China: wool fabrics, perfume, jewels, gold and silver coins and vessels, glassware, music, dances, foods, costumes, and animals and plants. Plants as we know now, like the corcassian walnut, cucumber, black pepper and carrot, were first imported from the Western Regions. Fine breeds of horses, like the Xijima from Usun and the Tianma from Dawan[1], were also brought to China, which helped with the amelioration of these breeds.

Besides silk and silk products, Chinese inventions, products and technology were taken to the west, including farming methods, paper-making and printing techniques, lacquerware, porcelain, gunpowder, and the compass. The Silk Road was a great contributor to the progress and spread of human civilization across the world.

Digging grottoes and engraving stone images and statues of the Buddha along the Silk Road prevailed from the Western Jin Dynasty (265-317), a trend supported by the royal household. The Yungang Grottoes, the Mogao Grottoes at Dunhuang, the Maiji Grottoes at Tianshui and the Grottoes of Bingling Monastery[2] all feature Wei (220-265) and Jin (265-420) Dynasty sculptures and paintings, which are considered treasure houses that contain China's Buddhist art. Flourishing Buddhist Cave Temples were an indication of the busy transportation along this route of trade.

The southward shift of the economic center necessitated by rapid growth of the shipbuilding industry and availability of convenient sea routes since the Song Dynasty saved people from making long, hard journeys that involved surmounting deserts and barren mountain ranges. This resulted in the gradual decline in the use of the Silk Road as a trade route linking China with the West.

Notes:

[1] The Xijima from Usun and the Tianma from Dawan: names of horses native to Usun and Dawan, two of the 36 states in the Western Regions in ancient China and producers of fine breeds of horses, the former located somewhere between Zhangye west of the Hexi (Gansu) Corridor and Dunhuang, and the latter located in Fergana in what is now Tajikistan Republic, then connecting Kangju in the north, and the Rouzhi in the south and southwest.

[2] The Grottoes of Bingling Monastery: located on Mount Jishi, 35 kilometers west of Yongjing County in Gansu Province; digging and repair projects were continued in the Dynasties of Northern Wei, Northern Zhou, Sui, Tang, Song, Western Xia, Yuan, Ming and Qing. It now houses 800 stone-engraved figures, clay sculptures and statutes, and over 1,000 square meters of painted murals.

MARCO POLO AND HIS TRAVELS TO CHINA

Marco Polo was born to a rich merchant's family in the northern Italian city of Venice, the "City of Water". In his time, the oriental civilization, epitomized by China's silk fabrics, had since long ago been introduced to Europe. To the Europeans, the Orient was mysterious and exotic, and was rich in gold and wealth.

In 1275, Marco Polo, then age 17, yielded to curiosity, and together with his father and uncle, embarked on his difficult and long journey to the East. They traversed desolate and uninhabited deserts, surmounted the Pamirs and turned east to pass Xinjiang and Gansu to finally arrive at Shangdu (northeast of Zhenglan Qi in Inner Mongolia), where they were well received and hospitably entertained by Emperor Kublai[1], who was at the time spending a holiday at a summer resort there.

Marco Polo stayed in China for 17 years. As he was intelligent and diligent, he learned to speak Mongolian and Chinese in a very short period of time, and familiarized himself with the country's systems of decrees and etiquette, which made a good impression on the imperial court and the masses. Later, he was appointed Governor-General of Yangzhou, a position which allowed him to come to see quite a number of urban and rural places in the country, and also to visit Java[2] south of Vietnam, Sumatra[3] and other places on the South Sea Islands.

In Hangzhou, he saw a city similar to his hometown of Venice, a city with some 12,000 bridges, and a beautiful lake. He saw people living in grand houses like those of European aristocrats. He was amazed to know that the city's residents would consume as much as 43 dan (a unit of weight equivalent to 123 pounds) of black pepper everyday, and on this basis he calculated how huge the daily consumption of other spices and necessities was for the residents in one single day.

In Chengdu, he saw lucid streams flowing through or surrounding this large city, some spanned by bridges lined with shops selling commodities of every conceivable kind. Here, bridges served three purposes: as venues for linking the river banks, for business transactions and for collecting transit tolls. Out of town, he marveled at the fact that farmers ran a variety of workshops, particularly those that produced fine-quality silk fabrics.

In Yunnan, he was amazed to see people making wine with wheat and rice, for it was his understanding that wine could be only brewed with grapes, while he did not know that spirits made from grain were the best wine which kept the body warm and effectively stimulated the spirit. Equally striking to his eyes was that in Baoshan area, the local people followed the custom of ornamenting their teeth with thin pieces of gold; almost everyone, men and women, young and old, had gold filled around their teeth so that when speaking or smiling they showed a mouthful of dazzlingly glittering teeth. Using expensive gold as decoration was actually pursuit of beauty.

After 17 years of living among the Chinese, Marco Polo returned to Venice in 1290. Before long, he joined in the sea warfare against Genoa and was taken prisoner. While in prison he dictated what he had seen and heard in the East, while his fellow inmates took down his dictation. What this brought about was the widely-read *Marco Polo Travels*, whose publication caused a stir in the western world. China provided a new frontier for the Europeans to explore, and the Chinese borderland in the southwest became a place of aspiration and admiration.

Notes:

[1] Kublai: (1215-1294), founder and the 5th emperor of the Yuan Dynasty with the posthumous title of Shizu; In 1271, Kublai came to the throne, changing the dynastic title to Dayuan, and planned an attack against the Southern Song Dynasty (1127-1279). In 1279, the Southern Song Dynasty was conquered and Kublai began his rule over the whole of China. During

his reign, Kublai established authority of a centralized government to bring the whole country under his dominance. Meanwhile, he adopted proactive policies to encourage agriculture and handicrafts, which helped the social orders and economy recover as well as aided in the development of the border areas.

[2] Java: name of an ancient state, the modern Java on the South Sea Islands.

[3] Sumatra: a large island lying west of Indonesia, separated by the Strait of Malacca and facing the Malay Peninsula in the northeast, with the South China Sea and the Sea of Java to the southeast and the Indian Ocean to the southwest, covering an area of 434, 000 square kilometers

ZHENG HE AND HIS VOYAGES TO THE OCCIDENT

Zheng He was a great navigator in ancient China, who led a huge fleet of ships to sail to the West on seven voyages between 1405-1433. In the history of navigation, their feat was unparalleled and an outstanding contribution to the friendship and cultural exchanges between the people of China and southeast Asia and Africa.

Zheng He (1371-1435), was born in Kunyang (what is now called Jinning), Yunnan. Of the Hui nationality, he was originally surnamed Ma with the nickname Sanbao. When the imperial army of the Ming Dynasty captured Yunnan in the late 14th century, Zheng He, still a young man then, became a eunuch against his will. As he was capable and hardworking, and with his courage and insight, Zheng He was completely trusted by Zhu Di, the Emperor. As a matter of fact, his new surname was given by Zhu Di when he was still King of the State of Yan, though he was still popularly nicknamed "Eunuch Sanbao" by the ordinary people.

In June 1405, Emperor Zhu Di (Chengzu) appointed Zheng He envoy to the West. The "West" that he was to sail to was not the continent of Europe, but the sea and coastal areas west of the South China Sea. He had a huge fleet of ships (62 in all) with some 28,000 people aboard, including soldiers and sailors, technicians and interpreters, doctors, blacksmiths and artisans. Their ships, nearly 150 meters long and 60 meters wide and equipped with nautical charts, were among the largest of their kind at that time, and what's more, they were laden with gold and silver, silk and satin, porcelain and many other valuable objects. Their voyage started from the Liujiahe River in Suzhou (what is now the Liuhe River in Taicang, Jiangsu Province), then they sailed past the coast of Fujian and continued southward.

The first voyage led Zheng He to various kingdoms including Zhancheng (now southern Vietnam), Java, Jiugang (or Old Harbor, on the southeastern bank of what is now Sumatra in Indonesia), Sumatra, Malacca[1], and Ceylon (now called Sri Lanka).

Upon his landing at each of these destinations, Zheng He would first present the Ming Emperor's letter to the king there and then distribute the gold, silver and jewels that he had brought with him to the local people as a gesture of goodwill. Knowing that Zheng and his men meant well and hoped to establish friendly relations with them, the local people gave them a warm welcome and kind treatment.

In October 1407, Zheng He headed for home, his fleet of ships loaded with ivory, black pepper, perfume and medicinal herbs. Zheng He's successful maiden voyage to the west was praised and highly honored by Emperor Chengzu. Later, Zheng He made six more voyages to the "Western" World, touring more than 20 countries and going as far as the east coast of Africa and the Red Sea.

Zheng He was 61 when he made his last voyage west in 1431. He died not long after he returned two years later. His seven daring voyages were an embodiment of ancient China's indomitable spirit of exploration,

Map of Zheng He's Voyages Routine to the Occident

and also proof of the country's highly developed navigational technology. These voyages helped further the friendly exchanges between China and the rest of the world.

Zheng He's stories are to this day circulating among the people of many countries and regions. Commemorations of this great man are evidenced by the creation of the Sanbao Port, Sanbao Temple and Sanbao Pagoda in Thailand, Sanbao City and Sanbao Cave in Indonesia, and Sanbao City and Sanbao Well in Malaysia.

Zheng He's voyages took place more than half a century earlier than those attempted by the Europeans. It was not until 1492 that Christopher Columbus discovered America. And in 1497, Vasco da Gama rounded the Cape of Good Hope to reach the Indian coast by sailing along western Africa. None of these fleets, or their voyages, could be compared with those led by Zheng He. Zheng He proved himself to be a truly great navigator and a successful goodwill ambassador—the man who bridged China with the world.

Notes:

[1] Malacca: ancient city in Malaysia, capital of the state by the same name, located at the southern section of the east coast of the Malacca Strait, on the aggraded valley plain between the east and west banks of the Malacca River; Most of its residents are Chinese in origin; built around 1400, Malacca was made capital of the Kingdom of Malacca in 1405. It was once an international trade center in southeast Asia. In 1511, Malacca became a colony of Portugal. In 1641, it was occupied by the Netherlands. And in 1826, it became part of the Straits Settlements of Great Britain. Settlers here included Chinese, Indians, Arabs, Siamese, and Javanese. The status of Malacca as a city declined as a result of the silting-up of the mouth of the Malacca River and the emergence of Penang and Singapore.

(English Author: Liu Guoqiang)

Afterword

Understanding the "Dragon": A Panorama of Chinese Culture (with DVD-ROM) is a project sponsored by the National Publication Foundation. It is quite gratifying that the book, through material selection, compilation, and all the way up to the postproduction, has finally come into publication. Following the principles of inheriting civilizations, accumulating cultures, serving for the contemporary society, and promoting the publishing industry, the editorial board has compiled this bilingual book for readers home and abroad with a view to carrying forward Chinese culture and enhancing cultural exchanges between China and the rest of the world.

To guarantee the book a tour de force, the editorial board invited many experts, pooling their wisdom to the work of compilation, translation and proofreading. Such dedication has ensured the Chinese version of concision, the foreign language versions of fluency, and the whole work of clarity. The Chinese version was compiled by Professor Zheng Tiesheng, who is of profound scholarship and voluminous authorship on Chinese culture and literature. The English version was done by teachers from Tianjin Foreign Studies University, who have accomplished many translation tasks for international conferences. Yang Zhongxian, former director of Tianjin Ancient Books Publishing House, proofread the Chinese version, and so did experts on English, Japanese and Korean to the foreign language versions.

In applying for the National Publication Foundation Project, we got generous support and recommendation from Professor Meng Zhaoyi, Vice President of the Chinese Comparative Literature Teaching Research Society. Sincere thanks go to Meng Zhaoyi, Yang Zhongxian, and those foreign experts who made their contribution to the publication of this book. The Scientific Research Department of Tianjin Foreign Studies University also gave great support to its publication. Moreover, some photos and materials in this book were selected from other related books. So, special thanks go to authors of those books. And the Copyright Agency of China (CAC) has been entrusted with copyright issues concerning this book.

The Editorial Board
August, 2010

(Translated by Ma Linlin)

参考书目

1. 李希凡 . 中华艺术通史［M］. 北京 : 北京师范大学出版社，2006.

2. 编委会 . 中国武术百科全书［M］. 北京 : 中国大百科全书出版社，1998.

3. 李泽厚 . 中国思想史论［M］. 合肥：安徽文艺出版社，1999.

4. 庞朴，刘泽华 . 中国传统文化精神［M］. 沈阳 : 辽宁人民出版社，1995.

5. 金景芳 . 周易讲座［M］. 长春 : 吉林大学出版社，1988.

6. 杜继文 . 佛教史［M］. 南京 : 江苏人民出版社，2006.

7. 卿希泰，唐大潮 . 道教史［M］. 南京 : 江苏人民出版社，2006.

8. 朱裕平 . 中国唐三彩［M］. 济南 : 山东美术出版社，2006.

9. 史树青 . 中国艺术品收藏鉴赏百科全书 · 铜器卷［M］. 北京 : 北京出版社，2005.

10. 史树青 . 中国艺术品收藏鉴赏百科全书 · 陶瓷卷［M］. 北京 : 北京出版社，2005.

11. 史树青 . 中国艺术品收藏鉴赏百科全书 · 书画卷［M］. 北京 : 北京出版社，2005.

12. 刘志雄，杨静荣 . 龙与中国文化［M］. 北京 : 人民出版社，1999.

13. 张道一，唐家路 . 石雕［M］. 南京 : 江苏美术出版社，2009.

14. 张道一，唐家路 . 木雕［M］. 南京 : 江苏美术出版社，2009.

15. 张道一，唐家路 . 砖雕［M］. 南京 : 江苏美术出版社，2009.

16. 彭信威 . 国货币史［M］. 上海 : 上海人民出版社，1965.

17. 千家驹，郭彦岗 . 中国货币演变史［M］. 上海 : 上海人民出版社，2005.

18. 石毓符 . 中国货币金融史略［M］. 天津 : 天津人民出版社，1984.

19. 李泽厚 . 美的历程［M］. 北京 : 文物出版社，1981.

20. 马伯英 . 中国医学文化史［M］. 上海 : 上海人民出版社，1997.

21. 池小芳 . 中国古代小学教育研究［M］. 上海 : 上海教育出版社，1998.

22. 尚衍鎏 . 清代科举考试试述录及有关著作［M］. 天津 : 百花文艺出版社，2005.

23. 徐诚北 . 京剧与中国文化［M］. 北京 : 人民出版社，1999.

24. 刘琦 . 京剧形式特征［M］. 天津 : 天津古籍出版社，2003.

25. 高新 . 京剧欣赏［M］. 上海 : 学林出版社，2006.

26. 于志钧 . 中国传统武术史［M］. 北京 : 中国人民大学出版社，2009.

27. 张炯，邓绍基，樊骏 . 中华文学通史［M］. 北京 : 华艺出版社，1997.

28. 黄帝内经［M］. 北京 : 万卷出版公司，2009.

29. 编委会 . 中国历史文化名城词典［M］. 上海 : 上海辞书出版社，1985 年 .

30. 许嘉璐 . 中国古代礼俗辞典［M］. 北京 : 中国友谊出版公司，1981 年 .

31. 南京大学历史系编委组 . 中国历代名人辞典［M］. 南昌 : 江西人民出版社，1982 年 .

32. 陈璧显 . 中国大运河史［M］. 北京 : 中华书局，2001 年 .

33. 沈福煦 . 中国古代建筑文化史［M］. 上海 : 上海古籍出版社，2001.

34. 蒋光福 . 中国美术史［M］. 北京 : 知识出版社，1982.

35. 林正秋，徐海荣 . 中国饮食大辞典［M］. 杭州 : 浙江大学出版社，1991.

附　录

中国历代纪元表
A Brief Chronology of Chinese History

<table>
<tr><td colspan="3">夏　Xia Dynasty</td><td>2070 ~1600 BC</td></tr>
<tr><td colspan="3">商　Shang Dynasty</td><td>1600 ~1046 BC</td></tr>
<tr><td colspan="3">周　Zhou Dynasty</td><td>1046 ~256 BC</td></tr>
<tr><td colspan="2" rowspan="2">周　Zhou Dynasty</td><td>西周　Western Zhou Dynasty</td><td>1046 ~771 BC</td></tr>
<tr><td>东周　Eastern Zhou Dynasty</td><td>770 ~256 BC</td></tr>
<tr><td colspan="3">秦　Qin Dynasty</td><td>221~206 BC</td></tr>
<tr><td colspan="3">汉　Han Dynasty</td><td>206 BC~AD 220</td></tr>
<tr><td colspan="2" rowspan="2">汉　Han Dynasty</td><td>西汉　Western Han Dynasty</td><td>206 BC~AD 25</td></tr>
<tr><td>东汉　Eastern Han Dynasty</td><td>25~220</td></tr>
<tr><td colspan="3">三国　Three Kingdoms</td><td>220~280</td></tr>
<tr><td colspan="2" rowspan="3">三国　Three Kingdoms</td><td>魏　Kingdom of Wei</td><td>220~265</td></tr>
<tr><td>蜀　Kingdom of Shu</td><td>221~263</td></tr>
<tr><td>吴　Kingdom of Wu</td><td>222~280</td></tr>
<tr><td colspan="3">晋　Jin Dynasty</td><td>265~420</td></tr>
<tr><td colspan="2" rowspan="2">晋　Jin Dynasty</td><td>西晋　Western Jin Dynasty</td><td>265~317</td></tr>
<tr><td>东晋　Eastern Jin Dynasty</td><td>317~420</td></tr>
<tr><td colspan="3">南北朝　Southern and Northern Dynasties</td><td>420~589</td></tr>
<tr><td rowspan="5">南北朝
Southern and Northern Dynasties</td><td colspan="2">南朝　Southern Dynasties</td><td>420~589</td></tr>
<tr><td rowspan="4">南朝
Southern Dynasties</td><td>宋　Song Dynasty</td><td>420~479</td></tr>
<tr><td>齐　Qi Dynasty</td><td>479~502</td></tr>
<tr><td>梁　Liang Dynasty</td><td>502~557</td></tr>
<tr><td>陈　Chen Dynasty</td><td>557~589</td></tr>
</table>

南北朝 Southern and Northern Dynasties	北朝 Northern Dynasties		386~581
	北朝 Northern Dynasties	北魏 Northern Wei Dynasty	386~534
		东魏 Eastern Wei Dynasty	534~550
		北齐 Northern Qi Dynasty	550~577
		西魏 Western Wei Dynasty	535~556
		北周 Northern Zhou Dynasty	557~581
隋 Sui Dynasty			581~618
唐 Tang Dynasty			618~907
五代 Five Dynasties			907~960
五代 Five Dynasties		后梁 Later Liang Dynasty	907~923
		后唐 Later Tang Dynasty	923~936
		后晋 Later Jin Dynasty	936~947
		后汉 Later Han Dynasty	947~950
		后周 Later Zhou Dynasty	951~960
宋 Song Dynasty			960~1127
宋 Song Dynasty		北宋 Northern Song Dynasty	960~1127
		南宋 Southern Song Dynasty	1127~1279
辽 Liao Dynasty			907~1125
金 Jin Dynasty			1125~1234
元 Yuan Dynasty			1206~1368
明 Ming Dynasty			1368~1644
清 Qing Dynasty			1616~1911
中华民国 Republic of China			1912~1949
中华人民共和国 People's Republic of China			Founded on October 1, 1949